History and Historians in
the Twentieth Century

Andrew Linn

Sheffield 2002

HISTORY and HISTORIANS

in the Twentieth Century

Edited by
Peter Burke

Published *for* THE BRITISH ACADEMY
by OXFORD UNIVERSITY PRESS

Oxford University Press, Great Clarendon Street, Oxford OX2 6DP

Oxford New York

Athens Auckland Bangkok Bogotá Buenos Aires Cape Town
Chennai Dar es Salaam Delhi Florence Hong Kong Istanbul Karachi
Kolkata Kuala Lumpur Madrid Melbourne Mexico City Mumbai Nairobi
Paris São Paulo Shanghai Singapore Taipei Tokyo Toronto Warsaw

with associated companies in
Berlin Ibadan

Published in the United States
By Oxford University Press Inc., New York

© The British Academy 2002
Database right The British Academy (maker)

British Library Cataloguing in Publication Data
Data available

ISBN 0–19–726268–6

Typeset in Europe by the Alden Group, Oxford

Printed in Great Britain
on acid-free paper by
Bookcraft (Bath) Limited
Midsomer Norton, Avon

In memory of
Roy Porter
(1946–2002)

Contents

Notes on Contributors

Stephen Bann, FBA is Professor of History of Art at the University of Bristol, and currently President of the Comité international d'histoire de l'art (CIHA). He has written extensively on the visual representation of history since the 1970s. His most recent books are *Paul Delaroche: History Painted* (1997) and *Parallel Lines: Printmakers, Painters and Photographers in Nineteenth-century France* (2001).

C. A. Bayly, FBA is Vere Harmsworth Professor of Imperial and Naval History at the University of Cambridge. He is the author of works on Indian history and British imperial history, including *Imperial Meridian: The British Empire and the World, 1780–1830* (1989) and *Empire and Information: Intelligence Gathering and Social Communication in India, 1780–1870* (1996).

John Breuilly is Professor of Modern History at the University of Birmingham. His main interests are in nationalism, modern German history, and comparative urban and cultural history in modern Europe. He is the author of *The Formation of the First German Nation-State, 1800–1871* (1996) and *Nationalismus und moderner Staat: Deutschland und Europa* (1999) and editor of *Nineteenth-century Germany* (2001).

Peter Burke, FBA is Professor of Cultural History, University of Cambridge, and Fellow of Emmanuel College. His studies of the history of historical writing include *The Renaissance Sense of the Past* (1969) and *The French Historical Revolution: The Annales School, 1929–89* (1990).

Peter Clark is Professor of European Urban History at the University of Helsinki and formerly Director of the Centre for Urban History, University of Leicester. He has written extensively on urban and social history and is general editor of the *Cambridge Urban History of Britain* (2000).

David Feldman is a Reader in History at Birkbeck, University of London. He is the author of *Englishman and Jews: Social Relations and Political Culture, 1840–1914* (1994). He is currently researching and writing a book provisionally titled *The Rights of Strangers: Migrants, Immigrants and Welfare since the Seventeenth Century*.

Ludmilla Jordanova works at the University of East Anglia and specialises in the long eighteenth century. Current research interests include portraiture, self-portraiture and the relationships between the visual arts and the history of science and medicine. Among recent publications are *Nature Displayed: Gender, Science and Medicine, 1760–1820* (1999) and *Defining Features: Scientific and Medical Portraits, 1660–2000* (2000).

Roy Porter (who died in 2002) was Professor of the Social History of Medicine at the Wellcome Trust Centre for the History of Medicine at University College, London. Recent books include *Doctor of Society: Thomas Beddoes and the Sick Trade in Late Enlightenment England* (1991), *London: A Social History* (1994), *'The Greatest Benefit to Mankind': A Medical History of Humanity* (1997), *Enlightenment: Britain and the Creation of the Modern World* (2000) and *Bodies Politic: Disease, Death and the Doctors in Britain, 1650–1914* (2000). He was co-author of *The History of Bethlem* (1997) and *Gout: The Patrician Malady* (1998).

Miri Rubin is an historian of late medieval Europe at Queen Mary, University of London. Her more recent books are *Corpus Christi: The Eucharist in Late Medieval Culture* (1991) and *Gentile Tales: The Narrative Assault on Late Medieval Jews* (1999). In them she explores her interest in religious cultures and social relations.

E. A. Wrigley was formerly Professor of Economic History, University of Cambridge and Master of Corpus Christi College, Cambridge. He was President of the British Academy 1997–2001. His research interests lie in the economic and demographic history of England during the early modern period and in the genesis of the industrial revolution.

Introduction

PETER BURKE

As part of the celebrations of its centenary, the British Academy decided to commission a retrospective volume about history and historians in Britain in the twentieth century. The idea was to produce a collection of essays which would present a historical and critical overview of historical thought and writing since 1900, emphasising recent developments. In a single volume of ten essays it was obviously impossible to cover all the areas which British historians had studied in the course of a century, so attention has been focused on a few major topics, whether periods (such as the Middle Ages), regions (such as 'the Orient'), disciplines (art history, historiography or historical demography), or themes (nation, class, disease, gender and so on).

This choice had its price. Economic history, for instance, despite its importance, especially in the middle years of the century, does not have a chapter devoted to it, nor does the history of political thought. The point was not to cover the ground and produce a kind of encyclopaedia, but to offer a series of reflective essays on a number of different fields, on the kinds of innovation which had been made, for instance, when and by whom. Contributors to the volume were also asked to engage, insofar as they considered it appropriate, with the question whether these fields or objects of study have been 'constructed' rather than discovered by the scholars working on them. In this introduction I should like to offer some more general comments on the problem of construction, together with an overview of the development of British historical writing in the twentieth century — its chronology.

The problem of construction

At first sight it may appear absurd to say that historians invent or construct what they study rather than choosing or finding it. At an individual level, at least, our experience is that of studying a past which exists outside ourselves and also of entering a field populated by scholars, a territory with its own customs and forms of organisation. On the other hand, we know that interpretations of the past — of the career of Napoleon, for instance — have their own history and even their own politics, as Pieter Geyl showed in Napoleon's case over half a century ago.[1] So some kind of construction is going on. The problem is to discover who is doing it — individual historians, the historical profession, or 'society'.

The question whether, or better, the extent to which, or the ways in which scholars construct their objects of study has itself turned into a major object of study and debate in the last two decades. It is a special case of what some philosophers and sociologists call the 'social construction of reality' — or, alternatively, the 'construction of social reality'.[2] One influential formulation of the 'constructivist' (or the 'constructionist' or 'constructionalist') position was offered by Michel Foucault when he defined 'discourses' as practices which 'systematically construct (*forment*) the objects of which they speak'.[3]

There are obvious links between this debate and a more general revolt against determinism, especially in its Marxist form, a revolt encouraged by events in Berlin in 1989 as it had been by events in Paris in 1968. It is unlikely to be an accident that these ideas have surfaced at a time when governments and corporations appear to be more concerned than ever before with their public images.

One area in which this scholarly debate has been particularly lively is anthropology, following the publication of Johannes Fabian's *Time and the Other: How Anthropology Makes its Object* (1983). Another is the history of science.[4] As scientists have explored phenomena which are more and more remote from everyday reality, they have asked themselves, for instance, whether electrons (say) have objective properties independent of their minds. Historians too have been asking this kind of question. If we see social reality as manipulable, we will obviously view both the past and historical writing in a different way from Ranke (say) or Braudel.

'Class', for example, which was once treated as an objective social category by Marxists and non-Marxists alike (however they might disagree

---

[1] Pieter Geyl, *Napoleon: For and Against* (London, 1949).

[2] Peter Berger and Thomas Luckmann, *The Social Construction of Reality* (New York, 1966); John R. Searle, *The Construction of Social Reality* (New York, 1995); Ian Hacking, *The Social Construction of What?* (Cambridge, MA, 1999).

[3] Michel Foucault, *L'archéologie du savoir* (Paris, 1969), p. 66.

[4] Jan Golinski, *Making Natural Knowledge: Constructivism and the History of Science* (Cambridge, 1998).

over its definition), is now, like 'caste' and 'tribe', increasingly regarded as a social or historical construct.[5] Feminists in particular have encouraged historians to treat 'gender' in the same way. Not to do so is to run the risk of being described as an 'essentialist', a term of abuse which has become increasingly common in the last ten years or so. As for 'nation', it is now regarded as a paradigm case of construction; witness the shelf of books about nations with the word 'invention' or 'inventing' in their titles, including the invention of Argentina, Australia, Canada, Ethiopia, France, Ireland, Japan, Paraguay, Scotland and Spain. A similar point has been made about Europe, Eastern Europe, Africa and America, about the 'Orient' and the 'North' (the Scandinavian *Norden*).[6]

The history of population, on the other hand, offers an obvious counter-example to the arguments of the constructivists. As T. S. Eliot's Sweeney memorably remarked, 'Birth and copulation and death; That's all the facts when you come to brass tacks; Birth and copulation and death.' In the debate about social construction, distinctions obviously need to be drawn. As the philosopher Ian Hacking most pertinently asks, 'The social construction of what?' His main point is to distinguish between categories and what lies behind them. To this question might be added two more: 'By whom?' and, no less important, 'Out of what?' Let us take these three questions in order.

The distinction between the concepts used by historians and the reality to which they refer is of course a traditional one. It was F. W. Maitland who remarked that 'were an examiner to ask who introduced the feudal system into England, one very good answer, if properly explained, would be Henry Spelman'. Again, the Swedish economic historian Eli Heckscher began his classic study of mercantilism with the words 'Mercantilism never existed in the sense that Colbert or Cromwell existed'.[7]

In the case of concepts or models such as 'mercantilism' or 'feudal system', scholars are generally conscious that they are the ones who are doing the constructing. The terms 'class', 'caste' or 'tribe' are more complicated in the sense that these concepts were used by at least some of the people whom historians of nineteenth-century Britain, or India, or Africa have been

---

[5] Adrian Southall, 'The Illusion of Tribe', *Journal of African and Asian Studies* (1970), 28–50; Jean-Loup Amselle, *Mestizo Logics: Anthropology of Identity in Africa and Elsewhere* (1990, English trans., Stanford 1998); Ronald Inden, 'Orientalist Constructions of India', *Modern Asian Studies*, 20 (1986), 401–46; Ronald Inden, *Imagining India* (Oxford, 1990).

[6] Edward Said, *Orientalism* (London, 1978); Øystein Sørensen and Bo Stråth (eds), *The Cultural Construction of Norden* (Oslo, 1997).

[7] F. W. Maitland, *The Constitutional History of England* (1888, posthumously published, Cambridge 1908), p. 142; Eli Heckscher, *Mercantilism* (1931, revised English trans., London, 1955), p. 19.

studying. They are part of the data, written into official documents such as the census, documents which helped form people's perceptions of their own society. That does not mean, of course, that they were necessarily the best, let alone the only possible social categories to use in the circumstances. In any case, other questions need to be asked: to what extent these classifications were successfully imposed from above, for instance, how they interacted with earlier classifications and whether they were reinterpreted from below.

Births and deaths may be 'brass tacks', but historians of population are among the most self-conscious and sophisticated employers of models and even flow charts of different 'demographic regimes'.[8] In similar fashion the language of 'models' became widespread among economic historians, following the economists, in the 1950s and 1960s, to refer to intellectual constructs which select and simplify, emphasising what is typical and translating social reality into a system of interdependent and often quantifiable characteristics.

If the construction of concepts is a fairly uncontroversial activity, some historians do not see the point of model-building. Still more would object to the suggestion that their 'sources' are constructed. All the same, the rise of oral history has made this problem impossible to ignore. It is obvious enough that oral historians choose whom to interview and also when to switch the tape recorder on and off. It is equally obvious that oral historians have a different relation to sources from their colleagues who work in archives, but their practices prompt questions about archives and documents which were not asked earlier, or were not asked so often and so insistently as they are today. The researchers may 'discover' the documents, but the archivists constructed the archive by arranging or at least rearranging it. The scribes or clerks who wrote the individual texts may also be described as having constructed them, and so may the officials who dictated letters or interrogated suspects.

A consciousness of the process by which documents are constructed is allied to a consciousness of gaps in the record, of silences or absences. Recent movements such as history from below, women's history and post-colonial history both express and encourage the awareness that much of the past is absent from official records, so that what can be found in the archive may be described as an official selection. If some of these absences are the result of deliberate attempts by officials to cover the traces of activities which might tarnish their reputations, others reveal what was once thought

---

[8] E. A. Wrigley, *Population and History* (London, 1969).

to be unimportant. Written genealogies, for instance, often suppress certain kinds of people, notably infants and women. This makes them at once unreliable sources for family reconstitution and valuable documents for historians of mentalities.

Beyond the archive, it is not difficult to identify further constructions of social reality. What the philosopher John Searle calls 'institutional facts', including 'money, property, government and marriages' all exist, as he puts it, 'only because we believe them to exist', where the term 'we' refers to a working social consensus rather than to the opinions of individuals.[9] In that sense, 'money', like 'England' or the 'middle class', may be regarded as a social construction. We might go on to say that these contemporary constructions are sometimes translated or reconstructed by historians, who may describe a society in terms of class even if the people themselves spoke in terms of 'estate' or 'order'.

In a more self-conscious way rulers, aided by their councillors, poets, painters and historians, have long been in the business of constructing favourable images of themselves. If Mrs Thatcher was the first British Prime Minister to go to Saatchi & Saatchi for help in this respect, what she was doing was no different in principle from the official 'fabrication' of (say) Louis XIV. Republics as well as rulers may construct official images of themselves. What historians describe as the 'myth of Venice' is simply a well-documented example of a process of myth-making in which many communities have engaged. Saints too may be described as collective fabrications in the sense that the image of the heroically virtuous miracle-worker is attached to a particular individual, first at a local level, and then, after canonisation, by the whole Church.[10]

It would of course be unwise to assume that everyone accepted these official images uncritically. Indeed, in the case of Louis XIV there is considerable evidence to the contrary. In his case, as in that of many other rulers, some people noted discrepancies between the official heroic image and the king's observed or unofficially rumoured behaviour. Constructivists surely need to confront the question of failed constructions. The failures to achieve heroic status — to be canonised, for example — raise an even bigger problem, that of the limits and constraints — mental, social, or material — within which the process of construction has to operate.

---

[9] Searle, *The Construction of Social Reality*, p. 1.

[10] Peter Burke, *The Fabrication of Louis XIV* (New Haven, CT, 1992); ibid., 'How to be a Counter-Reformation Saint' (1984, rpr. *Historical Anthropology of Early Modern Italy*, Cambridge 1987, pp. 48–62); Myron Gilmore, 'Myth and Reality in Venetian Political Theory', in John Hale (ed.) *Renaissance Venice* (London, 1973), pp. 431–44.

Speaking about 'process' raises the problem of change over time. The myth of Venice offered an image of that city-state as always the same, possessing the secret of resisting change, corruption, decay. Of course Venice, like any other community, was constantly changing, and to some extent the myth changed as well. In other words, both the city and its myth were involved in a process of what might be described as 'continuous construction' on the analogy of 'continuous creation'. A better term might be 'continuous reconstruction'. Its value is to emphasise the point that cultural construction does not take place *ex nihilo*, any more than the construction of buildings. The idea of a culturally blank slate is an illusion, ignoring the cultural heritage, the material (not 'raw' but 'cooked', not natural but cultural) out of which constructions are made.

For a case-study of both the value and the limitations of the constructivist approach we might turn to the 'invention of tradition', a phrase launched by Eric Hobsbawm and Terence Ranger at a *Past and Present* conference and adopted as the title of an internationally successful book first published in 1983. The phrase was of course originally designed to provoke, to demystify what was taken for granted. It was coined to refer in particular to a group of European festivals such as May Day and Bastille Day. In these cases, it is possible to say when the festivals began (in the later nineteenth century), who founded them and for what purposes.[11]

When the concept of the invention of tradition is extended more widely, however, problems quickly surface. Is it useful or possible to distinguish two kinds of tradition, the genuine and the invented? Or should all traditions be described as invented? Neither answer is satisfactory, because traditions change. To continue with the example of public festivals, it is odd to describe the Carnival of Venice as an invention, since it is impossible to say either when it was invented or by whom, and in any case the Venetian was only the most famous of many European carnivals. On the other hand, the description of the tradition of the festival as genuine or spontaneous has to be qualified, since practices changed over time and the Carnival of Venice was exploited for both political and commercial reasons. It makes a good example of continuous reconstruction.

To conclude this brief discussion, it might be said of historiography as of other disciplines that the idea of construction or invention was a liberating or demystifying one, especially when it was launched. It liberated historians from lingering assumptions that our concepts of periods such as the Middle

---

[11] Eric Hobsbawm, 'Introduction' to Eric Hobsbawm and Terence Ranger (eds), *The Invention of Tradition* (Cambridge, 1983).

Ages, regions such as France, or practices such as politics are natural and eternal rather than contingent and subject to change. However, as often happens in the history of ideas, 'construction' has become so popular a term that it seems to block thought rather than stimulate it. The concept itself is in need of reconstruction, if not deconstruction.

The problem of chronology

Looking back from the beginning of the twenty-first century, it is all too easy, especially for those of us who entered the historical profession in the 1960s, to judge the historiographical achievements of the twentieth century primarily by its second half, which we have experienced, and to assume that this was when the action really took place. There has indeed been a good deal of action, a good deal of change, in the last forty years. All the same, the dangers as well as the temptations of treating the years from 1900 to 1960 as a historiographical old regime against which to define new developments will be obvious enough. Of the contributors to this volume, Chris Bayly resists the temptation most strongly. Concerned to combat the assumption that serious studies of the Orient began with Edward Said, he prefers to emphasise the contribution made by early twentieth-century scholars. A similar point might be made in other fields as well.

Suppose one tried to list acknowledged masterpieces of British historical writing in the last century. The first titles which came to mind might well be from the second half of the century, from Richard Southern's *Making of the Middle Ages* (1954) and Edward Thompson's *Making of the English Working Class* (1963) to Keith Thomas's *Religion and the Decline of Magic* (1971). However, the first half of the century also had its fair share of classics, including R. H. Tawney's *Religion and the Rise of Capitalism* (1926), G. N. Clark's *The Seventeenth Century* (1929), and Maurice Powicke's *Henry III and the Lord Edward* (1947).

Turning to the fields privileged in this volume, women's history, for example, did not begin in the 1960s, although it was given increasing attention at that time. Alice Clark's *Working Life of Women in the Seventeenth Century* came out in 1919, and Eileen Power's *Medieval English Nunneries* in 1922. Although art history, as an academic discipline, was almost invisible in the middle of the twentieth century, Anthony Blunt had already published his *Artistic Theory in Italy* (1940) and Dennis Mahon his *Studies in Seicento Art and Theory* (1947), while E. H. Gombrich's best-selling *The Story of Art* made its appearance in 1950. In historical demography, a field in which the rise of new methods around 1950 is particularly clear, it would still be a pity to forget G. T. Griffith's *Population Problems in the Age of Malthus* (1926). As for economic history, one might contrast the years from around 1920 to around 1970, when it was in the vanguard of historical studies, to the years before and after, when it was somewhere in the rear.

Moving from fields to approaches, it may be worth noting that certain trends widely discussed in the 1980s and 1990s began to be practised considerably earlier. Take the case of 'microhistory', for instance, an approach which attracted considerable interest in Britain as in other countries following the success of two classics in the field, Emmanuel Le Roy Ladurie's *Montaillou* (first published in French in 1975) and Carlo Ginzburg's *Cheese and Worms* (which appeared in Italian a year later). British historians followed the trend. David Underdown's *Fire from Heaven* (1992), for example, a study of Dorchester in the seventeenth century by an English historian who has lived for many years in the USA, has been described as 'the English equivalent of Le Roy Ladurie's *Montaillou*'.

All the same, there were English precedents for studying the history of small communities as a way of understanding larger societies. Four examples from the 1950s are worthy of attention in this respect. Geoffrey Elton's *Star Chamber Stories* (1958) was an attempt to understand the Reformation by examining ordinary people in local settings, an approach pursued more systematically by Geoffrey Dickens in his *Lollards and Protestants in the Diocese of York* (1959). Still more remarkable for their time, in their concern with long periods of time as well as their attempt to approach the national through the local, are studies by J. H. Plumb and W. G. Hoskins. Published in 1954 and buried in one of the Leicestershire volumes of the *Victoria County History* is one of Plumb's most brilliant historical essays. Entitled 'Political History 1530–1885', the essay views the major political conflicts of that long period through the lens of Leicestershire politics, focusing on the struggle for mastery between the Grey and Hastings families.

Better known, even though it never achieved the cult status of *Montaillou*, is Hoskins' study *The Midland Peasant* (1957), in which the author uses a single Leicestershire village, Wigston Magna, from 1066 to 1900, as a way of exploring major themes in English economic and social history. The book was dedicated to Tawney, whose inaugural lecture at the LSE in 1932, discussed in a later essay of this collection, had already advised historians to practise the analysis of structures rather than the narrative of events. Enthusiasm for the changes in British and indeed in western historical writing between 1970 and 1999 should not lead us to imagine the years from 1900 to 1969 as an unchanging, conservative, old historiographical regime.

A still more difficult question, which will surface from time to time in the pages which follow, is the extent to which the history written in the last century reveals a distinctively English or British approach to the past. It is probably wise to leave to a foreign scholar the task of discussing the Englishness of English historiography, as it was left to the German refugee scholar Nikolaus Pevsner to discuss 'the Englishness of English Art'. Are English historians more insular, more individualist or more empiricist than their continental colleagues? Are these trends equally visible in Scotland, Wales or Ireland?

So far as this volume is concerned, it will be noted that in his discussion of art history, for example, Stephen Bann treats Britain as part of a larger unit which includes the USA. John Breuilly's discussion of the nation, though focused on the work of British historians, is even more broadly international in approach. This 'individualism' on the part of contributors was only to be expected and is surely to be welcomed. Such disagreements encourage readers to make up their own minds and draw their own distinctions.

The problem of progress

A hundred years ago, if a volume like this dealing with the previous century had been contemplated, it is likely that the editor would have offered some concluding remarks about the progress of historical studies. On the other hand, in a famous study of 'scientific revolutions' published some forty years ago, Thomas Kuhn criticised the assumption of progress in the sciences and suggested its replacement by the idea of 'paradigm change'. I think it is fair to describe the contributors to this volume, myself included, as conscious or unconscious Kuhnians, in the sense of being fascinated by change but reluctant to claim that it is necessarily for the better or even for the worse, although we may wish to speak of the costs as well as the benefits of a particular way of writing history.

It seems especially appropriate to assess quantitative history in these terms. Developed within economic history and historical demography, quantitative methods were extended in the 1960s and 1970s to other historical fields, to social, political and even cultural history, with the French and the North Americans in the lead and some British historians not far behind. As Miri Rubin reminds us in her essay, the history of piety was studied on occasion via the records for the number and weight of candles burned at particular shrines. Today, in the age of reaction against such methods, the costs are obvious, emphasising quantity at the expense of quality (as historians are the first to complain when the government tries to measure their 'productivity').

Despite these problems, the benefits to historical understanding as a result of bold attempts to use quantitative methods outside economic history should not be forgotten. The history of the book offers an outstanding example of such benefits. Launched in France in the 1960s, *l'histoire du livre* focused on statistics of editions, whether concerned with the popularity of a given book or the importance of a given city in the history of printing. In the 1970s and 1980s, this approach gave way to a qualitative, impressionistic 'history of reading', focused on micro-studies of individual readers. All the same, as multi-volume syntheses such as the *History of the Book in Britain* (still in progress) show, it is possible to combine the two approaches.

The increasing professionalisation and specialisation on the part of British historians in the course of the last hundred years of historical research and writing in Britain also deserves to be examined in terms of costs as well as benefits. For example, the vision of the past is now more fragmented than it used to be, not only among students but among their teachers as well. At one time it looked as if a split might develop between professional historians writing for one another and amateur historians writing for the general public. Today, some of the best academic historians, in Britain as in France or the USA, are read outside the profession. On the other hand, the tradition of the many-sided scholar appears to be in decline. In the early twentieth century, G. M. Trevelyan wrote books on topics ranging from England in the age of Wycliffe to Italy in the age of Garibaldi, even if he was better informed about the age of Queen Anne. In the middle of the century, Herbert Butterfield was still able to move with apparent ease from Machiavelli to Napoleon, from the history of science to the history of history. Today, it remains possible to name one scholar interested in what he calls 'scattered parts of a great subject', from Laud to Hitler, but it is regretfully necessary to admit that Lord Dacre (formerly Hugh Trevor-Roper) is in this respect the last of the dinosaurs.

CHAPTER ONE

The Middle Ages, or Getting Less Medieval with the Past

MIRI RUBIN

Medieval history: a history which is not one?

The British Academy's centenary is an apt moment for reflection on all that is novel and noble in and about our profession. This volume clearly attempts to embrace and explore the variety and richness of history making today. By noting that diversity it implicitly acknowledges others, too: that historians are not researchers alone, but teachers, administrators, collaborators in joint projects and sometime wielders of substantial resources; that historians are read and used, accessed and invoked by a very wide range of people, within and without academic frames, of varying degrees of historical training; that we are expected to be able to perform in several media — as lecturers, research supervisors, reviewers, experts for radio and television pro-grammes; and we are supposed to know *all* that is relevant to our sphere, without barriers of language or method, about increasingly complex prob-lems bursting out of the compartments of training and discipline which once held them in place. Most of these facets of the historian's life are to be welcomed, granted that they are experienced in an appropriate dosage. And all these aspects are particularly true for the group of historians to which my essay is devoted: those who study what has been known for over 500 years as 'the Middle Ages'.

The Middle Ages are unique inasmuch as dealing with them will always require a very protracted apprenticeship. The linguistic range and the generic diversity make clear demands on practitioners; the paucity and patchiness of documentary survival oblige historians to treasure and track down any relevant piece of evidence. Our increased awareness of what constitutes a conversation with the past means that few scholarly enterprises will satisfy if they are based on a single source, without a strong comparative dimension or a braided consideration of other, adjacent sources: liturgy with theology, wills with commemorative monuments, images with the devotions habitually directed at them,[1] legislation and law enforcement. And, as the set of questions we hope to answer has grown and diversified, so have the techniques we apply: ethnography, literary criticism, and the treatment of visual imagery have become part of the medieval historian's toolbox, requiring a life-long education and an extensive network of colleagues and friends for advice, correction and, sometimes, shared enterprises.[2] Medieval historians must read widely in order to discard readily. It is the recognition of these needs that has inspired some interesting projects of co-authorship, like that of Marilynn Desmond and Pamela Sheingorn, combining literary and art-historical skills.[3]

The twentieth century sustained a contest between the openness and the opacity which the Middle Ages offer their observers. For Marc Bloch it was not the Middle Ages which was 'a problem', but history itself, by its very nature, was *histoire-problème*. He wrote as readily, and as movingly, about eleventh-century northern France as he did about the First World War (which he experienced as a soldier), or the more recent and devastating Occupation of France.[4] Another medieval historian who died too young, Eileen Power, was similarly engaged in comparison and observation. Her travels in China illuminated her understanding of the English village; her thoughts on her own life as a women-historian, and a fellow of the first women's university college in Britain, projected insight into the lives of

[1] Virginia Reinburg, 'Popular Prayers in late Medieval and Reformation France', Ph.D. dissertation (Princeton University, 1985); see also eadem, 'Prayer and the Book of Hours', in *The Book of Hours in Medieval Art and Life*, ed. Roger S. Wieck (London, 1988), pp. 39–44.

[2] The word 'interdisciplinarity' is an extremely tired one; for its history see Roberta Frank, ' "Interdisciplinarity": The First Half Century', in *Words: For Robert Burchfield's Sixty-fifth Birthday*, ed. Eric G. Stanley and Terry F. Hoad (Cambridge, 1988), pp. 91–101; for a spirited suggestion of 'antidisciplinarity' as a rallying cry see Paul Strohm, *Theory and the Premodern Text*, Medieval Cultures, 26 (Bloomington, IN, 2001), pp. 33–7.

[3] Marilynn Desmond and Pamela Sheingorn, *Myth, Montage and Visuality in late Medieval Manuscript Culture: Christine de Pizan's Epistre Othea* (Ann Arbor, MI, forthcoming); for another fruitful collaboration, between a medievalist and a social scientist see J. W. Fentress and C. J. Wickham, *Social Memory* (Oxford, 1992). On collaboration see Judith M. Bennett, 'Our Colleagues, Ourselves', in *The Past and Future of Medieval Studies*, ed. John Van Engen (Notre Dame, IN, 1994), pp. 245–58, at pp. 252–3.

[4] On Bloch and the Great War see Carole Fink, *Marc Bloch: A Life* (Cambridge, 1989), pp. 54–78, 205–40. He wrote *Souvenirs de guerre, 1914–15* [*Cahiers des Annales*, 26 (Paris, 1969), trans. Carole Fink as *Memoirs of War, 1914–1915* (Ithaca, NY, 1980; Cambridge, 1988)] in 1915 while recovering from typhoid fever; he also wrote *L'étrange defaite: témoignage écrit en 1940* (Paris, 1957) [*A Strange Defeat*, trans. Gerard Hopkins (London, 1949)].

medieval religious women.[5] So it may be with us: our scholarship in hand, our subjects diverse and well-formed, medieval historians can and should contribute to wider historical discussion.[6] Medieval historians usually possess broader linguistic skills than others, and are trained at length in the art of textual appreciation. They read comparatively far more readily than other historians, and they are versed in dialogic strategies which historians of more modern periods might feel to be unnecessary. Their period is styled variously as 'middle', 'dark', 'of faith', 'of chivalry', or 'of cathedrals'; it far transcends the period 500–1500, and harbours the epitomes of human cruelty as well as human inventiveness and beauty. With the diversity that the last decades have unearthed, the Middle Ages emerge as an abundant cluster of opportunities. Defiant and evading labels, astonishing (the feats of oral literature, of architecture), repulsive (misogyny, anti-Judaism), and in some ways so mundane and familiar (court politics, taxation, the double standard), the Middle Ages have to be known. No historical education, nor survey of any field is complete without them. And in these Middle Ages of the future, I would like to situate not only Chaucer but Shakespeare, Augustine and Luther, Christine de Pisan as well as Queen Elizabeth I.[7] It is a long and broad set of traditions and affinities which defy naming.

The Middle Ages: women lived then, too

The medieval communities studied and taught in 2002 are substantially different from those taught, say, in 1952 or 1902. They are simply communities in which women as well as men worked, thought, believed, created, did most things which for generations have been seen as actions of men. The impact of

[5] Maxine Berg, *A Woman in History: Eileen Power 1889–1940* (Cambridge, 1996), ch. 4, pp. 83–109 and ch. 8, pp. 200–21; on Power and Marc Bloch see pp. 210–18.

[6] Although the *Historikerstreit* which rocked German intellectual and political circles in the 1980s dealt with historiographical issues medieval historians made no public contribution to it. See the documentation in *Forever in the Shadow of Hitler? Original Documents of the Historikerstreit, the Controversy concerning the Singularity of the Holocaust*, trans. Truett Cates (Atlantic Highlands, NJ, 1993).

[7] The problem of periodisation is a vexed one, and it is often discussed with irritation by medievalists. Attempt to transcend the dates 500 and 1500 are best chosen and demonstrated within the contexts of specific studies. Some journals have attempted to straddle the latter boundary, such as the *Journal of Medieval and Early Modern Studies* published by Duke University Press. On institutions which try to do the same see Randolph Starn, 'Who's Afraid of the Renaissance?', in *The Past and Future of Medieval Studies*, ed. John Van Engen (Notre Dame, IN, 1994), pp. 129–47. On alternative periodisations see Jacques Le Goff's views in Paul Archambault, 'An Interview with Jacques Le Goff', *Reflexions historiques*, 21 (1995), 155–85, at 173–4. On the terms which designate the 'Middle Ages' see Jacques Heers, *Le moyen âge: une imposture* (Paris, 1992), part 1, pp. 23–100.

the arrival of women — through the efforts of historians of women, who were usually women themselves — on medieval scholarship is not evenly spread, nor is it welcomed by all. But it has happened and is here to stay. Women are known and familiar, not only queens and mystics; and gendered properties of language, images, gestures and space are apparent in texts as varied as theological and mystical tracts, the statutes of craft-guilds and books of conduct. Gender is recognised as a formative way of thinking about the world, as gendered arrangements structured the religion of the parish, household, workshops, dynasty/lineages, as well as demographic patterns. Women did not habitually attend the meetings of city councils, nor the chambers of state. But even when absent the powerful presence of the feminine — that which was to be won, controlled, protected — constructed the world and actions of men, defining the duties of those councilmen, rulers, soldiers — to protect and provide, win and occupy those seemingly weaker and dependent.

The excavation of women's medieval past has occurred in tandem with other developments in historical practice. The moves in the last forty years or so, known as the 'new history', have legitimated investigation of family, community, the rural, the daily, the unexceptional, work, leisure, the study of images and material culture. In all these areas — as opposed to military, diplomatic, administrative histories and materials — women are more likely to loom large, and have done. Even so, a lot more work is to be done, particularly in the exploration of public and civic life, and in the reaches of vernacular literature and culture. But there is now a place, demand and recognition of such work, particularly in American, but increasingly in British universities. The intellectual achievement and the institutional provisions will not be lost, animated as they are not only by cohorts of bright and committed young scholars, but also by a constant stream of scholars who are recasting their histories so as to 'see woman' and think through issues of gender. Much good writing has chronicled the paths formed in recent decades.[8] Towards the end of this essay I shall comment on new directions which might be called 'after gender', which are discernible in work on religious imagery.

The dual heritage

Those involved in the study of the period 500–1500 entertain widely differing expectations from their work, in terms both of the intellectual and

---

[8] For a useful survey see Judith M. Bennett, *Medieval Women in Modern Perspective* (Washington, DC, 2000). I have written about some of these issues recently in Miri Rubin, 'A Decade of the Study of Women, 1987–1997', *History Workshop Journal*, 46 (1998), 213–39.

the physical aspects; and what is more physical than travel to archives and immersion in documents held there, reading of oversized codices and climbing ladders up to roof lofts and stained-glass windows? One possible relationship, probably the most pervasive in the structuring of educational curricula in schools and universities of Europe and the Americas, is that which acknowledges a link between present and past, and a need for comprehension of the medieval past in order to understand the present.[9] This can be cast in more or less nuanced fashions: habitual is the reference to the continuity of systems of rule (monarchy, parliament), regional identities (Bavarian, Welsh), landed entitlement (in those countries which never saw revolution or reformation, like Britain or Austria), civic and cultural endowment (as in the Tuscan cities, Paris, Flemish identity within Belgium).[10]

In a country like the United States, whose origins lie in the dualism of domination of indigenous people and slaves, as well as immigration of poor and/or persecuted Europeans, Europe represents a place left, abandoned,[11] away from poverty and persecution. Nonetheless a sizeable group of Americans maintained important cultural affinities with European Catholic religion.[12] As memory gave way to current prosperity and confidence, the 'old country' could exercise a nostalgic attraction, evident in relations to Britain and, more recently, to eastern Europe. It is interesting to note that today, as European immigration into the United States has given way to that from Asia, Central and Latin America and the Caribbean, a new-found enthusiasm for things medieval/European is flourishing, as witnessed in patterns of tourism, themed parks, invented village fêtes, and a wide circulation for toys, games and literature on

---

[9] See an interesting survey of teaching and comprehension of terms related to the Middle Ages in French secondary schools, Didier Lett, 'Le moyen âge dans l'enseignement secondaire français et sa perception par l'élève: entre mémoire scolaire et mémoire "buissonnière" ', *Revista d'història medieval*, 4 (1993), 291–320 and 5 (1994), 181–8.

[10] On some paradigms of self-understanding as related to the European past see Chris Wickham, 'Problems of Comparing Rural Societies in Early Medieval Western Europe', *Transactions of the Royal Historical Society*, 6, 2 (1992), 221–46, esp. 222–3.

[11] On medieval studies in places apart from the medieval European past see Roberts Frank, 'On a Changing Field: Medieval Studies in the New World', *South African Journal of Medieval and Renaissance Studies*, 4 (1994), 1–20, at 1. On a related theme see Gabrielle M. Spiegel, 'In the Mirror's Eye: The Writing of Medieval History in America', in *Imagined Histories: American Historians Interpret the past*, ed. Anthony Molho and Gordon S. Wood (Princeton, NJ, 1998), pp. 238–62, at pp. 239–41.

[12] Philip Gleason, *Keeping the Faith: American Catholicism Past and Present* (Notre Dame, IN, 1987), ch. 1, esp. pp. 11–34.

medieval themes.[13] Not unlike the current appropriation of commercialised 'country music' by white, middle-class suburbanites, as an alternative to rap music and other areas of popular culture perceived as African-American idioms, the medieval marks a space which is exclusively 'white'. Yet to gesture towards a medieval past, the heritage of white descendants of Europeans, is an unstable move. For the medieval defies such possession. It can be linked with roots and genealogy for Wasps, but it also denotes violence and horror. That is why Quentin Tarantino made 'getting medieval' the menacing threat which Marsellus Wallace uttered at his erstwhile tormentor–rapist in the film *Pulp Fiction*.[14] Yet by its very use, it becomes abundantly clear that the horror that is the 'medieval' — associated with torture, intolerance and rife interpersonal violence and official cruel and unusual death — is alive and present in 1990s Los Angeles, just as it is on death row in several American states.

The search and claim for medieval origins is dual; it is not only the work of conservative bodies, nor always the expression of a Whig–liberal sentiment. The Middle Ages have been the *locus classicus* for the grounding of counter-cultural movements, movements of liberation. Textbooks on women's history and feminism begin by acknowledging Christine de Pisan, and take pride in the feisty creativity of Hildegard of Bingen. Yet one person's liberation is another's oppression. A self-professed movement for liberation is the Italian *Lega Nord* (product of the recent fusion between *Lega Lombarda* and *Liga Veneta*), which claims affinity with central and northern Italian medieval communes. Its adoption

---

[13] Louise O. Fradenburg, ' "Absolutely Fabulous": The Historicity of Medieval Romance', unpublished opening plenary lecture, Medieval Academy, Austin, TX, April 2000. I am most grateful to the author for allowing me to cite her paper. On the 'return' of the Middle Ages and its many forms see Umberto Eco, *Travels in Hyperreality: Essays*, trans. William Weaver (San Diego, New York and London, 1986), pp. 61–85. On the proliferation of 'medieval' themes in popular culture see Matteo Sanfilippo, *Il medioevo secondo Walt Disney: come l'America ha reinventato l'eta di mezzo* (Rome, 1993); Kevin J. Harvey, *Cinema Arthuriana: Essays on Arthurian Film* (New York, 1991); Susan Aronstein and Nancy Coiner, 'Twice Knightly: Democratising the Middle Ages for Middle-class America', in *Medievalism in North America*, ed. Kathleen Verduin, Studies in Medievalism, 6 (Woodbridge, 1994), pp. 212–31. William C. Jordan's family contributed to a mapping of such medieval materials in children's culture, see William C. Jordan, 'Saving Medieval History: Or, the New Crusade', in *The Past and Present of Medieval Studies*, ed. John Van Engen (Notre Dame, IN, 1994), pp. 259–72, at pp. 265–8.

[14] Analysed in Carolyn Dinshaw, 'Getting Medieval: *Pulp Fiction*, Foucault, and the Use of the Past', in *Getting Medieval: Sexualities and Communities Pre- and Post-modern* (Durham, NC, 1999), pp. 183–206, at pp. 183–5. On 'medieval' as a pejorative adjective in current usage see Roberta Frank, 'On a Changing Field: Medieval Studies in the New World', *South African Journal of Medieval and Renaissance Studies*, 4 (1994), 1–20, at 3.

of the *carroccio* (the ceremonial wagon of the medieval communes) as a symbol, the founding demonstration in Pontida in 1991 (the site of oath-taking of the Lombard League in the Middle Ages), and the invocation of an ancestry from Alberto da Giussano appeal to schoolroom memories and suggest a renewal of autonomy and liberation (from the 'empire' of Brussels, from the burden of the *Mezzogiorno*). Similarly, Occitan separatists delight in macabre stories of suffering and defiance suffered by Languedoc's medieval Cathars;[15] and Greens and other European environmentalists attempt to reintroduce forest and resource management which is less intrusive and exploitative, just as medieval people managed their forests, streams and meadows.

Reflection on the Middle Ages and its many refractions within past and present cultures has become a distinct area of scholarship of which I do not mean this short essay to form a part.[16] What is less frequently emphasised is just how often it can give rise to political appropriation, for which we need quick answers and a political presence of mind. From the wishful thoughts of Hindu nationalists keen to establish their affinity with Aryan Balts,[17] to the scholarly debates on the 'Englishness' of the Anglo-Irish;[18] or the elaborations of what the left-wing journalist and novelist Edith Thomas — a supporter of the *résistance* against Vichy — called 'troubadourisme'.[19] Medieval historians are invoked and used; they may thus also be engaged with problems alive in contemporary political life — local, national and global — to which their expertise and ideas might be applied and within which they may find their words embedded.[20]

---

[15] Andrew Roach, 'Occitania Past and Present: Southern Consciousness in Medieval and Modern French Politics', *History Workshop Journal*, 43 (1997), 1–22.

[16] See for example Roger Dahood (ed.), *The Future of the Middle Ages and Renaissance: Problems, Trends and Opportunities for Research* (Turnhout, 1998); the following volume is the first in a series published by Brepols 'Making the Middle Ages', *Medievalism in the Modern World: Essays in Honour of Leslie J. Workman* (Turnhout, 1998).

[17] Douglas R. Spitz and William Urban, 'A Hindu Nationalist View of Baltic History', *Journal of Baltic Studies*, 24 (1993), 295–8, at 296.

[18] Art Cosgrove, 'The Writing of Irish Medieval History', *Irish Historical Studies*, 27 (1990), 97–111.

[19] Dorothy Kaufmann, 'Against "Troubadourisme" in Vichy France: The Diaries of Edith Thomas', *Journal of Medieval and Early Modern Studies*, 27 (1997), 507–19; see the definition of 'troubadourisme' at 510: 'Le troubadourisme est une maladie de l'art et de la littérature qui apparaît en période régressive et consiste en un attendrissement ingénu sur un passé imaginaire.'

[20] On the challenge which faced Johann in Huizinga see Willem Otterspeer (trans. by Lionel Gossman and Reinier Leushuis), 'Huizinga before the Abyss: The van Leers Incident at the University of Leyden, April 1933', *Journal of Medieval and Early Modern Studies*, 27 (1997), 385–444.

Medieval Europe: a vision of peace?

The relevance of medieval Europe to contemporary political projects is based
not only on the sense of continuity, but also on its value as a source for
alternative cultural and political forms. Thus, for Jacques Le Goff, medieval
Europe is a cultural system from which a post-national, post-Christian Europe
can find models for self-understanding and self-imagining.[21] Here the desire is
to remake those patterns of interaction, ease of movement, shared institutions
which facilitated intellectual exchange and commercial enterprise in the past,
without adopting those less desirable or even deadly heritages of religious
persecution, personal unfreedom, and political disenfranchisement experienced by almost all women and most men in that period. This 'opportunistic'
approach — picking and choosing from the medieval treasure trove — is
appealing, as long as it is clear that medieval institutions are examined each for
its merits and dangers, before they are disseminated through the powerful
cultural apparatus of, say, the European Union.[22] In all the cases mentioned
above we witness the intermeshing of political and affective desires, and the
gesture towards the medieval endows a new party or movement with dignity
and recognisable, legitimate symbolic currency.[23]

   In the aftermath of the First World War, medieval understandings and
medieval visions inspired some of those involved in the work of healing.
Among the American legation to the Paris peace talks in 1919 and 1920 was
the historian of the medieval monarchical state, Charles Homer Haskins,
whom Woodrow Wilson knew as part of a group of progressive Democrats

---

[21] See for example Jacques Le Goff's thoughts in Archambault, 'An Interview with Jacques Le
Goff'. For a vision of the medieval European heritage see Richard W. Southern, *The Making of the
Middle Ages* (London, 1953, new edn, 1993). Robert Bartlett inverts the perspective by looking at
Europe from its 'borders', see *The Making of Europe: Conquest, Colonization and Cultural Change,
950–1350* (Harmondsworth, 1994).

[22] On the 'dual' legacy see Le Goff's terms 'rosy' and 'dark' in Archambault, 'An Interview with
Jacques Le Goff', 168; Eco, 'Dreaming the Middle Ages', in *Travels in Hyperreality*, pp. 68–72; see
also Albrecht Classen, 'Warum und zu welchem Zweck studieren wir das Mittelalter? Deutsche
Literatur des Mittelalters im 20. Jahrhundert', *Wirkendes Wort: Deutsche Sprache und Literatur in
Forschung und Lehre*, 43 (1993), 7–25, at 8; on the 'light' and 'dark' Middle Ages see Hans-Werner
Goetz, *Moderne Mediävistik: Stand und Perspektiven der Mittelalterforschung* (Darmstadt, 1999),
pp. 47–54.

[23] On medieval history practised in Europe, seen by an American scholar, see Giles Constable, 'The
Many Middle Ages: Medieval Studies in Europe as seen from America', in *Bilan et perspectives des
études médiévales en Europe: Actes du premier congrès européen d'études médiévales (Spoleto
27–29 mai 1993)*, ed. Jacqueline Hamesse (Louvain-la-Neuve, 1995), pp. 1–22. For an interesting
collection of essays on the relation of Germans to 'their' Middle Ages see Gerd Althoff (ed.), *Die
Deutsche und ihr Mittelalter: Themen und Funktionen moderner Geschichtsbilder vom Mittelalter*,
(Darmstadt, 1992).

educated at Harvard. It was the vision of national states — which to Haskins seemed akin to Capetian France and Anglo-Norman England — that offered a vision of stability in a post-imperial age. Hence the models for Yugoslavia and Czechoslovakia, states large enough to be economically viable, and yet structured constitutionally to contain diversity.[24]

In the very same years another arm of American influence, the Rockefeller Foundation, wished to finance a new pan-European historical journal, through which historians of countries only recently at war would forge a shared enterprise. Marc Bloch and Lucien Febvre, who were the journal's initiators, approached Henri Pirenne to head it, but he refused to act so long as the editorial board included German historians. (At the outset of the war Pirenne had returned all his honours and resigned his membership of several German historical bodies.) Throughout the 1920s the enterprise was discussed in various international historical forums; the *Annales d'Histoire Economique et Sociale* was finally born in 1929, the progenitor of the *Annales: ESC* and today's *Annales: HSS*.

It is interesting for our discussion to note the prominence of medieval history in the process of post-war reconstruction of European culture. If a vision of a healed Europe was to be constructed and an idea of a peaceful European future created, then a history to serve it was required. This had to be a history of a collective European 'experience': a simple political, military, or diplomatic history, but one which addressed long-term trends in agrarian life, beliefs, demography, lordship and technology — and which thus touched the lives of the European multitudes. A history for those who paid the price of war. The medieval was the matter and the social–economic inquiry the form of which a European history was to emerge. Political history could not grapple with a European vision, nor, by 1929, with the current problems of Europe.[25] Moreover, the history Bloch and Febvre envisaged could not be compartmental, since life was not. Hence Lucien Febvre's rallying command 'abattre les cloisons' ('down with the compartments').[26]

Alterity or commonality: then or now

A powerful attraction to medieval culture has been generated by the appreciation of its radical difference, and the hope of generating from it

[24] Norman Cantor, *Inventing the Middle Ages: The Lives, Works and Ideas of the Great Medievalists of the Twentieth Century* (New York, 1991), pp. 245–86, esp. pp. 252–3.
[25] Fink, *Marc Bloch*, p. 130.
[26] Peter Burke, *The French Historical Revolution: The Annales School, 1929–1989* (Cambridge, 1990), p. 2.

inspiration for tired modern, postmodern, sensibilities. You may have noted that this essay is the only one in the volume devoted to a period, rather than to an area of practice or concept. Perhaps rightly, for the 'Middle Ages' is a concept and a problem. More than any other period it is 'another place', perceived alternatively as weird and wonderful.

Probably the most influential worker in this mode has been Caroline Walker Bynum. Her work on women's religious practices and the centrality of somatic mediation of faith and worship has emphasised the power of medieval symbols to offer balm for quintessentially modern discontents.[27] In the creation of rich inner worlds out of the materials of liturgy and hagiographical and mystical narratives, women in the Middle Ages are seen as taking control of their lives, and transcending the debasing and passing aspects of (female) physicality through an association with a different (yet not too different) sublime corporality, that of Christ's suffering body. Moreover, in a polemic against Leo Steinberg she has presented an understanding of the value of considering medieval ideas in our times: 'If we want to turn from seeing the body as sexual to seeing the body as generative, if we want to find symbols that give dignity and meaning to the suffering we cannot eliminate and yet fear so acutely, we can find support for doing so in the art and theology of the later Middle Ages.'[28] The Middle Ages are here seen as offering a plenitude of rich symbols of the kind we dearly need and have sadly lost. This plaintive tone and wistful desire for the Christian Middle Ages have inspired Bynum's own exceptional work, but where does it leave the rest of us? Who can share in it, and who cannot? Can it be approached without our bodies, ourselves? Bynum's

---

[27] Caroline Walker Bynum, *Holy Feast and Holy Fast: The Religious Significance of Food to Medieval Women* (Berkeley, CA, 1987); see also on the body *Fragmentation and Redemption: Essays on Gender and the Human Body in Medieval Religion* (New York, 1991); and *The Resurrection of the Body in Western Christianity, 200–1336* (New York, 1995). On this approach and related difficulties see Michael Camille, 'Art History and the Past and Future of Medieval Studies', in *The Past and Future of Medieval Studies*, ed. John Van Engen (Notre Dame, IN, 1994), pp. 362–82, at pp. 369–70; David Aers, 'The Humanity of Christ: Reflections on Orthodox Late Medieval Representations', in David Aers and Lynn Staley, *The Powers of the Holy: Religion, Politics and Gender in Late Medieval English Culture* (University Park, PA, 1996), pp. 15–42, at pp. 28–42; Kathleen Biddick, 'Genders, Bodies, Borders: Technologies of the Visible', *Speculum*, 68 (1993), 389–418, repr. in *The Shock of Medievalism* (Durham, NC, 1998), pp. 135–62; see also Paul Freedman, 'The Return of the Grotesque in Medieval Historiography', in *Historia a Debate — Medieval*, ed. Carlos Barros (Santiago de Compostella, 1995), pp. 9–19, at pp. 10–16.
    On the turn to the body see Miri Rubin, 'Why the Body and Why Now?', in *The Work of Jacques Le Goff and the Challenges of Medieval History*, ed. Miri Rubin (Woodbridge, 1997), pp. 209–19; for a discussion of these interests as reactions within a consumer-oriented culture see Doug Mann, 'The Body as an "Object" of Historical Knowledge', *Dialogue: Canadian Philosophical Review*, 35 (1996), 753–76.
[28] Caroline W. Bynum, 'The Body of Christ in the Late Middle Ages: A Reply to Leo Steinberg', *Renaissance Quarterly*, 39 (1986), 399–439.

expert hands have dealt deftly with texts and some visual material of a group of women who came to be remembered in *vitae*. Those very symbols also participated in other experiences of pain, and punishment and revenge, which cannot so easily be seen as offering us symbols of generation: pain, exclusion, revenge, suspicion are as much the matter of that religious universe as is nurture, and the relation between the two sets of symbols is a close, sometimes necessary one. The nourishing blood was also blood that called for revenge in the many stories of ritual murder and host desecration. Who is the 'we' in the call 'if we want to turn'? Not I.

The critical procedures which we bring to bear on our own cultural production must be allowed to work for those of other periods, as long as we employ them scrupulously. The call for empathy with past religious practices can exclude positions and interpretive possibilities.[29] Why should Leo Steinberg's position — that of a man schooled in traditional art history — be dismissed as not sufficiently medieval? If we have learned something from the mode of engagement practised by ethnography, it is not so much empathy, but 'being taken seriously', with attention to the many ways in which they are authored and made.[30]

It appears to me that a critical and knowing engagement with the traces of medieval societies and cultures is one which treats them, among other artefacts and phenomena, as useful sounding boards for contemporary, always historical, quests.[31] This is not to say that the medieval should be robbed of its historical specificities. Quite the contrary. For medieval images to be 'good to think with' they must be meticulously known and carefully searched. They are useful, since they combine familiarity pregnant with occasions for defamiliarising; images ubiquitous from postcards and children's games, and yet highly enigmatic. As instances within religious cultures, medieval cases offer a terrain for the understanding of ritual and symbols; located within a large geographic entity, they force us to reflect on regional difference and the nature of solidarity and cooperation; as an epoch of limited resources and a widespread subsistence economy, it offers a useful terrain for reflection on management of poverty, dearth and

---

[29] Such as those based on contemporary concerns, see Freedman, 'The Return of the Grotesque', p. 10.

[30] Aletta Biersack, 'Local Knowledge, Local History: Geertz and Beyond', in *The New Cultural History*, ed. Lynn Hunt (Berkeley, CA, 1989), pp. 72–96; James Clifford, 'On Ethnographic Authority', *Representations*, 1 (1983), 118–46. See also the collection *Writing Culture: The Poetics and Politics of Ethnography*, ed. James Clifford and George E. Marcus (Berkeley, CA, 1986).

[31] Peter L. Allen, 'A Frame for the Text? History, Literary Theory, Subjectivity and the Study of Medieval Literature', *Exemplaria*, 3 (1991), 1–25, at 2.

preservation of resources. All of these questions remain with us. This is of course also to say that the Middle Ages are not unique in offering these illuminating vantage points; but nor should it ever be said that they are less illuminating than other, closer periods.

Opposites and beyond: Latinate masculinity and the vernacular

All areas of knowledge and practice in the Middle Ages — medicine, religion, politics — are now recognised to have been extremely diverse, defying any simple set of opposing terms such as elite–popular, spiritual–materialist, literate–illiterate, personal–collective, mystical–parochial, and even male–female.[32] This is not to say that for a good number of years some of these terms have not been extremely useful in helping us arrive at current appreciation of complexity: 'elite' and 'popular' (or rather *savant/clericale* and *populaire*) were the necessary bolster for some of the edifices arising from *Annaliste* historiography in the 1970s.[33] These terms sanctioned and inspired the entry into discussion of a whole world of tale and practice — think only of the rigorous study of *exempla* and of images which have resulted[34] — which have transformed the range of beliefs we now know to have been held by medieval people.

This debate ultimately resulted in a recognition that 'elite' and 'popular' are categories so unstable that the intellectual effort required to shore them up could be much more effectively invested in reflection on, and analysis of, those contexts of use from which their meanings arose.[35] To say so is not to

[32] On such binaries in medieval studies see Anne Middleton, 'Medieval Studies', in *Redrawing the Boundaries: The Transformation of English and American Literary Studies*, ed. Stephen Greenblatt and Giles Gunn (New York, 1992), pp. 12–40, at p. 25.

[33] The editor of this volume, Peter Burke, was the first to consider systematically the terms and their historical significance in *Popular Culture in Early Modern Europe* (London, 1978). See Jean-Claude Schmitt, ' "Religion populaire" et culture folklorique', *Annales: ESC*, 31 (1976), 941–53; idem, 'Les traditions folkloriques dans la culture médiévale: quelques réflexions de méthode', *Archives de Sciences Sociales des Religions*, 52 (1981), 5–20.

[34] *Prêcher d'exemples: récits de prédicateurs du moyen âge*, ed. Jean-Claude Schmitt (Paris, 1985); Alain Boureau, *La Légende dorée: le system narratif de Jacques de Voragine (d. 1298)* (Paris, 1984); *Les exempla médiévaux: introduction à la recherche*, ed. Jacques Berlioz and Marie Anne Polo de Beaulieu (Carcassone, 1992). For a recent assessment of new directions in the field see Hans-Jörg Gilomen, 'Volkskultur und Exempla-Forschung', in *Modernes Mittelalter: Neue Bilder einer populären Epoche*, ed. Joachim Heinzle (Frankfurt and Leipzig, 1994), pp. 165–208.

[35] See the classic statement in Roger Chartier, 'Culture as Appropriation: Popular Cultural Uses in Early Modern France', in *Understanding Popular Culture: Europe from the Middle Ages to the Nineteenth Century*, ed. S. L. Kaplan, New Babylon: Studies in the Social Sciences, 40 (Berlin, 1984), pp. 229–53.

reiterate the sentiment held by several scholars — ranging from Leonard Boyle to Eamon Duffy — that, say, the faith of the prince and the pauper may have been very close indeed. It is, rather, to say something else. It occurs to me that every Humbert of Silva Candida, every Albert the Great, even a Stephen of Bourbon — monitors and producers of 'elite' culture — were reared and formed in childhood and boyhood within cultural frames that can only be described as local and vernacular. In the case of the last, the Dominican, this interest was maintained through a critical engagement in the ethnographic description of local practices, which he saw as abhorrent.[36] This is to say that before their formation turned them into the brilliant scholar, theologian, inquisitive friar, each with his imagined part in the building of a *societas christiana* through images of uniformity and ubiquity, they were versed in local traditions, cherished local saints, were lulled to sleep by lullabies mouthed in local dialect. These formative experiences and forms of knowledge were, moreover, mediated by people who were, by necessity, of lower social status, often by women (siblings, wet-nurses, servants, cooks). Becoming a man, a young cleric, a student, and then rising in the world, was thus a process of shedding that local vernacularity, a process of refashioning which is also one of loss and possible mourning.[37] By acquiring Latin, by discoursing in scholastic dialects, by training in a universal system of knowledge — in theology and law — by acquiring the skill and confidence with which to correct and chastise, through extensive travel across Europe, and sometimes beyond it — they became men. And this came about through a process of distancing from the early 'feminine' formation, and incorporation within a world which was almost purely male, predominantly celibate, and involved in system-building, forensic inquiry, and sometimes harmonising of difference.[38]

Yet something was always retained, and could be relived, re-experienced, as a re-sentiment. Jean Gerson negotiated deftly the layers of his *Bildung* and experience, the roles which the world awaited him to perform:

[36] Jean-Claude Schmitt, *The Holy Greyhound: Guinefort, Healer of Children since the Thirteenth Century* (Cambridge, 1982), 'The Inquisitor', pp. 9–35.

[37] On pedagogy and pain see Jody Enders, *The Medieval Theater of Cruelty: Rhetoric, Memory, Violence* (Ithaca, NY, 1999), pp. 129–52.

[38] Some defied that pull and devoted themselves self-consciously to immersion in the 'feminine'; see the career of Eckhard of Schönau, Anne L. Clark, *Elisabeth of Schönau: A Twelfth-century Visionary* (Philadelphia, PA, 1992). Another configuration of this trope may be discerned in the hagiographical theme ascribed to young male future saints, the rejection of the wet-nurse or an aspect of early nurture as sinful or distasteful even to the young infant; see Shulamith Shahar, 'Infants, Infant Care and Attitudes towards Infancy in the Middle Ages', *Journal of Psychohistory*, 10 (1983), 281–309, at 299. See also Burke, *Popular Culture in Early Modern Europe*, p. 28.

Chancellor of the University of Paris, parish priest, leading conciliarist, arbiter of the orthodoxy of dogma, prophecies, and mystical pronouncements. He contained and channelled the 'vernacular' into an overwhelming pastoral thrust and was both productive and imaginative in his pursuit of themes in religious affect, such as the cults of the new saint, St Joseph.[39] His embroidery upon the image of Joseph and Mary's marriage draws as much from his theology of faith as it does from an observation of conjugal daily life. His advice to his sisters on their devotional practices bespoke a domestic imagination, of an intimacy quite foreign to the milieu of university and council where he spent most of his time.

Multitude and meaning

Two strands of historical questioning were expressed in the quantifying thrust of the second half of the century. The triumph of American sociology, for a while, and in Europe the strong traditions of nineteenth-century statistics and historical geography, together with a guiding Marxist turn towards engagement with economies, often through the study of large bodies of data. All combined to a great sense of purpose and promise in quantifying work. Work on the peasantry, it was thought, could be done only through a careful serial approach to the sources which could reveal their lives: those of the manorial courts. Writing on families required painstaking attention to the lives and deaths which marked beginnings and ends and which for the period after 1536 are available in the form of parish registers in England and Wales. Quantification could raise the dead, and make the otherwise silent and unknown subjects of history speak. It could even delve into pious intention; *Annalistes* famously sought ways of making pounds of wax expended in religious practice represent hopes and fears about death, and the choices of testators in their wills express a religious sensiblity.[40] Most famously, it was the insights of a historical demographer, Philippe Ariès, that pro-

---

[39] See his advice to his sisters, and on St Joseph, Miri Rubin, 'Purity and Danger: Europe in the Later Middle Ages', *Transactions of the Royal Historical Society*, 6, 11 (2001), 101–24, at 113–14.

[40] On quantification in *Annaliste* history of the 1960s and 1970s, see Philippe Carrard, *Poetics of the New History: French Historical Discourse from Braudel to Chartier* (Baltimore, MD, 1992), pp. 166–81; Michel Vovelle, *La mort et l'occident de 1300 à nos jours* (Paris, 1983), quantification here addressed both the demographic trends and responses to it. For the influence of such method see Jacques Chiffoleau, *La comptabilité de l'au-delà: les hommes, la mort et la religion dans la région d'Avignon à la fin du moyen-âge, vers 1320–vers 1480* (Rome, 1980); Norman P. Tanner, *The Church in Late Medieval Norwich, 1370–1532*, PIMS Studies and Texts, 66 (Toronto, 1984).

posed one of the boldest theses about the nature of the medieval family.[41] For medievalists the move to quantify engulfed all types of sources: hagiography,[42] manorial court rolls,[43] canonisation processes,[44] tax returns,[45] customs records,[46] *exempla*,[47] personal names.[48] Yet after a while some fundamental problems with method, and a dissatisfaction with the types of results which such work could produce began to emerge.

The claims of similarity within large bodies of data became increasingly hard to sustain. My own attempt to follow up a study of medieval hospitals with a quantitative study of all English medieval hospitals came to a halt as it became clear that houses called 'hospital' in different places could be widely different institutions. How might one assess the impact of hospital formation when those that were counted varied from the minute and barely traceable to a large urban foundation?[49] Moreover, looking at words, how does one move from the sheer recurrence of an *exemplum* about the poor, or Jews, to an appreciation of the impact and tenor of such usage?[50] Quantification of entries in manorial court rolls has been revised through the recognition that whole

---

[41] In *Centuries of Childhood*, trans. Robert Baldick (London, 1962, repr. 1996). The thesis is mightily refuted in Shahar, *Childhood in the Middle Ages* (London, 1990). On the intellectual milieu from which Ariès' work arose see the collection of his autobiographical and methodological essays *Essais de mémoire 1943–1983* (Paris, 1993), part I.

[42] Donald Weinstein and Rudolph M. Bell, *Saints and Society: The Two Worlds of Western Christendom, 1000–1700* (Chicago, IL, 1987).

[43] *Medieval Rural Society and the Manor Court*, ed. Zvi Razi and Richard Smith (Oxford, 1996); on methodology see ch. 9. On different approaches see Zvi Razi, 'The Toronto School's Reconstitution of Medieval Peasant Society: A Critical View', *Past and Present*, 85 (1978), 141–57.

[44] André Vauchez, *Sainthood in the Late Middle Ages* (Cambridge, 1997).

[45] David Herlihy and Christiane Klapisch-Zuber, *Tuscans and their Families: A Study of the Florentine Catasto of 1427* (New Haven, CT, 1985); P. J. P. Goldberg, *Women, Work and Life Cycle in a Medieval Economy: York and Yorkshire c. 1300–1525* (Oxford, 1992), throughout, and see appendix on pp. 368–75.

[46] Maryanne Kowaleski, *Local Markets and Regional Trade in Medieval Exeter* (Cambridge, 1995).

[47] *Les exempla médiévaux: Exempel und Exempelsammlungen*, ed. Walter Haug and Burghart Wachinger, Fortuna vitrea, 2 (Tübingen, 1991).

[48] See the work of David A. Postles: 'Personal Naming Patterns of Peasants and Burgesses in Late Medieval England', *Medieval Prosopography*, 12 (1991), 29–56; idem, 'The Baptismal Name in Thirteenth-century England: Processes and Patterns', *Medieval Prosopography*, 13 (1992), 1–52; idem, 'Cultures of Peasant Naming in Twelfth-century England', *Medieval Prosopography*, 18 (1997), 25–54.

[49] For some critical thoughts about aggregating material on leper-house foundations see E. A. M. Satchell, 'The Emergence of Leper-houses in Medieval England, 1100–1250', D.Phil. dissertation (Oxford University, 1999).

[50] For an attempt to deal with *exempla* of Jews see Jacques Le Goff, 'Le Juif dans les *exempla* médiévaux: le cas de l'*Alphabetum narrationum*', in *Pour Léon Poliakov: Le racisme: mythes et sciences*, ed. Maurice Olender (Paris, 1981), pp. 209–20.

sections of village society were unlikely to be recorded. The reaction against quantification stemmed not only from the fear that it might simply be inaccurate, but rather that it created a false sense of rigour and a gold standard of soundness, which was increasingly difficult to sustain and out of keeping with more hermeneutic and textual approaches to historical materials.[51]

Quantitative work has thus not answered all the questions it had hoped to resolve, and its own evolution has seen a shift in its ambitions from quantitative coverage, to questions that are qualitative, regional and highly complex. The careful work on the annual movements of prices of agricultural produce, recently conducted by David Stone, illustrates the dilemmas of the reeve, steward of estates in late medieval England, in new and exciting ways.[52] To the unforgettable image of Chaucer's Reeve can now be added some painstakingly reconstructed realities of harsh vocational expectations and the related dilemmas. This case rewards closer scrutiny: after the Black Death there was widespread movement in estate management away from arable, but this was neither a straightforward nor a linear trend. Fluctuations in patterns of land-use are sometimes discernible over short periods of two-to-three years. A vigilant eye was monitoring the movement of prices and the levels of wages; that eye was the reeve's. Stone is able to show that decisions about cropping followed carefully perceived shifts in market prices. The picture is particularly dramatic in a monoculture, as Stone's work on a pastoral area demonstrates. Here the reeve had to decide how much work was to be bought in and how much care the ewes and their mothers deserved.[53] A constant cost-benefit analysis was under way on estates in early fourteenth-century England, without glittering calculators or the aid of trade magazines. The pressure from estate owners who were experiencing a decline in income was high, and was directed largely at those who tended their estates, their reeves.

This may seem to be a hidden corner of medieval life, so minor as to be negligible. But it is not. The pressures on reeves not only affected the quality

---

[51] I am grateful for a most useful conversation on these issues with Katherine Gill, of Boston College, the coordinator of the MATRIX project on female religious houses.

[52] David Stone, *Decision Making in Medieval Agriculture: Wisbech Barton in the Fourteenth and Early Fifteenth Centuries* (Oxford, forthcoming 2003); see also idem, 'Medieval Farm Management and Technological Mentalities: Hinderclay before the Black Death', *Economic History Review*, 54 (2001), 612–38; see also work by Chris Briggs, 'Rural Credit, Debt Litigation, and the Manor Court', unpublished Fellowship dissertation (Trinity College, Cambridge, 2000).

[53] On productivity see Bruce M. S. Campbell, *English Seigneurial Agriculture, 1250–1540* (Cambridge, 2000). The extraordinary subtlety of medievalists' work in quantitative methods relating to trade as well as to agrarian society has not been sufficiently noted by other historians. The very useful Pat Hudson, *History by Numbers: An Introduction to Quantitative Approaches* (London, 2000) uses only two examples of work on medieval sources, pp. 92–3, 101, 185.

of life of the majority of the population, made up of rural, agricultural workers. They also illuminate areas of life so often hidden, and which we know from current experience to be highly indicative of communal, domestic and personal well-being. Stress, insecurity in employment, anxiety about status, all affected levels of sociability, charity, stability, violence and cohesion within the rural communities — at once estate, village, parish — in which most people in most regions (the Low Countries and central and northern Italy being the exception) lived.[54]

Within the demographic realities emerging from quantitative work, we may proceed to ask how the experiences of marriage and childbirth were nonetheless unique and personal dramas. Demography in touch with feminist historical interests has yielded new social categories, such as the 'single-woman', the woman living alone or as head of household, which is to be understood as a mainstay of medieval communities, particularly in north-west Europe, one which poses not a *Frauenfrage*, but the opportunity to delve into worlds of work, sociability and sentiment.[55] Demographic trends are always experienced through the rhythms of ritual and the patterns of meaning, by people with local knowledge.[56] How did thinking about demography relate to other ways of quantifying the world and predicting the fortunes of families, towns, polities?[57] Numbers and words, science and art — still too separate in our practice — were not thus configured in several medieval contexts.

Culture, culture, and yet more culture

The sources now studied by medieval historians have, as I have suggested, multiplied greatly. This extension continues to express the desire for novelty, but also new appreciations of the possible. The effect of such broadening is, on the whole, empowering, and it tends to create new collaborative impulses. What a teacher may have dismissed as 'folkloric' when I was a student in the

---

[54] On Tuscan rural life see Duccio Balestrucci, *The Renaissance in the Fields: Family Memoirs of a Fifteenth-century Tuscan Peasant*, ed. Paolo Squatriti and Betsy Meredith (University Park, PA, 1999).

[55] See Maryanne Kowaleski, 'Singlewomen in Medieval and Early Modern Europe: The Demographic Perspective', in *Singlewomen in the European Past, 1250–1800*, ed. Judith M. Bennett and Amy M. Froide (Philadelphia, PA, 1999), pp. 38–81 and appendices on pp. 325–44.

[56] For an instructive example of the combination of quantitative/demographic and cultural understandings see the essays in Christiane Klapisch-Zuber, *Women, Family and Ritual in Renaissance Italy* (Chicago, IL, 1985).

[57] See the magisterial Peter Biller, *The Measure of Multitude: Population in Medieval Thought* (Oxford, 2000).

late 1970s, now forms the matter of serious reflection on symbolic systems and cultural forms.[58] Much of the new-found confidence in dealing with religion and culture has resulted from encounters with anthropology. The ethnographic impulse, the ethnographer's liminal situation within and without a culture, the respect for the telling detail which can reveal the lineaments of structure and meaning, are all grist to the mill of the questing medievalist and early modernists, intent on inclusion, expansion and unravelling of collective lives and everyday experience.

The passionate and productive embrace of history and anthropology occurred at a significant moment for the latter discipline. Historians could watch and learn, and, in the 1970s, a series of brilliant innovators devised ingenious ways of incorporating anthropological insight into the study of religion and culture. *Annalistes* read the classics, Marcel Mauss's *The Gift: The Form and Reason for Exchange in Archaic Societies*,[59] Emile Durkheim's *The Elementary Forms of Religious Life*;[60] they met and interacted with Claude Lévi-Strauss in the Maison des Sciences de l'Homme in Paris.[61] Georges Duby's *The Three Orders: Feudal Society Imagined* pays tribute to the influence of the comparative models of religion and language in Indo-European cultures developed by Georges Dumézil (1898–1979).[62]

In American universities cultural anthropology was energised by the confident and powerful vision of sociology in the 1950s and 1960s, by the social sciences as yet untroubled by the implications of decolonisation and the political dislocation which followed the inception of the Vietnam War.[63]

---

[58] On such habits see L. E. Boyle, 'The Future of the Past', *Florilegium: Carleton University Papers on Late Antiquity and the Middle Ages*, 13 (1994), 1–12, at 8; and the recent *Medieval Folklore: An Encyclopedia of Myths, Legends, Tales, Beliefs, and Customs*, ed. Carl Lindahl, John McNamara and John Lindow (Santa Barbara, CA, and Oxford, 2000). For a view which laments these developments see John Van Engen, 'The Christian Middle Ages as a Historiographical Problem', *American Historical Review*, 91 (1986), 519–52, esp. 535, 545, and see the response in Jean-Claude Schmitt, 'Religion, Folklore and Society in the Medieval West', in *Debating the Middle Ages: Issues and Readings*, ed. Lester K. Little and Barbara H. Rosenwein (Oxford, 1998), pp. 376–87.

[59] Trans. W. D. Hall (London, 1990). See enduring influence in Natalie Zemon Davis, *The Gift in Sixteenth-century France* (Oxford, 2000).

[60] Trans. and intro. Karen E. Fields (New York, 1995).

[61] From Durkheim they adopted *représentations collectives* which came to be *mentalité*, which never quite served historians with sufficient precision; see Robert Darnton, 'Intellectual and Cultural History', in *The Kiss of Lamourette: Reflections in Cultural History* (London, 1990), pp. 191–218, at pp. 215–16.

[62] Trans. Arthur Goldhammer (Chicago, IL, 1980), pp. 6–8; especially Georges Dumézil's *Mythe et épopée*, I (Paris, 1968). Jean-Claude Schmitt acknowledged a debt to ethnography in *The Holy Greyhound*, p. 8, and see the ethnographic report in ch. 8, pp. 124–44.

[63] On these developments see Adam Kuper, *Culture: An Anthropologist's View* (Cambridge, MA, 1999), ch. 5.

British and American scholars learned from British contemporaries Victor Turner and Mary Douglas.[64] Predominant in his impact has been, without doubt, the historical anthropologists' own patron saint, Clifford Geertz.[65] A particular gift for turning ethnographic gaze into historical anthropology was refined by Natalie Zemon Davis in her classic collection of articles *Society and Culture in Early Modern France*, while by the 1980s a fruitfully critical mode developed, in the further historicising applications of anthropology in the work of Bob Scribner.[66] Direct contact in certain academic settings further fostered the exchange albeit with very differing styles: would Keith Thomas have known Evans-Pritchard's work had he not come across a pamphlet of a lecture delivered by the anthropologist in 1961, while acting as editor of the local *Oxford Magazine*?[67] Would Robert Darnton's work have produced so sustained an engagement with anthropology but for the useful seminar, History 406, which he created in 1972 and then taught jointly for six years with Clifford Geertz?[68] In turn historians' creative work with anthropology allowed them to contribute to debates on methodology. Robust exchanges followed the appearance of Robert Darnton's *The Great Cat Massacre* in 1984, and, more recently, Marshall Sahlins and Gunanath Obeyesekere have been locked in exchanges which addressed essentially historical questions about the handling of written sources and the study of

---

[64] V. Turner, *The Ritual Process: Structure and Anti-structure* (Cambridge, 1969); *Celebration: Studies in Festivity and Ritual*, ed. Victor Turner (Washington, DC, 1982); Turner introduced into discussion the work of Arnold Van Gennep, *The Rites of Passage* (London, 1960); for use by a medieval historian see Patrick J. Geary, *Furta Sacra: Thefts of Relics in the Central Middle Ages* (Princeton, NJ, 1978, new edn 1990). Mary Douglas, *Purity and Danger: An Analysis of the Categories of Pollution and Taboo* (London, 1966, repr. 1984); eadem, *Natural Symbols: Explorations in Cosmology* (London, 1970, new edn 1996).

[65] On Geertz see Kuper, *Culture*, ch. 6; on Geertz and the historians see William H. Sewell Jr, 'Geertz, Cultural Systems and History: From Synchrony to Transformation', in *The Fate of 'Culture': Geertz and Beyond*, ed. Sherry B. Ortner (Berkeley, CA, 1999), pp. 35–55, esp. pp. 37–9.

[66] R. W. Scribner, *For the Sake of Simple Folk: Popular Propaganda for the German Reformation* (Cambridge, 1981, repr. Oxford, 1994); *Popular Culture and Popular Movements in Reformation Germany* (London, 1987).

[67] See Keith Thomas's own version of the forms of influence in an interview published in *The Many Faces of History*, ed. Maria-Lúcia Pallares-Burke (Cambridge, forthcoming 2002); this encounter led Thomas to explore his views in 'History and Anthropology', *Past and Present*, 24 (1963), 3–24, in reaction to E. E. Evans-Pritchard, *Anthropology and History* (Manchester, 1961). Thomas mentions his general debt to anthropologists in Keith Thomas, *Religion and the Decline of Magic: Studies in Popular Beliefs in Sixteenth and Seventeenth Century England* (London, 1971), p. ix, and pp. 339, 463, 566, 645. On Thomas and anthropology see Jonathan Barry, 'Introduction: Keith Thomas and the Problem of Witchcraft', in *Witchcraft in Early Modern Europe*, ed. Jonathan Barry, Marianne Hester and Gareth Roberts (Cambridge, 1996), pp. 1–45, at pp. 4–8.

[68] Robert Darnton, *The Great Cat Massacre: And Other Episodes in French Cultural History* (London, 1984), p. 9.

oral cultures, questions close to the heart of medievalists.[69] Moreover, the textual turn which historians have come to appreciate in considering their own sources has also touched anthopologists and ethnographers, creating a mutual ground for reflection. The ethnographer is thus coming to see her exchanges and notes as texts, just as historians are considering genre and production more intently.[70] In these, medievalists rarely led the way, but became cautious users once methods and examples were well-tried and tested.

The fruits of observing interactions within the symbolic realm of culture also became evident for those studying political change. It is such an understanding which has led early medievalists to explore ethnicity and identity as underpinnings of political change;[71] which moved Johannes Fried to describe and analyse political life in the Ottonian Empire as a game played by king, nobility, church and people, and to trace an ethnography of the court and contacts with it;[72] and which informs the reminder offered by Rees Davies in suggesting that political acts cannot be understood outside the world of 'political perceptions'.[73] For those historians who work on medieval violence and communal tensions, writing based on ethnographic observation of contemporary violence can yield useful comparative dimensions into the abyss, into traumatic experiences which most western academics will never personally encounter.[74]

Above all, anthropology has offered guidance into the world of medieval religion. Medieval people lived within religious cultures, in ways which most Europeans and many North Americans no longer do. While there are those — and this has been said to me on several occasions by eminent scholars — who believe that only members of a certain faith can truly penetrate its mysteries

---

[69] See Marshall Sahlins, *How 'Natives' Think: About Captain Cook, for example* (Chicago, IL, 1995); Gunanath Obeyesekereh, *The Apotheosis of Captain Cook: European Myth-making on the Pacific* (Princeton, NJ, 1994). For the Middle Ages see Matthew Innes 'Memory, Orality and Literacy in an Early Medieval Society', *Past and Present*, 158 (1998), 3–36. On the relation between history and anthropology see Renato Rosaldo, ' "From the Door of his Tent": The Fieldworker and the Inquisitor', in *Writing Culture: The Poetics and Politics of Ethnography*, ed. James Clifford and George E. Marcus (Berkeley, CA, 1986), 77–97.

[70] On ethnography and literary theory see *Culture/Contexture: Explorations in Anthropology and Literary Studies*, ed. E. Valentine Daniel and Jeffrey M. Peck (Berkeley, CA, 1996).

[71] Walter Pohl, 'Conceptions of Ethnicity in Early Medieval Studies', in *Debating the Middle Ages: Issues and Meanings*, ed. Lester K. Little and Barbara H. Rosenwein (Oxford, 1998), pp. 15–24.

[72] *Der Weg in die Geschichte: Die Ursprünge Deutschlands: Bis 1024*, Propyläen Geschichte Deutschlands, 1 (Berlin, 1994), esp. pp. 632–736. Another matter which reflects on history making in the Federal Republic of Germany is the fact that the prestigious series in which this book appeared, Propyläen Geschichte Deutschlands, comprised seven distinguished historians — each and every one, a man.

[73] Rees R. Davies, in a review in *Southern History*, 13 (1991), 132–4, at 134.

[74] See for example the work on Sri Lanka by E. Valentine Daniel, *Charred Lullabies: Chapters in the Anthropography of Violence* (Princeton, NJ, 1996).

and evoke its cultures, new approaches to religion 'as cultural system' offered a vantage point and a set of procedures which could be evaluated, acquired and applied, even by the 'impious'.[75] The anthropological impulse interacted fruitfully with the desire to include and expand the terrain (veritable *terrain*, in the French sense, ethnographic field work) of history, for it suggested ways in which religious symbols could be discussed in settings that were neither official nor normative,[76] and even in those which were rejected by the church. The procession, the fraternity, the creative inventions of saints and liturgies, the vernacular prayer, the failed charismatic, all came to be seen not only as part of a rich array of religious forms and experience, but as telling sites, revealing nodal points which we ignore at the peril of ignorance.

In the wake of the anthropological turn we are witnessing a revival of interest in liturgy — for so long the exclusive domain of learned priests and monks — among historians of social relations. This renewed interest in liturgy may avail itself of a strong tradition in British scholarship of historical liturgiology born in the midst of mid-Victorian religious revival and experimentation. The example of Edmund Bishop, who expounded a historical frame for liturgical study, influenced medievalists such as David Knowles, Richard Southern and Christopher Brooke.[77] They could appreciate the transmission of liturgical texts as intellectual and devotional subject matter, but also attend to the performance itself, within sacred spaces and among artefacts which antiquarians such as J. Charles Cox minutely (if not always accurately) described, drew and collected.[78] The work of Eamon

---

[75] Patricia Crone and Michael Cook, *Hagarism: The Making of the Islamic World* (Cambridge, 1997), p. viii; cited and discussed in Richard W. Bulliet, 'Orientalism in Medieval Islamic Studies', in *The Past and Present of Medieval Studies*, ed. John Van Engen (Notre Dame, IN, 1994), pp. 94–104, at p. 101.

[76] Sewell, 'Geertz', pp. 37–9. On anthropological discussion of that very terrain, moving away from the localised, local culture, see Lila Abu-Lughod, 'The Interpretation of Culture(s) after Television', in *The Fate of 'Culture': Geertz and Beyond*, ed. Sherry B. Ortner (Berkeley, CA, 1999), pp. 110–35.

[77] Edmund Bishop, *Liturgica Historica: Papers on the Liturgy and Religious Life of the Western Church* (Oxford, 1918); Nigel Abercrombie, *The Life and Work of Edmund Bishop* (London, 1959). Similarly inspired by a commitment to Catholicism, but deploying the most rigorous standards of historical method, without the slightest apologetic mood, is the excellent work of several French medievalists such as Nicole Bériou, Dominique Rigaux and André Vauchez. Following in some ways the example of Michel Mollat, they work within a paradigm quite different from the *Annaliste*: taking religion as a sphere *sui generis*, albeit situated historically within broad historical contexts, but not to be reduced or subsumed within other social and cultural processes. Their work arises from within the Catholic tradition, but is understood by them to be what the French call *laïc*.

[78] J. Charles Cox and Alfred Harvey, *English Church Furniture* (London, 1907, facsimile edn East Ardley, 1973); J. Charles Cox, *Bench-ends in English Churches* (Oxford, 1916); idem, *Churchwardens' Accounts: From the Fourteenth to the Close of the Seventeenth Century* (London, 1917); Edmund Bishop, *Edward VI and the Book of Common Prayer* (London, 1891).

Duffy may be seen as a feeding off this very tradition; like Bishop he follows his interest in medieval liturgy through the challenges and the changes of the Reformation.[79] The challenge I have already highlighted pertains here too: the historian's training does not get easier, but more demanding.[80] For, if anthropology and liturgy are to interact, then new combinations of skill and training must be acquired and sustained by practitioners.[81]

From structures and systems to people and places

In so much of the work proliferating in medieval studies there is an evident tension between the desire to identify and comprehend structure — the rules of engagement between actors — while at the very same time to value and chronicle variety of local or personal idiosyncrasy and choice. Magisterial surveys, such as Richard Southern's *Scholastic Humanism and the Unification of Europe*,[82] will form backdrops for the emergent under-standings of particularity within frameworks — Christianity, Latinity, empire — which allowed people from disparate regions an experience of mutual understanding, cooperation and self-recognition. Thus, while the structure of the sacramental world was defined by theology and structured around ritual, it is striking and important to observe the very many uses and extensions created within that structure, sometimes in ways which under-mined the structure itself.[83] A legal system such as canon law, which circulated by papal endorsement, accompanied by ever-growing authorised glosses, offered a seemingly homogenous and stable structure of procedure and jurisprudence. And yet study of its application reveals wide levels of variation in interpretation, application and social function.[84] We have yet to find the terms and means of expressing and discussing that wide diversity

[79] Eamon Duffy, *The Stripping of the Altars: Traditional Religion in England, 1400–1580* (New Haven, CT, 1992).
[80] On methodological diversity see Patrick J. Geary, 'Visions of Medieval Studies in North America', in *The Past and Future of Medieval Studies*, ed. John Van Engen (Notre Dame, IN, 1994), pp. 45–57.
[81] They will also have to develop an acute awareness of the possible clashes and incompatibilities of frames of reference which might be deployed in unison, and in ignorance; see the discussion of theory and its uses and the strategies of 'practical' theoretical work in Paul Strohm's introduction to *Theory and the Premodern Text*, pp. xi–xvi; and for the practice, read the book.
[82] I–II (Oxford, 1995–2000).
[83] Miri Rubin, *Corpus Christi: The Eucharist in Late Medieval Culture* (Cambridge, 1991).
[84] Richard H. Helmholz, 'Spanish and English Ecclesiastical Courts (1300–1500)', *Studia Gratiana*, 28 (1998), 415–35.

and locality which characterised the Europe of our studies, and an important catalyst to their emergence may be the need and desire to understand and incorporate central Europe, not only into the European Union of the twenty-first century, but into the histories of medieval centuries. To do so may sometimes feel dispiritingly like 'starting from scratch',[85] but our political awareness in this age beyond empires, and the facility of communication, offer opportunities for collaboration and comparison — diversely, daringly — as never before.

In search of experience within structures some scholars have chosen to inhabit the difficult location between cultures, which also means between affinities, traditions and frames of historiographical reference. One such locus is the challenging terrain of Christian–Jewish relations, between textual traditions, within neighbourhoods, through shifting grounds of bureaucratic provision and representation.[86] Jews seem to fit both within the story — of urbanisation, of growth in state competence — and without it, in the fears and discomfort they evoked, as they came to embody the very idea of boundary. Around Jews were discussed such fundamental issues as business practice,[87] charity,[88] bodily comportment,[89] honour,[90] marriage,[91] orthodoxy.[92]

The fruitful work which has established our recognition of the power of gender to classify people and construct their identities is offering the grounds for understanding of experiences which defy reduction to male

---

[85] Wickham, 'Problems of Comparing', 222.

[86] Robert E. Lerner, *The Feast of Saint Abraham: Medieval Millennarians and the Jews* (Philadelphia, PA, 2001); David Nirenberg, *Communities of Violence: Persecution of Minorities in the Middle Ages* (Princeton, NJ, 1996); Ivan G. Marcus, *Rituals of Childhood: Jewish Acculturation in Medieval Europe* (New Haven, CT, 1996); Sara Lipton, *Images of Intolerance: The Representation of Jews and Judaism in the Bible Moralisée* (Berkeley, CA, 1999). This area of research — like that of gender — has been animated by empathy and commitment of a personal nature, as noted in Jordan, 'Saving Medieval History', p. 261.

[87] In discussion of usury, see for example Michael H. Shank, *'Unless you Believe, you shall not Understand': Logic, University and Society in Late Medieval Vienna* (Princeton, NJ, 1988), chs 6–7.

[88] Vittorino Meneghin, *I monti di pietá in Italia: dal 1462 al 1562* (Vicenza, 1986).

[89] Diane Owen Hughes, 'Distinguishing Signs: Ear-rings, Jews and Franciscan Rhetoric in the Italian Renaissance City', *Past and Present*, 112 (1986), 3–59.

[90] R. T. P. Mills, 'Visions of Excess: Pain, Pleasure and the Penal Imaginary in Late Medieval Art and Culture', Ph.D. dissertation (Cambridge University, 2000), ch. 2.

[91] Alain Boureau, 'L'inceste de Judas: Essai sur la genèse de la haine antisémite au XII siècle', *Nouvelle Revue de Psychanalyse*, 33 (1986), 25–41; repr. in Alain Boureau, *L'evénement sans fin: Récit et christianisme au moyen-âge* (Paris, 1993), pp. 209–30.

[92] Lipton, *Images of Intolerance*. See also Kathleen Biddick, 'Bede's Blush: Postcards from Bali, Bombay, Palo Alto', in *The Past and Future of Medieval Studies*, ed. John Van Engen (Notre Dame, IN, 1994), pp. 16–44, at p. 16.

or female. This is a move beyond gender. For, following Judith Butler's logic, naming spheres, acts and artefacts as feminine and masculine, begs transgression, confusion and creative performance between, around and beyond these very concepts.[93] Not to acknowledge these possibilities is to foreclose and hide from view desires and thus identities which may be neither one nor the other, but built upon both. The work 'beyond gender' can be as simple as discovering and interpreting the world of Marian devotion current among German burgers of the fifteenth century, with their ancestral devotion to images of the Virgin which they carefully passed on to their sons;[94] or to appreciate that the abjection of St Sebastian's tortured body may bespeak not only suffering and sympathy, but a delight in the imaging of pain and its transcendence; that an image of an abused martyr such as St Barbara may produce defiance in viewers as well as compassion or erotic desire.[95] Such work is mapping processes which will have to be drawn out with care and scrutiny, but they are worth having.

Beyond region and locality too there beckons a set of emergent interests which have had a profound effect on our thinking. If Southern's great works concentrated on the thoughts of men who used Latin, a robust sense of the vernacular is now emerging. Vernacular here denotes more than texts in languages other than Latin; these have been dealt with amply by the traditional philological sections of medieval studies, and more recently by the 'new philology'.[96] Rather, vernacular is meant here as a location within communities, sometimes the language of complaint, of instruction, women's idiom of choice. A number of important innovators have taken vernacular writings seriously not only in the areas of romance, but in religious guidance literature,[97] even identifying a realm which until recently

---

[93] See for example Amy Hollywood, *The Soul as Virgin Wife: Mechtild of Magdeburg, Marguerite Porete, and Meister Eckhart* (Notre Dame, IN, 1995).

[94] As shown recently by Bridget Heal, 'A Woman like Any Other? Images of the Virgin Mary and Marian Devotion in Nuremberg, Augsburg and Cologne, *c.* 1500–1600', Ph.D. dissertation (London University, 2001).

[95] For reflections on positions in relation to Christ see David Aers, 'The Humanity of Christ: Reflections on Julian of Norwich's *Revelation of Love'*, in *The Powers of the Holy: Religion, Politics and Gender in Late Medieval English Culture* (University Park, PA, 1996), pp. 77–104, at pp. 95–102.

[96] *The New Medievalism*, ed. Marina S. Brownlee, Kevin Brownlee and Stephen E. Nichols (Baltimore, MD, 1991); *Towards a New Synthesis? Essays in the New Philology*, ed. Keith Busby (Amsterdam, 1993); on it see Lee Patterson, 'The Return to Philology', in Van Engen, *The Past and Future*, pp. 231–44.

[97] *Medieval English Writings for Women: Selections from the 'Katherine group'*, ed. Bella Millett and Jocelyn Wogan-Browne (Oxford, 1990).

may have been taken to be oxymoronic, that of 'vernacular theology'.[98] Here is more than the unearthing of new texts, although these are always extremely welcome;[99] it is a questioning of the assumed hierarchy within medieval culture — between Latin and other languages — and, as the case of Lollardy shows, one with strong political resonances. We can even apply the 'vernacular turn' to deal with the ramification of the choice, by distinguished Latin writers, of the medium of the vernacular, thereby discovering new valences, registers of personality and intellect, as the case of Bernardino of Siena and Jean Gerson would amply testify. Moreover, the vernacular, that which was used daily and by many, also means incorporation of what Jeffrey Hamburger has simply called 'the ugly', that which previous generations of art historians have not cherished as part of the artistic canon of the Middle Ages. Some of the images we now examine are 'vernacular': they were hand-held, locally made, modest in cost, small in size. They offer links to a user, within a world of work, prayer, seasons, all of which historians profess to desire.[100]

We cannot hope to accomplish all this without a practice which displays similar sentiments and procedures. Humility towards the text, critical engagement with personal and institutional dilemmas, questioning of hierarchy, inclusion of disparate voices — all these must in meaningful ways be reflected in our modes of exposition, discussion, teaching and

---

[98] Nicholas Watson, 'Censorship and Cultural Change in Late-medieval England: Vernacular Theology, the Oxford Translation Debate, and Arundel's Constitutions of 1409', *Speculum*, 70 (1995), 822–64; idem, 'Visions of Inclusion: Universal Salvation and Vernacular Theology in Pre-Reformation England', *Journal of Medieval and Early Modern Studies*, 27 (1997), 145–87; idem, 'Conceptions of the Word: The Mother Tongue and the Incarnation of God', *New Medieval Literatures*, 1 (1997), 85–124. On the vernacular and intellectual work see Alain de Libera, *Penser au moyen âge* (Paris, 1991), p. 13.

This is material which can be taught as exemplified in the anthology *The Idea of the Vernacular: An Anthology of Middle English Theory, 1280–1520*, ed. Jocelyn Wogan-Browne, Nicholas Watson, Andrew Taylor and Ruth Evans (University Park, PA, 1999); part 4 contains interpretative and programmatic essays by the editors. See on vernacular pastoral material Craig Fraser, 'The Religious Instruction of the Laity in Late Medieval England with Particular Reference to the Sacrament of the Eucharist', D.Phil. dissertation (Oxford University, 1995).

[99] New perspectives are not gained exclusively through access to new materials (the vernacular canon is expanding), but through rereadings of familiar texts, as noted in Freedman, 'The Return of the Grotesque', p. 17.

[100] Like dolls and jewellery, see Jeffrey F. Hamburger, *The Visual and the Visionary: Art and Female Spirituality in Late Medieval Germany* (New York, 1998), p. 23. On the need to integrate images into historical analysis rather than to keep them as a separate section for display and discussion, which is still common practice, see Michael Camille, 'Art History in the Past and Future of Medieval Studies', in Van Engen, *The Past and Future*, pp. 362–82, at p. 369.

interaction.[101] This is not always easy. For we inhabit institutional structures which are often hierarchical and constraining; university scholars are increasingly pressed for time; our practice is as different and unique as each of us is. And yet we meet more frequently than historians have ever done, and have means for keeping in touch and supporting each other as never before.[102] There are some shining examples which we may choose to emulate, and, above all, it is never too late to experiment, reflect and learn.

Note. I am extremely grateful to Christopher Brooke, Marilynn Desmond, Yitzhak Hen, Piroska Nagy and Gareth Stedman Jones for conversations which helpfully contributed to this essay. Peter Burke's acute and sympathetic reading generously produced suggestions for further exploration. Paul La Hausse de la Louviere very kindly acquired for me articles which appeared in the *South African Journal of Medieval and Renaissance Studies*.

[101] For an example of a scholarly volume intent on bridging research interests and pedagogy within a historical frame of reference see *Between Hope and Despair: Pedagogy and the Remembrance of Historical Trauma*, ed. Roger I. Simon, Sharon Rosenberg and Claudia Eppert (New York and Oxford, 2000).

[102] On such contact and communication see E. Ann Matter, 'The Future of the Study of Medieval Christianity', in Van Engen, *The Past and Future*, pp. 166–77, at p. 167.

CHAPTER TWO

The City

PETER CLARK

British city growth since the Victorians has been dynamic and sustained. Whilst the majority of the population already lived in town by 1851, if not earlier, by 1900 the proportion was over 75 per cent and in 1950 only 20 per cent still lived in places regarded as rural; at the start of the twenty-first century Britain is 'effectively an urbanised society in which towns set the pace and city dwellers imagine the countryside in forms that complement their own modernity'.[1] In comparison, the writing of urban history has had a more uneven, erratic career.[2] Rather, as with an elderly motor car, there have been times of an apparent loss of power; on other occasions, a sudden swerve in direction. The historical literature on the city has been shaped, perhaps more than in other fields, by external influences, both methodological and organisational. One can identify three distinct phases in the conceptualisation of the city in all its forms: the first before the First World War, when German and legal-cum-constitutional influences were strong; the second around the 1960s and 1970s when American and, to a lesser extent, French methodological ideas oriented British interests, along with an awareness of the growing problems of contemporary urban development; and, finally, the third phase up to the present time, in which a large part of the important intellectual momentum of the field appears, at first sight, to be self-generated, from within the academic world, though again external factors cannot be ignored. Outside this country, British scholars have made significant

[1] L. H. Lees, 'Urban Networks in Britain 1840–1950', in M. Daunton (ed.), *Cambridge Urban History of Britain, vol. 3* (Cambridge, 2000), pp. 67–8.
[2] For recent detailed bibliographical surveys of the field see D. M. Palliser (ed.), *Cambridge Urban History of Britain, vol. 1* (Cambridge, 2000), pp. 7–13; P. Clark (ed.), *Cambridge Urban History of Britain, vol. 2* (Cambridge, 2000), pp. 16–22; also Daunton (ed.), *Cambridge Urban History, vol. 3*, pp. 1–55.

contributions to the urban history of France, Germany and Italy. Their work, inevitably reflecting in part local historiographical traditions, is beyond the scope of this analysis, which is limited to work on Britain.[3]

The study of British towns and cities is much older than the twentieth century, of course. During the later Middle Ages England had a small civic chronicling tradition (largely confined to London) and this survived on a modest scale into the eighteenth century (mainly in provincial centres such as Bristol). But in the last years of Elizabeth's reign John Stow's new-style *Survey of London* was published; it began the tradition of town histories, by collating antiquarian material on buildings, town worthies and municipal events with descriptions of the contemporary community. Initially these histories were written for local elites and those genteel folk who flocked to town during the urban renaissance of the early Georgian era, but after 1760 dozens of these works appeared, increasingly sold to the middle classes.[4] As national integration brought towns more directly into competition with one another, town histories acquired a boosterism quality, lauding the industrial and commercial advancement, cultural life and public improvement of the community, articulating civic pride and identity. This tradition remained strong through the nineteenth century with municipal authorities not infrequently commissioning works, such as J. T. Bunce's *History of the Corporation of Birmingham with a Sketch of the Earlier History of the Town* (1878–85), which was sanctioned by a committee chaired by that apostle of municipal socialism Joseph Chamberlain.[5] From the early Victorian period there was also a second strand in the literature, which was concerned more with the pathology of cities, with their mortality, sanitation and social problems: these works were often written by medical men such as William Farr, J. P. Kay and William Duncan, or by lay students of physiology such as Edwin Chadwick or Charles Bray.[6] The town history tradition has continued into the twentieth century and has

---

[3] See for example R. Cobb, *Death in Paris* (Oxford, 1978); R. W. Scribner, *Popular Culture and Popular Movements in Reformation Germany* (London, 1987); L. Roper, *The Holy Household: Women and Morals in Reformation Augsburg* (Oxford, 1989); P. Burke, *Venice and Amsterdam: A Study of 17th-century Elites*, 2nd edn (Cambridge, 1994); B. Pullan, *Rich and Poor in Renaissance Venice* (Oxford, 1971); John Hale, *Florence and the Medici* (London, 1977).

[4] P. Clark, 'Visions of the Urban Community: Antiquarians and the English City before 1800', in D. Fraser and A. Sutcliffe (eds), *The Pursuit of Urban History* (London, 1983), pp. 105–24; also R. Sweet, *The Writing of Urban Histories in Eighteenth-century England* (Oxford, 1997).

[5] A. J. Vickery, 'Town Histories and Victorian Plaudits: Some Examples from Preston', *Urban History Yearbook* (1988), 58–64; B. I. Coleman (ed.), *The Idea of the City in Nineteenth-century Britain* (London, 1973).

[6] G. Davison, 'The City as a Natural System: Theories of Urban Society in Early 19th-century Britain', in Fraser and Sutcliffe (eds), *Pursuit*, pp. 349–70.

underpinned and cross-fertilised the academic writing of urban history which began shortly before 1900.

For James Tait writing in 1921, the twentieth century 'had opened with the brightest prospects for the study of early municipal history in this country'. He explained how Charles Gross (1857–1909), a professor of history at Harvard, had disposed of ignorance about the guilds through his important 1890 study *The Gild Merchant* (a few years later he published the still valuable *Bibliography of British Municipal History*); how Mary Bateson had revealed the great mass of borough law with her two edited volumes *Borough Customs* (1890–2), and a volume of Leicester borough records (1899); and, above all, how F. W. Maitland (1850–1906) had promoted the subject.[7] Trained as a barrister, Maitland became Downing Professor of English Law at Cambridge in 1888. His *Township and Borough* (1898), based on his Oxford Ford lectures, spelt out an early agenda for urban history, identifying 'the transition from rural to urban habits' and 'the corporateness and personality' of towns as vital topics for study. Maitland's wide-ranging interests and poor health precluded other major work on towns, but he warmly supported Gross's efforts and encouraged Bateson. Shortly before his death in 1906 Maitland declared his admiration for the first of Sydney and Beatrice Webb's many volumes on local government — their study *The Manor and the Borough* appeared in 1908.[8] As for the Webbs, it is likely that some of the inspiration for the new academic interest in municipal institutions came from the flurry of changes to urban government towards the end of the nineteenth century: the creation of the London County Council in 1888 and the new metropolitan boroughs soon after, the extension of provincial city boundaries, the issue of new royal charters, and the passage of legislation affecting many aspects of local administration.[9]

---

[7] J. Tait, *The Medieval English Borough* (Manchester, 1936), p. 339 (quotation from Tait's British Academy lecture in 1921); C. Gross, *The Gild Merchant: A Contribution to British Municipal History* (Oxford, 1890); *A Bibliography of British Municipal History* (New York, 1897, new edn, Leicester, 1966); M. Bateson (ed.), *Borough Customs* (Selden Society, vols 18, 21, 1904–6); idem (ed.), *Records of the Borough of Leicester* (Cambridge, 1899–1905).

[8] For Maitland see H. Damico and J. B. Zavadil (eds), *Medieval Scholarship: Biographical Studies on the Formation of a Discipline, vol. 1* (London, 1995), pp. 131–51; F. W. Maitland, *The Letters of Frederick William Maitland*, ed. C. H. S. Fifoot (Cambridge, 1965), pp. 214, 222, 277, 488.

[9] Sidney Webb was a member of the London County Council at this time and he and Beatrice had close links to ministers and politicians. *The Manor and the Borough* (London, 1908) was explicitly intended to promote local government reform, especially in the poor law: cf. N. Mackenzie (ed.), *The Letters of Sidney and Beatrice Webb, vol. 2* (Cambridge, 1978). G. Gordon (ed.), *Regional Cities in the UK 1890–1980* (London, 1986), pp. 69, 106, 155; R. Dennis, 'Modern London', in Daunton (ed.), *Cambridge Urban History, vol. 3*, pp. 101–2; J. Davis, 'Central Government and the Towns', in ibid., pp. 276–7; B. M. Doyle, 'The Changing Functions of Urban Government', in ibid., p. 288ff.

The Historic Manuscripts Commission (established 1870) increasingly turned its attention to cataloguing and publishing extracts from corporation records and this encouraged a number of councils such as the City of London, Nottingham and Leicester to commission editions of their own records.[10]

German influence was also important. From the 1820s and 1830s German scholars, both liberal and conservative, had concentrated their attention on the legal, political and economic institutions and constitutional authority of the medieval town, with important work by Friedrich Carl von Savigny, Heinrich Brunner and Otto Gierke. The work of the social philosopher Ferdinand Tönnies on community and society was also significant. This tradition was only one element in German research on the city before the First World War, as accelerating urban growth encouraged more sociological studies by Max Weber and Georg Simmel, but these had limited impact in Britain until after the Second World War.[11] In contrast, the institutional and legalistic methodology of von Savigny and others shaped the ideas of Gross when he studied at Gottingen, while Maitland, whose background included an upbringing by German governesses and travel in Germany, was equally conversant in the German literature. German work also inspired the study of George Unwin on the London guilds (1908).[12]

By the time that Tait wrote after the First World War, however, much of the initial impetus of research had been lost and prospects for further work had, in his words, 'become lamentably overclouded'. The early deaths of Maitland, Bateson and Adolphus Ballard, a student of borough charters, played their part: Tait himself completed Ballard's book.[13] Moreover, the German historiographical legacy was unpopular and unfashionable after 1918. Tait's own work *The Medieval English Borough* (1936) showed greater interest in economic and commercial explanations of early urban development and here the role of the distinguished Belgian historian Henri Pirenne may have been significant. Various studies by Pirenne appeared before the war, and in 1925 came his

[10] For example *HMC*: 9th Report, App., Vol. I; 11th Report, App. III. R. Sharpe (ed.), *Calendar of Letter Books of the City of London* (London, 1899–1912); *Records of the Borough of Nottingham* (Nottingham, 1882–1956); Bateson (ed.), *Borough Records*.

[11] A. Black, *Guilds and Civil Society in European Political Thought from the Twelfth Century to the Present* (London, 1984), pp. 198–9, 210–19; *The Blackwell Dictionary of Historians* (Oxford, 1988), pp. 53, 367–8, 444–5. I am grateful to Professor Heinz Reif for discussing with me the different German traditions before the First World War.

[12] *Dictionary of American Biography, vol. 4 (2)*, (New York, nd) p. 18; *DNB*, Second Supplement, Maitland, Frederick William. J. M. Winter (ed.), *History and Society: Essays by R. H. Tawney* (London, 1978), p. 7.

[13] Tait, *Medieval English Borough*, pp. v, 339; Palliser (ed.), *Cambridge Urban History*, pp. 8–9.

masterly *Medieval Cities: Their Origins and the Revival of Trade*.[14] But economic history, consecrated as a subject in British universities with R. H. Tawney's appointment to a chair at the London School of Economics in 1932, was also starting to have a broader influence in the inter-war period. For the later Middle Ages Eileen Power wrote a number of pieces on urban trade and social life, and her colleague at LSE, F. J. Fisher, produced the first of his seminal articles on London commerce in the sixteenth century (1934); in the same vein was W. G. Hoskins' study of the cloth trade in seventeenth-century Exeter (1935). However, probably the only major study of a town written by a British scholar in this period was Dorothy George's brilliant *London Life in the Eighteenth Century* (1925), which took as its central theme the transformation of metropolitan society through urban improvement.[15]

The weakness of urban study during the inter-war era reflected not only the general stagnation of British universities, but also the growing trend against cities in British culture. If the Garden City movement had begun as an urban attempt to reform the nature of suburban development, by the 1930s a wave of nostalgia for the countryside was afoot in the land, with an undercurrent of anti-urbanism. To some extent, this was a function of the motorcar revolution which opened up English villages and rural lanes to private travel by the middle classes. But it was also a reaction to the sprawl of suburbanisation, accelerating on a massive scale in the 1930s, and the mounting problems of traffic congestion in London and other big centres. Truly the city appeared on the point of engulfing and polluting all England. Compared to the paucity of work on towns, the decades after 1918 saw a continuing spate of books on rural history, seeking to preserve the record of a world that was seen as on the eve of extinction.[16]

[14] Tait, *Medieval English Borough*, p. vi; H. Pirenne, *Medieval Cities: Their Origins and the Revival of Trade* (Princeton, NJ, 1925). For Pirenne's work and its limited reception in Britain see Damico and Zavidal (eds), *Medieval Scholarship*, pp. 153–68.

[15] For Tawney's work at LSE and elsewhere see Winter (ed.), *History and Society*, p. 14 et passim. For Power, Damico and Zavadil (eds), *Medieval Scholarship*, pp. 219–28; F. J. Fisher, 'The Development of the London Food Market 1540–1640', *Economic History Review*, 1, 5 (1935), 46–64; idem, 'Commercial Trends and Policy in 16th-century England', *Economic History Review*, 1, 10 (1940), 95–117. Fisher's articles are now collected in F. J. Fisher, *London and the English Economy 1500–1700*, ed. P. J. Corfield and N. B. Harte (London, 1990). W. G. Hoskins, *Industry, Trade and People in Exeter* (Manchester, 1935); M. D. George, *London Life in the Eighteenth Century*, 2nd edn (London, 1965).

[16] P. Mandler, 'Against "Englishness": English Culture and the Limits to Rural Nostalgia', *Transactions of the Royal Historical Society*, 6, 7 (1997), 170–4. A. Sutcliffe (ed.), *Metropolis 1890–1940* (London, 1984), esp. pp. 13, 26–7, 244 ff. Agrarian history had grown up in the wake of the late Victorian agricultural depression, but for works during the inter-war period see, for instance, M. E. Seebohm, *The Evolution of the English Farm* (London, 1927); S. J. Madge, *The Domesday of Crown Lands* (London, 1938), H. S. Bennett, *Life on the English Manor* (Cambridge, 1937).

Immediately after the Second World War only limited change occurred — with two notable exceptions: Sir John Summerson's brilliant *Georgian London* (1945), an elegant architectural counterpart to Dorothy George's study, and Asa Briggs' work on Victorian Birmingham (1952). Although in a conventional format — the second volume of a town history commissioned by the city council — Briggs' book was the first important study of a modern British town. Although others appeared about this time — on Crewe and St Helens, for instance — what was especially valuable about Briggs' study was his recognition both that town histories had to grapple with wider themes, and that, conversely, generalisations about suburban growth, mass politics, and municipal government only made sense when investigated through the prism of the distinctive local community with its own structures and relationships.[17] This theme was orchestrated on a grander scale in Briggs' powerful and influential *Victorian Cities* (1963), which laid the foundations for urban history 'as a discrete field of historical studies'.[18]

Within a decade there had been an explosion of interest and research: the second historiographical breaker had hit the shore. Now the leading influence was not German but American, not so much law as sociology. In the 1920s the Chicago school had invented the first analytical model for the study of big cities, mainly from a socio-spatial perspective. Their theories had negligible impact in Britain during that period, but they made steady progress in the United States and after 1945 inspired a number of historical studies of Boston, Philadelphia and Los Angeles. Theoretical discussion of the city became fashionable, bringing together sociologists, historians, and economists in a number of conferences (at Chicago in 1954 and 1959, and at Harvard in 1961), and in publications such as Handlin and Burchard's *The Historian and the City* (1963) and Hauser and Schnore's *The Study of Urbanization* (1965).[19]

---

[17] J. Summerson, *Georgian London* (London, 1945); A. Briggs, *History of Birmingham, Vol. 2: Borough and City 1865–1938* (Oxford, 1952), p. 1; W. H. Chaloner, *The Social and Economic Development of Crewe 1780–1923* (Manchester, 1950); T. C. Barker and J. R. Harris, *A Merseyside Town in the Industrial Revolution: St Helens 1750–1900* (Liverpool, 1954).

[18] A. Briggs, *Victorian Cities* (London, 1963); D. Fraser (ed.), *Cities, Class and Communication: Essays in Honour of Asa Briggs* (London, 1990), p. 5.

[19] For a recent comprehensive review of the Chicago school and its impact see K. Plummer (ed.), *The Chicago School: Critical Assessments*, 4 vols (London, 1997); O. Handlin, *Boston's Immigrants*, revised edn (Cambridge, MA, 1959); S.B. Warner, *The Private City: Philadelphia in Three Periods of its Growth* (Philadelphia, PA, 1968); R. Fogelson, *The Fragmented Metropolis: Los Angeles 1850–1930* (Cambridge, MA, 1967); also S. Thernstrom and R. Sennett (eds), *Nineteenth-century Cities: Essays in the New Urban History* (New Haven, CT, 1969). O. Handlin, J. Burchard (eds), *The Historian and the City* (Cambridge, MA, 1963); P. Hauser and L. F. Schnore (eds), *The Study of Urbanization* (New York, 1965).

Briggs had spent a lot of time in the United States in 1953 where he was involved in the development of urban studies. He writes: 'my debt to the University of Chicago is immense. I knew personally everybody concerned with the development of the subject there'.[20] Another important vector of American ideas was H. J. (Jim) Dyos (1921–78) who, after Briggs moved on to other areas of research, became the doyen of the field, being appointed Professor of Urban History at Leicester University in 1971. Dyos made several visits to the United States and his papers reveal close and extensive correspondence with many American scholars. The 1960s saw a surge of Anglo-American contact in many scholarly and scientific areas as university systems expanded on both sides of the Atlantic, but for Dyos the multidisciplinary big-city vision of the Americans was fundamental to the conceptualisation of urban history in Britain. He noted that 'the Chicago school of sociologists ... had a headstart ... in the dynamic interpretation of the inherent structures and internal organisation of urban society'. As late as 1975, he was to declare that 'the United States remains the epicentre of our field'.[21]

Dyos was a brilliant organiser and entrepreneur; after 1963 he set about creating a structure for modern British urban history. With Sydney Checkland, Theo Barker, David Reeder and others, he established the Urban History Group as an offshoot of the Economic History Society — with annual workshops and a stencilled *Newsletter* (replaced after 1972 by the *Urban History Yearbook*). In 1966 he conducted at Leicester the first major conference on British urban history, including significant American participation. (The proceedings were published as *The Study of Urban History*, with a preface by Briggs.)[22] As David Cannadine has written, under Dyos the area 'combined the maximum of organisational centralisation with the minimum of intellectual dogmatism'. Following the American pattern, Dyos welcomed to the broad church of urban history sociologists, geographers, architects and planners, as well as historians. Though his main interests were in the nineteenth century he was encouraging and supportive to those working on earlier periods. In a time of increasing disciplinary experimentation but few new organisational structures Dyos's

---

[20] Personal communication from Lord Briggs. I am grateful to Lord Briggs for his advice.

[21] Fraser (ed.), *Cities, Class and Communication*, p. 6. H. J. Dyos Collection, Centre for Urban History, Leicester University. This collection has recently been catalogued by Ms D. Sheil with funding from the Pilgrim Trust and Aurelius Trust; I am grateful to Dymphna Sheil for her help and advice in my use of the Dyos Collection. For Dyos's US links and visits: Dyos Collection, 1/19/2, 3, 1/20/2, 1/23/2, 3; 3/11; 4/15. Quotations from 1/9/1.

[22] Dyos Collection, 1/2/4, 1/9/1; H. J. Dyos (ed.), *The Study of Urban History* (London, 1968).

brand of urban history offered one of the best shows in town for meeting and debating with a wide swathe of people working in urban-related fields.[23]

But it was not the only show in town. After the Second World War W. G. Hoskins, another Leicester historian (later at Oxford), began to revive interest in the early development of the town. Though (like Briggs) Hoskins' historical ambitions were diverse, his articles on Exeter, Leicester and provincial towns opened a new door to an area largely dormant since earlier in the century.[24] Interest in the medieval period benefited from the new contributions of archaeology to the subject, the Society of Medieval Archaeologists (established 1956) leading the way: early fruits included Conzen's analyses of town plans, the first British atlas of town plans, and the important excavations of Winchester by Martin Biddle (1961–7). Another boost to new work on the medieval and early modern town came from several volumes in the *Victoria County History* series — on York, Leicester, Warwick and Coventry, written now by academic historians and of a high standard. At Oxford, informal seminars at All Souls College, held among Hoskins' postgraduate students and others influenced by him (Paul Slack, Charles Phythian-Adams, David Palliser and Peter Clark), gave impetus to more critical comparative work on early modern towns, finally ending in the publication of a collected volume *Crisis and Order in English Towns 1500–1700* (1972).[25]

For the early modernists American sociological influences were less crucial than others nearer home. Though the French *Annales* school had originally focused on the countryside, by the 1960s rapidly accelerating French urbanisation and the intellectual exhaustion of rural studies led to a new preoccupation with towns, particularly their demographic and economic trends. Pierre Goubert's *Beauvais et le Beauvaisis de 1600 à*

---

[23] D. Cannadine and D. Reeder (eds), *Exploring the Urban Past* (Cambridge, 1982), p. 203. For Dyos's eclectic links and interests see the correspondence, passim: Dyos Collection, series 1.

[24] Hoskins taught at Leicester in the 1940s, was Reader in Economic History at Oxford (1951–65), and returned to Leicester (1965–8) as Professor of English Local History. W. G. Hoskins, *Provincial England* (London, 1963), esp. chs 3–5; idem, 'The Elizabethan Merchants of Exeter', in S. T. Bindoff, J. Hurstfield and C. H. Williams (eds), *Elizabethan Government and Society* (London, 1961), pp. 163–87. In an interesting review of the literature at the time Peter Burke drew attention to the importance of the Leicester and Chicago schools and the impact of the latter on the former, but he may not have distinguished enough the two strands in the Leicester approach: *Quaderni Storici*, 27 (1974), 816–26.

[25] Palliser (ed.), *Cambridge Urban History*, pp. 9–10; *Victoria County History*, Leicestershire, IV (1958), Yorkshire, City of York (1961), Warwickshire, VIII (1969); P. Clark and P. Slack (eds), *Crisis and Order in English Towns 1500–1700* (London, 1972).

1730 was especially significant in triggering British interest, along with Fernand Braudel's brilliant discursus on the European city in *Civilisation Matérielle et Capitalisme XV–XVIII siècle* (1967). But the new French approaches were also disseminated through the Cambridge Group for Population and Social Structure, which under Peter Laslett had an energising effect across the whole historical spectrum at this time. Inspired by Keith Thomas there was also considerable interest in the empirical research of British social anthropologists working in Africa and elsewhere, questioning whether the problems, processes and social responses of rapid urbanisation in contemporary developing countries bore resemblance to those experienced in pre-industrial towns.[26]

So the take-off in work on the British city in the 1960s revealed divergent methodological currents. Lurking behind this diversity, however, was a shared awareness that British towns were experiencing change of an especially radical order. Initially, anxiety was concentrated on London and how to contain the increasingly gargantuan metropolis, but by the late 1960s the problems seemed much more wide-ranging. Post-war economic growth, the rise of private transport, and the baleful influence of modernist architects and planners were leading to the rapid and destructive redevelopment, the trashing, of traditional city centres across the country. 'Everyday almost,' Dyos observed, 'some building or other of historical importance ... comes under threat from what is misleadingly referred to as urban renewal'. The growth of strong planning and architectural history perspectives on urban history about this time was in part a response to this frustration, which was also articulated through the Georgian Society (1937) and the Victorian Society (1958); Dyos succeeded Pevsner as president of the Victorian Society in 1976.[27]

In the United States and then to a growing extent in Britain, public opinion, the media and politicians were also exercised by the growing problems of social deprivation, poor housing, nascent ethnic conflict, and disorder. Fundamental in this country were structural changes: the decline of traditional staple industries in midland and northern towns and the general

---

[26] P. Goubert, *Beauvais et le Beauvaisis de 1600 à 1730* (Paris, 1960); also M. Garden, *Lyon et le Lyonnais au XVIII siècle* (Paris, 1970); F. Braudel, *Civilisation matérielle et capitalisme XV–XVIII siècle* (Paris, 1967); K. Thomas, 'History and Anthropology', *Past and Present*, 24 (1963), 3–24. For a later discussion see P. Burke, 'Urban History and Urban Anthropology of Early Modern Europe', in Fraser and Sutcliffe (eds), *Pursuit of Urban History*, pp. 69–82.

[27] G. E. Cherry, *Cities and Plans* (London, 1988), ch. 6; Dyos Collection, 1/9/1. See D. Olsen, *The Growth of Victorian London* (London, 1976); also C. W. Chalklin, *The Provincial Towns of Georgian England* (London, 1974).

exodus of population from inner-city areas either to the suburbs or
(eventually) further afield.[28]

All the signs are that the 1960s marked a watershed for modern British
cities and it is not surprising that urban historians should have been been
engaged, directly or indirectly, in these developments. Briggs for instance
gave evidence to the commission on the future of the London County
Council. In the case of Dyos, he not only spoke out on planning issues but
took part with the planner Peter Hall and others in government think-tank
discussions on social policy at Ditchley Park.[29] More indirectly, many of the
contemporary social issues and concerns have echoes in the new literature on
towns. For the pre-industrial period the editors of *Crisis and Order in
English Towns* argued in the introduction for a general crisis in English
towns in the Tudor and Stuart periods and so triggered a protracted debate
about the timing and nature of the economic and social problems at that time,
including industrial decline, depopulation and mounting poverty.[30] For the
nineteenth century some of the most interesting work included John Foster's
exploration of class conflict and tension in three English provincial towns,
Gareth Stedman Jones' powerful reconstruction of the social topography of
destitution in Victorian London, Ralph Samuel's wonderful evocation of the
world of the marginal classes, John Kellett's analysis of the urban upheaval
in central urban areas caused by the railways, and studies by Dyos and
Michael Thompson on housing and suburbanisation in the capital.[31] The
two-volume *Victorian City* (1973) edited by Dyos and the American scholar
Michael Wolff offered a wide-ranging panorama (including literary
discourses on reading the city), but again the main corpus of chapters —
on poverty, slums, suburbs, housing, migration and prostitution — chimed
with the contemporary agenda of public concern.[32]

---

[28] M. Castells, *The City and the Grassroots* (London, 1983), pp. 50–66; H. P. White, *The Continuing
Conurbation* (Farnborough, 1980), ch. 2; J. Herington, *The Outer City* (London, 1984), p. 2 ff;
S. MacGregor and B. Pimlott (eds), *Tackling the Inner Cities* (Oxford, 1990); D. Coleman and J. Salt,
The British Population: Patterns, Trends and Processes (Oxford, 1992), p. 102 ff.
[29] Communication from Lord Briggs. Dyos Collection, 1/19/5, 1/23/2. I am grateful to Sir Peter Hall
for confirming the Ditchley Park meetings.
[30] For a summary of the debate see A. Dyer (ed.) *Decline and Growth in English Towns 1400–1640*,
2nd edn (Cambridge, 1995).
[31] J. Foster, *Class Struggle and the Industrial Revolution* (London, 1974); G. S. Jones, *Outcast
London: A Study in the Relationship between Classes in Victorian London* (Oxford, 1971); R. Samuel,
'Comers and Goers', in H. J. Dyos and M. Wolff (eds), *The Victorian City: Images and Realities,
vol. 1* (London, 1973), pp. 123–60; J. Kellet, *The Impact of Railways on Victorian Cities* (London,
1969); H. J. Dyos, *Victorian Suburb: A Study of the Growth of Camberwell* (Leicester, 1961);
F. M. L. Thompson, *Hampstead: The Building of a Borough* (London, 1974).
[32] Dyos and Wolff (eds), *Victorian City*, esp. chs 4, 5, 15, 26, 29, 30.

By the late 1970s the second wave of British work had run its course. The original American impetus had largely evaporated with the collapse of the subject there. The explosion of research, the diversity of disciplines engaged, the widening time frame spawned, it seemed, a confused, confusing picture. One critic complained that urban history was 'a large container with ill-defined, heterogeneous and sometimes indiscriminate contents'; another declared that urban history (and urban sociology) had 'proved graveyards of generalisations about the town'. Meantime, other subject areas — social history, women's history and the like — were growing in organised competition. In the real world urban problems were mounting and with the collapse of public finances under the second Wilson government they seemed out of control, beyond resolution. On Dyos's sudden death in 1978 the 'organisational centralisation' noted by Cannadine lost much of its inspiration. The prognosis for the subject, as for the cities, seemed gloomy.[33]

Yet if there was a loss of momentum it was short-lived. Already in late 1978 the creation of the Pre-Modern Towns Group, linked to the Urban History Group, offered a new focus for the growing research on the medieval and early modern town.[34] From about that time a series of volumes opened up the area, including monographs on York, Norwich and Coventry, wide-ranging collections of articles, and notable general surveys by Susan Reynolds on the medieval period and Penelope Corfield on the eighteenth century.[35] On the modern period there were major studies by Derek Fraser on urban power relations, Cannadine on towns and landowners, and Martin Daunton on homes and housing; and the *Themes in Urban History* series, sponsored by the Urban History Group, published new doctoral work on key themes. Particularly encouraging for the health of the subject, the *Urban History Yearbook*, edited after Dyos by David Reeder, became a bright

[33] First quotation from Eric Hobsbawm cited by Dyos: Dyos Collection, 1/9/1. Second quotation from Philip Abrams in P. Abrams and E. A. Wrigley (eds), *Town in Societies* (Cambridge, 1978), p. 9. For the pessimistic view of Cannadine in the early 1980s see Cannadine and Reeder (eds), *Exploring*, p. 207.

[34] The first meeting of the Pre-Modern Towns Group (attended by twenty-seven people) was held at the Institute of Historical Research, London in December 1978 and was organised by D. Hey, P. Borsay, P. Corfield and P. Clark; the new group had been conceived at the Urban History Group conference earlier that year.

[35] D. M. Palliser, *Tudor York* (Oxford, 1979); J. T. Evans, *Seventeenth-century Norwich* (Oxford, 1979); C. Phythian-Adams, *Desolation of a City* (Cambridge, 1979). Abrams and Wrigley (eds), *Towns in Societies*; P. Clark (ed.), *Country Towns in Preindustrial England* (Leicester, 1981); S. Reynolds, *An Introduction to the History of English Medieval Towns* (Oxford, 1977); P. Corfield, *The Impact of English Towns 1700–1800* (Oxford, 1982).

beacon for new empirical research, publishing articles and reviews on all periods of the subject.[36]

By the late 1980s one can see the advent of a third cycle of historical research on cities with a surge of articles, books, research projects and data-sets. There were new trends in methodological approach, as well as new geographical, temporal and subject perspectives. In terms of methodology, one sees a distinct shift away from the analysis of towns through case-studies of individual communities towards thematic studies often looking at a range of towns. This wider perspective is also evident in the geographical coverage of towns being investigated. Although there had been a number of good earlier studies of Scottish towns, now there was a new momentum, with research extending from the medieval to the modern era.[37] By 1990 one also sees the first attempts to put British towns in a comparative European context. Already there had been some links between British scholars and continental colleagues. In the mid-1970s Dyos had toured the Netherlands and Italy promoting the subject, and during the following decade a number of British academics participated in the various international colloquia on towns organised by the Maison des Sciences de l'Homme in Paris. Now collaborative work began in earnest on European small towns, the petty bourgeoisie, urban population, and much else.[38] If such efforts suffered from the continuing failure of historians as a whole to develop an advanced conceptual framework for comparative analysis, still there was some useful preliminary research.

The *longue durée* of British urbanisation also came under the micro-scope. In place of the previous rather spotty preoccupation with Tudor and

---

[36] D. Fraser, *Power and Authority in the Victorian City* (Oxford, 1979); D. Cannadine, *Lords and Landlords: The Aristocracy and the Towns 1774–1967* (Leicester, 1980); M. J. Daunton, *House and Home in the Victorian City: Working-class Housing 1850–1914* (London, 1983); also G. Crossick, *An Artisan Elite in Victorian Society* (London, 1978). Among the volumes in the *Themes* series were F. M. L. Thompson (ed.), *The Rise of Suburbia* (Leicester, 1982) and R. Morris (ed.), *Class, Power and Social Structure in British 19th-century Towns* (London, 1986). David Reeder was editor of the *Urban History Yearbook* from 1978 to 1987; he was succeeded by Richard Rodger; in 1992 the *Yearbook* was transformed into the journal *Urban History*.

[37] G. Gordon and B. Dicks (eds), *Scottish Urban History* (Aberdeen, 1983); M. Lynch, *Edinburgh and the Reformation* (Edinburgh, 1981); M. Lynch, M. Spearman and G. Stell (eds), *The Scottish Medieval Town* (Edinburgh, 1988); E. Ewan, *Townlife in 14th-century Scotland* (Edinburgh, 1990); R. Houston, *Social Change in the Age of Enlightenment: Edinburgh 1660–1760* (Oxford, 1994); R. Rodger, *The Transformation of Edinburgh in the 19th Century* (Cambridge, 2001).

[38] Dyos Collection, 1/4/2, 1/9/1. Meetings in Paris began in 1978, and were strongly promoted by Maurice Aymard and Bernard Lepetit. Publications from the various projects included J. P. Poussou (ed.), *Les Petites Villes du Moyen Age à Nos Jours* (Paris, 1987); P. Clark (ed.), *Small Towns in Early Modern Europe* (Cambridge, 1995); G. Crossick and H.-G. Haupt (eds), *Shopkeepers and Master Artisans in 19th-century Europe* (London, 1984); G. Crossick (ed.), *The Artisan and the European Town 1500–1900* (Aldershot, 1997); R. Lawton and R. W. Lee (eds), *Urban Population Development in Western Europe from the late 18th Century to the early 20th Century* (Liverpool, 1989).

Stuart towns and Victorian cities, new work advanced on the later Middle Ages (and then on the preceding era), on the eighteenth century, and, to some extent, on the early twentieth century. Attempts were also made to bridge traditional chronological boundaries, as for instance in work on London and its hinterland which reached from the fourteenth century to the seventeenth century, or studies of the professions and voluntarism that ranged from the seventeenth century into the mid-nineteenth century. This enhanced consciousness of the underlying continuities in function, location and networking of towns, as well the recurrent disjunctures, led to the design of the *Cambridge Urban History of Britain* (2000) which in its three volumes offers the first sustained analysis of the period from the sixth to the late twentieth centuries.[39]

The widening arc of exploration became equally evident in the kinds of subject under scrutiny. Whereas the first wave of urban study was strongly institutional and the second was focused on socio-economic problems and spatial issues, the third has had a more pluralistic, apparently less focused character. There has been growing interest not just in the poor but in the middling and elite classes — their composition, networking, and cultural and political roles.[40] We are more aware of the variety of 'sub-cultures' in towns — of artisans, young men, women, homosexuals and prostitutes.[41] Economically, the stress has been less on industry, than on the tertiary sector — the professions, medicine, retailing and the like.[42] Urban governance has been examined in the context of the dynamic relationship between municipal institutions, the state, and the powerful voluntary sector with its dense mesh of sociable, philanthropic, political, educational,

[39] J. A. Galloway and D. Keene, *Market Networks in Transition: London, its Hinterland, and the Internal Trade of England 1300–1600* (forthcoming); P. Corfield, *Power and the Professions in Britain 1700–1850* (London, 1995); P. Clark, *British Clubs and Societies: The Origins of an Associational World* (Oxford, 2000). Palliser (ed.), *Cambridge Urban History, vol. 1*; Clark (ed.), *Cambridge Urban History, vol. 2*; Daunton (ed.), *Cambridge Urban History, vol. 3*.

[40] For example J. Barry and C. Brooks (eds), *The Middling Sort of People* (London, 1994), esp. chs 3–7; R. Morris, *Class, Sect and Party: The Making of the British Middle Class: Leeds 1820–1850* (Manchester, 1990).

[41] For example H. Swanson, *Medieval Artisans* (Oxford, 1989); P. Griffiths, *Youth and Authority: Formative Experiences in England 1560–1640* (Oxford, 1996); A. Clark, *The Struggle for the Breeches: Gender and the Making of the British Working Class* (London, 1995); T. Hitchcock, *English Sexualities 1700–1800* (Basingstoke, 1997), esp. ch. 5; T. Henderson, *Disorderly Women in 18th-century London* (London, 1999); J. R. Walkowitz, *City of Dreadful Delight: Narratives of Sexual Danger in late-Victorian London* (London, 1992).

[42] Corfield, *Power and the Professions*; S. Lawrence, *Charitable Knowledge: Hospital Pupils and Practitioners in 18th-century London* (Cambridge 1996); D. Reeder and R. Rodger, 'Industrialisation and the City Economy' in Daunton (ed.), *Cambridge Urban History, vol. 3*, pp. 553–92; W. Lancaster, *The Department Store: A Social History* (London, 1995).

religious, social and cultural associations.[43] The cultural life of towns, and its complex array of public and commercial entertainments, has been explored.[44] Again, the identity of towns, how people perceived them, particularly how successive generations of townspeople reformulated and refashioned local urban identities, have also been an important theme of research.[45]

Attention has moved away, at least in part, from the bigger cities which dominated study in the 1960s and 1970s. There has been growing analysis in the medieval and early modern periods (less so for the modern era) of the hundreds of small market towns which formed the basement of the urban system from the thirteenth century and which appear to have flourished in England, and later in Scotland, into the early nineteenth century (with a revival in the inter-war period).[46] Specialist tourist, spa and seaside towns have also attracted considerable attention, along with transport centres.[47] Where new work has been done on big cities such as London, it has been reconceptualised through attempts to disaggregate the metropolis, to identify different jurisdictions, neighbourhoods and spaces.[48] In all these ways the urban world has been unravelled.

How does one explain these later-twentieth-century visions of the city and its history? Once again there is evidence that they mirror organisational and institutional trends, as well as methodological innovation and the influence, however imperfect, of the contemporary urban scene. Urban

---

[43] J. Davis, *Reforming London* (Oxford, 1988); also idem, 'Central Government', in Daunton (ed.), *Cambridge Urban History, vol. 3*, ch. 9; R. J. Morris, 'Clubs, Societies and Associations' in F. M. L. Thompson (ed.), *Cambridge Social History of Britain 1750–1950, vol. 3* (Cambridge, 1990), pp. 405–43; Clark, *British Clubs*.

[44] P. Borsay, *The English Urban Renaissance: Culture and Society in the Provincial Town 1660–1770* (Oxford, 1989); P. Bailey, *Popular Culture and Performance in the Victorian City* (Cambridge, 1998).

[45] P. Borsay, *The Image of Georgian Bath 1700–2000: Towns, Heritage and History* (Oxford, 2000); H. Meller, 'Urban Renewal and Citizenship: The Quality of Life in British Cities 1890–1990', *Urban History*, 22 (1995), 63–84.

[46] C. Dyer, 'Market Towns and the Countryside in late Medieval England', *Canadian Journal of History*, 31 (1996) 18–35; P. Clark (ed.), *Small Towns in Early Modern Europe* (Cambridge, 1995), chs 5–6; A. Dyer and P. Clark, chapters in Clark (ed.), *Cambridge Urban History of Britain, vol. 2*, pp. 425–50, 733–73.

[47] P. Borsay, 'Health and Leisure Resorts 1700–1840', in Clark (ed.), *Cambridge Urban History, vol. 2*, pp. 775–803; J. Walton, *The English Seaside Resort* (Leicester, 1983); G. Shaw and A. Williams (eds), *The Rise and Fall of British Coastal Resorts* (London, 1997); D. Drummond, *Crewe: Railway Town, Company and People* (Aldershot, 1995).

[48] G. Rosser, *Medieval Westminster 1200–1540* (Oxford, 1989); J. Boulton, *Neighbourhood and Society: A London Suburb in the 17th Century* (Cambridge, 1987); P. Clark and R. Gillespie (eds), *Two Capitals: London and Dublin 1500–1840* (Oxford, 2002).

history remains a relatively well-organised field for its size. Nationally the two main urban history groups were joined in the mid-1980s by the foundation of two research institutes: the Centre for Urban History at Leicester University, and the Centre for Metropolitan History at the Institute of Historical Research, London. Both have been active in launching regional, national and international research projects, conferences and publications, seeking through teamwork to open new areas too difficult or complex for the individual scholar; the Leicester centre has been particularly keen to promote interdisciplinary studies. In addition to the availability of funds from the national research councils, in the late 1980s the European Commission began for a while to promote academic and research collaboration among European Community universities. Grants from Brussels enabled the setting up of the European Association of Urban Historians in 1989, a body in which British scholars have had a key founding and participatory role, forming the largest and usually one of the most dynamic contingents at the biennial conferences in different European countries.[49] This institutional impetus, along with political trends towards closer European integration, has reinforced greater awareness of the value of comparative work on British and continental cities. By contrast, those transatlantic comparisons so dominant in the literature of the 1960s are much less visible.

Methodologically, in fact, recent decades have seen negligible influence from overseas. Urban studies in this country have generated their own momentum. Particularly important has been the continuing significance of the interdisciplinary dimension, but the mosaic of disciplines contributing to the subject has changed. So important before, sociologists have withdrawn to their own disciplinary bunker and turned their attention almost exclusively to the contemporary situation; historical geographers have continued to work closely with historians though cultural geography has tended to eclipse earlier economic concerns.[50] Most striking, recent years have seen the greater impact of linguistic studies with postmodernist interpretations of urban class and social relations and also the new involvement by literary scholars (often inspired by new historicist theories), whether working on urban drama and ceremony in the Renaissance period,

---

[49] The European Association of Urban Historians was established with European Union funding in 1989; the founders were Herman Diederiks (Leiden), Bernard Lepetit (Paris) and Peter Clark (Leicester). Biennial open conferences have been held since 1992 at Amsterdam, Strasbourg, Budapest, Venice and Berlin.
[50] M. Ogborn, *Spaces of Modernity: London's Geographies 1680–1780* (New York, 1998); D. Cosgrove and S. Daniels (eds), *The Iconography of Landscape* (Cambridge, 1998).

or on the images and perceptions of Stuart and Hanoverian London.[51] These inputs have accentuated consciousness of the cultural aspects of British urbanisation. Archaeology, increasingly vibrant, has also contributed strongly to the excavation of the early medieval origins of British towns, but it also has much to offer to our understanding of residential occupancy and the economy of late medieval settlements and of the ways in which towns were overcoming their environmental problems by 1500.[52]

Despite the vitality and pluralism of the new literature on British towns from earliest times, the link to contemporary debates about the city is less clear than for earlier periods. The critical transformation of British towns in the 1980s and 1990s — the continuing decay of manufacturing (in part at least due to the forces of globalisation), the growth of poverty and social exclusion, high levels of crime and disorder — seems (by comparison to earlier periods) to have had less impact on the agenda of historians. To some extent this may reflect attitudes of government. Despite a plethora of official reports and programmes, such as the *Scarman Report* (1985) or *Action for Cities* (1988), ministers have shown scant interest in the historical or structural dimension to urban problems, most funding recognition being concentrated primarily on instant solutions to the most pressing current problems.[53] On the other hand, urban historians have been slow to come to grips with the long twentieth century. Despite the watershed for many communities of the 1960s most recent research has concentrated on the preceding era, and the study of urban change after 1970 has been left to the charge of sociologists, economists, planners and so forth.

Yet urban scholarship may have mirrored the contemporary urban world more than one might have supposed. Interests have been less oriented to the old agenda of concerns, to the structural problems of cities, than to what are increasingly seen as the remedies, the planks of the springboard that will recreate the urban economy and society, and so bounce British cities successfully into the twenty-first century. Here what is important is the

---

[51] P. Joyce, *Visions of the People: Industrial England and the Question of Class 1840–1914* (Cambridge, 1991). For long-running innovative work in this area see the *Records of Early English Drama* publications. L. Manley, *Literature and Culture in Early Modern London* (Cambridge, 1995); C. Wall, *The Literary and Cultural Spaces of Restoration London* (Cambridge, 1998); E. Copeland, 'Remapping London: Clarissa and the Woman in the Window', in M. A. Doody and P. Sabor (eds), *Samuel Richardson: Tercentenary Essays* (Cambridge, 1989).

[52] Palliser (ed.) *Cambridge Urban History, vol. 1*, esp. chs 1, 2 and 8; E. Jones, J. Laughton and P. Clark, *Northampton in the late Middle Ages: The Archaeology and History of a Midland Town* (Leicester, 2000).

[53] MacGregor and Pimlott (eds), *Tackling the Inner Cities*, p. 4 et passim; B. D. Jacobs, *Fractured Cities* (London, 1992), p. 94 ff.

growth of the service sector, the role of tourism, the new power of the voluntary sector in urban governance, the reinvigoration of the cultural image and identity of big cities through urban improvement and promotion, the spread of new industries to smaller urban centres. And these are the themes which, as noted earlier, have been taken up and espoused indirectly at least in some of the literature of this third wave of urban history. In the struggle to reconstitute the sense of community and identity of towns, historians have also contributed more directly. Since the 1980s a number of municipal councils, keen to overcome a sense of urban malaise and to promote civic recognition and pride, have commissioned or encouraged urban historians to produce new-style town histories — as for example on Glasgow, Nottingham, Maidstone and Leicester.[54] Here we see a marriage of rigorous, scientific approaches and insights with those older traditions of town literature with which we began this analysis.

The picture of British urban history in the twentieth century is a complex one. More perhaps than in most other areas of historical research there have been powerful institutional and external influences. Along with the physical palimpsest of towns and cities from early times, urban history in a primitive fashion already existed long before academic authors came on the scene. They did not invent or construct the field: indeed, it is arguable that they did not do enough initially to distance themselves from the early conceptual parameters. Yet as we have seen they have been pioneers among historians in developing not only comparative but interdisciplinary approaches. Above all, they have repeatedly sought to redefine, to reconstruct, and refurbish the field — the urban home. Whilst the first two phases of research were concerned with exposing the institutional foundations and socio-economic structures of the historic city, at the turn of the twentieth century we see much more of the whole building — the political and cultural walls and windows, the cracks and fault lines in development, the community not just in isolation (though, as Briggs showed, local identity is crucial, the city as both actor and acted upon), but in a wide-ranging regional, national and international perspective — its networks and relationships. At the same time, as we have seen, our picture is not a neat, perfect, photographic image. It is fragmented, disjointed, splintering. We should not be too surprised or unhappy at that, for urban

---

[54] T. M. Devine et al. (eds), *Glasgow*, 2 vols (Manchester, 1995–6); J. V. Beckett (ed.), *A Centenary History of Nottingham* (Manchester, 1997); P. Clark and L. Murfin, *The History of Maidstone* (Stroud, 1995); D. Nash and P. Jones (eds), *Leicester in the Twentieth Century* (Stroud, 1993).

history at last 'begins to look', as Jim Dyos prophetically wrote, 'rather like the cities themselves'.[55]

Note. I am very grateful to David Reeder, Charles Phythian-Adams, Richard Rodger and Peter Burke for their ideas and comments. The piece was written while I was a visiting fellow at the Netherlands Institute for Advanced Studies (1999–2000) and I am also much indebted to my colleague there, Marcel Cornis-Pope, for his suggestions.

[55] Dyos Collection, 1/9/1.

CHAPTER THREE

Historians and the Nation

JOHN BREUILLY

Introduction

The idea of the nation can be deployed by historians in different ways. At its minimum an historian of 'England' or 'France' or 'Germany' may use national terms as little more than framing devices. Going a little further an historian may treat the nation as a real historical force which in some way, for example through national character, helps account for what happens. Going yet further the historian might take as his or her theme the way in which a particular place and its inhabitants *become* national, turning the nation itself into an historical subject rather than the frame or unchanging basis of history.[1] Reacting against these attributions of reality to the nation are historians who treat it as myth, ideology, false consciousness or imagination, although some stress the capacity of myth or imagination actually to construct what it mythicises or imagines while others regard the nation as a fragile, even unreal subject. Finally, and less frequently, historians use 'nation' as a concept, like class, status, power or occupation, as a method of organising historical evidence rather than something which is either 'real' or 'imagined'.

In a short essay I can only sketch some ways in which these different conceptions of the nation have been deployed by historians. I will focus on British and European historians and proceed in a roughly chronological way.

British historians and the nation, 1900–45

By 1900 the acceptance of the 'nation' as both framework and basic assumption was most firmly established in English/British historiography. England/Britain displayed territorial and institutional stability and continuity

[1] See for example the essays collected in Geoff Eley and Ronald Suny (eds), *Becoming National: A Reader* (New York and Oxford, 1996).

which could also be taken as a key to its immense success in modern times. For Macaulay, the best known of nineteenth-century historians of England, the English, with their achievements of liberty, prosperity and power, were the most favoured of nations.[2] There was a problem — certainly for later observers — of how the terms 'England' and 'Britain', 'English' and 'British' were to be related to one another but that would have involved precisely the unpicking of the concept of nation which might have undermined this confident historiography. That historiography itself divided, for example, between Whig and anti-Whig views of the English past, but the framework and assumption of nation remained constant. A reading of English history as the story of progress might depict hindrances to national progress as alien; the inclination of the Stuarts to Catholicism, absolutism and close relations with France being a prime example. It could further be argued that legal codification, the laying down of a firm administrative structure, the Reformation, conflicts with European powers, the establishment of overseas empire, the growth of parliamentary power, the extension of the franchise — that all this and more strengthened and diffused a sense of nationality; in other words, that national history is a history of becoming *more* national. Nevertheless, the general assumption in this historiography was that this was a matter of growth rather than a transformation from some earlier, non-national condition, a growth whose origins can be traced back to the later Anglo-Saxon period.[3]

This ruling but largely unexamined assumption makes it profitless to explore the concept of nation within English/British historiography in the early part of this century. All one can do is register that the assumption is 'there' but that it has little to do with the active arguments and stories which are rather about such matters as internal political conflicts, constitutional development and diplomatic and military relations with other states. More interesting is how British historians treated the history of 'other nations'. I begin with the examples of G. M. Trevelyan and R. W. Seton-Watson.

Trevelyan is best known for his work on English history. In that body of work assumptions about the English nation, its sterling character, its achievements of liberty and self-determination, are deployed in particular and rich ways.[4] Trevelyan was in the Whig tradition, related to Macaulay

---

[2] James Vernon (ed.), *Re-reading the Constitution: New Narratives in the Political History of England* (Cambridge, 1996). See now Edwin Jones, *The English Nation: The Great Myth* (Stroud, 1998).

[3] See John Burrow, *A Liberal Descent: Victorian Historians and the English Past* (Cambridge, 1981).

[4] The study by David Cannadine, *G. M. Trevelyan: A Life in History* (London, 1992) provides a detailed and sympathetic account, including a vigorous rejection of criticisms of Trevelyan as gentleman–amateur, partisan Whig historian.

(from whom he took his middle name). He represents a late and somewhat romantic version of the school, being much more ambivalent if not hostile to modernity than Macaulay and contributing to pastoral ideals of England, for example his leading role in the early development of the National Trust.

However, his most optimistic and substantial pre-1914 work was a three-volume study of Garibaldi and his contribution to Italian unification.[5] In this study the concept of the nation is of central importance: as framework, assumed object and emergent reality. Garibaldi was the darling of radical and Whig circles in the mid-nineteenth century with his exotic combination of adventurer, fighter and romantic nationalist.[6] Trevelyan's detailed account — a brilliantly evocative narrative based on intimate knowledge of the terrain on which Garibaldi conducted his campaigns — skates over the complexities concerning national identity and action in the events culminating in unification, even while recognising that Garibaldi himself failed and was marginalised in the new Italy. Habsburg rule is depicted as German and wholly negative; national conflict is conveyed through picturesque but impressionistic passages which attribute stereotypical features to the Italian victim and the German/imperial oppressor. For example, Radetzsky's capacity to maintain an effective army in the far north of Italy after being forced to withdraw from Milan is in part put down to:

> The habits engendered by discipline, the fraternal bonds of *esprit de corps*, and above all that ignorant contempt for the Italians indigenous in the transalpine barbarian — a feeling old as Attila, old as Brennus — gave to Radetzky's troops a unity which was wanting to their assailants.[7]

Later, in his wonderful account of Garibaldi's retreat from Rome, Trevelyan notes, as any good historian must, that amongst his pursuers were Papal,

---

[5] *Garibaldi's Defence of the Roman Republic 1848–1849* (London, 1907); *Garibaldi and the Thousand* (London, 1909); *Garibaldi and the Making of Italy* (London, 1911).

[6] See the account of his visit to England in 1864 provided in *The Era of the Reform League: English Labour and Radical Politics 1857–1872: Documents Selected by Gustav Mayer*, ed. John Breuilly, Gottfried Niedhart and Anthony Taylor (Mannheim, 1995), ch. 2 and Derek Beales, 'Garibaldi in England: The Politics of Enthusiasm', in *Essays in Honour of D. Mack Smith*, ed. J. Davis and P. Ginsborg (Cambridge, 1990), pp. 184–216.

[7] *Garibaldi's Defence of the Roman Republic* (1935 edn), p. 54. A note to this passage remarks that 'the patriotic part of the Italian conscripts had deserted from the Austrian army'. So far as I can tell the index of patriotism is desertion so the sentence is a tautology. Compare these views with modern studies of Radetzky and the Habsburg army: Alan Sked, *The Survival of the Habsburg Empire: Radetzsky, the Imperial Army and the Class War, 1848* (London and New York, 1979); István Deák, *Beyond Nationalism: A Social and Political History of the Habsburg Officer Corps, 1848–1918* (New York and Oxford, 1990).

Tuscan, Neapolitan and French troops. But he wishes to register the national struggle above all and chapter 12 ends as follows:

> By the terrible march of the last night [16 July 1849], Garibaldi had finally thrown off the French, whom he did not see again for ten years, and then as his allies for the delivery of Italy. In crossing the Tuscan border he left behind all the armies of the Latin races; but there remained ahead of him a foe more formidable than the Spaniards and Neapolitans, more cruel than the French — the *Tedechi*, waging their war of extermination on Italian rebels. The network of Austrian armies, stretched across Italy through Florence, Siena, Perugia, and Ancona, had yet to be passed before he could reach the Adriatic, and stand by Manin in Venice.[8]

As befits a Whig approach connections are made to the present. Thus in the 1920 preface to reprints of the trilogy Trevelyan notes that when he first published the books 'I certainly did not expect that I was going to serve for more than three years with the Italian army, becoming intimate in the field with the sons and grandsons of men recorded in these pages, in the final war of the *Risorgimento*, waged, during its first year, against that very Kaiser Franz Josef whose soldiers hunted Anita and Garibaldi in 1849.' Problems such as the overwhelming role of France in unifying Italy in 1859–61 or the dependence upon Prussia in 1866 for the acquisition of Venetia are not analysed. 'Italian' resistance to unification, for example the role of Papal and Neapolitan troops in the repression of the 1848–9 revolution, are registered as facts but taken as emanations of Catholic and monarchical autocracy ('Pope and Bourbon'), somehow alien to the 'true' Italy. The perspective adopted is that of Garibalidi himself, a superb man of action but not one noted for reflection or analytical thinking. What we have is a projection of English national historiographical assumptions abroad: there *is* an Italian nation — a moral as much as a sociological fact — which wishes to be rid of foreign oppressors and where national self-determination will mean constitutional government along the lines a British Whig could support.

The case of Seton-Watson is instructively different.[9] Seton-Watson was a Scot and proud of it but who nevertheless unproblematically accepted the British state and identity. He was, like Trevelyan, a member of its confident intellectual elite (Winchester and Oxford whereas Trevelyan was Harrow and Cambridge). Since his first visit to Vienna in 1905 Seton-Watson had became interested in the national question in the Habsburg Empire. His

[8] *Garibaldi's Defence of the Roman Republic*, pp. 248–9.
[9] See the study by his two sons Hugh and Christopher Seton-Watson, *The Making of a New Europe: R. W. Seton-Watson and the Last Years of Austria–Hungary* (London, 1981).

concern initially was more with current politics than history and this informs much of his historical work. Initially, like many contemporaries, he did not envisage the break-up of the Habsburg state but rather its reform along federalist lines which would free other nations from German and Hungarian domination. Seton-Watson saw it as one of his tasks to explain to British public opinion and government why the cause of small nations should be supported.

Seton-Watson represents a move beyond classical Whig positions. As late as the 1860s such opinion was blind to the existence of these 'small' nations; if their existence was registered it was as cultural/ethnic groupings within larger political nations. The Magyar revolutionary Kossuth was as much a darling of Whig and radical opinion as was Garibaldi, both representatives of 'historic' nations subject to Habsburg rule.[10] For radicals the answer was not the federalisation of the empire or its break-up into many small states but the creation of a few constitutional and national states — Poland, Germany, Italy, Hungary — out of the dynasties of east-central Europe.[11] However, these views were soured by the transformation of Germany into a unified and threatening power, German–Czech disputes in the western half of the Habsburg Empire, and increasingly illiberal Magyar domination of the eastern half.

The problem that Seton-Watson faced was that there was less of a secure national identity and history available for small nations compared to the larger, dominant cultural groups possessed of political institutions and a 'high culture'. Crucial to nation building for these subordinate groups was the assertion of cultural identity through language reform, the cultivation of customs and historical intepretation. Seton-Watson in his various national histories presents such assertions to the English-speaking world. Carefully avoiding nationalist propaganda, he nevertheless draws upon it. For example, when discussing arguments about the origins of the Romanian nation (did it pre-exist Roman settlement or is it descended from those settlers?) he writes of the:

> long series of reliefs of Dacian captives and victorious legionaries. In modern times these memories have fired the imagination of the Roumanian race and are treasured as a kind of ancestral charter, in which the rival claims of Roman and of Dacian origin are blended and confused.[12]

---

[10] Marx and Engels were typical of this radical view; see Ian Cummins, *Marx, Engels and National Movements* (London, 1980).

[11] Detailed and documented in Breuilly et al. (eds), *The Era of the Reform League*, esp. ch. 2, 'British Radicalism and Foreign Affairs, 1861–67'.

[12] R. W. Seton-Watson, *A History of the Roumanians* (Cambridge, 1934), pp. 2–3.

Note the use of the term 'race' and the way in which he skates over internal arguments among Romanian nationalists. He goes somewhat further when, writing of the post-Roman period:

> A new and transformed nation was already in the making, when the Empire fell into decay and was driven on to the defensive. Unfavourable conditions arrested the process of many centuries, but the elements remained, and the emergence of the blade of wheat from the rich native soil of the Wallachian plain is the symbol of a mystery which we must accept by an act of faith, since we cannot hope to explain it by rational methods.[13]

Is further comment needed concerning Seton-Watson's emotional commitment? Problems such as whether 'Romanian' is a modern construct which deliberately rejects its Slavic culture and history; how a 'nation' can exist in an 'arrested' state for centuries; why any case for political justice in the present requires one to accept as an act of faith dubious assertions about a distant and largely unknowable past: these are ignored.

As members of the British intellectual elite Trevelyan and Seton-Watson could exert influence upon policy. Both men played a part in intelligence and other connections with Italy and nationalist oppositions to the Habsburg Empire during the First World War. There were conflicts when Croatians and Italians made incompatible territorial claims. The British government was ambivalent between such claims and also whether its principal policy should be to detach the Habsburg Empire from its alliance with Germany or foment internal nationalist opposition which aimed at the destruction of the empire.[14] Seton-Watson in particular was very important in shaping British policy once the course of the war forced events towards the latter conclusion.

For all their knowledge and love of the languages and cultures of these other nations and their careful and detailed research, one cannot help feeling that Trevelyan and Seton-Watson projected or sought the unproblematic acceptance of national identity built into British historiography onto these other countries. There is a telling example when a Croatian nationalist exiled politician, Supilo, writes to Seton-Watson from Edinburgh, declaring he is now in 'the Capital of your great north jugoslav Croatia and have seen your Agram'.[15] Seton-Watson did not dispute this analogy but a moment's consideration reveals its absurdity. If Edinburgh was the north Yugoslav capital, London was Belgrade. However, Belgrade and Agram were in

---

[13] R. W. Seton-Watson, *History of the Roumanians*, p. 4.
[14] Lloyd George combined the two by means of duplicity: support the nationalist oppositions but as one lever upon the Habsburg government. One typical story describes Lloyd George seducing exile Serbians with a speech in which he reminds them that he too hails from a small, oppressed nation, while simultaneously secretly authorising negotations with the Habsburg government. H. and C. Seton-Watson, *The Making of a New Europe*, pp. 224–5.
[15] Letter of 27 January 1916, quoted in ibid., p. 193.

separate states at war with one another. There were no institutions such as the great public schools, Oxford and Cambridge and parliament which could unify Croatian and Serb elites. To compare Croatians and Serbs with the Scottish and English, let alone to construct a south Slav identity which included them, presumably on analogous lines to the British national category, is utterly misleading.[16] Maybe the Habsburg Empire was beyond saving and successor states had to be constructed but such national arguments were intellectually weak instruments indeed for the purpose.

The real problems became clear when those successor states were established by the Versailles peace settlement. The revelation that 'Romanians' could be just as nasty towards Hungarians as Hungarians had been to them; that the 'Romanians' from the former Habsburg Empire had little in common with those from the Danubian principalities that had formed the original national state in 1878; that nationalist politicians were no more inclined towards democratic or constitutional politics than the dynasts they had displaced: all this made it increasingly difficult for British historians to retain their former enthusiasm. Trevelyan watched with sadness but also little comprehension as Italy turned fascist.[17] Seton-Watson did remain committed to the small-nation cause (and had played a key role in the establishment and early activity of the School of Slavonic Studies in the University of London) but in increasingly critical fashion.

A new kind of historian came to the fore, one much more sceptical of all things continental and of the capacity of any European nation to emulate the achievements of the English/British. The best example is Sir Lewis Namier, himself of Polish-Jewish origins. He had served in the same political intelligence unit as Seton-Watson during the First World War, advising on Polish affairs. Where Seton-Watson and Trevelyan were optimistic, Namier was pessimistic. Where they saw virtue and vice in political institutions, including the capacity to generate national identity, Namier saw Freudian psychology as the key to understanding human beings. Institutions would

---

[16] Here is part of the text of a manifesto in which Seton-Watson played a part drafting in May 1915: 'The Jugoslavs form a single nation, alike by identity of language, by the unanswerable laws of geography and by national consciousness.' H. and C. Seton-Watson, *The Making of a New Europe*, p. 131.

[17] However, in his note to the new impression of *Garibaldi and the Making of Italy (June–November 1860)* in 1947 Trevelyan writes that after 'forty years in the wilderness' for Europe, including Italy, there was now once again 'a free Italy, the old friend of England, and our hearts go out to her once more'. In the resistance movement of 1943–5 Trevelyan sees 'a revival of the Garibaldian tradition. Garibaldi was always the symbol to Italians of anti-Fascism and of friendship to this country. May that friendship never again be broken!'

largely reflect what individuals, their interests and their powers, dictated. Political values were so much chatter.[18]

The major chink in Namier's bleak view of human beings was his idealisation of the English landed elite as a group which, over a long and continuous history, had succeeded in constructing an ethos and system of rule which was stable and worthwhile. It was his innovative studies of this class as a political elite in eighteenth-century England which established his reputation as an historian. However, this only put the contrast with the continent more starkly. Nationalism in Europe was for Namier an ideology; ideology was a disastrous substitute for good habits of rule, an expression of psychological instability, the rendering of group identity into abstract and fantastic forms. Whereas the English cherished land in the concrete form of specific estates, farms and villages and the ways of life they sustained, nationalists cherished land in the abstract form of national territory and fantasised ways of life on the basis of an abstract vision of the nation.[19] Fascism for Namier was not a betrayal of the original liberal form of nationalism; rather it was the logical conclusion to what was always an inherently illiberal and fanatical current of thought. Whereas Namier analysed the British parliament in detailed terms of individuals and interests, his brief study of the German National Assembly of 1848–9 treated it in terms of intellectuals, ideologies and longings for power.[20] Namier built on the empirical tradition of British historiography but actually raised it to a theoretical principle, ironically preserving a continental tradition of generalised thought.[21]

British historians and the nation, 1945–70

Fascism and war discredited nationalism, the deliberate project of constructing nation-states. For optimists after 1945 the defeat of the Axis powers represented the end of the era of nationalism. E. H. Carr, who became a

---

[18] For studies of Namier see John Cannon, 'Lewis Bernstein Namier', in idem (ed.), *The Historian at Work* (London, 1980), pp. 136–53; and Linda Colley, *Namier* (London, 1989).

[19] It is therefore somewhat ironic that Namier was also an admirer and assistant to the Zionist leader Chaim Weizmann. Zionism was arguably the most abstract of nationalisms as the chosen people, for the most part, did not even live in the land claimed as the national territory.

[20] *1848: The Revolution of the Intellectuals* (London, 1944) began life as a lecture in wartime London. Namier's other writings on modern European history mainly took essay form which have been gathered together in various volumes such as *Europe in Decay* (1950), *Avenues of History* (1952) and *Vanished Supremacies* (1958).

[21] In this sense he belongs with a whole group of émigré intellectuals who provided a generalised and theoretical defence of British empiricism. See Perry Anderson, 'Components of the National Culture', originally published in *New Left Review*, 50 (1968) and reprinted in idem, *English Questions* (London, 1992), pp. 48–104.

somewhat fatalistic believer in progress who looked to the Soviet Union as representing a different way forward in history, caught this sense of hope in the title of his 1945 survey *Nationalism and After*.[22] By now the idea of nationalism as having run its historic course through various stages was being captured in synthetic historical works. These were generally not the product of British historians who were mainly too empirical and anti-theoretical to be able to write such works. Carr was an exception as were British Marxist historians as a small group, although the latter had much more to say about socialism and the labour movement than about nationalism and the national movement.[23] The most significant studies were those of the American historian Carlton Hayes and the German émigré historian Hans Kohn.[24] Hayes developed a typology based on doctrine, with nationalism moving through Jacobin, liberal and radical versions to forms of fascism. Kohn distinguished between eastern and western forms of nationalism based on the ethnic community and the willed political association, respectively. It was but a step to making choices between good and bad forms of nationalism or for reserving the term simply for the bad forms, i.e. illiberal and ethnic nationalism.

The failure of the 1919 peace settlement and the barbaric extremes to which nationalism had been taken up to 1945 made supranational values appear more attractive or at least stronger. Yet the structure of nation-states continued after 1945 with the major exception of divided Germany. Indeed, genocide and forced population movement rendered many post-war states ethnically more homogenous than before, ironically giving a greater reality to the idea of nation as ethnos just as its legitimacy was rejected. However, the incorporation of eastern European states into a Soviet bloc inclined even western observers, especially during the period of the Cold War, to downgrade the significance of national identity. Typically British historical

[22] Carr is best known for his multi-volume study of the early years of the Soviet Union and for his short work *What is History?* (1961). Easily as significant an historian as Trevelyan or Namier and at first glance as much an Establishment figure (Merchant Taylor and Cambridge, Foreign Office, assistant editor of *The Times*, posts at Balliol College, Oxford and Trinity College, Cambridge) Carr's combination of English empiricism and a rather determinist approach to history, though more in terms of the work of political elites than of nations or classes, as well as his semi-detached relationship to academic institutions, has marked him out as something of a maverick figure. Only recently has there been a study of him: see Jonathan Haslam, *The Vices of Integrity: E. H. Carr 1892–1982* (London, 1999).

[23] See Harvey Kaye, *The British Marxist Historians* (London, 1984). See below for the influence of E. P. Thompson on studies of modern colonial nationalism. More recently labour historians have extended their interests to national as well as class identity. See for example M. C. Finn, *After Chartism: Class and Nation in English Radical Politics, 1848–1874* (Cambridge, 1993).

[24] Carlton J. Hayes, *The Historical Evolution of Nationalism* (New York, 1931). Kohn wrote numerous works on nationalism, see for a good example *The Idea of Nationalism* (1944, repr. New York, 1967).

work on 'other nations' did not take the form of general and theoretically informed interpretations of the kind associated with Carr, Hayes and Kohn but rather of sceptical treatments of particular national histories.

Thus the doyen of post-war British historians of Italy, Denis Mack Smith, presented the story of Italian unification as a chapter of accidents marked by conflict and indeed the mutual personal loathing of the heroes of Risorgimento historiography — Garibaldi, Mazzini and Cavour.[25] The lack of national identity and unity in post-1861 Italy was a common theme in his work and has been in that of subsequent historians of Italy.[26] What is especially interesting, but beyond the scope of this essay, is the way Mack Smith's work became popular in Italy itself, although among Italian historians full-blooded critiques of Risorgimento perspectives came later and have remained weaker. Only now, with the development of acute regional conflict and despair over the integrity of the national state, does there appear to be a strong political incentive to look to non-national interpretations of modern Italian history.

Building on Namier's negative view of Germans and modern German history, A. J. P. Taylor represented a different kind of scepticism from that of Mack Smith, one which assumed a significant and widespread sense of German identity but saw this in terms of power drives and interest groups rather than traditions of radical or liberal nationalism or a commitment to the ideals of *Kulturnation* associated with Schiller and Goethe. German history had not 'gone wrong' after unification; rather it had unfolded its essential nature. Later, in his controversial work on the origins of the Second World War, this enabled Taylor to present Hitler as a 'normal' German.[27]

Even 'victim' nations were subject to this sceptical treatment, for example in R. F. Leslie's depictions of the Polish uprisings of 1830 and 1863 as the work of divided and incompetent aristocratic and intellectual elites with little understanding of or support from the mass of the people.[28] This debunking approach to the most romantic of all national movements in the nineteenth century was deepened with studies of the unsuccessful Galician uprising of 1846 when non-Polish speaking peasants turned against Polish gentry seeking

---

[25] Selecting from his numerous publications, see: *Cavour and Garibaldi, 1860: A Study in Political Conflict* (Cambridge, 1954); *Victor Emmanuel, Cavour and the Risorgimento* (London, 1971); *Mazzini* (London, 1994).

[26] See the historiographical survey by Lucy Riall, *The Italian Risorgimento: State, Society and National Unification* (London, 1994).

[27] A. J. P. Taylor, *The Course of German History* (London, 1945); *The Origins of the Second World War* (London, 1961). See also Chris Cook and Alan Sked (eds), *Crisis and Controversy: Essays in Honour of A. J. P. Taylor* (London, 1976).

[28] R. F. Leslie, *Polish Politics and the Revolution of November 1830* (London, 1956) and *Reform and Insurrection in Russian Poland, 1856–65* (London, 1963).

to throw off Habsburg rule. Nevertheless, the tendency to treat Polish history as the history of the Polish nation, rather than as the history of Polish-speaking groups within a variety of polyethnic social and political arrangements, continues in the work of Norman Davies. He has, however, more recently interestingly sought to view the history of Europe generally from an east-central rather than the normal western perspective and has questioned the use of the national framework for the long-run history of the British Isles.[29]

After 1945 the forces of progress were seen as supranational, not national: west European unity, Anglo-American cooperation, international socialism. Of course these projects were frequently supported or opposed in terms of national identity. The most popular histories of the post-war period in Britain again took up national themes. Churchill's *History of the English Speaking Peoples* [30] represented a last efflorescence of a romantic, racial and imperial approach to history, where white settlement and the virtues of the Anglo-Saxon race were equated with one another. However, although the racial underpinning of such an approach remained an important component in British culture, one should stress its looseness, its distance from scientific race theory.[31] Such an approach to nationality in history was becoming obsolete within historical scholarship with Britain about to lose its empire, the recognition that 'English-speaking' peoples included European immigrants into the USA and descendants of imported African slaves, and, somewhat later, the onset of mass immigration into the United Kingdom from various parts of the Commonwealth. Interestingly, the other great popular work, Trevelyan's *English Social History* (London, 1944), shifted away from themes of government, economy and international relations towards domestic themes, almost as if the British reading public wished to turn its back upon the more strenuous achievements of imperial glory. Churchill was overwhelmingly rejected at the polls in 1945 in favour of a party which was committed to welfare reforms, a holding position in Europe and a retreat from empire. Former imperialist Tories like Enoch Powell shifted to a 'little England' position.

---

[29] Norman Davies, *God's Playground: A History of Poland: Vol. 2, 1792 to Present* (New York, 1982); idem, *Europe: A History* (Oxford, 1996); idem., *The Isles: A History* (London, 1997). On this latter volume which refuses to use the term 'British' in its title, see the extensive review by Jeremy Black (including references to angry reviewers insisting on the retention of an English national perspective) in *The Times Higher Education Supplement*, 21 July 2000, 22–3.

[30] Winston Churchill, *A History of the English Speaking Peoples*, published in numerous volumes and editions.

[31] In the next section I will consider the way mainstream German historians took up connections with pseudo-scientific race theory in the Third Reich. The potential affinity was arguably present in other national historiographies as well.

Positive attitudes towards nationality and national movements focused on decolonisation. The use of categories such as 'liberal' or 'socialist', 'western' or 'civic' nationalism served to detach these national movements from the illiberal and ethnic forms of nationalism regarded as defeated once and for all in Europe. Figures such as Nehru and Nkrumah could be presented as the modern equivalents of Bolivar and Jefferson. It was a virtue that the colonial boundaries within which national liberation movements worked were arbitrary in relation to historic groups and boundaries: the modern national liberation movement was not based on ethnicity (where the pejorative word 'tribe' was deployed rather than 'nation') but on willed association committed to the achievement of freedom.

This approach to anti-colonial nationalism was buttressed by American modernisation theory as well as Soviet Marxism both of which presented the path towards freedom and modernity as a series of stages through which all societies must pass. It was important to ensure that the passage of the less developed world take the liberal/communist form. There was a stress upon the western/Soviet education of nationalist leaders; implicitly at least the very ideal of national self-determination in the form of a constitutional/socialist state was a western/Soviet transplantation.[32]

Since the 1960s with the growth of disillusion with independence and development there have been various shifts away from these progressive perspectives. One approach has been to equate non-European nationalism with European nationalism. Thus Kedourie, a conservative political theorist with Middle Eastern interests who worked in the tradition of Michael Oakeshott at the London School of Economics, presented nationalism generally as a pernicious doctrine peddled by a rootless intelligentsia to populations unsettled by the disruptions of war, revolution and rapid social change.[33] This conservative perspective, reminiscent of Namier's earlier work, was extended explicitly to the non-European world in a work in which Kedourie edited extracts from various Asian and African nationalist sources.[34] Many of the extracts took up irrational themes of tribe, religion and caste as providing the roots of national identity, thus emphasising the irrational, ideological character of national values.

[32] A classical example of the 'westernisation' approach to the general subject of decolonisation is R. Emerson, *From Empire to Nation* (Cambridge, MA, 1960). See also Thomas Hodgkin, *Nationalism in Africa* (London, 1956).

[33] Elie Kedourie, *Nationalism* (London, 1960). For a more extensive analysis of Kedourie's approach see John Breuilly, 'Nationalism and the History of Ideas', *Proceedings of the British Academy,* 105 (December 2000), pp. 187–223. This is the published version of the Elie Kedourie Memorial Lecture which I gave to the British Academy on 27 May 1999.

[34] Elie Kedourie (ed.), *Nationalism in Africa and Asia* (London, 1971).

This approach assumes the transformative grip of national ideology, even if presenting it in negative rather than positive terms. A different approach extended the sceptical view of nationalism beyond Europe. In a series of seminal articles and one influential book, *Africa and the Victorians*,[35] J. Gallagher and R. Robinson stressed the reluctant, transitory and limited impact of the British Empire upon the non-western world. Imperial arrangements were based on complex negotiations between colonial administrators and local interests; the rise of nationalism represented the breakdown of such arrangements and their redeployment in the form of movements claiming independence. The key figure was not the atavastic resister or the enthusiastic moderniser but the pragmatic operator who shifted from negotiated collaboration to negotiated opposition. The failure of the new states to realise western dreams was less to do with neo-colonialism or irrationalist national leaders than with the limited nature of independence. National rhetoric was more about providing the imperial power with a legitimate successor to untenable colonial rule than it was about any new form of political association or ideal. Especially in the work of the Cambridge school of Indian history this approach has generated detailed and productive research.[36]

All these perspectives — westernising, irrational, pragmatic — can be seen as demeaning from the non-western point of view. Another perspective, for example developed by historians of east-central Africa such as Terry Ranger, links modern nationalism to traditions of resistance, early responses to colonial incursion, and indigenous religious as well as Christian movements.[37] Critics of this school (one dubbed it the 'myth polishers of Dar es Salaam') have suggested that these historians follow in the footsteps of European historians who helped provide the historical arguments which are so essential to nationalist legitimation. Yet it is undeniable that this approach, alongside that of the Cambridge school, has shifted research effort from the imperial powers to the colonial society. Many of these historians were inspired by the work of E. P. Thompson on English labour history who sought to rescue various working-class oppositional movements from the 'enormous condescension of posterity'. The equivalent of 'history from below' was 'history from the periphery'; for 'class' read 'nation'.

[35] *Africa and the Victorians: The Official Mind of Imperialism* (London, 1961).

[36] For further details see chs 7 and 8 of John Breuilly, *Nationalism and the State*, 2nd edn (Manchester, 1993).

[37] See, for a short statement from the time he was in Dar es Salaam following deportation from the then Southern Rhodesia by the Smith regime, Terence Ranger, 'The Recovery of African Initiative in Tanzanian History', the University College Dar es Salaam Inaugural Lecture, 2 (Dar es Salaam, 1969).

Between 1900 and 1970 British historians of other nations moved from a European to a global perspective, from enthusiasm for national liberation to hostility or scepticism about such movements but also to more deeply researched work into the indigenous roots of specific movements. Most of this work did not seek to conceptualise nations and nationalism within a larger, theoretical framework but operated in specific, empirical ways, deploying at most conceptual frameworks limited to a small range of cases (for example, the continuity of pre-national and national movements, the shifting patterns of collaborator and oppositional networks). In the 1980s there was a resurgence of theoretical and general perpectives in which British scholars, historians and others, took a leading part. Before considering this phase and what followed it, I will turn briefly to non-British historiography. In the space available I cannot extend this beyond some elements of European historiography.[38]

European historians and the nation

Continental historians have never been able to take national identity for granted in the way that British historians have.[39] Divisions as to the proper nature of national identity were significant even in France, the most continuous of the continental 'nation-states'. Arguments about the legacy of the French Revolution are in part arguments as to whether national identity was something which had emerged suddenly in the modern period or whether the revolution itself represented a rupture with a more continuous national history. Alexis de Tocqueville had famously tried to overcome the division by arguing that the revolution had simply deepened and quickened the centralising, nationalising work of the *ancien régime* but that did not settle the matter. Arguments about the role of the Catholic church and the competing merits of republican, imperial and monarchical states all raised questions as to the proper nature of national identity. If national identity is in part generated by reacting against the 'other' it might appear that the history of major wars between France and its German neighbour at least provided a basis for consensus about the nation. Yet even here the establishment of the Vichy regime and the adoption of at least some of the racial themes of the Third Reich led to polarisation, although mainstream French historiography

---

[38] Some non-European work, such as the Indian Subaltern Studies school will be touched upon in the section on the resurgence of theory.

[39] For this whole section see *Writing National Histories: Western Europe since 1800*, ed. Stefan Berger, Mark Donovan and Kevin Passmore (London, 1999).

remained fairly distant from racial approaches to national identity. The more enduring divisions between left and right, pro- and anti-revolutionary views of national identity continued, as was made clear at the bicentenary of the French Revolution in 1989. By then debates concerning national identity had become linked to more general issues of modernist and postmodernist interpretations which I deal with in the next section.[40]

If such divisions were acute in French historiography, how much more so would one expect them to be in newly formed national states such as Germany and Italy, or in the multinational Ottoman, Romanov and Habsburg empires faced by the national challenges, or in the mutual rivalries of national movements and new nation-states after 1919? In a short essay I can only briefly treat of a few examples. Germany and Turkey will be selected as cases of new nation-states, the Habsburg Empire and the USSR as multinational states in which new approaches to the nation, especially linked to Marxism, were developed.

Germany was unified in part through division: the exclusion of Austrian Germany from the new state.[41] There rapidly developed an official historiography which legitimised this new state but it rather uneasily blended themes of Prussian and German identity, national and federal values. It was difficult for democrats, socialists and Catholics, and quite impossible for non-German speakers such as Poles and Danes and the inhabitants of Alsace-Lorraine, to identify with this Prusso-German state. Rejection of the official historiography was not necessarily rejection of the nation-state; radicals, socialists and Catholics as well as those who wished to see Austrian Germany included had their own, competing views of national history and identity, even if these were marginalised by establishment history and politics.

Yet the 'official' version did not remain static or unchallenged. The increasing importance of national institutions and experiences (east–west migration, urban and industrial growth, military service) signalled the decline of particularism, or at least its reduction to the harmless virtue of diversity within greater unity. The development of radical right nationalism with themes of anti-Semitism, race and expansion both in and beyond Europe in part influenced and in part challenged official national views. Yet it is difficult, certainly before 1914, to see these having a major impact on historiography which remained rather conservative, focused on the state as a force above society. Rather it was in newer disciplines such as sociology and economics that such ideas were most clearly mobilised. Attempts, for

[40] Generally see Robert Gildea, *The Past in French History* (London, 1994). More specifically see Steven Kaplan, *Farewell, Revolution: The Historians' Feud: France, 1789/1989* (London, 1995).
[41] See John Breuilly, *The Formation of the First German Nation-State, 1800–1871* (London, 1996).

example, to write about national history in terms of 'folk culture' were rejected and marginalised by the academic establishment.[42]

Nevertheless, the idea that Germany *did* represent a special culture and politics was elaborated through the dominant historiography which rejected comparison or social science approaches and, with its focus on state institutions, great men and *Ideengeschichte*, stressed ideas of uniqueness.[43] This idea of national uniqueness was emphasised by historians in pro-war propaganda from 1914 and was later used to condemn the Versailles peace settlement with its imposition of alien, western ideas of government upon Germany. The academic establishment remained little changed in Weimar, at best accepting the republic pragmatically and blocking the careers of liberal, democratic and socialist historians. It was not too difficult for most of this establishment, including historians, to come to terms with the Third Reich, especially where there were shared values on authoritarian rule and a policy of revising the peace treaty.[44]

More contentious was the question of how far the specifically racial theories of the regime could be combined with traditional national historiography. There was a radical implication in a focus on the racial *Volksgemeinschaft* rather than the authoritarian state which was set above society and, therefore, the *Volk*. In many cases the convergence was mainly at the level of opportunist rhetoric as well as in cases of academic historians offering advice on such matters as racial settlement in occupied eastern Europe. In other cases, some of the ideas of community, 'history from below' and a non-state-centred history arguably re-emerged, purged of race terms, in new currents of historiography that developed in post-1945 West Germany. This legacy of *Volksgeschichte* has recently led to controversy with suggestions that the work of innovative historians such as Werner Conze, Theodor Schieder and Otto Brunner is tainted by their origins in the Third Reich and that this in turn casts questions over the next generation of historians who trained under these men.[45]

[42] For a survey of German historiography see Stefan Berger, *The Search for Normality: National Identity and Historical Consciousness in Germany since 1800* (Oxford, 1997).
[43] For the special tradition of *Ideengeschichte*, see the example of Friedrich Meinecke, *Cosmopolitanism and the National State*, originally published in 1907 (Princeton, NJ, 1970). Generally on German historiography see George Iggers, *The German Conception of History: The National Tradition of Historical Thought* (Middletown, CT, 1968).
[44] See some of the essays in *British and German Historiography 1750–1950*, ed. Benedikt Stuchtey and Peter Wende (Oxford, 2000).
[45] See Hans Schleier, 'German Historiography under National Socialism: Dreams of a Powerful Nation-State and German *Volkstum* Come True', in Berger et al., *Writing National Histories*, pp. 176–88.

In my view such arguments have little merit, displaying much of the conservative approach to intellectual history (unique unit-ideas which migrate from one generation to the next and are expressed through the work of an intellectual elite) rather than treating ideas as concepts to be judged by their capacity to organise productive historical research. Far more intellectually significant as a critique, for example, of Conze's 'structural' history which hinged upon the transition from agrarian community to industrial society, was the Marxist view put long ago by Hartmut Zwahr that the approach failed to take account of the nature of class divisions within society and their influence upon politics.[46]

This debate provides a specific example of the two most important developments in post-1945 German historiography. In the German Democratic Republic Marxism was established as the official framework within which to conduct history. The traditional Marxist view adopted has notoriously encountered problems of understanding national identity and nationalism because of the primacy of value given to class identity. The effective denial, for example, of any continuity between capitalist Germany and socialist Germany, as well as any significant differences between the various kinds of capitalist Germany (Wilhelmine, Weimar, Nazi and West Germany) make it very difficult to explore themes of national identity and traditions.

In West Germany the development of the 'critical school of history' took the idea of a special German path but now treated this not as the virtuous uniqueness of conservative historiography but as a divergence from a normal path of western modernisation which could be explained in specific terms such as the character of German unification and the continued dominance of pre-industrial elites in power. The nation-state and national identity were, in such a framework, accepted as part of the normal pattern of development and not explored any further; instead explanatory effort was focused on accounting for the particular forms of German deviance. Amongst other things the results of this work was the explicit importation of social science concepts into historical work, the recognition that historical research was guided by contemporary values, the partial disengagement from state-centred history, and the partial commitment to comparative history.[47]

---

[46] For an account of the 'unit-ideas' approach to nationalism see Breuilly 'Nationalism and the History of Ideas'. For the Zwahr critique see his introduction to Hartmut Zwahr (ed.), *Die Konstituierung der deutschen Arbeiteklasse von der 1830er bis zu den 1870er Jahren* (Berlin (E), 1981).

[47] For a brief introduction see Mary Fulbrook, 'Dividing the Past, Defining the Present: Historians and National Identity in the Two Germanies', in Berger et al., *Writing National Histories*, pp. 217–29.

I say 'partial' because arguably the societal history which resulted
was still led by state-centred questions (for example, what are the social
causes or effects of the failure to develop liberal democracy?) and the
comparison with other countries was skewed both by the assumption that
this involved comparing 'norms' with a deviant case and also by a
discrepancy between the intensity of research into German history and the
superficial study of other national histories. Yet this historiography has
itself responded creatively to such criticisms, and at the same time those
critiques, both from Marxist and from conservative historians, have become
more sophisticated. Space does not allow for further consideration of such
debates.[48]

By comparison with this sophisticated historiography, the historiography
of the new nation-states tended to remain at the level of official propaganda.
Sometimes, given the novelty of the new state, this did involve considerable
intellectual innovation. For example, in the new state of Turkey the theorist
Ziya Gökalp drew from functionalist sociology and from western distinctions between 'culture' and 'civilisation', 'race' and 'nation' in order to
produce an elaborate framework within which the modernising policies of
the regime could be justified in relation to a concept of the Turkish nation.
Such ideas involved a sharp break with traditional Ottoman understandings
of history and politics.[49]

By contrast, the nationality disputes that had characterised late
Habsburg politics as well as the claims elaborated by the pre-1914 Balkan
states meant that the other successor states (with the glaring exception of
Austria, stripped of an empire but not integrated into the German nation)
had well-developed national ideologies on which to draw in the inter-war
period. Generally speaking historiography was an instrument of policy
and consequently is not of great intrinsic intellectual interest.

The one situation which did throw up interesting engagements with issues
of national identity and nationalism was rather amongst intellectuals in
multinational states trying to understand the recent eruption of nationality
disputes from a non-national perspective. Above all, the late Habsburg
Empire was rich in such endeavour. The Austro-Marxist school sought to give
concepts of nation and national identity an autonomy they did not possess

---

[48] On the value of comparison and how this relates to the work of the 'critical school' see the
introductory and concluding essays to John Breuilly, *Labour and Liberalism in Nineteenth-century
Europe* (Manchester, 1994). I have incidentally considered the specific contribution of British
historians to this historiography in 'Modern German History and British Historians', *German Studies
Library Group Newsletter*, 21 (November 1996), 11–29.
[49] See Ziya Gökalp, *Turkish Nationalism and Western Civilization: Selected Essays of Ziya Gökalp*
(New York, 1959).

within orthodox Marxism, arguing that national culture would in many ways become more significant as politics and economy became more democratic.[50] Freud began the tradition of spawning various psychological theories to account for nationalism. Intellectual émigrés from the Habsburg Empire or its successor states such as Karl Deutsch and Ernest Gellner have in turn developed new ideas about national identity and nationalism which link them to modern communications or economic systems.[51] Less theoretically innovative or influential but in practical ways more important were the ways in which the USSR accepted national and ethnic identities within its territory and sought to incorporate such identities into cultural policies.[52]

However, the main impact of such novel approaches to nation and nationalism tended to be upon disciplines other than history such as anthropology, sociology and ethnography. Historiography was increasingly nationalised from the late nineteenth century up to and beyond 1945 but intellectually the main effect was that the nation was accepted as an unproblematic, 'natural' category. There might be fierce arguments as to the appropriate form of the nation, or concerning conflicts within and between nations, but the idea that the history of modern Europe and subsequently the world was the fairly natural growth of national consciousness and its political expression in the form of a system of national states went largely uncontested.[53] This changed with the renewal of general theory from the 1980s and this in turn has had a profound impact on historical writing on nation and nationalism.

Modernity and nationalism

Anthony Smith has usefully outlined the key features of what he terms the 'classical modernist paradigm' of nationalism.[54] This takes the nation and/or

[50] Tom Bottomore, *Austro-Marxism: Texts Translated from the German and Edited by Tom Bottomore* (Oxford, 1978).

[51] Karl Deutsch, *Nationalism and Social Communication* (New York, 1953); Gellner is considered below but his writings include illuminating studies of various late Habsburg intellectuals. See for example essays in Ernest Gellner, *Encounters with Nationalism* (Oxford, 1994) and *Language and Solitude: Wittgenstein, Malinowski and the Habsburg Dilemma* (Cambridge, 1998).

[52] See for example Edward Allworth (ed.), *Soviet Nationality Problems* (London, 1971). From a more theoretical perspective see now Rogers Brubacker, *Nationalism Reframed: Nationhood and the National Question in the New Europe* (Cambridge, 1996).

[53] For a very fine and comprehensive study in this tradition see Hugh Seton-Watson, *Nations and States: An Inquiry into the Origins of Nations and the Politics of Nationalism* (London, 1977).

[54] Anthony D. Smith, *Nationalism and Modernism* (London, 1998). For another useful survey of modern theorising on the subject see Umut Özkirimli, *Theories of Nationalism: A Critical Introduction* (London, 2000).

nationalism to be both modern and 'real'. The nation is the real product of specifically modern forces. Thus Kedourie and Deutsch, in their very different ways, are modernists: the modern intelligentsia and modern forms of social communication respectively being the key forces which create national identity and its ideological expression, nationalism.

This modernist paradigm, according to Smith, reached its theoretical climax in the late 1970s and 1980s and intellectuals in the United Kingdom played an important role in this. One could see this as part of a more general process of the 'resurgence of general theory' within British intellectual culture, perhaps linked to the re-emergence of ideological polarisation and debate in the Thatcherite–Reagan years.[55]

Smith further distinguishes five variants on this modernist paradigm in which the central aspect of modernity is variously identified as industrialism, capitalism, political ideology, the state and imagination/invention. These should be treated as useful organising ideas; many of the writers analysed make connections across these categories. I will cite brief examples from each category.

The central figure focusing on industrialism is Ernest Gellner, a late example of a generalising émigré intellectual hailing from Prague where German–Czech tensions seem to have been responsible for much of the best theorising about nationalism.[56] Gellner had already adumbrated his main lines of thought in a 1960s text, *Thought and Change* (London, 1965), but developed this more fully in *Nations and Nationalism* (Oxford, 1983). For Gellner the transition from agrarian to industrial society led to unprecedented increases in social and geographical mobility which made it impossible to tie culture and identity to fixed social positions. Cultural identity, above all in the form of nationality, acquired autonomy and political meaning. The ideas are highly persuasive but have rarely been used as the leading concepts in historically researched studies of nationalism. Rather it has been more peripheral aspects of Gellner's arguments, for example the way in which different groups of immigrants into the modern city can come to construct mutually conflicting ethnic identities, which have been utilised in studies of cities such as Belfast, Prague and

---

[55] For a panoramic survey across the social sciences see Perry Anderson, 'A Culture in Contraflow', originally published in *New Left Review*, 180/182 (1990) and reprinted in idem, *English Questions* (London, 1992), pp. 193–301.

[56] See *The State of the Nation: Ernest Gellner and the Theory of Nationalism*, ed. John A. Hall (Cambridge, 1998).

Kampala;[57] or the way in which the construction of a public education system is used to propagate a view of national identity. Gellner himself sketched out a model of how a national culture is constructed/invented[58] but never sought to provide any detailed historical account. The most detailed work has been conducted on nationalist elites which elaborate the idea of national identity and use it to mobilise popular support but such work draws as much upon ideas of the modern state, intelligentsia and the invention of tradition as upon specific ideas about industrialism.[59]

Rather fuller historical accounts have come from the Marxist tradition which especially links nationalism to the development of capitalism, although that is also closely associated with industrialisation. These approaches were developed a little earlier, in the 1970s, in the face of radical critiques of neo-colonialism and the emergence of separatist nationalist movements in western Europe. Thus Nairn's view of colonial nationalism as a populist response to uneven and combined development; and Hechter's arguments about Celtic nationalism in the United Kingdom as a response to patterns of internal colonialism.[60] Rather different, and with a greater sense of contingency and irrationality, is Hobsbawm's argument that the dominance of ethnic nationalism in the twentieth century is more the product of the 'accident' of the First World War than something inscribed in the general development of industrial capitalism.[61] Clearly there are distinctions to be made between the nationalist movements of dominant cultural groups which had such success in the nineteenth century (the nationalisation of the British, French and Spanish states; the formation of

[57] For examples see P. Gibbon, *The Origins of Ulster Unionism: The Formation of Popular Protestant Politics and Ideology in Nineteenth-century Ireland* (Manchester, 1975); David J. Parkin, 'Social Structure and Social Change in a Tribally Heterogeneous East African City Ward', Ph.D. thesis (University of London, 1965); Gary B. Cohen, *The Politics of Ethnic Survival: Germans in Prague 1861–1914* (Princeton, NJ, 1981).

[58] See his very amusing account in *Nations and Nationalism* of how the Ruritanians in the land of Meglomania acquire a sense of national identity. As Smith points out (*Nationalism and Modernism*, p. 231, n. 3) Gellner's account draws upon the Habsburg Empire and his anthropological field work in Morocco.

[59] The 'elite plus mobilisation' approach is well represented in the work of Paul Brass; see his *Ethnicity and Nationalism* (London, 1991).

[60] Tom Nairn, *The Break-up of Britain: Crisis and Neo-nationalism* (London, 1977) and 'Marxism and the Modern Janus', *New Left Review* (1975), 3–29; Michael Hechter, *Internal Colonialism: The Celtic Fringe in British National Development 1536–1966* (London, 1975).

[61] Eric Hobsbawm is another example of a generalising émigré, in his case from Germany, although his sweeping historical works are characterised by vast knowledge and respect for the evidence as well as being located within the Marxist tradition. See his *Nations and Nationalism since 1789* (Cambridge, 1990) and *Age of Extremes: The Short Twentieth Century, 1914–1991* (London, 1994). The point about the contingency of ethnic nationalism and the First World War is also made in Anthony Giddens, *The Nation-state and Violence* (Cambridge, 1985).

the Italian and German states) and those of subordinate cultural groups
which underpinned the formation of most of the nation-states formed in
1919. So far as these small nations are concerned, perhaps the most
important historical contribution from within the Marxist tradition is that of
Miroslav Hroch (yet another Prague intellectual!). Hroch assumes the reality
of national identity (for example, in the form of distinct languages and
cultures) and also of class identity, and in a detailed, comparative study has
shown how these acquire greater salience in regions where commercial and
industrial capitalism first penetrates. Yet Hroch's work has not been
emulated by anyone else — perhaps because of the (unreasonable)
discrediting of Marxism since the collapse of the USSR and communism
but also because of the special combination of linguistic range, research
energy and theoretical acumen which his work displays.[62]

I will not spend much time on the approach which focuses on political
ideology because I have already discussed this in relation to the work of
Namier and Kedourie. This type of interpretation is usually located within
a conservative tradition which regards generalising and abstract ideologies
with hostility and associates their impact with the formation of a dedicated
intelligentsia which sometimes can take power in revolutionary situations.
This approach has also been applied to the rise of communism, for
example in the work of Talmon and Schapiro, one stressing ideology, the
other the organisational power of a political intelligentsia. Just as National
Socialism is treated as the extreme but logical destination of nationalism
within this framework so too is Stalinism or Maoism treated as the
destination of communism. After 1945 such work could be used to bracket
together the Third Reich and the Soviet Union, contrasting these as
'totalitarian' regimes to the liberal democracies of the west.[63]

Much more significant in more recent historical accounts has been the
emphasis on the state, often though not necessarily taking the form of elite-
focused studies. The figures on whom Smith concentrates attention include
Anthony Giddens, Charles Tilly, Michael Mann and myself, all working
within a tradition of historical sociology. I have argued that nationalism
produces national identity rather than the other way around and that
the development of nationalism is closely related to the emergence of the

[62] Miroslav Hroch, *Social Preconditions of National Revival in Europe* (Cambridge, 1985). More
influential has been his 'three-stage' view of nationalism. For a succinct statement see idem, 'From
National Movement to the Fully-formed Nation: The Nation-building Process in Europe', *New Left
Review,* 198 (1993), 3–20, repr. in *Mapping the Nation*, ed. Gopal Balakrishnan (London, 1996), pp. 78–97.
[63] J. L. Talmon, *The Myth of the Nation and the Vision of Revolution* (London, 1981); Leonard
Schapiro, *The Russian Revolutions and the Origins of Present-day Communism* (Harmondsworth,
1985) and idem, *Totalitarianism* (London, 1992).

modern, participatory and sharply territorial state which nationalists claim for their own — whether through reform of the present state, unification of a number of smaller states or separation from the existing state. In *Nationalism and the State* I tried to underpin this general argument with a series of historical case-studies drawn from Europe, the Middle East, Africa and Asia. Those case-studies are utterly dependent upon a good secondary literature and in this short essay I can do no better than refer readers to that literature. I would stress, however, that I sought, as did the other theorists mentioned, to relate the development of the modern state to more general patterns of modernisation in which political, economic and cultural functions came to be increasingly concentrated into the operations of specialised institutions such as bureaucracies, parliaments, political parties, firms, markets, churches, schools, museums, theatres and the mass media. Any particular history of the development of the modern nation, national identity and nationalism must therefore relate state and politics to economy, society and culture. My argument simply is that for any *general* account of modern nations and nationalism (as opposed to the very diverse, specific histories of particular cases) it is the state–nation relationship that is particularly illuminating.

The emphases of Tilly, Mann and Giddens are somewhat different. Tilly stresses the formative role of the state and in numerous studies has sought to bring out the various roles of war-making, urbanisation and capitalism in this process.[64] Giddens also makes much of war and violence as well as the surveillance powers of the modern state.[65] In both cases there is a strong emphasis upon the sharply delineated territory of the modern state. Mann still has to publish the third volume in his planned trilogy on the 'sources of social power' which will deal with the twentieth century but he has already indicated the way in which he sees the nation-state and the associated ideology of nationalism as the appropriate power unit under modern conditions, a unit which shows no signs of decline in the near future.[66]

---

[64] Amongst his many works see *Coercion, Capital, and European States, AD 990–1992* (Oxford, 1992); (ed.), *The Formation of National States in Western Europe* (London, 1975).

[65] Amongst his many works see *A Contemporary Critique of Historical Materialism: Vol. 2, The Nation-state and Violence* (London, 1985). I have critically assessed this work in 'The Nation-state and Violence: A Critique of Giddens', in *Anthony Giddens: Consensus and Controversy*, ed. Jon Clark et al. (London, 1990), pp. 271–88, 291–93; repr. in *Anthony Giddens: Critical Assessments of Leading Sociologists*, ed. C. Bryant and D. Jary, 4 vols (London, 1996), vol. 3, pp. 302–23.

[66] The first two volumes of his major work are *The Sources of Social Power: Vol. 1, A History of Power from the Beginning to AD 1760* (Cambridge, 1986) and *The Sources of Social Power: Vol. 2, The Rise of Classes and Nation-states, 1760–1914* (Cambridge, 1993). For a more contemporary assessment see his essay, 'Nation-states in Europe and Other Continents: Diversifying, Developing, Not Dying', in *Mapping the Nation*, ed. Gopal Balakrishnan (London and New York, 1996), pp. 295–316.

The works cited above have been written both by generalising historians and historical sociologists and seek to advance general interpretations within what Smith calls the 'classical modernist' paradigm. Most historians tend rather to borrow from such understandings of modernity in order to analyse particular cases. The best such historical work combines a focus on the modern state with an understanding of the modernisation of economy, society and culture. A good example is Eugene Weber's study *Peasants into Frenchmen: The Modernisation of Rural France, 1870–1914*.[67] Weber's argument is that a common and widespread sense of national identity only became possible in France under the modern conditions of the centralised state, mass politics, public education system, and greater social and geographical mobility associated with commercialisation, industrialisation and urbanisation. Only under such conditions can one get the language standardisation and extensive social communication which alone give meaning, beyond certain educated elites, to the idea of 'Frenchness'. Only in this period, for example, did large numbers of people in western and southern France adopt French as their first language, acquire literacy and start voting in national elections.

In a very different way, with a greater focus on religion and warfare, Linda Colley has argued that a British (as opposed to a specifically English) identity was forged out of Protestantism and conflict with the Catholic powers of France and Spain in the eighteenth and early nineteenth centuries.[68] The earlier formation of central political institutions (above all administrative, legal and representative), widespread commercialisation, social and geographical mobility (even seventeenth-century studies indicate a very high proportion of people who at some point at least visited London), and a more vigorous civil society — all this can be added to Colley's account to explain why a widespread sense of British identity can already be traced back to the eighteenth century.

Similar arguments can be developed for Germany and Italy, although increasingly the emphasis is placed upon the very late and limited development of national identity. I have sketched out such an argument in relation to Germany between 1800 and 1871 and many recent studies have emphasised the limited penetration of national identity beyond certain bourgeois elites before unification. Conversely, many studies have implicitly followed Eugene Weber's approach in stressing how the massive socio-economic

[67] London, 1979. Weber is yet another example of cross-national links, a Romanian–American who in addition to his work on modern French history has also written on fascism and right-wing politics in twentieth-century Romania.

[68] Linda Colley, *Britons: Forging the Nation, 1707–1837* (London, 1992).

transformation of Germany into an urban/industrial society by 1914, along with the growth of mass education, politics and warfare was what made a reality of the nation in the period up to 1918.[69] By contrast, the stress in Italian historiography has been upon the failure of the new state to 'make Italians', linked to the relative lack of modernisation of politics, education, economy and society.[70]

My own view is that one or another of these paradigms of classical modernism provides the best departure point for study of the particular histories of modern nations, nation states and nationalism. However, of far greater importance in recent historical work has been the modernist approach associated with processes of imagination and invention and this in turn has moved towards postmodern interpretations in which such discursive processes are detached from any allegedly 'real' conditions. The two seminal books are *The Invention of Tradition*, edited by Eric Hobsbawm and Terry Ranger (Cambridge, 1983) and, above all, Benedict Anderson's *Imagined Communities: Reflections on the Origins and Spread of Nationalism* (London, 1983; second and revised edition, 1991). As Smith emphasises, both these books are modernist in that they place the activity of inventing traditions and imagining nations firmly within the framework of the modern state, politics and capitalism. At the same time, by paying careful attention to the specific conditions under which traditions can be invented and people can come to imagine that they are all members of the same nation, these historians were able to respond to the criticism of other forms of modernism that they reduce nationalism to a reflex of another aspect of modernity. There is still something of this quality in some of the contributions to the Hobsbawm–Ranger volume; invention takes the form of elite manipulation which in turn is explained in terms of class and other interests.

One can partly explain the immense influence of Anderson's work — without doubt the single most cited general text on nationalism — by the manner in which he avoids this reductionist trap. For example, his account of how a readership of a newspaper can, although consuming the newspaper as a set of dispersed individuals, at the same time imagine themselves as part of that collective body of readers, enables us to see the way in which what he calls 'print capitalism' can make its own autonomous and indispensable contribution towards the formation of national identity.

---

[69] For a good recent overview in English see David Blackbourn, *The Fontana History of Germany 1780–1918: The Long Nineteenth Century* (London, 1997) as well as John Breuilly (ed.), *Nineteenth-century Germany* (London, 2001).

[70] Riall, *The Italian Risorgimento*.

   Without wishing to seem churlish, however, or in any way detracting
from the merits of a brilliant and illuminating study, one can also see other
less intellectually impressive reasons for the impact of this book. It is much
easier to study the work of nationalist intelligentsias (and almost all the
historical studies following Anderson equate the activity of imagining the
nation with the published work of intellectuals) than, for example, to
construct indices of national identity (such as language use, voting patterns,
associational habits) and to correlate these with the spread of modern
practices such as schooling, commercial employment, urban immigration
and trade unionism. To some extent Anderson's work has created a new
legitimacy for an older style of intellectual history. Whereas Kedourie
presented nationalism as an 'invented doctrine', placing the origins of the
subject within the history of ideas, Anderson with his focus on the 'imagined
community' shifts the focus to a more broad-based cultural history. Once
that cultural history is detached from its modernist context, it can appear as a
rather less precise kind of intellectual history than that practised by
Kedourie.
   On the positive side much recent work advances such cultural history,
for example by extending its range of interests to what might be called
'public culture'. The Hobsbawm–Ranger volume called attention to the
way tradition was crystallised into such activities as festivals, the construction of monuments and buildings designed to express a sense of national
identity, the formation of associations whose purpose was to cultivate
national memory and pride. The proliferation of such studies in the last
twenty years is far too great to be considered here. The best of such
work rigorously contextualises such subjects. A good example is Charlotte
Tacke's comparison of the movements which constructed monuments and
festivals to Vertingetorix in eastern France and Arminius/Hermann in
western Germany.[71] By means of comparison Tacke demonstrates that, for
all the surface differences in the national myths that were presented (French
civic versus German ethnic nationalism; French defeat by versus German
victory over Rome) the social bases and aesthetic styles of the two
movements were very similar. However, the worst of such work simply
provides descriptions of particular 'imaginings' without context, leaping
assertively from such descriptions to their presumed impact upon national
identity.

---

[71] Charlotte Tacke, *Denkmal im sozialen Raum: nationale Symbole in Deutschland und Frankreich*
(Göttingen, 1995).

This separation of imagining from its context reaches its apogee in postmodernist approaches.[72] The act of imagining the nation is not given its meaning within a 'modern' context which alone both enables such imagining to take place and to produce important effects, but is rather seen as what actually gives the nation any significance that it has. Anderson's autonomous sphere of imagination has become detached and self-sufficient.

There is some value to some of the accounts this has produced with titles such as *Nation and Narration* and numerous references to imagining or inventing nations.[73] They draw attention to the discursive construction of national identity, emphasising the ways in which the nation is presented as the subject of a story and becomes manifest within the conventions of such story-telling. This approach can help us understand why there can be so many discontinuities, fractures, conflicts and multiple forms of national identity. If one assumes that the nation is a real group constituted through common language, customs, associations or interests (whether or not this real group precedes or is the product of modernity) it can be difficult to grasp this volatility and changeability in national identity. A particularly important branch of this approach dealing with colonial nationalism and its aftermath has elaborated notions of 'post-colonialism' and, especially in the Subaltern Studies work on India, has produced a significant historiography.[74]

Yet, except possibly in the study of multiculturalism in the most advanced of today's societies, I would argue that this approach suffers from crippling defects. A significant and widespread sense of national identity and its expression through such institutions as nationalist parties and nation-states *is* a specific feature of the post-1800 world, one which was only generalised on a global scale in the twentieth century. One can locate imaginations of the nation before 1800 but rarely are they associated with such broader changes. Equally, comparisons across time and place make it clear that only some such imaginings have had a significant impact since 1800 and take remarkably similar forms despite the strenuous national(ist)

---

[72] See ch. 9, 'Beyond Modernism?' in Smith, *Nationalism and Modernism*.

[73] The title of a book edited by Homi Bhaba (London, 1990). See also *Imagining Nations*, ed. Geoffrey Cubitt (Manchester, 1998) and the fascinating study by Maria Todorova, *Imagining the Balkans* (Oxford, 1997). There are numerous books about invention or imagination (not by any means the same thing, although the German translation of Anderson's book turns 'imagined' into 'invented'); almost at random one can cite titles such as *The Invention of Argentina* (Shumway), *The Invention of Scotland* (Pittock) and *Inventing Ireland* (Kibberd).

[74] For example in the work of Partha Chatterjee: *Nationalist Thought and the Colonial World: A Derivative Discourse* (London, 1986); *The Nation and its Fragments* (Cambridge, 1993); 'Whose Imagined Community?' in Balakrishnan, *Mapping the Nation*, pp. 214–25.

insistence on uniqueness. It seems fairly obvious, therefore, that one must place such imaginings within a larger context which can help account both for their existence and, more importantly, significance. Generally speaking the non-contextualising and non-comparative postmodernist approach is incapable of grasping such large truths.

That still leaves a good deal open to debate. First, there are important differences within the 'modernist' camp. How does one variously balance industrialisation, imperialism, class conflict, the interventionist state, elite manipulations of mass politics, interstate warfare, the formation of a public culture and much else in both general accounts of national formation and in historical accounts of specific cases?

Second, there is the perennialist response to modernist accounts. Many theorists as well as historians argue that modernists have been too quick to stress the modernity of nations. Was there really no sense of national identity, for example, amongst the Jews of the Old Testament, or the English people about whom Bede wrote in the eighth century? Terms such as English, German, French have a lineage which extends well before the modern era, no matter how generously we understand that period. Recently, for example, Adrian Hastings has energetically argued that English national identity and even nationalism can be traced back to the late Anglo-Saxon period.[75] John Armstrong in *Nations before Nationalism* (Chapel Hill, NC, 1982) elaborated a more general case based on the way identity is constructed through self–other interactions. Anthony Smith has argued that ethnicity, understood not in terms of an 'objective' reality such as language or common ways of life but rather in terms of patterns of symbolic communication which are passed on down from one generation to another, forms the basis upon which modern nations and nationalism build.[76]

Such work needs to be distinguished from nationalist myth-making which projects back current claims about national identity on to carefully selected fragments of the past to create an apparently seamless national history which culminates in the present. These writers are well aware of much that is specific to the modern conception of the nation — for example legal, political and economic unity, mass loyalty and mobilisation, an extensive public culture, the absence of competing religious or dynastic legitimations of authority. Their claim is rather that modernity is not so clear a rupture from what went before and that indeed, without the earlier ties created through pre-

---

[75] Adrian Hastings, *The Construction of Nationhood: Ethnicity, Religion and Nationalism* (Cambridge, 1997).
[76] Apart from *Nationalism and Modernism* see his *The Ethnic Origins of Nations* (Oxford, 1986). For a more detached survey see also Özkirimli, *Theories of Nationalism*, ch. 5, 'Ethno-symbolism'.

modern national identity, one cannot understand why this rather than that conception of nationality came to prevail and how such identities play important roles in countering the fragmenting effects of modernisation.

This debate has been extensive and there is no need to repeat it here. Presented in a general form it is difficult to object to the perennialist argument. Furthermore, there is much good historical work drawing upon ideas of self–other interaction, ethno-symbolic communication, and more generally the elite uses of concepts of nationality in the pre-modern period. The problem really arises in trying to make specific connections between pre-modern and modern forms of national identity. For example, there is a body of work on pre-eighteenth-century France which can show how the monarchy and even some of its opponents deployed ideas of France and the French to legitimise their claims and policies. There is also a body of work which can point to the creative role of intelligentsias in imagining a new kind of France in the later eighteenth century.[77] Yet at some point one must then make the shift to the construction of new institutions in the Napoleonic period, the impact of mass conscription, and then the modernisation to which Eugene Weber refers. Beyond registering that there were competing concepts of the French nation up to 1800 how, in any active way, can this pre-modern history be linked to the ideologies, movements and modernising forces which made a reality of mass national identity by 1914?[78] Furthermore, one must stress the pre-modern context in which the nation was usually understood in a socially very limited way, in which national ideas were often subordinate in significance to regional identity and were often only tapped in episodic, xenophobic and negative ways at times of interstate conflict. This changing context alters the meaning of specifically national identity claims. In the modern era each generation so transforms whatever is 'handed down' to it by the previous generation, so selects from that legacy, that there is little general to be said beyond stating that there was some minimal inheritance. What is more, as Gellner forcefully argued in a debate with Smith, we only have to find one nation without a 'navel' to be able to claim that modern nations do not require pre-modern identities. There are many historians of modern Asian, African and American 'nations', let

---

[77] For example Keith M. Baker, *Inventing the French Revolution: Essays on French Political Culture in the Eighteenth Century* (Cambridge, 1990).

[78] A good historiographical survey which places this fashionable political culture approach to the French Revolution in context is Peter Jones (ed.), *The French Revolution in Social and Political Perspective* (London, 1996); and for an excellent study which draws attention to modernising institutions in the post-Revolution period see I. Woloch, *The New Regime: Transformations of the French Civic Order, 1789–1820s* (New York and London, 1994).

alone of various European 'nations', who would agree that there is precious little in the way of such navels.[79]

Conclusion

I have not considered the question of how far historians and their work are themselves part of the history of becoming national, that is the historical rather than historiographical significance of national historical writing. It is an important story.[80] The nation is usually understood as an historical construction. For most nationalists, establishing the appropriate historical credentials of their nation virtually amounts to legitimating national demands for autonomy. Historians therefore have played an important intellectual as well as political role in shaping modern national identity and commitment. The regimes of many nation-states seek to produce and impose an official view of national history and historians are involved in such projects. Conversely, oppositional national movements challenge such histories and propose rival versions.

However, there is not space to explore this theme. Rather I have considered historians and the nation in terms of historiography, that is in terms of the ways in which the nation has figured in the work of academic historians who do not regard themselves in the first instance as propagandists for their or any other nation. I will conclude by asking what directions such work is likely to take in the future and whether historians will continue to write in distinctively national ways.

Following the theoretical resurgence in the late 1970s and 1980s there has been a more 'practical' interest in nationalism stimulated by the break-up of the USSR and its replacement by national states, themselves frequently challenged by yet further national movements. This has led to an explosion of historical and other publications although much of it rather descriptive and drawing upon the various paradigms discussed in the last section. Much of this work also links to political divisions within the post-Soviet states.

Smith rather optimistically concludes his book *Nationalism and Modernism* by sketching out an agenda in which various competing approaches to the history of nations and nationalism can be productively combined. I am

---

[79] Ernest Gellner, 'Do Nations have Navels?' *Nations and Nationalism*, 10 (1996), 366–70.

[80] For a range of useful essays on the subject see Berger et al., *Writing National Histories*. I have briefly addressed the issue in the published version of my inaugural lecture at Birmingham University, *Myth-Making or Myth-Breaking? Nationalism and History* (Birmingham, 1997).

more sceptical. I do not think the sheer range of cases and aspects to be considered allow any overarching framework to be developed which could command widespread consensus. For example, it is difficult to see how one can reconcile modernist and postmodernist approaches, or integrate a history of ideas treatment of the subject with one that stresses elite manipulation or focuses on ethno-symbolism. We must simply register the fact of pluralism in approaches to the subject. This is especially evident in the particularising work of historians who do not seek a general overview of the subject.

Some approaches are currently more fashionable than others. The history of the nation as a process of imagining or inventing engages a great deal of attention; perennialist or modernist paradigms seem less attractive. In the longer term I suspect that historians will increasingly return to those other paradigms which provide a context within which discursive processes of imagining or inventing nations can be placed and which can offer some intelligible account of how and why some of those processes are more significant than others.

It may be that the processes of European integration and more generally globalisation will have an impact on national historiography. The move away from territorially demarcated nation-states possessed of sovereignty towards shared and overlapping powers and citizenship rights encourages historical explorations of pre-nation-state sovereignty and territoriality.[81] The extent to which national identity is bound up with the construction of national citizenship in legal, political and social terms (and therefore might decline with the unravelling of those terms) is also becoming a subject of historical research.[82] The growth of regional identity and power, as well as of cooperation between adjacent regions in different states, is another stimulus to historical work. All these concerns can lead to an emphasis upon the multiple and changing forms of identity, not just at the discursive level but also in terms of 'real' groups and institutions.

There may be less productive trends as well. The processes of devolution and multiculturalism in the United Kingdom quite understandably lead to challenges to the dominant English/British view of national history. Yet these will not be fruitful if they are simply replaced with a 'four nations/two islands' approach to our history. One national teleology will simply have

---

[81] On territoriality and boundaries see as a general overview Malcolm Anderson, *Frontiers: Territory and State Formation in the Modern World* (London, 1996). The most celebrated of modern studies is Peter Sahlins, *Boundaries: The Making of France and Spain in the Pyrenees* (Berkeley, CA, 1989).
[82] See for example Rogers Brubaker, *Citizenship and Nationhood in France and Germany* (Cambridge, MA, 1992) which has itself stimulated various critical responses from historians studying the history of the emergence of modern forms of citizenship in France and Germany.

been replaced by four. There is also a distinct danger that a 'little England' approach will simply be replaced by a series of 'little England/Ireland/ Scotland/Wales' approaches. The modern history of Britain cannot be understood outside the context of conflict with Europe and the establishment of overseas empire, and the unravelling of previously dominant conceptions of national identity must be linked to reversals of both those historical trajectories.[83] Even less promising will be a desperate stress on British/ English identity against the trends towards European integration and this will be especially deplorable if built into a national curriculum for school history teaching.

Historians should treat the 'nation' not as a 'real' object with a real history but equally not as a work of invention or imagination. Rather they should treat it as a social science concept, rather like other group concepts such as class or occupation. In doing so they will need explicitly to borrow from the social sciences as well as various cultural disciplines in order to make sense of the subject. Some might look to political theory concerning the state or elites; some to anthropology and the formation of identity through self–other interactions; some to sociology and economics, especially those aspects of the subject which themselves adopt historical perspectives in order to understand the nature of modernity and its impact upon the nation. Whatever directions the subject takes, however, one can be fairly confident that the historiography of the nation will be a lively and contested field for the foreseeable future.

However, I think such historiographical debates, even if *about* the nation, will be less and less the product of distinctively national styles of historical interpretation. In the early part of the twentieth century, especially before 1914, it was possible to regard the British nation as something which really existed and was a good thing. Such an assumption in turn informed the way in which British historians approached the history of other 'nations'. Historians like Trevelyan and Seton-Watson, for all their interests in other nations, were intellectually formed through a distinctive British cultural and educational system. The inter-war period began to undermine such an understanding which increasingly took on a romantic or nostalgic or more narrowly British form. Attention shifted from the nation as a natural human unit to nationalism as a modern and formative force, for good and evil.

---

[83] Fortunately there is also recent work which reverses the depressing descent into overly 'internalist' analyses of British/English history which arguably was one unfortunate legacy of the work of Elton and Namier. See for example John Brewer, *The Sinews of Power: War, Money and the English State, 1688–1783* (London, 1989) and C. A. Bayly, *Imperial Meridian: The British Empire and the World, 1780–1830* (London, 1989).

Explicit theory, often imported into British historiography and social science by émigrés, came to underpin further historical work, even if sometimes used to shore up an idealisation of the English and their admirable pragmatism and empiricism. Disillusionment, engagement in European conflict and intellectual emigration was already undermining distinctively British styles of understanding.

Those phases of Whiggism, romantic nostalgia, and the principled construction of a unique British national identity are over. Mass immigration, economic interdependence and European integration all work to undermine the credibility of distinct national identity. More specifically, the internationalisation of intellectual activity erodes national styles of academic history work. Many of the most influential 'British' historians and theorists of the nation of the last decades were not born in Britain at all (Eric Hobsbawm, Lewis Namier, Geoffrey Elton, Ernest Gellner). Even historians of Britain born in Britain have moved abroad during the period in which some of their major work has been produced (John Brewer, David Cannadine, Linda Colley, Michael Mann). Some indeed have no fixed national abode but rather move from one country and one academic institution to another. Even those normally resident in Britain often obtain visiting professorships or fellowships or extensive periods of research leave in academic institutions elsewhere. Many 'British' historians are leading historians of other countries, often plying their craft in those countries (for example Paul Ginsborg in Italy), or in third countries such as the USA or Australia (for example Simon Schama, Geoff Eley, David Blackbourn, John Davis). Some of the most influential modern work on British history which has adumbrated ideas of a specific type of national identity has been written by foreign historians, for example the influential study by the American Martin Wiener, *English Culture and the Decline of the Industrial Spirit 1850–1980* (Cambridge, 1981). Although there remain distinct national intellectual styles associated with different kinds of media and universities, this constant movement and communication across national boundaries means that these are sharply declining in significance, certainly at the level of sustained academic research activity. British historians did once take a distinctive approach towards the nation, albeit one which I think was inferior to that of many European historians by virtue of its lack of explicit theorisation. That has largely ceased to be the case. In future one can expect good historical work (as opposed to political propaganda) on this or that nation to take on a cosmopolitan character.

CHAPTER FOUR

The Orient: British Historical Writing about Asia since 1890

C. A. BAYLY

This essay examines the work of British scholars of Asia in the century since 1890 and especially writers who reflected on the history of the Islamic world, India, China and Japan. Before the mid-1950s great advances were made in the retrieval and organising of historical data from Asia, but the dominant aim of the writers of history was to chart a continuing religious and racial drama. This was true not only of official historians who wrote of oriental corruption and the coming of British law, but also of many of the oriental scholars, educationists and missionaries who wrote with sympathy of Asian aspirations. The Second World War and the triumph of nationalism created a true British social history of Asia which privileged impersonal forces: demography, trade and the play of local political systems. Such a version of social history has remained dominant until today, while in other English-speaking countries postmodernist and post-colonial themes have occupied the high ground. One reason is that British historians of Asia see in the post-colonialist preoccupation with the oppressed, the 'fragment', the pre-colonial community and popular resistance a moralising paradigm similar to the one from which they have only too recently escaped.

Imperial experience and the 'redemptive mode' of historical writing

In many ways, historical writing on Asia over the last century certainly manifested a will to 'dominate, restructure and have authority over the Orient' in the famous words of Edward Said.[1] Said argued that since

---

[1] Edward Said, *Orientalism: Western Conceptions of the Orient* (1978, repr. London, 1991), p. 3.

the Middle Ages, European writing about Asia had tended to construct Asia, and the Arab world in particular, as Europe's inferior 'other'. Ronald Inden developed this critique of oriental knowledge further in the case of India.[2] He wrote that in emphasising the unchanging village, the caste or the religious community as the essence of India in their analyses, European historians depicted Indians as beings incapable of individual action, their weak polities always on the point of being overwhelmed by the amoral community. This critique has been less obtrusive in east Asian studies, but in the 1970s self-styled 'concerned' scholars, protesting against the Vietnam War, claimed that European and American historiography had belittled the Asian capacity to develop independently and thus indirectly served the interests of imperialism.[3]

The reader will find a good deal in this essay to support such claims. Even radical and anti-imperialist historians believed in some form of western civilising mission in Asia. Up to 1950, those who were not themselves former imperial officials were usually missionaries, educationists or business people who moved easily in official circles. The London School of Oriental Studies (SOS), which generated much of the most important historical scholarship, was itself founded in 1911 specifically to train cadres of colonial officials in oriental languages and culture.

Even after the Second World War, the new generation of professional historians of Asia was educated by men who had direct experience of war and government in the former empire and inherited some of their assumptions. Until very recently Asian history continued to be built around a narrative which had served to make European dominance appear the natural consequence of the weakness of oriental government and the factionalism of its politics. Oriental historiography generally developed in stultifying isolation from another genre which bore an equally clear imprint of Britain's imperial experience. This was Commonwealth or 'white empire' history, inaugurated in the 1880s by Sir John Seeley and lavishly endowed with chairs at Oxford, Cambridge and London in the first half of the twentieth century.[4] Commonwealth history was the history of progressive British settlement and constitutional benevolence and was studied in history faculties. Asian history was the record of civilisations which ultimately

---

[2] Ronald Inden, *Imagining India* (Oxford, 1990); see also T. R. Metcalfe, *Ideologies of the Raj* (Cambridge, 1994).

[3] Paul A. Cohen, *Discovering History in China: American Historical Writing on the Recent Chinese Past* (New York, 1984), pp. 91–3.

[4] See Robin R. Winks (ed.), *Historiography, vol. 5* of *The Oxford History of the British Empire*, ed. Wm. Roger Louis (Oxford, 1999).

failed. It was relegated to the exotic terrain of oriental faculties. The natural relatives of Asian history were comparative religion, literary studies and archaeology, rather than European history.

Yet to stress the relationship between colonial power and oriental knowledge can only take us so far. Even in the latter days of empire, histories were the product of a more complex dialogue between several different levels of political interest and aesthetic sensibility. Intellectual changes in the metropolis reflected much more than the brute experience of empire. We will see that artistic taste influenced attitudes to the great civilisations of the East, particularly after the Victorian Arts and Crafts movement alerted the British public to chinoiserie and Japanese art.[5] A figure such as E. Denison Ross, first director of the London School of Oriental Studies, as it then was, became interested in the history and culture of Asia because exotic art and languages were fetishes of the social circles he frequented in London and Cambridge.[6] Only later was he exposed to the colonialist assumptions of the Calcutta Madrassa and the Archaeological Survey of India when he joined their staffs.[7] During his period in India in the 1900s he always maintained a distance from the old India and China 'hands' and their understandings of oriental culture even though he eagerly attended their balls and dinner parties.

Besides art, another critical component of metropolitan sensibilities about Asia was late Victorian and Edwardian religious attitudes, and these were often quite ambivalent.[8] Some historians of the Christian Orient were influenced by the contemporary Islamophobic rhetoric associated with W. E. Gladstone. Anti-Catholicism directed their interest to the history of the ancient apostolic churches of the East and Russia. But the 'Eastern Question' also generated its own mavericks and rebels, including E. G. Browne,[9] who deliberately took up the Islamic, Arab and Persian causes and, like Edward Gibbon a century before, believed Islam at its best to be a rational religion which perceived the Unity of God.

For most of the historians treated in this essay religious experience was the spur to historical understanding. It provided the organising principle for many of the histories themselves. This was not religion in the sense of

---

[5] John M. MacKenzie, *Orientalism: History, Theory and the Arts* (Manchester, 1995).

[6] Sir E. Denison Ross, *Both Ends of the Candle: The Autobiography of Sir E. D. Ross* (London, 1941), pp. 169–72 ff.

[7] Ibid.; the Calcutta Madrassa was founded by Warren Hastings in 1781 in order to associate Muslim learning with British rule.

[8] This point has been brought out for an earlier period in Geoffrey A. Oddie, 'Orientalism and British Protestant Missionary Constructions of India in the Nineteenth Century' *South Asia*, 17, 2 (1994), 27–42.

[9] See below, pp. 93–4.

theology. The writers considered here ranged in their beliefs from Presbyterians through High Anglicans to apparent agnostics. All, however, believed that religion provided a key to human experience and that all men were imbued with a sense of deep spirituality. Most of them also believed that the quality or character of individuals and peoples was manifest through their morality and altruism.[10] In 1976 Hayden White wrote of the 'tragic' and 'organicist' modes of nineteenth-century history writing which were so clearly signalled at its beginning by G. F. Hegel himself.[11] In this reading of history as tragedy, civilisations rose and fell because puny human energies and failing reason proved inadequate to maintain their complex fabrics. Yet the narrative and emplotment which was dominant in British writings about Asia until the 1950s is better described as 'redemptive'. Whether they were formally Christian or not, most of these historians, along with practitioners of other humane disciplines, believed that civilisations and races declined and fell as a consequence of moral corruption. But they also considered that a kernel of redeeming social vision or racial virtue survived this Fall. To many, it was obvious that redemption would be born of the supposedly Christian civic culture of the British conqueror. But, for other writers, Asian civilisations would rise again in response to the deep religious feelings of indigenous races themselves. The Indian historian Edward Thompson, indeed, wanted the British to redeem their own souls from past sins of genocide by building a new empire of morality in company with enlightened natives.[12] In the striking case of Joseph Needham's studies of Chinese civilisation, the salve of religion would be applied in equal measure with the purge of Marxist revolution to raise China from its decline.[13]

Race was the third main component of metropolitan sensibility which influenced history writing after aesthetics and religion. For late Victorian writers, the Comte de Gobineau had pointed the way by analysing the history of west and central Asia in terms of ascending and declining racial essences.[14] Some aspects of Gobineau's scheme survived through into the work of Oswald Spengler and his British compère, Arnold Toynbee, whose evolutionist *A Study of History* was the most important text for many of the Asian historians of the first half of the twentieth century. Yet racialism at this

---

[10] See Stefan Collini, *Public Moralists: Political Thought and Intellectual Life in Britain 1850–1930* (Oxford, 1991).

[11] Hayden White, *Metahistory: The Historical Imagination in Nineteenth-century Europe* (Baltimore, MD, 1976, repr. 1990).

[12] See below, pp. 103–4.

[13] See below, pp. 109–11.

[14] Joseph Arthur, Comte de Gobineau, *Histoire des Perses d'apres Les Auteurs Orientaux, Grecs et Latins* (Paris, 1869); *Trois Ans en Asie (Paris, 1859).*

period was a large arena for intellectual contention and not simply a set of reactionary or imperialist opinions.[15] The relationship between race, religion and culture was delineated with creative vagueness. Religious and cultural excellence were seen as outward signs of inner racial fibre. Radicals believed that inherent racial energies would reinvigorate oppressed colonial peoples. Pessimists, including Lord Curzon, believed that British racial energies were themselves waning. The discourse of race could be as subversive as it was supportive of the imperial order. It could also direct admiration to Asian races rather than simply 'other' them. In Asian historiography, a new British interest was stimulated by the Japanese emergence as a 'master race' following their war with Russia in 1904–5. Some British intellectuals saw themselves as the civilisers of the raw energies of this young giant.[16]

While metropolitan aesthetic sensibilities played a dominant role in setting the agenda and providing the plots for history writing, most historians were indeed influenced by the intellectual traditions of a different order: the institutions of the colonial periphery. These provided them with data, native informants and critics, ways of viewing the past, but also positions and prejudices to work with or against. The institutions included Christian missions, the Chinese Maritime Customs Service, the Indian and Sudan civil services and the Anglo-Persian Oil Company. They operated in complex ways both to discover and to construct history. No simple seamless amalgam of oriental knowledge and oriental power was anywhere visible. In many of these institutions embodied knowledge had suffered a time-lag. Even in the twentieth century, for instance, some of the assumptions and prejudices of the eighteenth-century Scottish Enlightenment thinkers were still evident in the periphery. The idea that climate dominated human character had not given way to race theory here. Metropolitan and colonial knowledge moved at different speeds, creating lacunae and tensions. Again, much of the writing produced through these local colonial institutions reflected the scholarly interests of learned individuals, betraying little or no ideological bias. These products of enlightened antiquarianism were the staple from which the broader histories were made.

Finally, indigenous voices played an increasing role in forming historical understandings both at the metropolitan level and in Asia. The British historical tradition and its indigenous critics worked on each other in complex ways. In some cases, British historians reacted violently against national and cultural self-assertion of Asians. In others, as, for instance, in

[15] See Susan Bayly, 'Caste and Race in the Colonial Ethnography of India', in Peter Robb (ed.), *The Concept of Race in South Asia* (Delhi, 1995), pp. 165–218.
[16] This point was suggested by Dr Peter Kornicki, see below pp. 107–8.

those of the Indian reformer C. F. Andrews,[17] Asian demands forced an agonising Christian reappraisal on them. The essay goes on now to develop these themes through the examples of historical writing on Islamic west Asia, India and the Far East.

Religion and polity in Persia

E. G. Browne must be the starting-point for the modern history of Persia in Britain, even though he would have regarded himself pre-eminently as a literary and textual specialist. For Browne and many others of his generation, Iran represented an exotic, living eastern Greece and Browne quickly identified himself as its Byron. Following Gobineau, Browne believed that in Iran 'Aryan freedom' had been overcome by 'Arab steel' in the early years of the Islamic expansion but that nevertheless 'the most striking feature of the Persians as a nation is their passion for metaphysical speculation'.[18] Sufi mysticism, which he initially saw as a largely Persian creation, represented the 'revolt of the Aryan Spirit against a semitic religion imposed by force of arms on an Aryan people'.[19] The religious creativity of ancient Persia had been manifested in Zoroastrianism and Mithraism. In modern times, it was the millenarian Babi Rebellion of 1848, ruthlessly suppressed by the Qajar regime, which represented Persia's enduring capacity to create new patterns of belief within Islam. That revolt, whose spirit was indirectly inherited by the Bahai movement, would in time mark the beginnings of a new World Religion. For in its transcendental claims as much as in the suffering of its martyrs, Babi-Bahaism recalled the rise of Christianity. Apparently without formal religious beliefs himself, Browne nevertheless warmed to the urge of 'the Brahmin sage, the Greek philosopher, the Persian poet or the Christian pietist to be at one with God'.[20] Thus modern Persia, like ancient Greece, was in the vanguard of the West's spiritual development. Browne once heard a lecture by George Bernard Shaw on the 'Religion of the Future'. Shaw prophesied that the faith of the coming superman would be a good healthy, western religion, not 'the rags of oriental systems of religion'. Browne dissented; it was ironic, he noted, that 'this brilliant modern thinker of the

---

[17] See below, p. 103.

[18] E. G. Browne, *A Year among the Persians* (London, 1893), p. 122.

[19] E. G. Browne, *Sufism (Religious Systems of the World)*, bound pamphlet, Oriental Studies Faculty, Cambridge, n.d., p. 2.

[20] Browne, *A Year*, p. 121.

West could not evolve a religion which the East had not already formulated'.[21]

In his literary and historical work, Browne was also preoccupied with Persia as a nation struggling to be free: 'Again and again Persia has been apparently submerged by Greeks, Parthians, Arabs, Mongols, Tartars, Turks and Afghans, yet she has always re-emerged as a distinct nation with peculiar and well-marked idiosyncracies.'[22] Religious history was also national history. For it was the suffering of the Babis and Bahais which demonstrated that the Persian was not cowardly, as racist commentators said, but on the point of asserting his nationality against the domineering British and Russians. Browne's *The Persian Revolution* (Cambridge, 1910) charted the re-emergence of this national essence.

This particular British vision of Persian race and religion persisted into the inter-war period and beyond in the work of Browne's pupil A. J. Arberry, whose teleology of Iranian history was equally marked: 'At the time when Greece turned back the hordes of Xerxes, the Persians had already a certain attitude of mind which runs through the changing pattern of the ages like bright unfading thread.'[23] Thus Iranian Aryan culture was not 'saharized' or dessicated by the arid Arab spirit. On the other hand, when it ventured south of the Hindu Kush, these bright threads of reason were quickly corrupted by the 'bombast, servility and typical lushness of India'.[24] Ironically, in view of the century-old tradition of espying Aryans in India,[25] Arberry needed to look no further than the baroque forms of medieval Indian Persian to perceive the bad effects of Indian racial turpidity.

These sensibilities in turn influenced the post-war generation of British interpreters of Persia, though in subtler form. Peter Avery wrote in his *History of Modern Persia* of mullahs producing 'a fanatical attitude among the masses; an attitude basically alien to the Persian character, though less so to the Turkish'.[26] Echoing Browne's and Arberry's hostility to the westernisation of Iran, Avery stated that, had Reza Shah Pahlavi's twentieth-century reforms been more ruthless and hence successful, 'he would have had to eradicate most of the features which make Iran wiser and more civilised than many other nations'.[27] It would have been reduced to

---

[21] E. G. Browne, *Materials for the Study of the Babi Religion* (Cambridge, 1918), p. xxii.

[22] E. G. Browne, *The Persian Revolution of 1905–1909* (Cambridge, 1910), p. xiii; see his letters about the Persian constitutional movement, Cambridge University Library.

[23] Introduction in A. J. Arberry (ed.), *The Legacy of Persia* (Oxford, 1953), p. vi.

[24] Arberry on 'Persian Literature', ibid., p. 207.

[25] See for example Thomas R. Trautmann, *Aryans and British India* (Berkeley, CA, 1995).

[26] Peter Avery, *Modern Iran* (London, 1965), p. 52.

[27] Ibid., p. 284.

'barbarism' in order to successfully compete with the 'materialistic civilisation of the West'.

The second great theme of British historians of Persia, as of the rest of the East, was the malformation, and hoped for redemption, of the state. The trope of decay and decline of civil society was almost universal, though liberals tended to indict malign foreign influence as well as Persian corruption. The main lines of the argument had been set as early as 1815 by Sir John Malcolm,[28] who had transposed many of the categories of his history of central India to Persia which he had visited as an envoy of the East India Company. In Malcolm's version, the failures of tyranny and religious fanaticism tended to unleash the tribal predator into Persian cities on a cyclical basis. More interesting were Malcolm's categories of human geography in Persia: the northern mountains, the desert east, the Arab littoral and the central plains.[29] These were drawn from the Scottish Enlightenment understandings of the relationship between culture and nature, but survived through into the twentieth century. In most respects, George Curzon merely revised Malcolm in his very influential *Persia and the Persian Question* of 1892. Arnold Wilson and Percy Sykes, two widely read amateur historians with military and administrative experience of Persia before and during the First World War,[30] drew on both Curzon and Malcolm. Sykes painted a simple picture of corrupt and lascivious dynasties falling periodic prey to hard men from the deserts and mountains. Here he also drew on Ibn Khaldun, the medieval Arab historian. Wilson, representing the colonial knowledge of the periphery, pressed Malcolm's categories into action to argue, in classic Anglo-Indian style, that there was no such thing as the 'Persian character', merely a congeries of tribes and local cultures evolving from the Russian north to the Baluchi south-east. E. G. Browne, he wrote acidly, knew little of Persia, having spent a mere year in Persia and then thirty years speaking Persian in Cambridge.[31]

This theme of the cyclical corruption of Persian polity also influenced writers who were more sympathetic to the rising nationalist tide. Lawrence Lockhart — pupil of Browne and a brilliant photographer and connoisseur of Persian art — turned scholarly attention to the eighteenth century in his *Fall of Safavi Dynasty* and *Nadir Shah*. Lockhart's theme was the decline of what

---

[28] Sir John Malcolm, *The History of Persia from the Most Early Period to the Present Time* (London, 1811).

[29] Malcolm Yapp, 'Two British Historians of Persia', in Bernard Lewis and P. M. Holt, *Historians of the Middle East* (London, 1962), pp. 344–50.

[30] Ibid.; Sir Percy Sykes, *A History of Persia*, 2nd edn (London, 1921) and Sir Arnold T. Wilson, *Persia* (London, 1932).

[31] Arnold T. Wilson, *South West Persia: A Political Officer's Diary 1907–14* (London, 1941), p. 136.

was commonly regarded as the last great Persian dynasty in the early eighteenth century. He took much of his analysis of harem influence, the debauchery of royalty and the revolt of the tribes from the work of the celebrated Russian Iranologist and former Tsarist intelligence official V. F. Minorsky, who fled to Paris, and eventually Cambridge, after the 1917 Revolution.[32] Minorsky had personally witnessed the fall of the Qajar dynasty in Iran after 1908 and it seems that his observations influenced the way he understood eighteenth-century history. Both Minorsky and Lockhart were also influenced by the experience of the Russian Revolution. Lockhart was attracted to the study of Nadir Shah, the brilliant usurper who had seized the Persian throne and gone on to sack Delhi in 1739. He saw in Nadir, as in Tamerlaine and Genghis Khan, 'one of the great conquerors who overran vast stretches of country, ravaging, killing and destroying'. This phenomenon was 'a characteristic of the East'.[33]

In the 1930s, however, Reza Shah's land reforms had initiated British discussion of a different and more pragmatic aspect of Iranian history, the relationship between landlord and peasant. Anne Lambton's work of this name, published by the Royal Institute of International Affairs as a monograph after the Second World War, was a comprehensive survey of Persian land revenue policy from the Arab conquests to the twentieth century.[34] It drew on medieval Persian ethical literature to delineate norms of good government and made extensive use of medieval and modern tracts on fiscal practice. Lambton interviewed contemporary Iranian revenue officials; she also consulted the Indian revenue expert Sir Malcolm Darling and W. H. Moreland's *The Revenue System of the Indian Moghuls*.[35] At this point, however, British scholarship had made little contact either with social anthropology, which was then asserting its independence of history, or with the French *Annales* school. The perspective in these works was downward, from lord to peasant. Peasant society was not, at this time, seen to have an existence independent of the policies of the state. The tribes were not analysed as social entities. It is revealing that the single general historian mentioned in Lambton's bibliography was Arnold Toynbee. Twenty years later Lambton herself was in the forefront of writing the new social history of Iran.[36]

[32] 'Vladimir Fedorovich Minorsky, 1877–1936', *Bulletin of the School of Oriental and African Studies (BSOAS)*, 29, 3 (1966), 694–9.

[33] Lawrence Lockhart, *Nadir Shah: A Critical Study based mainly on Contemporary Sources* (London, 1938), p. 1.

[34] Anne K. S. Lambton, *Landlord and Peasant in Persia: A Study of Land Tenure and Land Revenue Administration* (Oxford, 1953).

[35] Ibid., p. vi; see below, pp. 101–2.

[36] See below, p. 114, n. 105.

Islam and the Arabs

By the beginning of the twentieth century an independent tradition of British studies of Islamic history had established itself. But this was definitely Islamic history, rather than Arab or Persian history, in that it privileged a certain vision of Sunni Islamic integrity and of a civilisation driven, like medieval Christendom, by religious confession. In this interpretation, political organisation strove hard to embody the dictates of an overarching faith, and often failed. The dominant figure for much of the century was Sir Hamilton Gibb. Gibb spent his early years in Egypt where his father was director of the Aboukir Land Reclamation Company.[37] Gibb, however, like Browne, spent most of his life teaching in the West, in his case in London at the School of Oriental and African Studies (SOAS), Oxford and Harvard. He made major contributions to the early history of the Khilafat, medieval Islam and, with the Ottomanist Harold Bowen, to the study of Islam's confrontation with the West.[38] A critical influence on his views appears to have been his religious faith, not as with so many of his contemporaries Anglicanism, but Scots Presbyterianism. Christianity was for Gibb the highest form of religion and it must co-exist with a vibrant civil society. Equally, in Islam, 'The Muslim church and its members constitute a similar composite, each forming and reacting on the other, so long as Islam remains a living organism.'[39]

This idealist version of west Asian history created a powerful tool against anachronism. Gibb was able to interpret Ibn Khaldun, not so much as a typologist of states, anticipating modern political science, but as a thinker attempting to reconcile the demands of God's Law (Sharia) with the pressure of Man's instinctive desires. But Gibb's was also an essentialist version of history in which Islamic societies rose and fell like living organisms. As with many others of his generation, he admired Toynbee.[40] An important flaw in this approach was that Shi'ism, Sufism, heterodox religious movements and Arab scientific rationalism were all pushed to the margins in this story of endless dialogue between Islam's religious essence and an overarching ruling institution, whether Arab or Ottoman. While religion was the key determinant, race was also a factor. For Gibb seems to have acquiesced in Bowen's view that the Ottoman Empire declined in the eighteenth century because vigorous Balkan Christians were progressively excluded from office, which was not in

---

[37] Anne K. S. Lambton, 'Sir Hamilton Gibb, 1895–1971', *BSOAS*, 35, 2 (1972), 338–45.

[38] H. Gibb and H. Bowen, *Islamic Society and the West*, 2 vols (London, 1954).

[39] Cited by Lambton, 'Sir Hamilton Gibb', 343.

[40] Albert Hourani, 'Sir Hamilton Gibb', *Proceedings of the British Academy* (*PBA*), 68 (1972), 504.

fact the case.[41] Gibb was also uneasy with modernity. He saw western
influences, socialism and atheism as corrosive rusts on the surface of Islam.
He disliked the creation of a national home for the Jews and the Jewish State,
reflecting in a moderate form one trend within British history writing on Asia
which saw British and French intervention in west Asia as a Jewish plot.[42]

Sir Thomas Walker Arnold, holder of the chair of Arabic and Islamic
Studies at SOS before Gibb, provides us with an important link between the
Arab and the Indian worlds, as also a link between metropolitan sensibilities
and the institutions of the colonial periphery. Arnold had introduced Gibb to
the massive textual scholarship of the German orientalist tradition. But
Arnold's own initiation into a new world had been accomplished at the hands
of the Indian Muslim scholars of the Mahommedan Anglo-Oriental College
at Aligarh in north India. Recruited from the Cambridge Classical Tripos by
its founder Sir Sayyid Ahmed Khan along with several other young
Britons,[43] Arnold taught for some years alongside noted Muslim modernist
intellectuals before moving on to the Punjab Education Service.[44] Like Sir
Sayyid himself, Arnold believed he was helping to raise a fallen race, the
Indian Muslims, by combining western and Islamic teaching. But his
approach differed substantially from the official Anglo-Indian one and also
from much contemporary British discussion of the Islamic world.

In his major work, *The Preaching of Islam*, Arnold sought to portray the
enlightened, spiritual side of the Islamic faith. In this he opposed himself to
the position taken by Sir William Muir, a Scots evangelical and former
lieutenant-governor of the North-Western Provinces of India. Muir's
experience of the Indian Mutiny of 1857 when he was chief intelligence
officer in the rebellious North-Western Provinces[45] may have confirmed him
in his view that Islam had risen through blood and iron. Of the early years of
the Prophet's mission, Muir wrote 'the whole Arabian people, both town and
bedawi, were riveted to Islam by a common bond — the love of rapine and
the lust of spoil'.[46] Arnold tried to give scholarly respectability to the
rebuttal of this kind of interpretation, already made through pamplets and

[41] See review of *Islamic Society* by N. Itzkowits, 'Eighteenth-century Ottoman Realities', *Studia
Islamica* (1962), 73–95; see review of same by B. Lewis, *BSOAS*, 16 (1954), 598–602.
[42] For example Hon. J. M. Balfour (late chief assistant to financial adviser to the Persian
government), *Recent Happenings in Persia* (London, 1922), p. 298.
[43] David Lelyveld, *Aligarh's First Generation: Muslim Solidarity in British India* (Princeton, NJ,
1978).
[44] Sir Aurel Stein, 'Sir Thomas Walker Arnold', *PBA*, 16 (1930), 439–74.
[45] C. A. Bayly, *Empire and Information: Intelligence Gathering and Social Communication in India
1780–1870* (Cambridge, 1996), pp. 325–6.
[46] Sir William Muir, *The Caliphate: Its Rise, Decline and Fall* (1st edn 1885, new and revised edn by
T. H. Weir, Glasgow, 1915), p. 42.

press articles in British newspapers by Sayyid Ameer Ali and Sayyid Ahmed Khan. *The Preaching of Islam*, first published in Aligarh in 1894, was designed as 'a record of missionary efforts, not a history of persecution'[47] and a protest against 'prejudice and unfairness'.[48] Arnold broke with many conventional perspectives on Islam. He insisted that it was a religion of the rights of man and that its spread was materially influenced by the piety of women. In Spain and north Africa, Islam was propagated by saintly teachers not by soldiers and its absence of racial prejudice against blacks marked it out from the Christian West. In Arnold's work, the theme of oriental corruption and decadence was turned against the priests of the eastern Christian churches, rather than against Muslims.

Arnold's views of Islamic history were nourished by direct personal connections with Muslim intellectuals and a detailed study of south Asian local sources. But he was also influenced by a mystical vision of human brotherhood which appears to have warmed to quietist spiritual teachers in all faiths. He translated *The Little Flowers of St Francis*. As with many in this tradition, he was deeply influenced by medieval and renaissance European art.[49] It was this that turned him in his later years to the study of Persian and Indian miniature painting which had hitherto been regarded as pedestrian decorative arts.[50]

Arnold's early years at Aligarh made him receptive to voices from the Muslim world. But he also reflected a more general shift of liberal British and European opinion about the direction of and hence the history of the Muslim world. In the preface to the second edition of *The Preaching of Islam*, published in 1913, he pointed to the explosion of new work on Islam in ten languages and especially the French liberal journal *Revue du Monde Musulman* and the journal *Christian Missions in Muslim Lands*.[51] The spectre of pan-Islamism and Islamic nationalism turned European attention from medieval west Asia to its modern encounter with the world powers. Arnold ended his study of the Caliphate (1924) with the observation that though the great movement in India in defence of that office (1919–23) had

---

[47] T. W. Arnold, *The Preaching of Islam: A History of the Propagation of the Muslim Faith* (1895, 3rd edn London, 1935), p. 8.

[48] Stein, 'Arnold', 439.

[49] Ibid., 472–4; see Ross, *Both Ends*, p. 170. The only modern study of Arnold is K. M. Watt, 'Thomas Walker Arnold and the Re-evaluation of Islam *c.* 1864–1930', M.Phil. dissertation, University of Cambridge, 2000, Seeley History Library, Cambridge (a version of this thesis is forthcoming in *Modern Asian Studies*).

[50] For example T. W. Arnold, *The Old and New Testaments in Muslim Religious Arts* (Oxford, 1932); *The Library of Chester A. Beatty* (London, 1936).

[51] Arnold, *Preaching*, preface to 2nd edn.

failed along with the Ottoman Khalifa himself, Muslims would retain the vision of an ideal state governed by Sharia.[52]

The theme of Islamic degeneration which had preoccupied historians of the high Victorian period was gradually dispelled by the availability of new sources and also through the efforts of indigenous historians of west Asian and Indian societies. In Egypt, for instance, the modernist literary revival of the late nineteenth century was accompanied by history writing which deplored the British occupation.[53] These writers adapted many themes from western writers on race and religion, depicting the Egyptian nation as descendants of the Pharaonic Egyptians, and hence as progenitors of European civilisation. The Anglican church's predilection for ancient apostolic churches outside the Roman communion had brought considerable academic attention at Oxford and Cambridge to bear on the Egyptian Copts.[54] Writers in this tradition often asserted that it was only Coptic Christians who were really the sons of the Pharaohs; other Egyptians were descendants of Arab plunderers who had prevailed in the ancient race wars of the Near East. Rather as in the case of the Indian Muslims, this sort of argument was easily used by scholar officials to justify the claim that Copts were a distinct people and should therefore have a separate political status outside the Egyptian nation. Egyptian nationalist writers and historians[55] vigorously rejected this attempt at 'divide and rule'.

Official histories and redemptive histories in India to the 1960s

In India itself the lines of fracture between contested histories had long been apparent and indigenous voices were already directly influencing British formulations before the end of the nineteenth century.[56] British official histories had evolved in depth and were supported by a range of literary and antiquarian studies unmatched in the rest of Asia and the Middle East. But several British historians, influenced once again by a particular interpretation of race and religion, had stepped across the racial divide and produced interpretations closer to those of the emerging nationalist historiography.

[52] T. W. Arnold, *The Caliphate* (Oxford, 1924), p. 182
[53] For example Salama Musa, *The Education of Salama Musa*, trans. L. O. Shuman (Leiden, 1961); Duse Mohamed Ali, *In the Land of the Pharaohs* (London, 1911).
[54] Mrs E. L. Butcher, *The Story of the Church in Egypt*, 2 vols (London, 1897); Revd M. Fowler, *Christian Egypt, Past Present and Future* (London, 1901).
[55] For example Salama Musa, *The Education of Salama Musa*.
[56] For reactions to nationalism, see Eric Stokes, 'The Administrators and Historical Writing on India', in C. H. Philips (ed.), *Historians of India, Pakistan and Ceylon* (London, 1961), pp. 387–95.

This section first briefly examines the varieties of official historical writing. It then moves on to examine the writings of three of these maverick historians: E. B. Havell, C. F. Andrews and Edward Thompson.

Just as John Malcolm had provided in 1815 the rail-tracks on which many histories of Persia would continue to move until the 1930s, so Mountstuart Elphinstone's *History of India*, written in the years before his death in 1856,[57] became the dominant text for late Victorian and Edwardian Britain. Elphinstone instituted the classic division of India's history into ancient, Muslim and modern sections. He painted a somewhat more favourable view of Hindu character and political institutions than James Mill. He also diverged from the common view that Aryans invaded India, believing, as modern Hindu supremacists do, that they had always inhabited the subcontinent. Vincent Smith, an Anglo-Irish member of the Indian Civil Service (ICS), followed in Elphinstone's path, though drawing on the textual collections of H. M. Elliot and the work of the archaeological survey of India which had been completed in the time since Elphinstone's death. Smith's, however, was a bleak picture of tribal and caste division in India and one which tended to deny even those broad civilisational unities which Elphinstone had perceived. His extreme anti-nationalist stance owed something to his upbringing as a Dublin Protestant.[58] In Smith's version, dynasty after dynasty succumbed to corruption, harem influence or listless self-indulgence. British rule, the salvation of India, could never be relaxed. Possibly because of their Oxford imprimatur, Smith's histories continued, ironically, to be the staple diet in Indian colleges and British universities until well after Independence.[59] Other official historians furnished similar multi-volume studies, while Cambridge University Press brought the whole dying tradition triumphantly together in its *Cambridge History of India* of 1929–31,[60] which included the work of many British civil servants and one Indian, Sir Jadunath Sarkar.

In contrast to this stood the work of W. H. Moreland, former director of Land Records of the United Provinces. Moreland is widely regarded as the pioneer of Indian economic history and the writer who provided, if only negatively, the essential scaffolding for the Indian Marxist historians of

[57] Mountstuart Elphinstone, *A Report on the Territories lately Conquered from the Paishwa* (Calcutta, 1823); *History of India*, 2 vols (London, 1856); J. S. Grewal, *Muslim Rule in India: The Assessment of British Historians* (Calcutta, 1970); Peter Hardy, *Historians of Medieaval India* (London, 1960).

[58] A. L. Basham, 'Modern Historians of Ancient India', in Philips, *Historians of India*, pp. 266–74.

[59] V. A. Smith, *Early History of India* (London, 1904); *Oxford History of India* (London, 1919); *Indian Constitutional Reform Viewed in the Light of History* (London, 1919).

[60] *The Cambridge History of India*, vols 3–6 (London, 1928–34).

Aligarh University after Independence.[61] Moreland drew on the greatest
British contribution to Indian historiography, not the grandiose but
pedestrian political narratives, but the huge volume of land settlement
reports and antiquarian investigations carried out by the scholar officials of
the ICS. He wove these into a broad analysis of medieval Indian history
which centred on the extraction of cash revenue from the peasantry.
Moreland appreciated the efficiency of early Mughal government. But he
was no crypto-nationalist, insisting like his contemporary, the Dutch
anthropologist–historian C. H. van Leur, that most pre-colonial trade was of
the 'peddling' variety and limited to luxury items. He discovered none of the
(aborted) sprouts of capitalist development in the subcontinent discussed
later by his critic and follower Irfan Habib.

The Indian bureaucracy and its expatriate fellow-travellers was,
however, an extention overseas of the British public at large and so it threw
up its own collection of radicals, mavericks, spiritualists, vicarious
nationalists and Christian oddities, who transgressed the bounds of the
official historical narrative. If Vincent Smith and most scholar officials all
warned ceaselessly that historic Indian divisions precluded modern Indian
nationhood, then E. B. Havell turned the argument on its head. Havell had
been an official in charge of Indian handicrafts and was an apostle of an
Indian Arts and Crafts movement. The 'Mother of Parliaments', he wrote in
a romantic version of Sir Henry Maine, 'had an Aryan relative in India'.[62]
Indians deserved progressive self-government because they instinctively
recognised in British representative institutions 'the same humanitarian laws,
which guided our ancient Aryan ancestors'. Eschewing the views of Smith
and most officials that Muslim India moved on a separate trajectory from
Hindu society, he believed that 'Islam did not alter Indian aesthetic
principles or add to them, but was the unconscious instrument of giving
Indian art a new impetus'.[63] In his interpretation, the Mughal Emperor
Akbar, a Turk, became an honorary Aryan. Racial theory in Havell's work
acted to subvert and not to confirm British dominance in India. India would
be redeemed by the ancient racial memory of democracy.

These disagreements among British historians of India mirrored the
conflicts in Persia and Egypt between the proponents of a fractured view of
oriental tribal and religious identity and those who thought that the East, like
the West, provided examples of submerged nationhood. But in India

[61] J. B. Harrison, 'Notes on W. H. Moreland as Historian', in Philips, *Historians of India*, pp. 310–18.
[62] E. B. Havell, *A History of Aryan Rule in India from the Earliest Times to the Death of Akbar*
(London, 1918), p. xiii.
[63] Ibid., p. 329.

vigorous indigenous schools history appropriated some of these debates and
their influence was increasingly felt by the last group of expatriate historians
discussed here, the liberal imperialist and Anglican writers of the first half of
the twentieth century.

It was against the intellectual background of Indian nationalism that
Charles Freer Andrews wrote his numerous works on India and Christian
redemption. A bearded twentieth-century Wilberforce, Andrews campaigned
for indentured labourers and Indians in South Africa.[64] Influenced by Gandhi,
he moved from an early empire loyalism to become a pale, worried co-worker
of the Mahatma. As Gandhi retreated to his ashram, so Andrews walled himself
up in the Cambridge Mission to Delhi. In his *Zakaullah of Delhi*, Andrews
depicted the great intellectual tradition of the Indo-Muslim age, battered by the
British guns on Delhi Ridge in 1857, but now emerging again under the
reforming influence of Christian moral education in the Delhi College. His
History of the Indian National Congress (1933) gave great prominence to
Christianity in the transition from the corrupted India of the eighteenth century,
through the Hindu reform movements of the nineteenth to the Congress which
was their culmination. For in India 'more than in any other country we have
always to notice those movements which spring directly out of the religious
spirit of the people'.[65] Evidently, the old theme of the British moral mission in
India lived on here, but, set amidst an awareness of British greed and violence,
it had been narrowed down to a kernel of fructifying Christian piety.

A more probing historical intelligence was revealed in the work of
Edward Thompson, a Methodist missionary and the father of E. P. Thompson,
the historian of the English working class.[66] The elder Thompson helped
develop a version of Indian history which still retains some credibility in the
academy. His best work, on the abolition of widow-burning in 1829 by Lord
William Bentinck, along with his study of the contemporary liberal
administrator Sir Charles Metcalfe, developed the idea of what became
known later as the 'Age of Reform' of the 1830s. It seemed to suggest,
following Andrews, that even within a corrupt racialist administration there
worked the spirit of progress. In the wake of the British massacre at Amritsar
in 1919, Thompson argued that the British should seek their own redemption
through social uplift. He especially emphasised the brutal suppression of the
Indian rebellion of 1857 and charted it in *The Other Side of the Medal*.

[64] Hugh Tinker, *The Ordeal of Love: C. F. Andrews and India* (Delhi, 1979).
[65] C. F. Andrews and Ginja Mukherji, *The Rise and Growth of the Congress in India* (London, 1938),
p. 59; C. F. Andrews, *The Renaissance in India: Its Missionary Aspect* (London, 1912).
[66] Sumit Sarkar, 'Edward Thompson and India: The Other Side of the Medal', in Sumit Sarkar,
Writing Social History (New Delhi, 1997), pp. 109–58.

The concept of Christian atonement was expressed here through the Sanskrit term *prayaschita* which implies a purging from ritual pollution. Thompson's evangelical sensibilities attuned well with the moralising Indian thought of the age and he acted as an interpreter to the West of the Bengali writer Rabindranath Tagore.

Just as Gibb carried some aspects of the Edwardian organicist understanding of Islam into the post-Second World War era of professional history and area studies, T. G. P. Spear was a linking figure in Indian history. While Gibb was a high academic orientalist, Spear was a popular writer who deplored histories written without imagination and pace.[67] And yet through *The Twilight of the Moghuls*, his *Penguin History of India* and numerous articles, lectures and doctoral examinations in Oxford, Cambridge and London he acted as a midwife to post-colonial British writing on the subcontinent and has some influence in the United States and India. Spear, like Andrews, was closely associated throughout his life with the High Anglican Cambridge Mission to Delhi. He lectured at St Stephen's College, Delhi where he taught or worked with many of the post-war generation of Indian and Pakistani historians. During the war he was seconded to the government of India as deputy secretary in the Department of Information and Broadcasting where he played an important, but still obscure role in counter-propaganda against both the Japanese and the Indian National Congress.

Spear developed the views of Andrews and Thompson. Eighteenth-century East India corruptions were banished by early nineteenth-century reformers who were animated by a new sense of British duty with Christian undertones. The Victorian generation of ICS officers and educationists wished to work for India. But racial feeling, deepened by the Indian Mutiny, produced an inevitable reaction in the form of the Indian National Congress. To Spear, India after 1750 had thrown up two traditions which derived from the operation of Christian liberalism in an Asian religious environment. First, there was the Anglo-Hindu liberalism of the moderate Congressmen. Second, Spear discerned a modernist Muslim tradition, nurtured by the pre-1857 Delhi College, but drawing on Mughal traditions of tolerance and rationalism. In his understanding of the earlier Indo-Muslim synthesis of the Mughals, he was heavily reliant on the work of Indian friends.[68] Finally,

---

[67] Spear Papers, Centre of South Asian Studies Cambridge, which contain a mass of letters, examiner's reports, reviews, etc.

[68] For example I. H. Qureshi, the historian of Muslim India; see Qureshi to Spear, 18 October 1947, Spear Papers, Box 9; and see letters from A. Batty and others to Spear during 1947–8, Box 9; these letters contain some riveting accounts of the communal riots of that year which perhaps helped form Spear's idea of the inevitabilty of Partition.

there was Hinduism which he saw, in common with Havell, as a sponge-like, cellular entity, capable of assimilating foreign influences, but firmly resistant to them.[69] Ultimately, in his view, the modernist Muslim tradition hived off naturally into Pakistan. Much of contemporary Indian history, Spear thought, masked a struggle between neo-Hinduism and Anglo-Indian liberalism. The contrast between Gandhi and Nehru reflected this polarity. After Independence the principles of hierarchy and leadership represented by the Hindu essence broke through the carapace of Anglo-Indian liberal institutions. Maintaining his status as speaker on all things Indian, Spear believed that Mrs Gandhi's dictatorial rule during the Emergency of 1974 reflected the re-emergence of Hinduism's traditions of 'authority, religious, social and political, concentrated and defined, but not absolute'.[70]

Some tension or at least re-evaluation was apparent here. Spear had once written, in a banal metaphor, that while the Mughal ship of state had foundered 'the British ship sailed on under Captain Nehru'.[71] Yet the myth of continuing progress often seemed to be no more than a slight liberal consolation plucked out from his more profound belief that something called Hinduism was resuming its glacier-like progress through Indian history erasing the traces of Islam and Christian piety. This tension between hope of reform and fear of the immutability of Hinduism recalls the moral agonising of a thousand missionaries since the first Jesuits set foot in the subcontinent. For, at heart, the liberal imperialist historians of British India were more often missionaries searching for redemption than straightforward handmaidens of imperial power.[72]

Money and faith in far eastern historiography

In 1989 T. H. Barrett commented on the 'singular listlessness' of the British historiographical tradition on China, neatly reversing this common British characterisation of the Chinese.[73] To him, the commercial secretiveness of the East India Company had given way to the commercial

[69] Inden, *Imagining India*.

[70] Spear, 'India since Independence', Spear Papers, Box 4.

[71] Spear, original drafts for 'Ideas of Duty among the British in India', 'W. G. Archer Memorial Lecture', 'India after Independence', 1970s–80s; A. T. Embree, 'Percival Spear's Vision of India', Spear Papers, Box 4.

[72] Spear's genealogy in the tradition of C. F. Andrews was quite clear; he wrote to Hugh Tinker on 28 August 1980, 'I lived, as it were, with his legend for years in Delhi', Spear Papers, Box 5.

[73] T. H. Barrett, *Singular Listlessness: A Short History of Chinese Books and British Scholars* (London, 1989).

myopia of high empire and neither of these had produced a significant
body of Chinese literary or historical studies. The few chairs of Chinese in
British universities were filled with 'superannuated old China hands',
exemplified by the mythical, but only too readily recognisable Cambridge
professor of the 1930s who used to chase away prospective students with
his walking stick.

Barrett's depressing reading of this track record perhaps understates two
specifically British contributions to Chinese history. There was, first, the
diplomatic and commercial history of the Far East which arose from the very
British avariciousness he properly berates. But, second, we must consider the
east Asian history of science, engendered by Joseph Needham, which
returned indirectly to those interests in race and religious redemption which
run like a thread through the history of British oriental studies. Neither of
these interests has ever seemed quite pucka to students of Chinese language
and literature.

Metropolitan aesthetic sensibilities helped to form the relatively sickly
British historiography of China and Japan as they had done in other parts of
the Orient. Display of the loot from the sacking of the imperial palace in
Peking in 1860 had produced a surge of interest. The Boxer Rebellion and
the strange accounts of the Chinese court of Sir Edmund Backhouse[74]
accomplished another revival in the early years of the twentieth century.
Laurence Binyon's *Painting in the Far East* (1908) was one among a number
of new art histories produced at this time. Throughout the inter-war years,
Arthur Waley, a wealthy businessman turned oriental expert, kept alive an
interest in Chinese art from his base in the British Museum. His translations
distantly nourished historical writing in the 1930s and 1940s. Something
similar happened in the case of Japan. The first English translation of the
'Tale of Genji' had been accompanied by a Victorian and Edwardian passion
for Japanese design. It was revealing that the most prolific British exponent
of Japanese history in the inter-war period, Sir George Sansom, was not only
commercial counsellor to the British Embassy, but also an internationally
renowned connoisseur and collector of Japanese art. Art, religion and culture
were inseparable in his eyes. Sansom saw in Japanese art, particularly Zen
Buddhism, an 'intuitive emotional approach' communicated pre-eminently
through art which spoke to the 'spirit of its civilisation'.[75]

Nevertheless, 'the word "trade" is written large in the history of the
British connection with China', as Barrett observes.[76] In the same way that

---

[74] Hugh Trevor-Roper, *A Hidden Life: The Enigma of Sir Edmund Backhouse* (London, 1976).

[75] George Sansom, *Japan: A Short Cultural History* (London, 1946), p. 1; see p. viii.

[76] Barrett, *Listlessness*, p. 113.

the Anglo-Persian Oil Company and the Indo-European Telegraph Company provided the local context and background for histories of west Asia, so the Chinese Maritime Customs Service, staffed by a line of Ulstermen and Americans, taught a generation of Chinese historians. H. B. Morse, originally a Harvard graduate, but one who drifted more and more into British circles, wrote the *International Relations of the Chinese Empire* and *The Trade and Administration of the Chinese Empire* (Shanghai, 1907), two works which provided much of the underpinning of the 'challenge and response' school of Chinese history. Though the Harvard historians put much more emphasis on autonomous Chinese action, it was John King Fairbank in the 1950s and 1960s who brought this tradition to its apogee.[77] The leading idea here was that the western intrusion into China in the century after the Opium War of 1842 was the key event of its modern history, signalling imperial decline, modernisation and revolution. Morse's careful use of the East India Company and Crown foreign-policy documents anticipated much that was later written on European relations with China and Japan, including the work of C. R. Boxer[78] on earlier European contacts and conflicts.

Religion, that other typical British preoccupation besides commerce, also raised its head in Morse's work. Writing of the leader of the millenarian Taiping Rebellion of the 1850s, Morse observes that he could have become a 'Mohamed, or at a lower plane a Joseph Smith' but he became instead 'a John of Leyden with eighty-eight consecrated wives and his innumbered concubines'.[79] The threat to far eastern commerce supposedly posed by xenophobic religious sectaries neatly brought the two preoccupations together and became a major concern after 1900. Several commentators interpreted early Chinese communism in this light. It is revealing that the best British history of the Boxer Rebellion was written in the 1960s by Victor Purcell, a former Malayan colonial official and expert in Malayan Chinese secret societies. Yet Purcell did not easily fit the stereotype of imperialist orientalism. He believed that the Boxers were a patriotic movement rather than a group of millenarian fanatics.[80] In a similar vein, he had argued that British policy in Malaya after 1945 would need to accommodate the expectations of local radical nationalists.[81]

---

[77] Paul A. Cohen, *Discovering History in China: American Historical Writing on the Recent Chinese Past* (New York, 1984) provides an excellent analysis of this dominant school since *c.* 1950.

[78] C. R. Boxer, *The Christian Century in Japan 1549–1650* (Berkeley, CA, 1951).

[79] H. B. Morse, *The International Relations of the Chinese Empire* (London, 1910), p. 433.

[80] V. Purcell, *The Boxer Uprising* (Cambridge, 1965); *The Chinese in Southeast Asia*, 2nd edn (London, 1980).

[81] V. Purcell, *Memoirs of a Malayan Official* (London, 1965); see T. N. Harper, *The End of Empire and the Making of Malaya* (Cambridge, 1999), p. 58.

The sudden emergence of Japan on the world stage as a result of its wars with China and Russia caught British historiography unawares. Against the background of a few art histories, James Murdoch, a Scots classicist working with the Legation in Kobe, wrote a history of Japan. Murdoch displayed in his detestation of Christianity and Buddhism almost the reverse of the usual British stance. But he resoundingly endorsed Japan's emergence as a modern state. He argued that Japan's rise was as important as the Italian Risorgimento and German unification.[82] Murdoch's work raised interest in a kind of Anglo-Japanese special relationship which influenced historians up to and even after the Second World War.[83]

While these writers should not be scorned, Barrett is surely right to point to the absence of strong British traditions of historical writing on east Asia. This may reflect not only lack of funding and training, but also the alienness of the region to the broad historical sensibilities which we have been describing. Ordinary educated Britons appear to have had some difficulty in fitting the Far East into the classic theories of race and religion with which they had marked out the rest of the world. Whatever the Japanese were (and they were at different times taken to be Sumerians, Dravidians and Mongolians), they were certainly not Aryans. Again, while Theravada Buddhism had received much attention from Sanskrit and Pali scholars, the practice of Mahayana Buddhism, Taoism, Shinto and Confucianism baffled many British writers of this era[84] who did not have the long tradition of Jesuit scholarship or the pioneering efforts of the Ecole Française de l'Extrême Orient to fall back on, as did the French. Intellectual puzzlement, as much as listlessness or avarice explains the patchy history of British writing on the Far East, though the engagement with Japanese cultural history may have been deeper than that with China until the 1930s.

One other comparative point should be considered. Unlike the case of India and west Asia, in east Asia Europeans were confronted with a highly developed, westernised historical profession in Japan by 1900 and in China by 1925. After the Meiji reforms following the restoration of 1868, the Japanese avidly absorbed first Ranke and then Marx. Even French, German and American historians before the 1960s were only able to make original

---

[82] James Murdoch, *History of Japan, 1* (London, 1910), pp. 1, 5.

[83] For example F. V. Dickins and S. Lane-Poole, *The Life of Sir Harry Parkes: Sometime H. M. Minister to China and Japan*, 2 vols (London, 1894) and later Grace Fox, *Britain and Japan* (London, 1969); Olive Checkland, *Britain's Encounters with Meiji Japan* (London, 1989).

[84] This was not true of the work of W. G. Aston, a major interpreter of Shinto; see his *Shinto (The Way of the Gods)* (London, 1905). Even Aston, however, wanted to see Shinto as a text-based religion like Christianity or Islam.

contributions in relatively few areas.[85] It is not surprising that, in their studies of east Asia, the Japanese historians left standing many of their contemporaries in the other island kingdom and many of its domestic historians, too.

Throughout the inter-war years, British historical writing on east Asia remained the preserve of 'old hands' and a few gifted individuals who thrived in an atmosphere of academic obscurity. In the later 1930s the arrival in Britain of some central European Jewish and liberal scholars helped revivify the study of oriental languages in Britain as did their colleagues in the physical and chemical sciences. One important, post-war development had its roots in the 1930s, however. This was Joseph Needham's vision of a global history of science. Needham, a biochemist, had been awakened to an interest in China by two of his Chinese colleagues in the Cambridge laboratories of the 1930s and had taken up the study of Mandarin under Gustav Haloun, one of these European émigrés.[86] Needham's period (under Sansom's patronage) as head of the British Scientific Mission to the Nationalist Chinese government based at Chunking during the Second World War gave him the local knowledge and contacts with Chinese scientists which were essential for his project. These allowed him to trace the history of Chinese skills in dyeing, printing, gunpowder and horology which he believed were later diffused to the West.

Yet the underlying philosophy of the East Asian History of Science project was already in place in the 1930s. Needham, an Anglo-Catholic Christian, wanted to integrate at the level of world history the following dominant British concerns: scientific eugenics, Marxist historiography and human religious experience. Needham was influenced by the philosophy of Herbert Spencer[87] and the history of Spengler and Arnold Toynbee. He vigorously rejected a simple biological version of the survival of the fittest, arguing that communities could only progress, like cellular organisms, through cooperation. According to Needham, Spencer had rightly understood that societies evolve as organisms and that social altruism, manifested in philosophical religion, provided an essential evolutionary motor. Spencer was incomplete, however, Needham argued, because he should have

[85] W. G. Beasley and E. G. Pulleyblank, *Historians of China and Japan* (London, 1961), pp. 19–21.

[86] J. Needham (H. Holorenshaw, pseud.) 'The Making of an Honorary Taoist', in C. M. Teich and R. Young (eds), *Changing Perspectives in the History of Science: Essays in Honour of Joseph Needham* (London, 1973), p. 11.

[87] J. Needham, *Integrative Levels: A Reevaluation of the Idea of Progress* (Oxford, 1937); see Mansel Davis (ed.), *A Selection from the Writings of Joseph Needham* (London, 1985), pp. 393–4; Holorenshaw (Needham) in Teich and Young (eds), *Changing Perspectives*. The evolution of Needham's ideas at this early period can be followed in the Needham Papers in Cambridge University Library.

integrated the need for revolutionary ruptures into his model. From time to time, the dead cells needed to be stripped away, as it were. The class structure, Needham wrote, 'suppresses genetic worth'[88] by privileging aggression. Revolution would release 'cooperative genetic material' at the level of civilisations. Chinese civilisation had once been a thriving cooperative organism, contributing, as had the Indian and Semitic-occidental civilisations, to the scientific development of the 'world mind'. It would do so again once the feudal class structure had been rooted out.

Needham had been introduced early to the history of science by E. G. Browne, who lectured on Arabic and Persian science to the St Luke's Society for Anglican Natural Scientists in Cambridge.[89] His understanding of the relationship between science and social revolution was confirmed by his study of the English scientific revolution of the seventeenth century. A pseudonymous pamphlet on the subject written by Needham had a considerable effect on the young Christopher Hill.[90]

Even before the end of the Second World War, Needham was beginning to challenge the simplistic historiography of the rise of the West. He took up the work of a few earlier missionaries and textual scholars such as James Legge, who had tried to bring the Confucian and Taoist world within the Aryan–Semitic mindset of British historians. He became, as he put it, 'an honorary Taoist'. But, despite the many academic outcomes in the later twentieth century, Needham's work still bore the marks of its Edwardian roots. It was teleological and organicist and some aspects of the notion of the diffusion of science and knowledge from East to West merely reversed the polarities of the old Eurocentric model. Needham's view of the atrophy of Chinese science after the end of the Ming dynasty and the concurrent rise of western science acted to post-date rather than relativise European scientific rationality.

Gibb, Needham and Spear represent, at very different levels of intellectual achievement, the links between the Victorian age and that of post-colonial scholarship in their continuing emphasis on the organic development of race-as-religion. But this paradigm now came under sustained assault. It is to the ruptures in British oriental history caused by the Second World War and the onset of mass higher education in the 1950s that the next section turns.

---

[88] From 'Time the Refreshing River', in Davis (ed.), *Selection*, p. 373.

[89] J. Needham, *Science and Civilisation in China, 1* (Cambridge, 1954), p. 7.

[90] Gary Wersky, *The Visible College* (London, 1978), p. 169.

War and institutional change

The Second World War acted in many ways to revolutionise Britain's view of its place in the world and consequently of world history. The grip of the 'old hands' on oriental studies was abruptly loosened. Thousands of young servicemen, some of them university educated, poured into the British and Indian armies and were scattered across Asia. Many of the following generation of historians of India gained experience of war in the East and pondered on[91] the caste system, the Indian Muslim question and the power of the government of India. The failure of understanding of Japan which was revealed by the Singapore debacle of 1942 forced a reappraisal of the need for oriental studies on even the most diehard politicians and military men. The cryptographical efforts against Japanese signals intelligence initiated at Bletchley Park were extended to the new-found menace of Chinese communism after 1949. Historians of east Asia, therefore, reaped the benefit of a total immersion in Asian languages before they embarked upon the historical study of the new civilisations they had discovered as conscripts.[92] In west Asia and north Africa old patterns of colonial administrative scholarship persisted for a time in the Arabian peninsula and the Sudan. But the young men became more aware of its politics as communism, Nasserism and Islamic revolution menaced. The next generation of historians of the Middle East saw the modern state sweep into the Arab lands and later wrote its history.[93]

War cracked the edifice of colonial officialdom and many of the attitudes to race, religion and history associated with it. Browne, Spear and Arnold had come from commercial rather than gentry backgrounds, but the academy now broadened further. Hebrew and Arabic speakers of Jewish and middle eastern origins, Albert Hourani, Elie Kedourie and Bernard Lewis, were to transform west Asian history writing. Eric Stokes, from a Cockney working-class family,[94] and C. H. Philips,[95] son of a train driver on the old East Indian Railway, built up schools of Indian history. Both men remained interested in the history of Indian reform as pioneered by Andrews and Thompson; Stokes was a strong Christian. But those who had fought in the

---

[91] For example Kenneth Ballhatchet, Hugh Tinker, Peter Hardy, Eric Stokes, Ralph Russell.

[92] Interview with Professor D. C. Twitchett, Cambridge, 22 September 1999. Besides Twitchett himself, one could mention here Michael Loewe, Carmen Blacker, Lawerence Picken and W. G. Beasley.

[93] For example P. M. Holt, *The Modern History of the Sudan* (London, 1961).

[94] C. A. Bayly, 'Eric Thomas Stokes', *PBA*, 97 (1997), 467–500.

[95] Sir Cyril Philips, *Beyond the Ivory Tower: The Autobiography of Sir Cyril Philips* (London, 1996), p. 3.

Asian dust and rains were more sceptical of the older history of religious and
racial essences. Change was not universal, of course. The old hands
maintained their grip on Oxford, and in London the myopic English
medieval historian V. H. Galbraith railed against the dilution of the graduate
student body by 'bloody niggers'.[96] But, by the 1960s, significant numbers of
south Asian, African and Chinese scholars were teaching in British history
departments.[97]

Government policy was forced to change by the impact of war and the
dissolution of empire. The immediate post-war Scarbrough Commission and
the Hayter Commission of 1961 increased the number of posts in oriental
languages and latterly introduced the American concept of modern area
studies to the universities.[98] In much of this development, SOAS took a
leading role, now transformed from a specialist institute to an organ of mass
higher education. In the 1960s, large numbers of Commonwealth citizens
were attracted to London by its rich holdings of oriental materials and by its
status as a centre of youth culture. The heart of east Asian studies had
probably already moved from Europe to the east coast of the United States,
but American students still came to London to study south Asia, Africa and
China. There was thus something of a counter-flow of academic emigration
to the brain drain of leading British historians of Asia to the United States in
the 1970s and 1980s.[99]

From redemptive history to social history

In the years after the Second World War, British historians of Asia
discovered social and economic history. Of course, scholars such as
Moreland and Morse had written much about society and economy earlier in
the century. But the categories 'society' and 'economy' had hardly been
subject to much theoretical scrutiny. British historians had generally failed to
notice the existence of their distinguished contemporaries who had virtually
created the fields of modern anthropology and economics. This was in
contrast to the situation in France where sociology and human geography
had melded with history long before the foundation of the journal *Annales* in

[96] Philips, *Autobiography*, p. 163 (Philips is an absolutely reliable witness).
[97] For example Z. H. Zaidi, S. Gopal, T. Raychaudhuri, A. Seal in south Asia, for China see below n. 105.
[98] See n. 97.
[99] SOAS at this time had the services of Stuart Schram, Jerome Ch'en and Wang Erh-min, all international authorities in Chinese history.

1929 and the work of Marc Bloch.[100] In Britain, the faculty structure of the old universities froze disciplines into rigid isolation.

This began to change after the mid-1950s. Current social debates on the Welfare State and overseas development turned academic attention to processes in social and economic history. The influence of Marxism began to be felt, directly in the case of historians such as Needham and Owen Lattimore (an American émigré from McCarthyite persecution), and indirectly through the influence of domestic British and Japanese Marxist historiography. Since R. H. Tawney's *Land and Labour in China* (1925), leftist circles at the London School of Economics and elsewhere in the capital had been interested in reforming, not simply in recording Asia's culture. The vision of contemporary Maoist reconstruction turned historians' interests more and more to the study of economic change.

While historians certainly constructed a new history in the days of the Bandung Pact and the Vietnam War, history was also definitely revealed to them in quite precise ways. Changes in historical writing reflected new cultural constructions of the past, but they were even more driven by an unparalleled access to archives. Bernard Lewis and his pupils and contemporaries penetrated the Ottoman records for the first time. The huge oriental and Indian record of the East India Company and the British Crown were exploited by British and Asian students on Commonwealth grants who came to study at SOAS.[101] Meanwhile the new linguistic competence of British historians of China and Japan made it possible for them to work on the Japanese domestic archive and the huge historical record built up in the 1920s and 1930s by the Manchurian Railway Company for the mainland.

The result was that the organicist and redemptive paradigm gave way very quickly in all the three regions we have discussed, to be replaced by what Hayden White calls a mechanistic form of Marxian or social history.[102] Gibb's vision of a Sunni church, for instance, was reinterpreted from the perspective of other communities — Shia, Jewish, Christian, Druze and so on. Likewise the understanding of the Islamic ruling institution was replaced by a picture of networks of decentralised power. Consequently, the relationship between government and Islam appeared to be more complex. Class divisions between tribesman and town, bourgeois and artisan became clearer. Beneath the surface of the onset of modernity, Albert Hourani

---

[100] Peter Burke, *The French Historical Revolution: The Annales School 1929–1989* (London, 1990).
[101] Particularly the Indian historians A. L. Basham, Kenneth Ballhatchet, J. B. Harrison and Peter Hardy.
[102] White, *Metahistory*, pp. 3–10.

perceived a deeper shift from an age of the notables to an age of popular mobilisation.[103] The theme found an echo in Egyptian history writing, where the class of village sheikhs or notables emerged in the historiography of the 1960s as a critical social formation between state and peasant.[104] The considerable British official and anthropological expertise on tribes and nomadism began, finally, to make its impact felt on history, first in studies of the Arabian peninsula then of Iran and Syria. Anne Lambton's later work on eighteenth-century Iran, when Zand and Qajar tribal dynasties successively took power, broke with the centralised, civilisational approach of earlier historians, including her own.[105] A new urban history of the Middle East also began to emerge under the tutelage of Lewis[106] and Hourani. The latter's pupil at St Antony's, Oxford, the French historian André Raymond initiated a detailed study of the quarters of Cairo.[107] Sufi shrines emerged as an important binding force in these cities now that the devotional and genealogical material in local histories was better known, further complicating the relations between church and state.

South Asian history also moved down a register from large political formations to district and local studies. In the years after 1955 some of the earlier interests were maintained. E. T. Stokes wrote about the Age of Reform in his magnum opus, *The English Utilitarians and India* (Oxford, 1959). The study of the interaction between Christianity and Asian religions persisted in some of the work of the American historian Robert Frykenberg on south India,[108] and in Judith Brown's work on Gandhi.[109] But more and more theses at Oxford, Cambridge and London concentrated on small units, cities or communities. There was a strong practical imperative here. Graduate students could be handed out manageable chunks of data from the India Office records and then despatched for a year's field work to some relatively inexpensive Indian district town. Ideological changes did play a role, however. Stokes, in particular, had been made aware of the 'peasant problem' through service in India, Malaya and East Africa. The Indian Marxist generation who took power after Independence pictured rebellions under the Raj as peasant movements

---

[103] Albert Hourani, *Political Society in the Lebanon: A Historical Introduction* (London, 1986).

[104] Gabriel Baer, 'Social Change in Egypt, 1800–1914', in P. M. Holt (ed.), *Political and Social Change in Modern Egypt* (London, 1968), pp. 135–62 ff.

[105] See for example A. S. K. Lambton, *Qajar Persia: Eleven Studies* (Austin, TX, 1988).

[106] Bernard Lewis, *The Jews of Islam* (Princeton, NJ, 1984); *Race and Slavery in the Middle East* (New York, 1990); (ed.), *Christians and Jews in the Ottoman Empire* (London, 1982).

[107] André Raymond, *Le Caire* (Paris, 1993).

[108] This is now made explicit in R. E. Frykenberg, *History and Belief: The Foundations of Historical Understanding* (Grand Rapids, MI, 1996).

[109] J. M. Brown, *Gandhi: Prisoner of Hope* (New Haven, CT, 1989).

betrayed by the self-interest of elites.[110] Stokes and his students tried to make this process more complex by drawing on the insights of the *Annales* school and of historians of medieval England.

Meanwhile, a new Indian urban history emerged from influences as diverse as contemporary histories of Victorian cities and the work of Hourani on notables.[111] In so far as caste, that ancient incubus of the historians of redemption, was examined, it was seen more as an institutional redoubt against agrarian change, than as an essence of Indian history. K. N. Chaudhuri's studies of the East India Company and the trade of Asia[112] followed in a tradition which went back to the official historians of the 1930s, but the emphasis was placed on indigenous merchants and mercantile institutions as much as it was on company trade. Peter Marshall's work on East India Company fortunes showed the detailed prosopographical methodology associated with Lewis Namier and Ronald Syme blended with a new social history of trade.[113]

The view of the world from the perspective of notables, urban quarters and peasants greatly changed post-war understandings of Asian national-isms, but in quite contradictory ways. Some of the work of Hourani and his school stressed large ideological forces such as concepts of the nation and the struggle of middle eastern thinkers with the idea of modernity within an Islamic context. But the tendency to study fragments also threw doubt on the salience of these large themes. In both the Middle East and India, an ironic style of writing about nationalism emerged. Elie Kedourie, a Jewish conservative of Iraqi origin, who was uneasy with post-Ottoman modernity, argued that the appeasement of the western powers had created Arab nationalism, which was an entirely illegitimate construct of office-seekers and marginal ideologues.[114] A similar view emerged from the so-called Cambridge school of Indian history in the 1970s, which reacted against both

---

[110] E. T. Stokes, *The Peasant and the Raj* (Cambridge, 1978); *The Peasant Armed* (Oxford, 1986).

[111] Christine Dobbin, *Urban Leadership in Western India: Politics and Communities in Bombay City 1840–85* (London, 1972); C. A. Bayly, *The Local Roots of Indian Politics: Allahabad 1880–1920* (Oxford, 1975); Rajat K. Ray, *Urban Roots of Indian Nationalism: Pressure Groups and Conflicts of Interest in Calcutta City Politics, 1875–1939* (Delhi, 1979) which was originally a Cambridge dissertation; and, more recently, R. S. Chandavarkar, *The Origins of Industrial Capital in India: Business Strategies and the Working Classes in Bombay 1900–1940* (Cambridge, 1994).

[112] K. N. Chaudhuri, *The Trading World of Asia and the English East India Company 1660–1760* (Cambridge, 1978).

[113] P. J. Marshall, *East Indian Fortunes: The British in Bengal in the Eighteenth Century* (Oxford, 1976); and, more recently, Catherine Manning, *Fortunes à Faire: The French in Asian Trade 1719–48* (Aldershot, 1996).

[114] E. Kedourie, *The Chatham House Version and other Middle-eastern Studies*, new edn (London, 1984); Maurice Cowling, *Religion and Public Doctrine in Modern England* (Cambridge, 1980), pp. 316–28 for an admiring portrait of Kedourie's anti-nationalism.

the Marxist and the liberal traditions of the previous generation, much to the anger of some Indian nationalist scholars.[115] The rather complex ideological affiliations of this group are now less significant than the impetus that its work gave to the study of localities, notables and municipalities.

Some similar trends can be seen in history writing about the Far East, though here the influence of Japanese and American historiography meant that they reflected much broader scholarly realignments. Maurice Freedman, an anthropologist at SOAS, influenced the attitudes of a whole generation of historians in Britain and indirectly in the United States.[116] Local social institutions became the focus of attention. D. C. Twitchett's studies of Tang institutions in the journal *Asia Major* during the 1960s[117] depicted the complex organisation of local imperial bureaucracy as it meshed with landholding gentry, clan and local religious institutions. Meanwhile, Michael Loewe pressed on with the creation of a 'strictly realist' history of early China, delinked from concerns with racial origins or religious essence.[118] These scholars drew on their readings of the *Annales*, but more so on Japanese scholarship, even as indigenous Chinese scholarship was crushed under the weight of the Cultural Revolution. The American interest in the local roots of China's nineteenth- and twentieth-century peasant rebellions and how its gentry responded to social crisis found an echo in Britain.

As the Needham project progressed, some of the earlier organicist and teleological ideas on which it had been premised began to be questioned and, by the end of the 1980s, much doubt was even being shed on the supposed collapse of Chinese science after about 1500. The 'challenge and response' model of Japanese history had already come under the scrutiny of Sir George Sansom, who argued that the Japanese feudal society was crumbling from within before the 'western summons' was heard from without. In the years after 1955 British historians of Japan also attempted to strike a balance between internal and external factors in the country's modernisation and industrialisation.[119] Adverse comparisons between Britain's and Japan's

[115] T. Raychaudhuri, 'Indian Politics as Animal Politics', *Historical Journal*, 23, 3 (1979), 747–63; a representative work of this school was B. R. Tomlinson, *The Indian National Congress and the Raj* (London, 1976).
[116] Freedman, for instance, was an influence on the leading American historian of China, Philip Kuhn, who spent some time at SOAS.
[117] D. C. Twitchett, interview September 1999; another writer in this vein was E. G. Pulleyblank, *Chinese History and World History* (Cambridge, 1955), his inaugural lecture at Cambridge.
[118] Michael Loewe, *Imperial China: The Historical Background to the Modern Age* (London, 1966), p. 1; Mark Elvin, *The Pattern of the Chinese Past* (London, 1975) was a later work in a similar vein.
[119] For example W. G. Beasley, *Great Britain and the Opening of Japan* (London, 1954) and *Japanese Imperialism 1894–1945* (Oxford, 1987); and Ian Nish, *The Anglo-Japanese Alliance* (Oxford, 1966).

industrial development directly stimulated the work on Japanese entrepreneurship.[120]

From social history to postmodernism — or not?

At the broadest level three interconnected themes run through the scholarship of the years after about 1980. First was the proliferation of sub-fields. Histories of Asian law, science, ecology, demography and architecture were later joined by women's history. Second, there was the gradual internationalisation of study which meant that by the end of our period it would be difficult to argue that there was a distinctive British history of Asia. By the 1990s North Americans, continental Europeans, Indians and Chinese held many key posts in the major research universities, while many Britons had moved to the United States, Canada, Australia and New Zealand. British scholarship had to consider issues and positions which derived from American academia and even, in the case of some Asian Marxist and subaltern history, from the Asian continent itself.

Third, the radicals of the 1960s and 1970s began to be perceived as conservatives. Social history began to appear as suspect in some eyes as the history of race and redemption had appeared to the post-war generation. Leftist and women's historians argued that the poor and women had been marginalised in Asian social history more thoroughly than had been the case in European history. But Edward Said's critique went much further by apparently throwing doubt on the whole epistemological basis of western studies of the Orient. What if it was not only the monolithic understanding of the Sunni church and Hinduism or Buddhism which were western constructs, but caste, tribe and village and the other staples of supposedly modern social history? What if all these units were no more than scholarly impositions born from the exercise of imperial power and imperial classification? Said's original assault was made from the position of a middle eastern liberal. However, it was soon overtaken by and merged with the radical relativism born out of the bizarre marriage of Jacques Derrida and Michel Foucault with the gurus of American ethnic politics. At their most extreme, the proponents of postmodern history seemed to argue that, since all signs were fluid and randomly assigned to entities through the operation of power, the

---

[120] R. P. Dore, *Taking Japan Seriously: A Confucian Perspective on Leading Economic Issues* (London, 1987).

whole corpus of historical writing on Asia could safely be cast aside. Only the unmediated voice of the oppressed 'native' or female could be authentic.

The Indian Subaltern Studies group, which influenced research in Britain and also in parts of the former colonial world outside the subcontinent, illustrates some of these trends.[121] It arose out of the need felt by young Indian post-doctoral fellows at Oxford and elsewhere to break away from the elite-centred studies of the Cambridge school and their coevals. The Subaltern historians equally scorned the economistic Marxism of their Indian contemporaries. Subaltern Studies in turn proved to be a good 'sales logo' for the many able young Asian scholars who wished to establish their positions in the United States through an appeal to academic novelty. Intellectually, the Subaltern collective drew, first, on the work of E. P. Thompson and the British homespun Marxist tradition and, later, on the radical relativism of Foucault and literary historians influenced by Derrida. Several left-leaning British historians of India were associated with the work of the Subaltern collective, though more in its mode as radical social history than in its linguistic 'turn'.[122]

Yet, on the other hand, some purely national idiosyncrasies in scholarship retained their hold. This was so even after the massive expansion of higher education, the internationalisation of knowledge and the relative decline of historical research in Britain which followed the Thatcherite attack on the universities. Historians of Asia working in Britain have remained largely within the social and economic history school which arose in the 1960s and 1970s and which has been broadly represented by general historical journals such as *Past and Present* or *The Economic History Review*. They have been much more resistant to the rise of radical relativism, discourse studies and postmodernist theory than many of their colleagues in North America and Australasia. Even the new 'history from below', associated with the Subalterns, has appeared more as a garnish to existing courses and research agendas than as a harbinger of an academic revolution.

Why is this? Institutional conservatism clearly plays a part here. But this resistance also has a distinct intellectual history, even justification. Because of its lack of documentary depth in many areas, British historiography of Asia between 1890 and 1950 was dominated, perhaps even more than that of other European countries, by the style of redemptive history of race and

---

[121] Ranajit Guha et al. (eds), *Subaltern Studies*, 10 vols (New Delhi, 1982–99); see also Vinayak Chaturvedi (ed.), *Mapping Subaltern Studies and the Postcolonial* (London, 2000).
[122] David Hardiman, *Feeding the Bania: Peasants and Usurers in Western India* (Delhi, 1996); *The Coming of the Devi: Adivasi Assertion in Western India* (Delhi, 1987); David Arnold, *Colonizing the Body: State Medicine and Epidemic Disease in Nineteenth-century India* (Berkeley, CA, 1993).

religion which has been the main theme of this essay. One reason why various forms of post-colonial cultural history, which are fashionable in other English-speaking societies, have not caught on to the same extent in Britain, is that, to many historians, they seem to embody precisely those types of essentialised thinking which sustained the older paradigm. Though much of the postmodern historiography speaks of fragments and claims to decentralise narratives or challenge meanings, it often revives, in effect, a concept of culture which is as organicist and undifferentiated as were the old categories of race and religion.[123] By privileging peasant revolts and community forms of action, this work often seems to be subscribing to a history of moral rectitude in which Sons of the Soil redeem the People from western colonialism much as Christian-influenced reformers were supposed to be doing for writers of an earlier period. A large part of the British historical profession remains sceptical of political moralising of this sort and of grand statements about community, culture or modernity. In view of its own history, it has good reason to be suspicious.

Note. This essay has benefited from the careful reading of many friends in different areas of Asian and imperial history, especially Dr Ronald Hyam, Dr Peter Kornicki, Dr Charles Melville, Professor Dennis Twitchett and Dr Hans van de Ven. Professor Burke and Dr Susan Bayly helped greatly, as did the staff of the Café des Deux Garcons, Aix-en-Provence. None of them is in any way responsible for my misreadings.

---

[123] See D. A. Washbrook, 'Colonial Discourse Theory', in R. Winks (ed.), *The Oxford History of the British Empire, vol. 5* (Oxford, 1999), pp. 596–611.

CHAPTER FIVE

Gender

LUDMILLA JORDANOVA

Introduction

Only twenty years ago 'gender' seemed a new, modish, and, to some, a distinctly scary term. Now it is used in just about every field of history and most historians feel more or less comfortable with it. However, its integration into the fabric of our lives does not mean that it is always used precisely or generatively. For example, the word gender is often used to refer to whether a person is male or female — a matter of their chromosomes, of what some scholars prefer to call 'sex', rather than of gender. It is a controversial distinction that continues to elicit passionate reactions. But, however defined, 'gender' refers to social and cultural phenomena, which are relational in character, and hence demand some measure of comparative analysis. The styles of masculinity, femininity and androgyny that people adopt concern gender, since they involve engagement with and relationships between these cultural modes. Masculinity, for instance, is never a homogenous, free-standing phenomenon; it is in perpetual conversation with femininity.[1] Furthermore, masculinity, like femininity, is manifestly a highly complex, even elusive phenomenon, and that is why the use of gender as an analytical term in historical practice remains challenging.[2]

---

[1] A pioneering volume remains J. Tosh and M. Roper (eds), *Manful Assertions: Masculinities in Britain since 1800* (London, 1991); see T. Hitchcock and M. Cohen (eds), *English Masculinities 1660–1800* (London and New York, 1999) and D. Hadley (ed.), *Masculinity in Medieval Europe* (London and New York, 1999). I have explored some issues concerning gender and historical practice in *History in Practice* (London, 2000). Readers should note that no attempt has been made to provide a literature survey in the notes. My thanks to Alison Rowlands and Clare Haynes for their kind help, and to Leonore Davidoff for reading an earlier version.

[2] Joan Scott's influential article, 'Gender: A Useful Category of Historical Analysis', was first published in 1986; it is reprinted in J. Scott, *Gender and the Politics of History* (New York, 1988), ch. 2 and in R. Shoemaker and M. Vincent (eds), *Gender and History in Western Europe* (London, 1998), pp. 42–65, which brings together much useful material.

It is important to note that the precise subject matter of gender history is underdetermined: much that is published under its name is in fact women's history, which is not quite the same thing, although there certainly are overlaps between the two fields. If gender concerns every aspect of masculinity and femininity, then it is likely to inform virtually all of human existence in one way or another. Hence it is difficult to say exactly what gender history includes. In this respect gender shares important properties with race and with other forms of social difference that are constitutive of a given society.[3] It follows, then, that any historical method, theory or approach could in principle be applied to the study of gender in the past. Here is an excellent example of thematic history, which illustrates perfectly both the potentials and the pitfalls of using wide-ranging concepts as the focus for research.[4]

I want to be explicit about the implications of working with such broad themes. If gender is ubiquitous, it calls into question traditional divisions and hierarchies within scholarship. For example, gendered phenomena cut across social, political and economic history, and also possess significant intellectual and cultural components. It is hardly coincidental that historians of science and medicine, who chart some of the most authoritative ideas and practices with respect to putatively natural differences, have made important contributions to gender history.[5] Yet these sub-fields have rarely been seen as 'mainstream' history. There certainly are historians who work on gender predominantly from an economic, social or political perspective, but these divisions seem especially artificial when considering a historical phenomenon of this kind — one where values and associations are pervasive. Indeed, it could be

---

[3] See the special issue of *Eighteenth-century Studies*, 23, 4 (1990), 'The Politics of Difference'; C. Hall, *White, Male and Middle-class: Explorations in Feminism and History* (Cambridge, 1992); C. Hall, J. Rendall and K. McClelland, *Defining the Victorian Nation: Class, Race, Gender and the Reform Act of 1867* (Cambridge, 2000).

[4] Especially useful is the special issue of *Gender and History*, 11, 3 (1999), 'Gender and History — Retrospect and Prospect'. Longman's series 'Women and Men in History' indicates some of the ways in which gender has been handled as a theme in recent historical writings, for example R. Shoemaker, *Gender in English Society, 1650–1850: The Emergence of Separate Spheres?* (London and New York, 1998); M. Wiesner, *Gender, Church and State in Early Modern Germany* (London and New York, 1998); J. C. Brown and R. C. Davis (eds), *Gender and Society in Renaissance Italy* (London and New York, 1998); E. Foyster, *Manhood in Early Modern England: Honour, Sex and Marriage* (London and New York, 1999); P. Carter, *Men and the Emergence of Polite Society in Britain 1660–1800* (London and New York, 2000).

[5] For example D. Haraway, *Primate Visions: Gender, Race and Nature in the World of Modern Science* (New York and London, 1989); E. Fox Keller, *Reflections on Gender and Science* (New Haven, CT, and London, 1985); N. Stepan, 'Race and Gender: The Role of Analogy in Science', *Isis*, 77 (1986), 261–77.

said that these divisions were already being called into question long before the advent of gender history. But the capacity of gender to suffuse social relations brings their artificiality into yet sharper relief.

Formulating a crisp problem as a research focus is particularly important and also correspondingly exacting given the properties of 'gender' that have already been mentioned. A related issue is that of sources. It follows from what I have said that a huge range of materials bears on gender in one way or another. The rise of interest in gender has gone along with an expansion in the range of topics that historians consider and with more concerted efforts to use local records in case-studies that shed light on larger problems. Within 'local', I include court records, wills, records of births, marriages and deaths, family papers and parish records. This has not precluded a strong interest in other kinds of sources — fiction, poetry, drama, art, prescriptive literature, for example.

However, historians are increasingly concerned about the status of their sources, of their limitations, and of the need to be particularly scrupulous in basing wider claims upon them. The awareness of what sources do *not* reveal has been growing among members of the historical profession. Perhaps such scepticism is linked with the increasing influence of social constructionist views in the 1980s, which emphasised the means through which views of the world are actively shaped by interest groups.[6] Accordingly, advice books, for example, should not be assumed to passively reflect social practices; rather, they actively construct attitudes and worldviews. Hence they cannot be used to establish what people did, although they do reveal how specific constituencies thought and felt about the world. The problems of using such sources in relation to gender are particularly acute. Because gender is implicated in so many aspects of human existence, the tendency to manage this through pontification, which is precisely what prescriptive and didactic materials involve, has been especially marked. The urge to pronounce is itself historically revealing; it is a form of what I have called 'cultural effort'.[7] The danger remains, however, and it is especially serious in relation to scientific and medical writings, that claims, discursive structures, acquire a status they do not deserve.

In this essay I discuss some of the issues surrounding gender and historical practice. I am concerned to probe the concept, to examine how it has been used, and to explore its role in broad historiographical trends. It is a controversial area for historians, touching as it does on many sensitivities

---

[6] P. Berger and T. Luckmann, *The Social Construction of Reality: A Treatise in the Sociology of Knowledge* (London, 1991, first published in 1967).

[7] L. Jordanova, *Nature Displayed: Gender, Science and Medicine 1760–1820* (London, 1999), ch. 1. The passionate debates about midwifery and especially about the propriety of men acting as midwives are excellent examples of 'cultural effort', see chs 2 and 12.

that are at once personal, professional and political. I want to invoke a number of types of politics here: movements that agitate directly for change; the activities of groups that feel themselves to be marginalised and under threat; and conflicts within the academy, whether ideological, professional or institutional. More specifically, the use of gender in historical practice relates directly to feminism and its impact upon received views of the past, to sexuality, to race and the intense debates about the understanding and representation of sexual orientation and racial difference, and to discussions about 'theory', which have divided the profession and called into question the status of historical knowledge.

Terms of engagement

Before exploring the politics of gender history a little further, I want to offer a preliminary discussion of the term 'gender' itself. Gender is the name we give to our understanding of masculinity and femininity and of the relationships between the constellations of attributes and metaphors associated with those terms.[8] Since it involves the study of relationships, it invites a special form of comparative history. This history is not about genitals or chromosomes in themselves, but about all those traits, experiences and entities that are linked to masculinity and femininity, male and female roles. The predominant forms of linkage are through associations of ideas, metaphors, and the social practices that sustain them. Such linkages have a material dimension — distinctions between men's work and women's work, for example, are tangibly manifested in pay structures and union organisation. None the less, the mechanisms by means of which certain kinds of labour and skills are tagged as 'for women' or 'for men' are cultural. Or to put the same point in a different manner, material life and cultural life are inseparable.

Some flexibility or play with respect to gendered mindsets is clearly possible, while at the same time there are associations that persist for centuries. Notions such as daintiness, softness and prettiness are not inherently linked to women, they are so contingently through historical processes, however persistent and natural they come to seem; yet many such notions do change over time. New gender norms constantly arise, some of them are operative for

---

[8] For a range of perspectives on gender compare, C. MacCormack and M. Strathern (eds), *Nature, Culture and Gender* (Cambridge, 1980); S. Garrett, *Gender* (London and New York, 1987); I. Illich, *Gender* (London, 1983); J. Butler, *Gender Trouble: Feminism and the Subversion of Identity* (New York and London, 1990).

sub-groups rather than for entire societies. However large or limited its reach, the constellation of phenomena we are calling 'gender' has two important properties. First, it exists through languages — verbal, visual, aural — and hence demands appropriate types of analysis. Second, it is insinuating, which is to say that it makes us what we are; it is constitutive of our very being and exists at levels of consciousness not easily amenable to conventional historical analysis. These two properties in part account for the significance for (some) gender historians of literary approaches (including critical theory) and of psychoanalysis.[9]

As a result, 'theory' can be a highly contentious issue for historians who study gender. I wish to signal here that it is problematic both to lump a number of frameworks and approaches together and call them 'theory', and to imply a clear-cut division between theory and something else — empirical work or practice. Indeed many recent trends have encouraged their subtle integration. Historians of gender are particularly reliant on conceptual frameworks because of the very nature of gender as an abstraction that cannot easily be handled simply as a variable, although some historians have sought to do just that. When they do so, however, they are not fully grasping gender as a concept. Hence work on gender demands a particularly self-aware blend of 'theory' and 'practice'. It is hardly unique in this respect, but it is worth remarking that political practices such as feminism, with their emphasis on consciousness raising, can be seen as akin to the emphasis on reflexivity that has become prominent in humanities disciplines since the late 1960s.

Politics

With these points in mind, let us return to the question of politics. Virtually all practitioners of gender history acknowledge their debt to feminism, a political movement that, by definition, had to consider men and women in relation to one another. It is significant that early feminism did so by

---

[9] J. Mitchell, *Feminism and Psychoanalysis* (Harmondsworth, 1975, new edn London, 2000); C. Weedon, *Feminist Practice and Poststructuralist Theory* (Oxford, 1987) and *Feminism, Theory and the Politics of Difference* (Oxford, 1999); B. Fay, P. Pomper, R. Vann (eds), *History and Theory: Contemporary Readings* (Malden, MA, and London, 1998), part VI, 'Gender, Sexuality, Sex'; A. Green and K. Troup (eds), *The Houses of History: A Critical Reader in Twentieth-century History and Theory* (Manchester, 1999), ch. 10.

deploying an abstract discourse of rights that derives from Enlightenment political thinking.[10] Although still widely used in practical politics, such notions have come under increasing critical scrutiny precisely because their liberal abstractness appears not to do justice to the profound intricacies of all forms of social difference. Feminist traditions have tended either to assert the entitlement of women to rights simply by virtue of being human or to use their distinctive moral and maternal qualities to make a special case.[11] There have been important changes in the ways in which scholars have approached the position of women over the last thirty years or so. For instance, they have begun to explore the limitations of atomistic, abstract approaches to rights. Furthermore, we are coming to appreciate how many forms of 'feminism' there have been.[12] Those of the late twentieth century were notable in the attention they paid not just to the diverse class experiences of women, but to racial, ethnic, linguistic and religious distinctions.

Politics works at many levels, hence historians have also been keen to show how important the micro-politics of gender relations are. Negotiations within the household, local protest and the use of legal procedures have all been investigated with the power relations between men and women in mind.[13] If it is permissible to generalise about such studies, I would say that they show women to be more politically aware, more adept at managing their immediate environment than had previously been recognised. They do so in

---

[10] Mary Wollstonecraft, with her two *Vindications*, one of women's, the other of men's rights, of 1792, exemplifies the point beautifully: M. Wollstonecraft, *Works*, ed. J. Todd and M. Butler, 7 vols (London, 1989).

[11] J. Rendall, *The Origins of Modern Feminism: Women in Britain, France and the United States, 1780–1860* (London, 1985); J. Mitchell and A. Oakley (eds), *The Rights and Wrongs of Women* (Harmondsworth, 1976); M. Freeman, 'Human Rights and the Corruption of Governments, 1789–1989', in P. Hulme and L. Jordanova (eds), *The Enlightenment and its Shadows* (London, 1990), pp. 163–83; M. Ostrogorski, *The Rights of Women: A Comparative Study in History and Legislation* (Philadelphia, PA, 1980).

[12] G. Bock and S. James (eds), *Beyond Equality and Difference: Citizenship, Feminist Politics and Female Subjectivity* (London and New York, 1992); C. Sowerine, *Sisters or Citizens? Women and Socialism in France since 1876* (Cambridge, 1982); J. Rendall, *The Origins of Modern Feminism: Women in Britain, France and the United States, 1780–1860* (London, 1985); K. Anthony, *Feminism in Germany and Scandinavia* (New York, 1915); R. Strachey, *The Cause: A Short History of the Women's Movement in Great Britain* (London, 1928); R. Evans, *The Feminists: Women's Emancipation Movements in Europe, America and Australasia 1840–1920* (London, 1977); S. Kemp and J. Squires (eds), *Feminisms* (Oxford, 1997); J. Scott (ed.), *Feminism and History* (Oxford, 1996).

[13] J. Tosh, *A Man's Place: Masculinity and the Middle-class Home in Victorian England* (New Haven, CT, and London, 1999); A. Clark, *The Struggle for the Breeches: Gender and the Making of the British Working Class* (London, 1995); A. Erikson, *Women and Property in Early Modern England* (London, 1993); M. Arnot and C. Usborne (eds), *Gender and Crime in Early Modern Europe* (London, 1999).

part by showing that women in the past were far better informed about their
legal situation, and more able to turn it to their advantage, than had
previously been thought.[14] In effect, a critique is being offered of those
who take women's *theoretical* position before the law as sufficient evidence
of passivity and/or victimhood. The impulse behind much work in this vein
was, on the one hand, 'feminism' and, on the other, a concern with 'gender'.
Recent studies also reveal the centrality of men to the home and to the
family. In its early years, the history of the family gave some scholars
a chance to pay special attention to women and children; now, when
masculinity seems to be in crisis and when gender has seeped into the
collective consciousness, the role of men in family life is receiving scholarly
attention.[15]

One consequence of these new intellectual and political impulses is, to put
it bluntly, that it is no longer clear what is meant by the term 'woman'
in a scholarly context, only that it should be interrogated.[16] By extension,
'man' has been subjected to similar scrutiny, although there is a significant
asymmetry here. In many past societies 'woman' has been a contested
category.[17] But the long-standing asymmetry between male and female has
meant that the latter was taken as peculiarly problematic, the former as
relatively straightforward.[18] It is ironic how this asymmetry has worked itself
out in the ways in which 'masculinity' and 'femininity' are now used.

---

[14] However, Davidoff and Hall point out that women's economic power could be much more limited
than appeared on the surface because they could rarely be active users of their resources. Thus, the
close attention to actual behaviour does not always show women to be stronger than had previously
been thought: L. Davidoff and C. Hall, *Family Fortunes: Men and Women of the English Middle
Class 1780–1850* (London, 1987), esp. part 2 and epilogue.

[15] L. Tilly and J. Scott, *Women, Work and Family* (New York, 1978) is an influential work on women
and family; there are countless others on this subject. However, it could be argued that many
demographers and historians of the family have been relatively blind to gender. A. Clare, *On Men:
Masculinity in Crisis* (London, 2000) is a sensitive exploration of recent issues.

[16] D. Riley, *'Am I that Name?' Feminism and the Category of Women in History* (Basingstoke,
1988).

[17] What counts as acceptable womanliness is invariably a contested matter, varying with class, race,
age, occupation and religion. In some periods, debates about Woman have been important. The
capital letter signifies a type, a category that has been used as a way of managing the complexities of
gender relations: for example J. Michelet, *La Femme* (Paris, 1860); H. H. Ploss, M. Bartels and
P. Bartels, *Woman: An Historical, Gynaecological and Anthropological Compendium*, 3 vols
(London, 1935, first published in German in 1885). I discuss this issue in *Sexual Visions: Images of
Gender in Science and Medicine between the Eighteenth and Twentieth Centuries* (Hemel
Hempstead, 1989), esp. ch. 4.

[18] One manifestation of this asymmetry is what is known as 'the double standard': K. Thomas, 'The
Double Standard', *Journal of the History of Ideas*, 20 (1959), 195–216. Another manifestation may
be found in the development of medical specialisms, for example O. Moscucci, *The Science of
Woman: Gynaecology and Gender in England, 1800–1929* (Cambridge, 1990).

'Masculinity' signals an important new area of historical research that is increasingly fashionable. By contrast 'femininity' sounds normative, stereotypical and perhaps therefore tainted with an older view of womanhood. Masculinity, it seems, is now ubiquitous in scholarship. Feminist historians are not surprised by the irony — they still want to insist on the continued unthinking use of gendered languages that, for example, refer to men when they mean people.[19] Furthermore, there is still much to be done on what we might call silent masculinity, for instance on those institutions like the army and the church, which depend on particular kinds of maleness. It is 'silent' because it generally not articulated as such.

Social categories

What is new is the realisation that a sophisticated account of how social categories are forged is a necessary foundation for virtually all forms of history. There are no simple formulae governing the form the interrogation of such categories should take, although there are two main possibilities. The first involves deploying one of the many theoretical perspectives, which scholars from a number of humanities and social science disciplines have developed.[20] We should note in passing, however, that few practising historians could be called feminist *theorists* or vice versa. Neither feminism nor gender history has in fact done much to change the fundamental relationships between historical practice and theory: the former tends to engage with detailed case-studies, the latter to be the prerogative of other disciplines. None the less, the prominence of theoretical debates about 'woman', sexuality and gender has put some pressure on historians at least to acknowledge and engage with more abstract questions. Inevitably, which theoretical perspectives are to be adopted, and precisely how, remain contentious issues.[21]

[19] Thus, when a historian such as Keith Thomas writes a book entitled *Man and the Natural World* (London, 1983) hearts sink.

[20] It is surely significant that historians with a background in the social sciences have made particularly strong contributions to gender history — the work of Leonore Davidoff being a prime example: *The Best Circles: Society, Etiquette and the Season* (London, 1986); *Worlds Between: Historical Perspectives on Gender and Class* (Cambridge, 1995) and, with Catherine Hall, *Family Fortunes: Men and Women of the English Middle Class, 1780–1850* (London, 1987).

[21] We should acknowledge the marked national (and disciplinary) differences with respect to the use of theory in historical scholarship. For example, many commentators argue that British historians are more empiricist than those, say, on mainland Europe.

The second possible route for interrogating the category 'woman' is more historical. It involves placing the very notion of 'woman' in a specific historical context, it thereby accepts that such matters are contingent, and that the meanings of womanhood and manhood have to be constantly replenished, given meaning and renegotiated in each historical situation. Yet this route is not as straightforward as it sounds. What kinds of evidence bear on the understanding of 'woman' at any given moment? There has been a tendency to treat certain areas as privileged indices — the law, science and medicine, and religion for example. If we want to trouble concepts of 'woman' and 'man', then a wider range of materials and perspectives is required.[22] In part this is because such concepts are felt, internalised, embedded in consciousness, not just thought about or managed explicitly. Increasingly, gender historians want to probe how abstract categories relate to and are informed by lived experience. Thus, although the growth of interest in gender is often taken as indicative of the rise of cultural history, it also bears eloquent testimony to the continued vitality of social history in its concern with the daily lives of large swathes of the population.

I have discussed feminism, politics and 'woman' here in order to signal important sources of energy for gender history. There are other sources. While many historians have taken masculinity to be relatively unproblematic, a number of groups have a strong interest in subjecting it to critical scrutiny. Gay men in particular were concerned to chart not just the troubled history of how men who were erotically drawn to other men were treated, but the very means by which notions such as 'the homosexual' were constructed.[23] Although, like feminist history, such initiatives could be seen as serving minority interests, that would be a limited and ungenerous response. It is true that, especially when gender and cognate concerns were seen as new and modish, such reactions were common. Now it is more widely recognised that, as a political question hinging on gender, sexual orientation is of broad historical significance. Feminism and women's history helped to give prominence to lesbian experiences,

---

[22] See J. Butler, *Gender Trouble: Feminism and the Subversion of Identity* (New York and London, 1990).

[23] Jeffrey Weeks has been a pioneer: *Coming Out: Homosexual Politics in Britain from the Nineteenth Century to the Present* (London, 1977); *Sex, Politics and Society: The Regulation of Sexuality since 1800* (London, 1981). See also his *Making Sexual History* (Cambridge, 2000). Other interested groups may be less easy to define, but men who are particularly committed to active fatherhood have wanted to make the history of family focus less on wives and mothers and more on husbands and fathers.

although this category — lesbian — also needs critical scrutiny. Just as naturally a desire for recognition, for some kind of legitimacy, has shaped gay and lesbian history.[24] But there is a wider point to be made. However insinuating and pervasive gender is, each society at any given time uses a specific and limited range of issues and phenomena as focal points through which difficulties relating to gender, masculinity and femininity are worked through. Very often these involve what is perceived at the time as some kind of deviance or abnormality.[25] It is as if these issues carry burdens on behalf of others, allowing them to be used to give access to much more general phenomena. That these 'selections', which are never fully conscious, are revealing is neatly demonstrated by the different histories of male and female homosexuality in Britain, especially with respect to the law.[26]

Like other forms of political-cum-intellectual engagement, feminisms are directly relevant to the practices of gender historians by virtue of their attention to relations of power. There are many possible accounts of power, and historians need to critically evaluate them.[27] Accordingly, it should be a matter of concern that Michel Foucault's approaches have been so widely and uncritically adopted.[28] The accuracy of his historical claims has been widely contested, but more worrying is the tendency to apply his ideas to a huge range of settings for which they may not be especially apt. Let me make the same point by saying that one pressing issue for historians here is what we could call the period effect.

[24] For example M. Duberman, M. Vicinus and G. Chauncy (eds), *Hidden from History: Reclaiming the Gay and Lesbian Past* (London, 1991).

[25] Infanticide is a particularly revealing example since it bears on sexuality, femininity and motherhood: see for example P. Hoffer, *Murdering Mothers: Infanticide in England and New England 1558–1803* (New York and London, 1981); L. Rose, *The Massacre of the Innocents: Infanticide in Britain 1800–1939* (London, 1986); R. Schulte, *The Village in Court: Arson, Infanticide and Poaching in the Court Reports of Upper Bavaria 1848–1910* (Oxford, 1994); M. Jackson, *New-born Child Murder: Women, Illegitimacy and the Courts in Eighteenth-century England* (Manchester, 1996).

[26] L. Moran, *The Homosexual(ity) of Law* (London and New York, 1996), esp. pp. 12–14.

[27] S. Lukes, *Power: A Radical View* (London, 1974) remains a classic; S. Lukes (ed.), *Power* (Oxford, 1986); N. Fraser, *Unruly Practices: Power, Discourse and Gender in Contemporary Social Theory* (Cambridge, 1989). See M. J. Maynes et al. (eds), *Gender, Kinship and Power: A Comparative and Interdisciplinary History* (London and New York, 1996) and S. K. Kent, *Gender and Power in Britain, 1640–1990* (London and New York, 1999).

[28] A selection of Foucault's writings and of responses to him may be found in P. Rabinow (ed.), *The Foucault Reader* (New York, 1984) and C. Jones and R. Porter (eds), *Reassessing Foucault: Power, Medicine and the Body* (London, 1994) respectively.

Period effects

Vocabularies are hardly period neutral, they have histories of their own and simply may not fit with some historical situations. Arguably 'feminism' is one such case; I would prefer to see its use limited to the nineteenth century onwards. It is now deployed in writings on the eighteenth century, although it can hardly be said to constitute a political movement in that period.[29] Historians have become increasingly conscious of the dangers of anachronism. This is a particular problem when ideas, concepts and theories are derived from political movements that are pursuing strong agendas of their time and place. I would suggest that 'rights', taken by some to be a universal category, would be an instance of this point. However, it does not follow that key terms never shed light on historical situations that antedate them. For example, once it is granted that there is something to psychoanalysis, then it can certainly be used in the study of eras before the late nineteenth century. If the unconscious exists in the ways psychoanalytic thinkers posit, then it did not spring into being with Freud.[30]

The larger point might be thought to apply to 'gender' itself — can we be gender historians of societies innocent of the term? My answer is a resounding yes, because gender is a productive term of analysis, not an actors' category, and because the phenomena it embraces can be shown to have existed in many places over long periods of time.[31] Admittedly it then follows that historians have to work deftly to show how the languages current at any given time relate to 'gender' and to demonstrate that it is worthwhile to bring diverse phenomena together in this way.

There is more to be said about gender and period. Like most forms of history, gender history has shifted the centre of gravity of the discipline towards the present day by paying particular attention to the Victorian era and subsequent periods. At one level this is quite understandable; it is a form of modernism that takes its lifeblood from the need to trace the immediate antecedents of our own preoccupations. Yet studies of earlier periods have

---

[29] For example A. Browne, *The Eighteenth-century Feminist Mind* (Brighton, 1987); V. Jones (ed.), *Women in the Eighteenth Century: Constructions of Femininity* (London, 1990); see 'Feminism and Enlightenment' project, Department of History, Royal Holloway, University of London.

[30] P. Gay, *Freud for Historians* (New York and Oxford, 1985) remains a persuasive account, see also *History Workshop Journal*, 26 and 45 (1988 and 1998, respectively) for innovative historical work using psychoanalytic ideas.

[31] In recent years gender *has* become an actors' category, so that most people would now understand what was meant by 'gender-bending' and would encounter instances of it in popular culture. For earlier periods, it is essential to examine extremely carefully the cognitive frameworks and vocabularies that existed in relation to what we now call 'gender'.

been energised by the growth of interest in gender: medieval, early modern and the long eighteenth century. Despite a few attempts to build bridges between these periods, they tend to operate as distinct sub-fields. In medieval and early modern history, the presence of unusually juicy topics, such as saints, mystics and witches, has made a gender perspective particularly compelling. The case of the long eighteenth century is noteworthy. While it is not immediate to our current concerns in the ways that the post-1850 period is, it does possess some historical movements that make it of special significance: the industrial revolution, the French Revolution, in the case of Britain an era of intense class formation, and so on. However, I see little evidence of sustained challenges to received forms of periodisation from historians of gender, but rather continuing debates about the precise significance of given eras for gender relations.[32]

Feminisms

To return once again to feminism: debates about both the position of women within the historical profession and the place that politicised history should play within the academy have made it of immediate relevance to gender historians. In North America, far more than in Britain, feminist politics have had an impact upon the courses taught in universities and the employment of female historians. This is consistent with the more overt and polarised identity politics especially in US universities by comparison with Britain. Feminism is after all an international movement, and in each situation its impact upon institutions of higher education has been different. For example, it is fair to say that in Scandinavia gender perspectives have been particularly successfully established in universities, much less so in France and other European countries.[33]

Gender is not the only issue that raises these questions, but, like race, it does so quite acutely. It is certainly no coincidence that there has recently been a flowering of interest in women historians in the past — Maxine Berg's biography of the medievalist Eileen Power is a case in point.[34] Indeed Bonnie Smith's recent book, *The Gender of History*, seeks to develop a

---

[32] J. Warren and M. Dickie, *Challenging Boundaries: Gender and Periodization* (Athens, GA, 2000).
[33] M. Riot-Sarcey, 'The Difficulties of Gender in France: Reflections on a Concept', *Gender and History*, 11 (1999), 489–98.
[34] M. Berg, *A Woman in History: Eileen Power 1889–1940* (Cambridge, 1996); see the 'Foremothers' series in *Gender and History*, 3 (1991), 4 (1992), 6 (1994), 8 (1996) and 10 (1998).

wide-ranging account of the ways in which the historical profession itself is gendered.[35] The claim that knowledge is gendered through and through is not a new point but has in fact been at the heart of work on science and medicine for some time now.[36] Smith's claims are hardly uncontentious. She discusses, for example, the fantasies of male historians, to indicate that the production of historical knowledge was deeply sexualised, imaginatively speaking. Along with this, she claims, went more or less systematic attempts to marginalise women historians. Thus, when the debt of gender history to feminism is acknowledged at least three political issues are present. The first is a commitment to understanding the power relations between men and women from a critical vantage point. Second, the question of how such relations are best conceptualised is passionately debated. Third, the implications of a feminist analysis for the professional lives of practitioners of history are a constant presence.

There is another hotly disputed issue that is related to feminism and gender. Women's history has a long tradition; by the end of the eighteenth century a number of works had been published that were recognisably in this mould, some of them by female authors.[37] Notable works were composed earlier in the twentieth century even if the big growth in the field has been since the Second World War.[38] By contrast, gender history is a relative newcomer, a phenomenon of the 1980s. So what should the relationship between these two fields be?[39] One response would be to focus on the differences between 'women' and 'gender' as concepts. Women are a social constituency of a particular kind, hence women's history might be expected to study all aspects of the persons who make up that constituency. 'Gender' is an abstract, comparative term and accordingly gender history focuses less

---

[35] B. Smith, *The Gender of History: Men, Women, and Historical Practice* (Cambridge, MA, and London, 1998); see J. Scott, *Gender and the Politics of History* (New York, 1988), esp. ch. 9.

[36] C. MacCormack and M. Strathern (eds), *Nature, Culture and Gender* (Cambridge, 1980); B. Easlea, *Fathering the Unthinkable: Masculinity, Scientists and the Nuclear Arms Race* (London, 1983); L. Jordanova, *Sexual Visions: Images of Gender in Science and Medicine between the Eighteenth and Twentieth Centuries* (Hemel Hempstead, 1989); L. Shiebinger, *Nature's Body: Gender in the Making of Modern Science* (Boston, MA, 1993); M. McNeil (ed.), *Gender and Expertise* (London, 1987).

[37] For example Ann Thicknesse (neé Ford), *Sketches of the Lives and Writings of the Ladies of France*, 3 vols in 2 (London, 1780–1); W. Alexander, *The History of Women, from the Earliest Antiquity to the Present Time*, 2 vols (London, 1779); M. Hays, *Female Biography; Or, Memoirs of Illustrious and Celebrated Women, of all Ages and Countries*, 6 vols (London, 1803).

[38] A. Clark, *Working Life of Women in the Seventeenth Century* (London, 1917, third edn 1992); I. Pinchbeck, *Women Workers and the Industrial Revolution 1750–1850* (London, 1930). See P. Sharpe (ed.), *Women's Work: The English Experience 1650–1914* (London, 1998).

[39] See. G. Bock, 'Women's History and Gender History: Aspects of an International Debate', *Gender and History*, 1 (1989), 7–30.

on the social history of persons and groupings than on the cultural history of femininity and masculinity *in relation to each other*. Yet a moment's reflection reveals that these projects cannot be so neatly separated, and it is worth noting that the premier journal in the field, *Gender and History* (founded 1989), has published a great deal on women.[40]

Another response would tackle the question somewhat differently. It would attend to the different political freighting of 'women' and 'gender', and the intellectual priorities that might follow. These are emotive matters. There are, for instance, historians who believe that gender history takes away a special emphasis on women, which is still needed.[41] That is, gender history can be perceived as depoliticised, a turning away from feminism. According to this view, the growing enthusiasm for gender robs women of the attention to which their previous neglect entitled them. Precisely by being relational, it could be said that 'gender' allows masculinity and men back in, thereby returning, albeit unintentionally, to a situation where history effectively means the history of men because they were more important and significant, the central term against which women should be compared. I can discern no simple patterns in the women-versus-gender discussions, although some would suggest that historians of women tend to be less theoretically orientated than those who work on gender. I suspect there are simply some historians for whom gender feels right and others for whom it does not. I would argue for a highly flexible approach. Categories of historical analysis should always mesh convincingly with the project in question. It follows that sometimes gender will work well as the leading concept, while at others woman or women may be more appropriate. It is up to historians to show, in each instance, that they have thought through these issues.

Agencies

Since women are a social constituency, one furthermore with which many practitioners identify, it might be assumed that women's history is better at revealing the agency of people, and especially females, in the past as well as being a more effective political instrument. However, I do not think it follows that historians who use gender as an organising term are either less attentive

---

[40] See *Journal of Gender Studies* (1991 onwards); *Journal of Women's History* (1988 onwards) and *Women's History Review* (1992 onwards).
[41] This, for example, is June Purvis's position. Her publications include *Hard Lessons: The Lives and Education of Working-class Women in Nineteenth-century England* (Cambridge, 1989).

to agency and social action or less politically engaged. But it does follow that they are open to work on men and masculinity. This must be a good thing given, for instance, the importance of men within the family, and of notions of patriarchy for traditions of social and political thought.[42] Indeed nationhood, war and empire would be examples of historical phenomena of the highest importance where the nature of masculinity was at their very core. Hence, bringing masculinity into focus should shed new light on them. So the point can be made quite strongly: with a gendered perspective, familiar historical phenomena of the broadest significance can be understood in fresh ways.

The categorisation and treatment of soldiers who failed to conform in one way or another during the First World War would be a case in point. A number of historians pointed out some time ago that the categories used for officers and men were different; thus, 'shell-shock' carried class connotations and was more often applied to officers.[43] To a class-based analysis we can add one based on gender; for example, we could note how closely related notions of mental illness were to contemporary assumptions about competence, sensitivity and femininity. It is no exaggeration to say that the First World War radically called into question what it meant to be a man, and that it continued to have an impact upon gender relations long after the participants returned home and attempted to build new lives.[44] It has become clear that masculinity is a theme of general historical importance, hardly something to be taken for granted or understood as a sectional interest.

A similar transition has, of course, occurred in relation to women. Women's history was construed by those opposed to it as a form of special pleading, and at best as a highly specialised, particular, limited concern that, as it were, the discipline might well grow out of. In recent years it has become clear that women's history has the capacity to transform our understanding of general historical themes — the burgeoning of interest in

[42] R. L. Griswold, *Fatherhood in America: A History* (New York, 1993); M. B. Norton, *Founding Mothers and Fathers: Gendered Power and the Forming of American Society* (New York, 1996); J. Elshtain (ed.), *The Family in Political Thought* (Brighton, 1982) and *Meditations on Modern Political Thought: Masculine/Feminine Themes from Luther to Arendt* (New York and London, 1986); G. J. Schochet, *Patriarchalism in Political Thought* (London, 1975).

[43] A. Babington, *Shell-Shock: A History of the Changing Attitudes to War Neurosis* (London, 1997) is a basic account, which does not, however, take a gendered perspective.

[44] J. Bourke, *Dismembering the Male: Men's Bodies, Britain and the Great War* (London, 1996); M. Higonnet, J. Jenson, S. Michel and M. C. Weitz (eds), *Behind the Lines: Gender and the Two World Wars* (New Haven, CT, 1987); S. K. Kent, *Making Peace: The Reconstruction of Gender in Interwar Britain* (Princeton, NJ, 1993); S. Grayzel, *Women's Identities at War: Gender, Motherhood and Politics in France during the First World War* (Chapel Hill, NC, and London, 1999); G. Chauncey Jr, 'Christian Brotherhood or Sexual Perversion? Homosexual Identities and the Construction of Sexual Boundaries in the World War I Era', in M. Duberman, M. Vicinus and G. Chauncey Jr (eds), *Hidden from History: Reclaiming the Gay and Lesbian Past* (London, 1991), pp. 294–317.

queenship in the medieval period would be a case in point.[45] So, these new perspectives can be used in a number of ways: to give fresh and fuller accounts of the past; to transform the very categories with which the past is studied; and to criticise received views.

New fields

It is worth noting how quickly standard topics become established in new fields. In relation to gender history, a particularly striking one is the distinction between public and private; perhaps it took hold precisely because it seems to be already gendered. In terms of public/private in general, the work of Habermas has been fundamental, but in relation to gender specifically, the prominence of these ideas as structuring terms in political thinking has been especially important, precisely because, at least from classical times onwards, the link with gender was perfectly explicit.[46] Sometimes historians have been tempted to read the distinction as a direct description, and it is commonplace to hear comments about women being confined to the private sphere. In fact the very word 'sphere', which suggests clear boundaries, reinforces ideas about separate domains for the sexes, yet a moment's reflection reveals that, in so far as we go along with the public/ private distinction as a *social* phenomenon, there must be constant movement between the two for both men and women. The very *idea* of the private appears to carry gendered connotations, but then the burden is on us to draw out what this means in practice for any given historical situation. What conceptual status do we give to 'public' and 'private'? The danger of reification is ever present. In this case concepts in political thinking, terms in

---

[45] P. Stafford, *Queens, Concubines and Dowagers: The King's Wife in the Early Middle Ages* (London, 1983) and *Queen Emma and Queen Edith: Queenship and Women's Power in Eleventh-century England* (Oxford, 1997); A. Duggan (ed.), *Queens and Queenship in Medieval Europe* (Woodbridge, 1997); J. Nelson, *Rulers and Ruling Families in Early Medieval Europe* (Aldershot, 1999).

[46] J. Habermas, *The Structural Transformation of the Public Sphere: An Inquiry into a Category of Bourgeois Society* (Cambridge, MA, 1989, first published 1962); C. Calhoun (ed.), *Habermas and the Public Sphere* (Cambridge, MA, 1992); J. Elshtain, *Public Man, Private Woman: Women in Social and Political Thought* (Oxford, 1981); J. Rendall, 'Women and the Public Sphere', *Gender and History*, 11 (1999), 475–88; A. Vickery, 'Golden Age to Separate Spheres: A Review of the Categories and Chronology of Women's History', *Historical Journal*, 36 (1993), 383–414; L. Davidoff, *Worlds Between: Historical Perspectives on Gender and Class* (Cambridge, 1995), esp. ch. 8; J. Landes, *Women and the Public Sphere in the Age of the French Revolution* (Ithaca, NY, 1988); D. Castiglione and L. Sharpe (eds), *Shifting the Boundaries: Transformation of the Languages of Public and Private in the Eighteenth Century* (Exeter, 1995).

ideological debates, can all too easily be treated not just as descriptions of past states of affairs, but as terms within which historical work is organised. It is possible that public and private appealed to scholars because of broader aspects of the setting in which history is practised. Many women have been agitating to play a more prominent part in public life, while the issue of women's status as citizens is being debated in numerous parts of the world. At the same time, the relationships between public and private life, for example in relation to state intervention, have become hot political topics. This is partly because of intense conflicts over child abuse, abortion, reproductive technologies, arranged marriages and genital mutilation, for instance, in which feminist scholars have been active. So, perhaps it was overdetermined that the public/private distinction would become important for scholars concerned with gender since it could be taken to mediate such a wide range of relevant issues.

There are other topics that have become central to historical work on gender and on the sexes: birth control, abortion, adultery, disease and especially mental illness, and divorce. They appear to go to the very heart of gender and of the institutions, such as the family, the state, and medicine, which manage it in most modern societies.[47] And I say 'modern' advisedly because much of the pioneering work in these areas concerned the later nineteenth and twentieth centuries. Naturally other central topics include economic phenomena, such as patterns of employment, but it is noticeable that in a good deal of so-called cutting-edge work, economic history has been seen as marginal.[48] This is certainly a mistake, and the phenomenon is not confined to gender but is a feature of the discipline of history more generally.[49]

If new fields quickly fall into established patterns, they also bring innovations. One that is particularly striking in gender history is the range of sources. It is true that most historians prefer to concentrate on a limited number of types of evidence, but, if we take gender history as a field, the diverse materials upon which it draws is striking, and perhaps derives from

[47] For example J. Lewis, *The Politics of Motherhood: Child and Maternal Welfare in England, 1900–1939* (London, 1982); A. McLaren, *Birth Control in Nineteenth-century England* (London, 1978); E. Showalter, *The Female Malady: Women, Madness and English Culture, 1830–1980* (New York, 1985); L. Stone, *Road to Divorce: England, 1530–1987* (Oxford, 1990); B. Brookes, *Abortion in England, 1900–1967* (London, 1988).

[48] There are exceptions, the distinguished work of Sonya Rose, trained as a sociologist, would be a case in point: *Limited Livelihoods: Gender and Class in Nineteenth-century England* (Berkeley and Los Angeles, CA, 1992). See also *Adapting to Capitalism: Working Women in the English Economy, 1700–1850* (London, 1996) by Pamela Sharpe, trained as both an economic historian and a demographer.

[49] I draw attention to the detrimental effects of this change in perceptions of the significance of economic history in *History in Practice* (London, 2000), esp. pp. 202–3.

the very nature of gender itself as pervasive and insinuating. This range of materials is linked with the range of topics — cross-dressing, consumption, music, gestures, kissing, eating, for example — now studied as part of a cultural history that often has holistic aspirations.[50] These topics were hardly virgin territory for historians, but when we place them under gender as an umbrella the kind of historical vision that results is indeed strikingly capacious.

Conclusions

In pulling the threads of this essay together, I want to insist on the importance of giving 'gender' its status as a complex concept, an abstract analytical term. Concepts are human constructions, so, in making the obvious point that gender is a concept, we remember that it was invented for doing certain kinds of business at particular times and places. A sharp reminder of this comes from scholars in France, many of whom remain suspicious of the term as an Anglo-American imposition, a form of intellectual imperialism. Gender was originally used in relation to grammar. The agents of its extension were initially psychologists and anthropologists, and in its early uses it carried a social constructionist claim. Women, as Simone de Beauvoir famously said, are made and not born; that is, the possession of female genitals does not make one a woman.[51] Womanhood is a cultural phenomenon that occurs through social processes; gender is the name we give to, as it were, the whole system, to the ways in which masculinity and femininity work. Gender, then, is an idea that is used to refer to and to analyse a wide range of phenomena that are of central importance for all historians. This is because gender necessarily touches everyone. Let us be clear, however, about what such a claim does and does not involve.

---

[50] For example V. Hotchkiss, *Clothes Make the Man: Female Cross-dressing in Medieval Europe* (New York, 1996); M. Garber, *Vested Interests: Cross-dressing and Cultural Anxiety* (London, 1992); V. de Grazia and E. Furlough (eds), *The Sex of Things: Gender and Consumption in Historical Perspective* (Berkeley, Los Angeles, CA, and London, 1996); R. Leppert, *Music and Image: Domesticity, Ideology and Socio-cultural Formation in Eighteenth-century England* (Cambridge, 1988); J. Bremmer and H. Roodenburg, *A Cultural History of Gesture* (Cambridge, 1991), ch. 9 (on the kiss) and ch. 10 (on gesture and masculinity); C. Walker Bynum, *Holy Feast and Holy Fast: The Religious Significance of Food to Medieval Women* (Berkeley, CA, 1987).
[51] S. de Beauvoir, *The Second Sex* (London, 1953, first published in French, Paris, 1949); E. Fallaize (ed.), *Simone de Beauvoir: A Critical Reader* (London, 1998). De Beauvoir has been a highly influential figure for feminists, perhaps because of her emphasis on the fabrication of gender roles. Cross-dressing is a topic that has allowed historians to explore the fluidity of such roles and hence to demonstrate their constructed nature. See the works cited in n. 50.

It touches everyone because it is among the most fundamental means
through which identity is established, selves constructed and relationships
conducted. It does not follow that all historians should be preoccupied with
or even use this concept, although it is extraordinarily insidious and we are
all implicated by it. Gender manifests itself unevenly across a society and
across time; it is obvious that within the family, for example, in notions of
fatherhood and motherhood and of marital relations, it is central.

It is worth insisting on the conceptual status of gender for another reason.
Some intellectual traditions, especially those in the English-speaking world,
tend to privilege concreteness and to be suspicious of what is abstract. What
is the material referent of gender? Perhaps it is because it does not have one
that some historians insist on women's history as a more useful rubric. But
the elusive and abstract nature of gender has to be embraced not denied. It
constitutes a huge intellectual challenge for historians used to adopting a
common-sense approach to the past that trades on a rather crude notion of
what can be directly recorded. The Anglo-Saxon preference for straightforward 'facts' makes 'essentialism' a problem. We tend to want gender to be
something tangible, material or object-like, for there to be, in other words,
certain essential, definitive qualities of women and men, womanhood and
manhood, femininity and masculinity. One of the greatest achievements of
recent historical work on gender is to consistently call essentialism into
question. This has entailed research into the intricacies of both lived and
conceptualised gender, if I can put it this way. Yet, much remains to be done
in integrating these insights into historical practice.

Furthermore, there is still what can be called the 'and' problem to be
tackled. I refer to the tendency simply to place terms in apposition — gender
and history, gender and anthropology, gender and crime, gender and the
state — as if the mere juxtaposition were doing the work. 'And' is a weak
form of association; it suggests that the precise relationships between the two
terms are underconceptualised. In fact, 'gender and ...' is rather mechanistic.
Thus, it is not surprising that the most articulate, creative and far-sighted
historians of gender want to stress its capacity to be a transformative
framework. Perhaps this is most neatly summed up by the increasing use of
gender as a verb. When we say that a phenomenon is gendered, two
suggestions are being made. The first is that human activities are constantly
and actively suffused with ideas and practices that relate to the differences
between masculinity and femininity. The second is that historians'
perceptions are changing as a result of studying such processes. I have
indicated that there are a number of ways in which we can understand this
potential for transformation: through political movements such as feminism,

through fresh theoretical and methodological perspectives, through revisions of major events and of periods, through the engagement with unfamiliar sources.

It would be neither possible nor appropriate to present a summary of new findings or research in an essay of this kind. The work that is now being done on gender is so diverse with respect to time, place, themes and sources, that it would be impossible to do it justice. Necessarily there is no consensus on central matters pertaining to gender in the past. For example, some historians find 'patriarchy' a useful term, whereas I am sceptical about its usefulness.[52] The sources that bear on this subject are both vast and diverse; accordingly, historians have to make difficult decisions about the level at which their research should be pitched. As I have tried to indicate, it is possible to treat gender as a micro-phenomenon, pursued largely through local records, but it is also possible to think in terms of slow change and persistent continuities when drawing on sources that reveal enduring mentalities and persistent inequalities.[53] Thus, gender history includes extremely carefully focused studies, works that cover the *longue durée*, and much else besides. The nature and pace of shifts that relate to gender remain a matter of debate. Some historians have been keen to identify periods of crisis with respect to masculinity and femininity, although, by the very nature of the subject, it is difficult to be convincing on the point.[54] There are two reasons why the crisis approach generally lacks plausibility in my view. First, the phenomena that make up 'gender' are varied, uneven and slow moving, whereas the very notion of crisis implies a crisp, widespread and general sense of alarm. Second, since gender implicates everyone and is used as a means of exploring so many other concerns, the sense of 'crisis' around masculinity and femininity occurs fairly frequently in relation to one issue or another. Subjectively, then, perceived crises around gender seem to be sufficiently common that claims about general ones lack analytical bite.

Throughout the essay I have emphasised the complexities of gender history as an enterprise. For example, its origins lie both in feminism and in

---

[52] For example A. Fletcher, *Gender, Sex and Subordination in England 1500–1800* (New Haven, CT, and London, 1995), esp. introduction and ch. 20. L. Gowing, *Domestic Dangers: Women, Words, and Sex in Early Modern London* (Oxford, 1996) is insightful on received approaches to patriarchy.

[53] Discussions on the question of continuities may be found in P. Sharpe (ed.), *Women's Work: The English Experience 1650–1914* (London, 1998), section 1.

[54] For an illuminating discussion of one particular 'crisis', see L. Roper, *Oedipus and the Devil: Witchcraft, Sexuality and Religion in Early Modern Europe* (London, 1994), ch. 2, 'Was there a Crisis in Gender Relations in Sixteenth-century Germany?' A different approach to gender and periods of crisis may be found in K. Honeyman and J. Goodman, 'Women's Work, Gender Conflict, and Labour Movements in Europe, 1500–1900', *Economic History Review*, 44 (1991), 608–28.

historical scholarship. It is intellectually distinct from while unavoidably bound up with women's history. It has had to engage with theoretical questions, but individual scholars have done so to markedly different degrees, and there is absolutely no consensus on which perspectives are most generative for the field. Generally speaking, historians of gender have neither slavishly followed particular theories, nor have they made contributions that are primarily theoretical — in these respects they are no different from other historians. Although the very notion of gender is viewed differently in different countries, scholarship has over the last few years become an increasingly international phenomenon just as issues such as women's rights have become 'globalised'. Britain has a distinguished record in gender history, although there does not seem to me to be a 'British' take on the subject. It is inevitable that there have been particularly extensive contacts between British and North American historians, but, as a journal such as *Gender and History* testifies, there are sustained efforts to make the field genuinely international.

I have heard one distinguished historian say that she was 'bored' with gender. It may be that, as a relatively new concern for professional historians, it became modish, part of a litany built around the holy trinity of class, race and gender. As such it may have appeared tiresome, a ritualistic gesture to political correctness. But it is not a phenomenon historians can afford to ignore — we do not have the option of being bored by the very nature of humanity. Human beings come in two basic forms, male and female; societies work with those forms and give them meanings in highly elaborate ways that lie at the core of both the past and our understanding of it. Gender is central to different parts of history in different ways, but the existence of this form of social difference, and of the structures that are built around it, is inescapable. Since it will never go away, historians had better make sure they can handle it — over the last twenty years a promising start has been made.

Note.   Like so many people interested in gender, I owe a special debt to Leonore Davidoff, to whom this essay is affectionately dedicated. I have enjoyed the benefits of her wisdom, support and stimulating company for more than two decades now, for which I remain deeply grateful.

CHAPTER SIX

Population History

E. A. WRIGLEY

If the British Academy had been founded two centuries ago rather than in 1902 it would have been abundantly clear that any survey of population history over the lifetime of the Academy should begin with the writings of Malthus. Even in a survey confined to the twentieth century it makes good sense to set the scene by referring to the questions which he brought into prominence since his analysis of the nature of the mutual interdependence of the economic, social, and demographic characteristics of societies, whether accepted or dismissed, has continued to provide the background to much discussion throughout the whole period since the publication of the *Essay on Population*.[1]

The Malthusian legacy

In considering Malthus's work it is essential at the outset to take into account a point which is too often ignored or inadequately acknowledged. The world which Malthus discussed was a pre-industrial world.[2] His writings therefore have far more relevance for an historian concerned with the medieval or early modern period than for an historian of, say, the twentieth century. The reason is simple. Malthus advanced two 'postulata': that food is necessary for life and that the 'passion between the sexes' could be regarded as a constant. He further argued that the ability of a society to increase its supply of food was at best restricted to the equivalent of an arithmetic progression whereas, given his second postulate, which implied relatively high and

[1] T. R. Malthus, *An Essay on the Principle of Population* (London, 1798).

[2] In common with the other classical economists, notably Adam Smith and David Ricardo, Malthus envisaged the future path of economic growth as more likely to be asymptotic than exponential. Therefore when speculating about the future he assumed that the constraints which had characterised societies in the past would continue to be experienced and might well become more acute.

invariant fertility, an unchecked population would rise by geometric
progression. However small the initial population and however abundant
the initial resources of land, this must eventually give rise to a tension
between production and reproduction which would rein in the growth of
population, probably through heightened mortality and by the agency of
famine, disease, or war.[3]

This characterisation of Malthus's views, though only marginally unfair
to the position which he adopted in the first *Essay*, is a caricature of his
understanding of the question in later years when he was far better informed,
but it is immediately clear both why his 'model' of the relationship between
production and reproduction is relevant to any study of traditional societies
and why it is largely irrelevant to the world that came into being in the wake
of the industrial revolution. The maximum rate at which human populations
can grow is quite modest. In the later twentieth century there have been some
instances of national populations growing by 3 per cent per annum or more.
These are countries in which fertility has remained very high but mortality
has fallen to levels not far short of those prevailing in the wealthy West.
Such rates of growth are, in general, a recent phenomenon. Historically, rates
of growth as high as 1 per cent per annum were highly unusual except where,
as in colonial North America, land was abundant and sparse settlement kept
mortality relatively low.[4] Before the industrial revolution, however, even
such modest rates of growth were substantially higher than their economic
equivalents. Hence the tension which caught Malthus's eye. After the industrial revolution, in contrast, production could easily outstrip reproduction.
Rates of growth in gross national product in excess of 2 per cent per annum
became commonplace in due course; and in some countries, such as Japan
in most of the second half of the twentieth century or the Asian 'tiger' economies more recently, rates in excess of 5 per cent per annum have been
sustained over substantial periods of time.

The tension which was the starting point for Malthus's analysis therefore
disappeared. Indeed the tension was, so to speak, reversed. Whereas he had
assumed that increasing prosperity, *ceteris paribus*, must lead to higher rates

---

[3] Malthus, *Essay on Population*, ch. 5.

[4] In colonial North America the population roughly doubled in each generation from natural increase
for the first century and a half of settlement. This was known to Malthus and it appears that the
contrast between rates of growth in the English settlements in North America and those in England
itself greatly influenced his thinking.

The certainty that average growth rates were extremely low for the great bulk of human history
comes home forcibly when it is considered that a rate of growth as low as one-tenth of 1 per cent per
annum implies that a population will grow almost 22,000-fold over a period of time as brief as
10,000 years.

of population growth by causing a fall in death rates and, in most instances, a rise in fertility, the reverse proved to be the case in the new world brought into being by the industrial revolution. The advent of effective and affordable methods of controlling fertility both within and outside marriage caused increasing prosperity to become associated with falling fertility and declining growth rates, to the point where very few wealthy countries today have sufficiently high levels of fertility to ensure that each new generation will be equal in size to its predecessor.[5] It is not uncommon for prevailing fertility rates to suggest that, ignoring the distorting effect of immigration or emigration, successive generations will shrink by as much as one-third: Italy, Spain, Germany, and Japan, for example, all fall into this category. Over a century such populations will decline by roughly 70 per cent unless replenished by immigration.

Population characteristics are of fundamental importance to the social and economic life of societies in all periods and places, including those of the post-industrial revolution world. In Victorian times, for example, such topics as the struggle to make cities safe to live in, or the immense population flows across the North Atlantic from Europe to the United States (and on a lesser scale to Canada, Latin America, and Australasia) were among the most significant of the issues of the day. In the later twentieth century both the hazards of surging population growth in south Asia and sub-Saharan Africa and the acute problems of the ageing of populations in western countries have caused great public concern and have produced a vast scholarly literature, to which the proliferation of journals devoted to demography bears witness.[6] In this period, too, as in the preceding century, international migration flows have produced great changes and, at times, great tensions. However, it remains the case that it has been in work on the period before the industrial revolution, an area where Malthus's writings continue to cast a long shadow, that the most exciting developments have taken place. I propose, therefore, to devote the remainder of this essay to this topic and to an issue which arises readily from

---

[5] The initial fall in fertility in most western countries was not, however, due primarily to new methods of birth control. Rather it was the combination of the practice of withdrawal and of abstention combined on occasion with procured abortion which accounted for the bulk of the fall in countries such as Britain or France until the Second World War.

[6] Leading journals such as *Population Studies* and *Population* were founded just after the Second World War. The scale of publication generally in demographic journals is illustrated graphically by the number of books, articles, etc. listed each year in *Population Index* which has aimed to cover the subject exhaustively since its first publication in 1935. In 1999, ironically the last year of its publication since electronic search facilities have undermined its *raison d'être*, a total of 4,060 publications were listed in its four quarterly issues.

it, that of the logical status of the findings of historical demography which offer some points of contrast with those of other areas of economic and social history.

The obstacles to progress: problems of stock and flow

The developments in historical demography which have transformed the study of early modern population history relate both to substantive issues and to matters of technique. As with any other subject for historical investigation, in the study of the demographic characteristics of communities in the past the nature of the sources available conditions the scope and precision of description and analysis which is feasible. All demographic statistics relate either to structure or to process or to some combination of the two. The structural characteristics of a population are revealed in sources of which the archetypal form is the census. Such sources almost invariably include data on matters such as the size of the population, its age structure, its division by sex, its occupational structure, *et sim.*, but may also include a plethora of additional information on, for example, educational attainment, religious affiliation, wealth, income, birthplace, ethnic character, or settlement size. Depending on the extent of cross-classification of the data and the degree of regional and local subdivision of the national whole, a census may provide a tolerably comprehensive and detailed picture of a population at a point in time. It will not, however, except by indirect implication, enable much to be said about process: how rapidly the population is growing, the level and trend in death rates, whether rapid urbanisation is in train, and so on.[7] To enable such issues to be addressed there must be information about flow as well as stock. In a modern state the registration of births, deaths, and marriages provides this information. Just as with the census, the information recorded in relation to each event may either be scanty or voluminous and this in turn will determine whether or not complex and sophisticated analysis of, say, fertility is possible; but the taking of censuses and the recording of vital events between them ensure that in many states today both structure and process, stock and flow, can be described and analysed. Where one type

---

[7] Much can, of course, be inferred about process from a succession of censuses which cannot be gleaned from a single census. See for example the early examination of what is possible using the census as a source in United Nations, Department of Social Affairs, Population Division, Population Studies no. 7, *Methods of Using Census Statistics for the Calculation of Life Tables and other Demographic Measures, with Application to the Population of Brazil* (New York, 1949). Even in the case of a single census, the relative size of successive age groups may provide a clue to recent growth rates.

of source is missing, and *a fortiori* where both are missing, the range and precision of analysis which is possible is greatly reduced, sometimes to the point where research is incapable of yielding anything of significance.[8]

The study of pre-industrial populations did not fail to attract attention in the first half of the twentieth century.[9] But it did not seem possible to come to grips effectively with many of the questions which were of greatest general interest. There appeared to be an impasse caused by the lack of appropriate source material. Accurate and comprehensive national censuses were essentially a nineteenth-century innovation. Previously, detailed and reasonably complete listings of populations were rare even for small populations and almost unknown for large areas. The size and structure of past populations could sometimes be inferred from sources created for a variety of purposes, though chiefly either for taxation or for the monitoring of religious adherence or observance, but the margin of error was normally wide. For example, a tax on households or on adult males characteristically involves both difficulties in establishing an appropriate multiplier and uncertainty about the extent of exemption or evasion. Similarly, it was only in the nineteenth century that states began to register vital events systematically, but, in contrast with the situation concerning censuses, there were extensive and sometimes relatively reliable and complete records of such events for earlier centuries. In both Catholic and Protestant Europe the parochial registration of baptisms, burials, and marriages became commonplace from Reformation times onwards. In the case of England Thomas Cromwell instituted such a system in 1538 and the Anglican church attempted with varying success to achieve a full coverage of Anglican events from then onwards.[10] Over the three centuries

---

[8] It is, of course, possible to overemphasise the distinction between censuses and vital registers as sources of information about population behaviour. If successive censuses are taken at sufficiently brief intervals the lack of a vital register is much less restrictive than where successive censuses are widely spaced. In Tokugawa Japan, for example, the *shūmon aratamechō* were compiled annually. These listings recorded everyone living in a village except infants born after New Year's Day. Assuming complete registration, and ignoring the complications introduced by migratory movement, therefore, a source of this type would enable many demographic measures to be derived which would normally only be calculable from a combination of a listing and vital registers. The possibilities offered by the *shūmon aratamechō* are vividly illustrated in T. C. Smith, *Nakahara: Family Farming and Population in a Japanese Village, 1717–1830* (Stanford, MT, 1977).

[9] The most notable publication was perhaps G. T. Griffith, *Population Problems of the Age of Malthus* (Cambridge, 1926), but see also M. C. Buer, *Health, Wealth and Population in the Early Days of the Industrial Revolution* (London, 1926) and J. Brownlee, 'The History of Birth and Death Rates in England and Wales Taken as a Whole from 1570 to the Present Time', *Public Health*, 29 (1915–16), 211–22, 228–38.

[10] The classic survey of this source is that of J. C. Cox, *The Parish Registers of England* (London, 1910), but see also D. J. Steel, *National Index of Parish Registers, vol. 1: Sources of Births, Deaths and Marriages before 1837 (I)* (London, 1968).

between 1538 and the inception of civil registration in 1837, therefore, there existed a source which offered the promise that much could be learned about demographic processes during the centuries leading up to the industrial revolution in England. But it was a promise which it proved difficult to realise.

The problem which, in the first half of the twentieth century, frustrated those interested in population change in early modern England will be obvious. The parish registers provided information about flow but there was no equivalent of the census to provide information about stock. Yet to calculate any *rate* — and all serious analysis requires a knowledge of rates — it was essential to know the population at risk as well as the frequency with which a given class of event was occurring. A doubling in the number of deaths during a half-century period, for example, is perfectly consonant with a fall in mortality if the population at risk has more than doubled. Rates are needed to remove uncertainty. The absence of censuses or their equivalent does not prohibit all types of analysis. It is no accident that there was much early work on mortality crises and their concomitants. A population may grow or decline substantially over half a century but it can change only slightly in the course of a single year. If, therefore, the number of deaths doubles between one year and the next, it is a safe inference that the underlying age-specific mortality rates, which express the phenomenon with greater precision, must also have roughly doubled. The absolute level of the rates may remain unknown but there will be no doubt that they have risen very sharply. As a result, certain short-term relationships can be studied effectively, such as that between a harvest failure and the concomitant jump in the price of food grains and any sympathetic movement in the number of deaths, or the sensitivity of marriage totals to price movements, or the strength and nature of any relationship between short-term movements in the three series of baptisms, burials, and marriages.[11] Lacking the ability to measure stock as well as flow, however, scholars were not well placed to test effectively the validity of many aspects of the model of the interrelationships between economic, social, and demographic movements which Malthus had adumbrated.

For much of the twentieth century work on the population history of pre-industrial England was constrained by the difficulties which have just been described and, perhaps paradoxically, also by a shortage of appropriate data. There was no shortage of raw data. There are about 10,000 ancient parishes in England. Many runs of registers for individual parishes are incomplete but

---

[11] See for example D. S. Thomas, *Social and Economic Aspects of Swedish Population Movements, 1750–1933* (New York, 1941), pp. 81–111.

some thousands appear to be continuous, or largely continuous, from some point in the sixteenth century onwards. Closer investigation often reveals flaws in registration but the scale of the surviving material is impressively large. Though the raw data were voluminous, however, one exercise in data assemblage dominated the field. Its existence is a tribute to the energy and breadth of interests of John Rickman under whose direction the first four censuses were conducted. (He also largely planned the fifth, that of 1841, though he died before it was taken.) When the first census was taken in 1801 he required the Poor Law officers to conduct a count of the inhabitants of each parish while at the same time enjoining each incumbent to make a return of the totals of baptisms, burials, and marriages recorded in his parish registers for every tenth year from 1700 to 1780 and for every subsequent year down to 1800. Nor did he rest content with the mass of data returned to him under this directive. As a result of a question addressed to each incumbent in 1831, by 1836 he knew the date of the earliest registers in each parish. Once more he made use of the good offices of incumbents in the subsequent census, asking every minister in parishes in which the registers began before 1600 to return the totals of events in each of the three series for three-year periods centring on 1570, 1600, 1630, 1670, 1700, and 1750, and in addition the totals for 1800. The returns which he secured on this occasion became the prime empirical basis for the bulk of the work carried out on English demographic history in the early modern period until the later decades of the twentieth century.

The returns obtained by Rickman remain of the greatest value even today. The quantity of information which he collected dwarfs any subsequent exercise, and he had a purpose in mind in imposing so much labour upon the Anglican clergymen of the day. Making a variety of assumptions about the relationship between the totals of baptisms, burials, and marriages which Rickman had assembled and the size of the population which had produced them, his successors, as part of the 1841 census exercise, made some highly influential estimates of the size of the population of England at each of the points in time for which he had secured totals of events.[12] The estimates were, and in some degree still are, influential. Despite its many virtues, however, this work did not provide a satisfactory foundation for the examination of production and reproduction in the past. Indeed, in 1970 Flinn characterised the results of Rickman's work bluntly as 'unacceptable for the purposes of modern scholarship'.[13] There were problems relating to evasion, to the

[12] *1841 Census*, Enumeration Abstract, *P.P.* 1843, XXXII, pp. 34–7.
[13] M. W. Flinn, *British Population Growth* (London, 1970), p. 20.

spread of nonconformity, to the varying frequency of defective or deficient registration in different periods, to the accuracy of the primary returns and still more of the clerks who tabulated and consolidated them, and, of course, to the fact that the returns were totals of baptisms and burials rather than births and deaths. But the fundamental difficulty lay elsewhere. In the absence of information about stock, the size of the population at risk, there was a severe limitation to what could be deduced from information about flow, the number of vital events occurring. Estimating population totals from the totals of vital events, as was done in 1841, involves circularity of argument since, in the absence of independent evidence about population size, the estimates spring directly from the assumptions made about the level of prevailing demographic rates whose denominator is population size.

Family reconstitution

The crucial advance which for the first time overcame this problem stands principally to the credit of Louis Henry. It affords a telling instance of an innovation devised to attack a particular problem proving to have applications of great importance in a very different context. Henry wished to establish a better understanding of the basic characteristics of human fecundity and fertility. He was frustrated by the fact that, in general, countries which collected full and accurate information of the type which he wanted were countries in which fertility was already heavily affected by the practice of birth control. This meant that he could not secure from them the information of greatest interest to him, while countries in which birth control was largely absent did not collect full and reliable fertility data. Henry had begun work on fertility and fecundity in the period immediately following the Second World War and by the late 1950s had discovered that he was more likely to find what he wanted by exploiting historical material than by using contemporary data. He turned first to a rich existing genealogical source for the Genevan bourgeoisie covering the period from the sixteenth century to the twentieth.[14] This study showed conclusively that data of this kind were suitable for his purpose: it also brought to light coincidentally a striking and unexpected finding — that the bourgeois families of Geneva were already controlling the size of their families by some form of effective birth control as early as the second half of the seventeenth century.[15] But it was Henry's

---

[14] L. Henry, *Anciennes familles genevoises: Etude démographique: XVIe–XXe siècles* (Paris, 1956).
[15] Henry, *Anciennes familles*, esp. pp. 75–110.

next venture into historical demography which represented the decisive breakthrough. It ensured that the Norman parish of Crulai would achieve a lasting fame. He used the information contained in the parish registers of Crulai to reconstruct the lives of the individual families resident in the village in the eighteenth century.[16] The technique which he used has come to be termed family reconstitution. Its advent transformed the possibilities open to historians of population because it made possible for the first time the calculation of accurate and detailed measures of fertility, mortality, and nuptiality in the past.

Henry's originality did not lie in defining the mechanics of family reconstitution itself. Genealogists and family historians had reconstructed the histories of individual families time out of mind, and scholars in Scandinavia had made use of family reconstitution to throw light on the demography of communities in the past from early in the twentieth century.[17] Until Henry's Crulai monograph, however, those intent on using family reconstitution lacked appropriate rules to enable them to avoid introducing bias into the measurement of demographic rates. The fundamental point is simple. Family reconstitution offers the possibility of achieving a solution to the stock and flow problem because, if, say, a family is in observation over a nine-year period during which four births take place, combining information about the period in observation with information about the number of events occurring during that period gives the equivalent of the information given by the census and the vital registration system. In the case of the latter, if 300 births occur to 1,000 married women aged 25–29 in a given year, the age-specific marital fertility rate for that age group in that year is said to be 300 per 1,000. Similarly, in the case of the former, if a group of married women in a reconstituted population live for a total of 1,000 years while aged 25–29 and produce 300 births during those years, then, too, their marital fertility in the age group 25–29 is 300 per 1,000. The reconstitution data relate to a cohort whereas rates derived from combining census and vital registration data are normally period rates, but this is a side issue without relevance to the basic point.[18]

To be able to use reconstitution data in this way with confidence, however, depends upon devising a set of rules to determine the period of time during which a given family may properly be regarded as in observation

---

[16] E. Gautier and L. Henry, *La population de Crulai paroisse normande* (Paris, 1958).

[17] K. A. Edin, 'Studier i Svensk fruktsamhetsstatistik', *Ekonomisk Tidskrift*, 9 (1915), 251–304; H. Hyrenius, *Estlandssvenskarna: Demografiska studier* (Lund, 1942).

[18] The reconstitution data are generated in cohort form but may be converted into period form without difficulty.

for the type of measurement undertaken. It would be fatal to the exercise, for example, if a family with many children were taken to be in observation for a longer period than a family, otherwise having identical characteristics, which had fewer children or vice versa. The bias-free period of observation differs for the measurement of different aspects of fertility, mortality, and nuptiality. Henry's great achievement was to have identified the nature of the problem and to have propounded a series of rules which, if observed, would result in unbiased estimates of a wide range of demographic variables.[19]

The Crulai monograph was published in 1958. The next few decades saw the publication of a flood of studies using Henry's methods. Most European countries possess parish registers whose contents are suitable to be used for family reconstitution, though from widely varying dates. Their exploitation meant that the wide diversity of the demographic regimes to be found in different countries, or in different regions within the same country, could be described for the first time. As a result the appearance of the land-scape of historical demography changed and some assumptions of long standing had to be modified or abandoned. Levels of marital fertility, for example, proved to vary substantially even though the communities in ques-tion all displayed the characteristics of 'natural' fertility (that is, there was no evidence of attempts to restrict fertility because of the growing number of living children in a family). The overall level of marital fertility in parts of Bavaria in the south of Germany, for instance, was 40 per cent higher than that in East Friesland in the north. Differences in the prevalence and length of breastfeeding proved to be especially influential in producing such large differences in marital fertility. The very high rate in parts of Bavaria was a direct consequence of the practice of weaning children at birth, a practice which also resulted in appallingly high infant death rates, in some parishes in excess of 350 per 1,000.[20]

---

[19] M. Fleury and L. Henry, *Des registres paroissiaux à l'histoire de la population: Manuel de dépouillement et d'exploitation de l'état civil ancien* (Paris, 1956). See also L. Henry, *Techniques d'analyse en démographie historique* (Paris, 1980) and M. Fleury and L. Henry, *Nouveau manuel de dépouillement et d'exploitation de l'état civil ancien*, 3rd edn (Paris, 1985). A description of the technique of family reconstitution modified to be applicable to English registers may be found in E. A. Wrigley, 'Family Reconstitution', in E. A. Wrigley (ed.), *An Introduction to English Historical Demography from the Sixteenth to the Nineteenth Century* (London, 1966), pp. 96–159.

[20] The level of I_g (an age standardised index of marital fertility) in the Bavarian villages in the period 1750–1849 was 0.95; in the East Friesland villages 0.68. J. E. Knodel, *Demographic Behaviour in the Past: A Study of Fourteen German Villages in the Eighteenth and Nineteenth Centuries* (Cambridge, 1988), tab. 10.1, p. 250. Infant mortality data for the same settlements may be found in ibid., tab. 3.1, p. 44.

The new demographic landscape

The most striking feature of the west European society brought to light by family reconstitution was its distinctive marriage system. Elsewhere marriage for women came early in life and was virtually universal. Soon after attaining sexual maturity most women married unless seriously handicapped in body or mind. In England, and in much of the rest of western Europe, however, for many centuries before the industrial revolution marriage was late for both sexes. In England the average age at first marriage for women varied between about 24 and 27 during the early modern period. Moreover, a substantial fraction of each new generation of men and women never married. In combination these two attributes kept overall fertility relatively low. Furthermore, since the decision to marry or to refrain from marriage was strongly influenced by economic circumstance, and since both age at marriage and the proportion never marrying varied over time, this feature of west European demography implied the possibility of a very different relationship between economic and demographic fluctuations from that prevailing elsewhere.[21]

Perhaps the most influential single article dealing with population history to be published during the post-war surge of interest in the subject was that by Hajnal on the distinctiveness of European marriage patterns.[22] Its appearance was happily timed in relation to the development of the technique of family reconstitution since it suggested a host of questions about European populations in the past whose potential significance was clarified by Hajnal's work, but which could not be pursued effectively without much new, reliable empirical data about nuptiality. Even earlier Habakkuk had shown great percipience in pointing to the possibility that fertility rather than mortality might have engendered the sudden acceleration of population growth in England in the middle and later decades of the eighteenth century, though he lacked the information to decide the issue one way or the other.[23] The flow of publications thereafter steadily gathered momentum. A range of different aspects of the relationship between social, economic, and demographic change was explored both empirically and theoretically in the writings of scholars such as Glass, Ohlin, Schofield, Eversley, Kussmaul, Smith, Laslett and Mendels during the quarter-century

---

[21] E. A. Wrigley and R. S. Schofield, *The Population History of England 1541–1871: A Reconstruction* (London, 1981), ch. 10.

[22] J. Hajnal, 'European Marriage Patterns in Perspective', in D. V. Glass and D. E. C. Eversley (eds), *Population in History: Essays in Historical Demography* (London, 1965), pp. 101–43.

[23] H. J. Habbakuk, 'English Population in the Eighteenth Century', *Economic History Review*, 2, 6 (1953), 117–33. Another valuable publication of this period is D. E. C. Eversley, *Social Theories of Fertility and the Malthusian Debate* (Oxford, 1959).

following the publication of Hajnal's article.[24] While almost every possible aspect of the relationship was explored, it was common for marriage to command the centre of the stage. Its sensitivity to economic and social influences attracted much attention and brought to light many features of early modern society which have proved instructive or suggestive.

Reconstitution studies also led, of course, to the reconsideration of many other aspects of the received wisdom about the demography of pre-industrial societies. For example, new and detailed information about their mortality characteristics has called in question the assumption that, in general, higher social status and higher income were associated with lower mortality. This is especially the case in relation to infant mortality. Infant mortality, like the level of marital fertility, was strongly influenced by breastfeeding customs, and, since in some communities babies were breastfed much longer by those in the lower echelons of society than by the elite, infant mortality was sometimes considerably less severe among the former than among the latter.

Family reconstitution provides remarkably detailed information about populations in the past, often fuller than the comparable data for more recent times. For example, since the Registrar-General collected only rather sparse information about fertility until well into the twentieth century, more is now known about some aspects of fertility in the parish register period

[24] Glass's career spanned the two halves of the century. Before the war he had published several articles on historical topics, as for example D. V. Glass, 'Marriage Frequency and Economic Fluctuations in England and Wales, 1851 to 1934', in L. Hogben (ed.), *Political Arithmetic* (London, 1938), pp. 251–88, but he remained prolific in the third quarter of the century publishing both intriguing notes such as D. V. Glass, 'Notes on the Demography of London at the End of the Seventeenth Century', in D. V. Glass and R. Revelle (eds), *Population and Social Change* (London, 1972), pp. 275–85 and undertaking extensive and valuable reviews of major topics as for example in D. V. Glass, *Numbering the People: The Eighteenth Century Population Controversy and the Development of Census and Vital Statistics in Britain* (Farnborough, 1973). A flavour of the work of other scholars published in the period is given by the following: P. Laslett and R. Wall (eds), *Household and Family in Past Time* (Cambridge, 1972); P. Laslett, *Family Life and Illicit Love in Earlier Generations* (Cambridge, 1977); R. S. Schofield, 'The Relationship between Demographic Structure and Environment in Pre-industrial Western Europe', in W. Conze (ed.), *Sozialgeschichte der Familie in der Neuzeit Europas* (Stuttgart, 1976), pp. 147–60; R. M. Smith, 'Fertility, Economy and Household Formation in England over Three Centuries', *Population and Development Review*, 7 (1981), 595–622; A. Kussmaul, A *General View of the Rural Economy of England 1538–1840* (Cambridge, 1990); H. J. Habakkuk, *Population Growth and Economic Development since 1750* (Leicester, 1971); F. Mendels, 'Proto-industrialisation: The First Phase of the Industrialisation Process', *Journal of Economic History*, 32 (1972), 241–61; P. G. Ohlin, *The Positive and Preventive Check: A Study of the Rate of Growth of Pre-industrial Populations* (New York, 1981).

The authors listed in the previous paragraph all published in English. A list which included leading scholars of comparable distinction publishing in French, German, Italian, Spanish, Dutch, and Scandinavian would, of course, be many times as long. An important general survey of work in historical demography in the past half century may be found in O. Saito, 'Historical Demography: Achievements and Prospects', *Population Studies*, 50 (1996), 537–53.

(1538–1837) than is known about the first century during which the state recorded vital events and conducted censuses.[25] But, for all its attractions, family reconstitution is not without serious limitations. If carried out by hand, it is inordinately time consuming. Because of this problem, and even with the resources available to a substantial research institute, the Institut National d'Etudes Démographiques in Paris drew a sample of only one-tenth of one per cent of the 40,000 French rural parishes when embarking, in 1959, on its study, using family reconstitution, of the historical demography of France in the eighteenth century. Electronic aids can greatly reduce the time necessary for data input, and all subsequent record linkage and statistical analysis can now be carried out by program, but it remains unrealistic to attempt to cover large populations.[26]

Moreover, parish registration was instituted for a different purpose from that which lay behind the creation of state registration systems in the nineteenth century. As a result, the available data often differ from those which would have been most helpful to historical demography. In England, for example, the parish registers record the dates of baptisms and burials but seldom add the associated dates of birth and death. During the seventeenth and eighteenth centuries the conventional delay between birth and baptism grew wider and wider, increasing the danger that the birth of a baby who died young might escape the registration system. The rise of nonconformity tended to reduce the proportion of the population covered by the Anglican registers. In addition, until the position was regularised by the passage of Rose's Act, which came into force only at the beginning of 1813, the degree of detail recorded when an entry was made in a parish register varied greatly from place to place, and in the same place over time.[27] These considerations severely limit

[25] In particular the fact that it was not until 1938 that such details as the age of the mother and the parity of the child were recorded severely limits the analysis of fertility decline during the period when family limitation became widespread whereas, of course, age-specific marital fertility rates are readily calculable from family reconstitution data. Similarly, although infant mortality rates are available from the inception of civil registration in 1837, it is rarely possible to secure a detailed breakdown of deaths within the first year of life from the Registrar-General's *Annual Reports* in the nineteenth century and therefore changes, for instance, in the level of neonatal mortality are not so readily identified as is possible using family reconstitution data for the early modern period. Both these and many other related issues are considered in R. Woods, *The Demography of Victorian England and Wales* (Cambridge, 2000), esp. pp. 110–40 and 247–95.

[26] The progress which has been made in transferring the bulk of the burden from manual to electronic methods in family reconstitution is described in R. Schofield, 'Automated Family Reconstitution: The Cambridge Experience', *Historical Methods*, 25 (1992), 75–9.

[27] It should be noted that, although it was not until the coming into force of Rose's Act that pro forma registration of baptisms and burials was prescribed, Hardwicke's Act of 1753 had earlier secured such treatment for marriages.

the number of registers which provide sufficiently detailed information to permit reconstitution to be undertaken successfully. There is also the general problem that reconstitution provides much more information about those who were born in a parish and remained there for the rest of their lives than it does about those who left the parish as emigrants or moved into it as immigrants. In some continental regions where a large fraction of the population was immobile, this feature of family reconstitution as a technique causes little difficulty since the bulk of the population is covered, but, in England where high levels of local migration were widespread, it constitutes a significant problem both in the sense that it is necessary to try to establish the scale and nature of demographic differences between the mobile and the immobile, and in the sense that because the ratio of metal to ore, so to speak, is low, the effort needed to produce a given quantity of useful information is high.[28]

Complementary technical advances

A quarter of a century after the study of population history was revolutionised by the advent of family reconstitution, another technique was developed which also overcame the problem posed by the absence of a source of information about stock to balance the information about flow afforded by parochial registration. This technique was initially termed back projection and was used to produce the bulk of the material published in the *Population History of England 1541–1871*. It was developed by Oeppen and represents an attempt to improve on the method of inverse projection devised by Lee.[29] Subsequently Oeppen has developed further the method embodied in back projection to produce the system known as generalised inverse projection (GIP).[30] The technique is complex and does not lend itself to brief summary. It is enough to note that its strengths and limitations are generally

---

[28] A discussion of the nature and strength of the various reservations which have been expressed about the fallibility of the technique of family reconstitution and the problems posed by the deficiencies of parochial registration may be found in E. A. Wrigley, 'How Reliable is our Knowledge of the Demographic Characteristics of the English Population in the Early Modern Period?', *Historical Journal*, 40 (1997), 571–95.

[29] R. D. Lee, 'Estimating Series of Vital Rates and Age Structures from Baptisms and Burials: A New Technique with Applications to Pre-industrial England', *Population Studies*, 28 (1974), 495–512.

[30] J. Oeppen, 'Back Projection and Inverse Projection: Members of a Wider Class of Constrained Projection Models', *Population Studies*, 47 (1993), 245–67 and 'Generalized Inverse Projection', in D. S. Reher and R. S. Schofield (eds), *Old and New Methods in Historical Demography* (Oxford, 1993), pp. 29–39.

the opposites of those of family reconstitution to which, therefore, it is complementary. The data needed for GIP are not laborious to secure. Annual totals of births and deaths stretching backwards from an endpoint for which there is a reliable census will suffice, though additional information, such as, for example, a population count at some intermediate point to 'anchor' the exercise is helpful. One of the most valuable features of GIP is that all the estimates of demographic variables which it generates are constrained to be mutually consistent. GIP produces estimates of population totals at any required dates, of fertility in the form of gross reproduction rates, of mortality in the form of estimates of expectation of life at birth (and related sets of the age-specific death rates), and of net migration totals. When combined with other information, further aspects of demographic experience may also be covered, such as the proportion of a given cohort which never married. Compared to family reconstitution, therefore, generalised inverse projection produces only a rather limited range of relatively crude demographic measures. Where both techniques can be applied to the same population, however, there are few aspects of population behaviour which cannot be studied effectively.[31]

As a result of the technical advances of the last forty years, the date which divides the demographic dark ages from the period of relatively complete knowledge has been pushed back substantially. Whereas it was once the inception of state registration of vital events combined with the taking of a decennial census which marked the beginning of the age of demographic enlightenment, it is now the date from which it is possible to construct a tolerably reliable annual series of births (baptisms) and deaths (burials). This will permit the use of GIP, though the requirements for the successful prosecution of family reconstitution work are more searching. In the case of England the date in question, as we have already noted, is 1538. The comparable date in other European countries varies widely not only because parochial registration began at varying dates but also because registration was sometimes seriously incomplete for many decades after its start. For example, in many Catholic countries the burials of children who died before they were of age to receive communion were not entered in the register in the early decades of registration.[32]

---

[31] Unless the population in question is small, however, it will normally be possible to reconstitute only a fraction of the whole population since family reconstitution is so labour intensive.

[32] In France, for example, it was very common for the poor registration of the burial of young children to continue until the early decades of the eighteenth century, though in particular parishes satisfactory coverage may date back well into the seventeenth century. Fleury and Henry, *Nouveau manuel*, p. 18.

Malthus reconsidered

Was Malthus right about England in the early modern period? It is now feasible to give a much more confident answer to this question than would have been possible half a century ago, still more than was possible when the *Essay on Population* was published. His fundamental proposition, that there was a necessary tension between production and reproduction, seems just. It has proved, indeed, to have a remarkable resonance extending well beyond the study of human society: reading Malthus's essay appears to have been the event which suggested to Darwin in the late 1830s the mechanism which would drive the process of natural selection. Since it is now possible to trace the size of the English population between the sixteenth and nineteenth centuries, and since evidence about the course of real wages over the same period also exists, the degree to which living standards were affected by the pace of population growth can be assessed. Figure 1 demonstrates the closeness of the relationship and illustrates its nature.

   In periods when population growth was rapid, real wages came under severe pressure. Broadly speaking, the experience of the early modern period suggests that the economy was able to sustain a rate of population growth of about 0.5 per cent per annum without prejudicing living standards, but that when the growth rate exceeded this level living standards were depressed. Symmetrically, when population grew slowly or declined, as in the later seventeenth century, real incomes rose. The closeness of the link between growth rates and real wages over a period of a quarter of a millennium from *c.* 1550 to *c.* 1800 is striking but it is equally striking that, just at the time when Malthus was drawing attention to the importance of the link between these two variables, it was on the point of disappearing. The nineteenth century saw a continued rapid growth of population which would, if the old relationship had maintained, have caused a sharp fall in real wages, but, in the event, the nineteenth century proved to be a period of improvement in living standards, hesitant initially but marked during the second half of the century. The nature, timing, cause, and even the reality of the 'industrial revolution' has been the subject of much discussion in recent decades. If it were adequate to define it simply as the point in time at which the inverse relationship between population growth rates and real incomes disappeared definitively, the evidence of Figure 1 might seem to leave no room for doubt either about its reality or its timing. It is, of course, unwarranted to claim that the link between living standards and population growth rates depicted in Figure 1 held true for all pre-industrial societies. There are very few periods or places for which the data exist to permit an exercise of the type

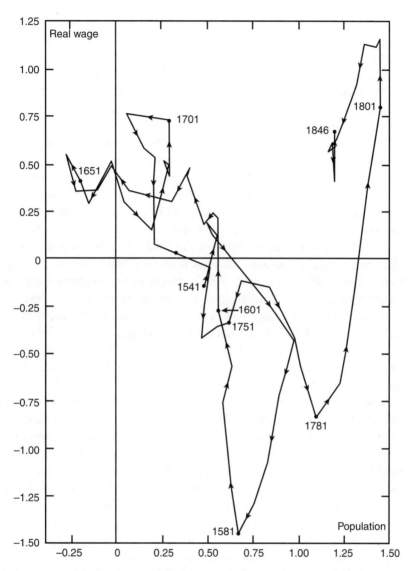

Figure 1. Annual percentage rates of growth of population and of a real-wage index.
Note: The rates of growth of the two variables are measured over a 25-year period extending forward in time from a given date shown in the graph.
Source: Wrigley and Schofield, *Population History of England*, fig. 10.4, p. 410.

summarised in Figure 1 but studies which have focused on this issue have often come to a similar conclusion, though the empirical evidence precludes the same type of quantitative analysis.[33]

Other aspects of Malthus's initial treatment of the interplay of economic and demographic change appear less prescient when confronted with the evidence provided by the recent advances in the techniques used in population history. In particular it is notable in the case of England that his supposition that deteriorating economic circumstances would be accompanied by worsening mortality is not borne out by the available evidence. During the later seventeenth and early eighteenth centuries real incomes were rising strongly in England. The average craftsman or labourer was substantially better off than his predecessors in the later sixteenth century, yet expectation of life at birth was at a nadir of about 33 years in the later decades of the seventeenth century though it had been substantially higher a century earlier and was also significantly higher a century later (in the range between 36 and 40 years in both cases), though living standards were then more depressed.[34] It was fertility rather than mortality which was responsive to economic signals. Fertility rose when prospects improved and declined when real incomes fell. This did not occur, however, because the fertility of married women changed significantly but because when times improved nuptiality increased either because marriage age fell or because fewer women remained unmarried or from a combination of the two.[35]

That changes in nuptiality could have a major impact on fertility is easy to exemplify for early modern England. Assuming that, in this period, the proportion of women never marrying varied between 5 and 20 per cent and that age at marriage varied between 23 and 26 years, then, at the age-specific marital fertility rates typical of the period and with constant adult mortality, the number of children born to an average woman might be 50 per cent higher in a period of high nuptiality than at the other extreme.[36] If, therefore, nuptiality was responsive to economic 'signals' the leverage which nuptiality

---

[33] As for example in three early classic examinations of this and cognate issues: P. Goubert, *Beauvais et le Beauvaisis de 1600 à 1730*, 2 vols (Paris, 1960); E. Le Roy Ladurie, *Les paysans de Languedoc*, 2 vols (Paris, 1966); B. H. Slicher van Bath, *Een samenleving onder spanning: geschiedenis van het platteland in Overijssel* (Assen, 1957).

[34] Wrigley and Schofield, *Population History of England*, fig. 10.5, p. 414.

[35] Ibid., pp. 417–35.

[36] This calculation was based on the marital fertility rates given in E. A. Wrigley, R. S. Davies, J. E. Oeppen and R. S. Schofield, *English Population History from Family Reconstitution 1580–1837* (Cambridge, 1997), tab. 7.1, p. 355 and the adult mortality rates to be found in ibid., tab. 6.20, p. 291. In the latter case adult mortality was taken as the mean of the rates prevailing in 1640–89 and 1750–1809. These rates are close to those in the Princeton tables for model North level 6, and the female rates in this table were used for the mortality element in the calculation.

could exert upon growth rates was very great. There is strong evidence both that the link existed and that it had a dominant effect upon growth rates.[37] In the later seventeenth century the intrinsic growth rate of the English population hovered close to zero. In the early decades of the nineteenth century it had risen to a peak of 1.5 per cent per annum, an exceptionally high rate for any population in a long settled country in the period before the great fall in death rates consequent upon the better nutrition, improved sanitary and public health facilities, and medical advances of the later nineteenth and twentieth centuries. Approximately three-quarters of the acceleration which occurred is attributable to higher fertility rather than lower mortality and the great bulk of the fertility rise was a consequence of the increase in nuptiality rather than a rise in marital or extra-marital fertility.[38]

Few would deny the fundamental importance of a knowledge of their demographic attributes to the understanding of the functioning of societies in the past. The tension between production and reproduction conditioned much of social and economic life in all organic societies, those, that is, where the land provided almost all the material needs of the population and where, therefore, the fact that the productivity of the land could only be raised slowly and uncertainly necessarily caused such a tension to exist. But, though no society could escape this tension, both the nature and the degree of tension varied widely. Early modern England was relatively fortunate in this regard. The country stood much less close to the Malthusian precipice than many others. The last occasion on which a poor harvest and a consequent rise in grain prices produced a significant parallel rise in mortality on a national scale was in 1596–7. England escaped the heavy famine mortalities of the 1690s which caused grievous suffering in countries as close as France and Scotland.[39] Further afield on the continent severe famine mortality

---

[37] The link is described in Wrigley and Schofield, *Population History of England*, tab. 7.29, p. 267 and accompanying text. It should be noted that the apparent time-lag between economic 'signal' and demographic 'response' has attracted much attention. The issues involved are complex and defy brief summary. See Wrigley and Schofield, *Population History of England*, paperback edn (Cambridge, 1989), introductory note, pp. xix–xxx for a description of the views of the chief protagonists and for a discussion of the merits of the various positions adopted.

[38] There is a general discussion of this range of issues in E. A. Wrigley, 'The Growth of Population in Eighteenth-century England: A Conundrum Resolved', *Past and Present*, 98 (1983), 121–50.

[39] See for example the description of the crisis of 1693–4 in the Beauvaisis whose characteristics led Goubert to remark: 'l'identité de la crise céréaliére et de la crise démographique est absolue'. Goubert, *Beauvais et le Beauvaisis, I*, p. 52. His discussion of the general question of mortality crises of the classic kind associated with harvest failure may be found in ibid., pp. 45–59. For Scotland, see M. Flinn (ed.), *Scottish Population History from the 17th Century to the 1930s* (Cambridge, 1977), pp. 164–85 and R. E. Tyson, 'Famine in Aberdeenshire, 1695–1699: The Anatomy of a Crisis' in D. Stevenson (ed.), *From Lairds to Louns: Country and Burgh Life in Aberdeen, 1600–1800* (Aberdeen, 1986), pp. 32–51.

remained a threat until much later. There were serious famines in Scandinavia at intervals during the eighteenth century and the problem extended into the early years of the nineteenth century.[40] In Finland the last such episode occurred as late as 1868 and was notably severe.[41] And no one living in the British Isles needs to be reminded that Ireland, with a population of about eight millions, suffered approximately one million additional deaths from starvation and related diseases in the potato famine of the later 1840s and lost a further one million to emigration during the same period.[42]

The fact that the English economy had developed to the point where famine had ceased to be a major threat before the end of the sixteenth century is a tribute to its growing productivity and sophistication, but it did not imply that the feedback between economic and demographic trends was of lesser importance than elsewhere. Attention has already been drawn to the close linkage of population growth rates and the living standards of the mass of the population. Many other comparable linkages existed: those between economic growth, urbanisation, migratory movements, and increasing mortality afford another instance of the same phenomenon, for example.

The logical status of the findings of historical demography

In conclusion, it may prove of interest to develop further a point made *en passant* earlier in this essay. Because of the immense quantity of relevant data contained in Anglican parish registers and the success with which techniques have been developed to make use of this information, more is now known, and more accurately, of population changes and of the trends in fertility, mortality, and nuptiality which caused them than of any other aspect of the economic and social life of England in the early modern period which depends upon statistical data for its elucidation. There are no price, wage, or production series of comparable detail or authority to those of population size, of expectation of life at birth, or of reproduction rates. And if more

---

[40] For example Drake writes of Norway: 'A number of the major peaks in the death rate (1741–2, 1748, 1773) occurred in years when the grain harvest failed over large parts of the country and it is noticeable in each that the Akershus diocese, where the diet was based more on grain than elsewhere, suffered particularly badly. Other failures in 1762–3, 1784–5, 1808 and 1812 also made their mark.' M. Drake, *Population and Society in Norway 1735–1865* (Cambridge, 1969), p. 71. 1773 was also a particularly bad year in Sweden whose experience in general was not dissimilar to that of Norway.
[41] K. Pitkänen, 'The Patterns of Mortality during the Great Finnish Famine in the 1860s', *Acta Demographica* (1992), 81–101.
[42] C. Ó Gráda, *Black '47 and Beyond: The Great Irish Famine in History, Economy, and Memory* (Princeton, NJ, 1999), ch. 3.

refined information is required, such as, for example, age-specific fertility and mortality rates, intrinsic growth rates, or estimates of endogenous and exogenous infant mortality rates, it is often readily available. Few if any statistical series, whether historical or relating to the contemporary world, are perfectly reliable and those relating to the population of early modern England are no exception to this rule. Complex problems exist relating to the deficiencies of Anglican registration and to a variety of possible sources of bias in the data themselves or which may be introduced by the methods of analysis used, and doubts of a more sweeping kind have occasionally been expressed, but the general soundness of the body of findings which have been published in the past three or four decades is widely acknowledged.[43] It is not, however, this feature of historical demographic data which is most important in relation to the logical status of the material, but rather one which stems directly from the nature of demographic processes.

It is a platitude to remark that all social processes are interrelated. Sometimes the tie is very close. A sharp rise in the output of coal, for example, must almost certainly imply a matching increase in the volume of heavy goods traffic. Other links are much looser. An increase in the proportion of children attending school, a rise in literacy, and a surge in the purchase of books and other reading matter are likely to be associated but the linkage is less certain, while the relationship between, say, a rise in the proportion of the population at work on Saturdays and a decline in the proportion of ice cream sold on that day is far from necessary. But there are very few if any other aspects of social and economic behaviour where the interrelationship between the chief variables is as tight as that which obtains in demographic matters. Although the point is, in some degree, self-evident, its implications are not always realised. In a closed population, for example, if there is an increase in fertility with no change in mortality but there is no alteration in the prevailing rate of population growth (positive or negative), it is an inescapable conclusion that one or more of the variables in question is incorrectly measured.[44] Or, to take the simplest possible case, if, in a closed

[43] The most telling reservations about the possible biases introduced into demographic measures based on family reconstitution by the fact that no parish is a closed population were those formulated by S. Ruggles, 'Migration, Marriage, and Mortality: Correcting Sources of Bias in English Family Reconstitution', *Population Studies*, 46 (1992), 507–22. Razzell has frequently expressed doubts of a more diffuse nature as for example in P. Razzell, 'The Growth of Population in Eighteenth-century England: A Critical Reappraisal', *Journal of Economic History*, 53 (1993), 743–71. The validity of such reservations is reviewed in Wrigley, 'How Reliable is our Knowledge'.

[44] This statement is strictly true only of a stable population, and few populations have experienced unchanging fertility and mortality long enough to have achieved stability, so that, although it is true in principle, it is a fallible guide in many empirical situations.

population, after a lengthy period in which numbers were stable, successive population counts suggested that the population was rising but there was no apparent change either in fertility or mortality, it would be clear that the three variables were not compatible with each other. In a population which was not closed the position is more complicated since migration must be taken into account, but, assuming that information on migration is available, it, too, must be consonant with other demographic variables. Otherwise, it will be evident that something must be amiss with the data. It is also true, and of great value in establishing the course of change in the past, that if it can be demonstrated that estimates of certain variables can be relied upon, then it may also be possible to make confident estimates of the value of another variable about which there is no information. If, for example, to revert to the second example given above, there is no reason to doubt either the estimates of fertility, mortality, or population size, it must follow that net immigration is occurring and its scale is readily established.

The identity which encapsulates the relationships referred to in the last paragraph is known as the population balancing equation.[45] Its implications are immensely productive in enabling a hypothesis to be rejected or, more commonly, in requiring a modification in a hypothesis to make it consistent with current empirical knowledge. Although the equation itself deals only with the simplest and most elementary of demographic variables, the principle that underlies it, that the nature of the relationship between different aspects of demographic behaviour places close limits upon the degree to which any one variable can change without implying sympathetic change elsewhere in the system, enables inferences to be made in a manner not paralleled in most other areas of historical study. For example, in a population in which there is little or no practice of birth control a fall in age at marriage for women must be expected, other things being equal, to cause overall fertility to rise. If this does not happen either one of the two measures is faulty, or there must simultaneously have been a change in behaviour which reduced fertility within marriage, as might happen, for example, as a result of a change in breastfeeding customs. If women were breastfeeding longer this might, in principle, offset the effect of marrying earlier. The fact that demography lies at the interface between the social and the biological sometimes makes it feasible to draw inferences not only about one demographic variable from another but also about social activity from

---

[45] Expressed in its most elementary form the identity in the balancing equation is given as: $P_t - P_0 = B - D + I - E$, where P_t is the population at the end of a period, P_0 the population at its beginning, while B represents births, D deaths, I immigration and E emigration during the period. H. S. Shryock and J. S. Siegel, *The Methods and Materials of Demography*, 2 vols (Washington, 1971), I, p. 6.

the characteristics of demographic variables. Enough is known about the effect of breastfeeding in delaying the resumption of the normal monthly cycle, for instance, to enable estimates to be made, in a non-contracepting population, of the normal length of breastfeeding by utilising information about the difference in the average length of birth intervals following an infant death compared with the average of those following the birth of children who survived.[46]

The nature of the balancing equation has implications for the logical status of information about populations in the past. The raw data in an Anglican parish register are just as likely to suffer from inaccuracy and incompleteness as any other historical source material. Individual entries may be inaccurate either intentionally or unintentionally. They are frequently incomplete and may be entirely missing in the sense, for example, that a death and subsequent burial in the churchyard may have taken place without there being any matching entry in the register. But their deficiencies are less likely to escape notice and correction than with most other statistical sources. If, for example, for any reason, in a closed population, the record of births (baptisms) is less complete than that of deaths (burials) so that estimates of fertility are too low relative to those of mortality and there is also evidence of the scale of population increase or decrease between two points in time, the pieces of the demographic jigsaw will fail to fit together and by a process of elimination it will frequently be possible to identify which element is at fault.

At the national level, if a claim is made about the extent of the fall in mortality in eighteenth-century England, and if there is no room for doubt about the scale of population growth during the period, with two angles of the triangle determined the size of the third angle is also determined, or, in other words, the scale and direction of any implied change in fertility will be calculable.[47] If the best existing estimates of fertility are not in conformity with this inference, if, using the same metaphor, the third angle had been previously estimated as different from that implied by the other two, one or more of the three estimates must be in error. In detail the constraints of the balancing equation can give rise to arguments of great complexity, but the point of principle is simple and implies a rigour which is either absent or less exacting in other areas of economic and social history. This constitutes a considerable strength. Any given assertion about population characteristics

[46] Wrigley et al., *English Population History*, pp. 477–92.

[47] This point is simply demonstrated in terms of population totals and crude birth and death rates but such an analysis leaves unclear, of course, what the underlying changes in fertility and mortality may have been which brought about the change.

in the past may be in error. Indeed all may simultaneously be in error, but, within the limits set by the nature of the balancing equation, it is possible to ensure that the characteristics are mutually consistent. The same does not normally hold good elsewhere in social and economic history. The principal practical reason for uncertainty about most production series in the early modern period, for example, lies straightforwardly in the absence or very poor quality of the surviving source material, but, even if this were not the case, the absence of the equivalent of the population balancing equation would restrict the confidence with which the existence of good series for certain products could be used to make inferences about the other related series. The mutual consistency of such series is, in general, harder to establish than is the case with demographic series.

Malthus's work, which was to prove so provocative and productive in many fields, also illustrates the same point. When he asserted that a population which was untroubled by resource constraints would tend to grow geometrically and at the same time assumed that there must be a ceiling to the possible growth of population because of resource constraints, he was justified in drawing the inference that either fertility must fall or mortality rise or that there would be a combination of the two. Because of the nature of the balance equation, either the positive or the preventive check or both must come into play. However, when he also asserted that at best the output of food would grow arithmetically, he was making an assumption that was far more contingent upon the uncertainties of technological change. Although, therefore, the inferences which he drew from the comparison of arithmetic and geometric growth rates may be sound, at least for pre-industrial societies, the differences in the nature of the economic and biological constraints on human behaviour made his assumption about the growth of food production more uncertain than that about population growth. Reproduction, understood broadly as the process by which one generation is replaced by the next, looks to biology, so to speak, whereas production looks to technology and economics. In consequence, the relation of demographic variables to each other is much more tightly constrained than the comparable relationship of technological or economic variables to each other. One of the fascinations of population history might be said to lie in finding ways of exploiting the nature of the balancing equation.

CHAPTER SEVEN

Disease and the Historian

ROY PORTER

In the West various intellectual hierarchies continue to exercise their accustomed sway. Head is over hand, and theory is reckoned better than craft or empirical knowledge — something recently reiterated in the humanities by the arguments used by advocates of postmodernism and other forms of cultural and literary criticism. In the sciences for their part, physics has been superior to biology, and biology for its part prized above medicine (as theoretical knowledge over know-how or practical knowledge).

Historical and philosophical investigations into the nature of scientific knowledge have, at least until recently, overwhelmingly focused on the physical sciences. Is science empirical? cumulative? objective? Does it proceed through a succession of paradigms? Is the path of science progressive? How are discoveries made? The answer has been: Turn to Galileo! Take a case-study from Lavoisier! On the whole, the life sciences and medicine have received prestige only insofar as they have assimilated themselves to the models of the physical sciences, as in molecular biology.

In these contexts pertaining to the philosophy of science there has customarily been scant discussion of the status of medicine.[1] And perhaps with good reason. After all, medicine always has been a hodgepodge, an amalgam of knowledge pure and applied, of art, craft and science — and the proof of the pudding has always been taken to be in the healing. In 1950 the UK experienced 26,000 infant deaths; within half a century that had fallen by 80 per cent. Deaths in the UK from infectious diseases nearly halved between 1970 and 1992. As answers to the questions posed above, such facts have been thought, by spokespeople for the medical profession at least, to speak for themselves. That is, however, no reason for neglecting the philosophy and history of medicine.

---

[1] H. T. Engelhardt Jr, 'Philosophy of Medicine', in P. T. Durbin (ed.), *A Guide to the Culture of Science, Technology and Medicine* (New York, 1980), pp. 364–451; idem, *The Foundations of Bioethics*, 2nd edn (Oxford, 1996).

This essay addresses certain issues in the history and philosophy of medicine. I do not intend to retread certain ground that has been much trodden. I shall not rehearse, yet again, the rejection of Whiggish triumphalism, or revisit the impact of feminist history, of structuralism, of Foucauldian *savoir-pouvoir*, postmodernism, Derridean textual analysis and the wider 'linguistic turn'.[2] These tendencies and counter-tendencies have been discussed and debated from San Diego to St Petersburg.[3]

I hope to steer my philosophical, methodological and historiographical ship between two reefs. On the one hand, I shall not write abstractly of clashes between 'isms' and 'ologies'. That would not only be tedious, it would also be misleading, because work in the history of medicine — in Britain at least — has not in reality been ideologically polarised into doctrinaire warring sects, but has been characterised by a healthy eclecticism, pluralism and diversity: amongst historians of medicine at least, English individualism still rules OK.[4]

On the other hand, I shall avoid discussing minutiae and will not load this essay with fleeting and instantly forgettable references to hundreds of names, topics and titles. My plan, rather, is to address in some detail a few big issues, so as to avoid intellectual indigestion.

By way of scene-setting, it will be useful to say something about the institutional developments underpinning the scholarly analysis of the history of medicine in Britain. When I started out as a research student in the late 1960s, the history of medicine in Britain was generally thought an intellectually lacklustre pursuit, holding no fascination for brash and bumptious apprentice historians of science like myself: it had no big issues, no clashes of the kind provoked by Popper, Lakatos, Kuhn or Feyerabend. It seemed to be the unproblematic chronicle of how dreadful diseases had been conquered by great doctors.

All this was to change. Over the last thirty years, new diseases like AIDS have challenged the once unquestioned saga of progress, while public

---

[2] G. H. Brieger, 'History of Medicine', in Durbin (ed.), *Guide to the Culture of Science*; idem, 'The Historiography of Medicine', in W. F. Bynum and R. Porter (eds), *Companion Encyclopedia of the History of Medicine* (London, 1993), pp. 24–44; L. Jordanova, 'The Social Sciences and History of Science and Medicine', in P. Corsi and P. Weindling (eds), *Information Sources in the History of Science and Medicine* (London, 1983), pp. 81–98; idem, 'The Social Construction of Medical Knowledge', *Social History of Medicine*, 8 (1995), 361–82; M. Pelling, 'Medicine since 1500', in Corsi and Weindling (eds), *Information Sources*, pp. 379–407.

[3] R. Evans, *In Defence of History* (London, 1997); J. Geyer-Kordesch, 'Women in Medicine', in Bynum and Porter (eds), *Companion Encyclopedia*, pp. 884–910; C. Jones and R. Porter (eds), *Reassessing Foucault: Power, Medicine and the Body* (London, 1994).

[4] A. Macfarlane, *The Origins of English Individualism: The Family, Property and Social Transition* (Oxford, 1978).

attitudes towards scientific medicine and the medical profession have grown critical. As an inevitable consequence, the history of medicine has itself been problematised.[5]

British scholars have been particularly well placed to participate in and take advantage of such new ferments thanks to two developments. The discipline has been energised during the last quarter-century thanks to the founding and flourishing of the Society for the Social History of Medicine, an initially radical group which brought together younger historians, social scientists and left-leaning health professionals. Its thrice-yearly journal, *Social History of Medicine*, is now well into its second decade.[6]

A comparable stimulus has come from the Wellcome Trust. By supporting the Wellcome Institute (from October 2000, the Wellcome Centre) in London, units in Edinburgh and Cambridge (both now closed), Oxford, Manchester, Glasgow and East Anglia, and lectureships in approximately thirty universities, the Wellcome Trust has set study of the history of medicine — once largely conducted by retired or Sunday doctors — on to a proper academic footing. Most Wellcome appointees are trained historians working in or alongside history departments. That has its pros and cons — arguably certain research topics really do require professional medical expertise and experience. But it has ensured that the history of medicine has been exposed to the trade winds of academic scholarship and is now undertaken with due historiographical sophistication.

The problem of disease: philosophical issues

In this section I shall survey attempts by western medical thinking to define and delineate the nature of disease. Here questions of everyday language immediately intrude. The term 'disease' is commonly used synonymously with 'illness', yet they may also be differentiated. We can say of somebody with a tumour, 'he's got cancer, but he's not sick', and we call mouldy apples 'diseased' but never 'ill'. In contemporary English-language parlance, 'disease' depicts an objective state, commonly triggered by a virus or similar pathogen, and marked by familiar signs such as a rash or a raised temperature. Illness, on the other hand, tends to denote something subjective, feelings of malaise or pain. Such distinctions give clues to changes in thinking and meaning over time. The term 'disease' itself has developed

---

[5] I. Illich, *Limits to Medicine: The Expropriation of Health* (Harmondsworth, 1977).
[6] D. Porter, 'The Mission of Social History of Medicine: An Historical Overview', *Social History of Medicine*, 8 (1995), 345–60; Jordanova, 'The Social Construction'.

from 'dis-ease' (and similarly malaise from 'mal-aise', ill at ease); hence within the modern, scientific concept of disease, older and more subjective connotations are contained and perhaps fossilised.[7]

Fundamental contrasts may be drawn between the concepts of health and disease advanced by western scientific medicine and those typical of the small, pre-literate communities studied by anthropologists. In tribal societies, sickness (especially if spectacular, unusual or fatal) is commonly viewed as personal, an evil wilfully worked by a sorcerer, ghost, ancestor or demon. Sickness thus often involves bewitchment or possession, malevolently inflicted through spells or curses. Such sickness does not strike randomly but may be a reprisal or punishment, targeted against a specific individual or group, in retribution for some such act of commission or omission as taboos breached or a god unpropitiated.[8]

Where illness is regarded as the outcome of personal or community behaviour, healing is too important to be left to healers alone. It involves the collectivity, and requires rituals to cleanse the polluted, lay ghosts and make reparation. Ceremonies are thus intrinsic to healing. All such features are at odds with the rationales espoused by official medicine in the West, which views disease as an impersonal event of nature and its remedy likewise.

The key medical beliefs of the great Asiatic cultures show some affinities to the thinking which emerged in the West. In ayurvedic medicine, health is the supreme foundation of virtue, wealth and enjoyment, while diseases are the destroyers of health. In China, health and disease were incorporated into the Taoist philosophy, with its binary principles of yin and yang. Health and disease are inflections of the human microcosm reflected in the heavens.[9]

On their clay tablets and papyri the archaic civilisations of Mesopotamia and Egypt left written evidence of their beliefs about disease. These record descriptions of many different symptom complexes, frequently localised in a particular body part and connected with specific demons and deities. Such images form the basis for prognostications (death or recovery) and for therapy. Especially in Mesopotamia, maladies were understood as omens, and disease was thought to derive from the hand of a deity.

---

[7] A. L. Caplan, H. T. Engelhardt and J. J. MacCartney (eds), *Concepts of Health and Disease* (Reading, MA, 1981).

[8] A. Kleinman, *Patients and Healers in the Context of Culture: An Exploration of the Borderline between Anthropology, Medicine, and Psychiatry* (Berkeley, CA, 1980); M. Last, 'Non-western Concepts of Disease', in Bynum and Porter (eds), *Companion Encyclopedia*, pp. 634–60.

[9] F. Bray, 'Chinese Medicine', in Bynum and Porter (eds), *Companion Encyclopedia*, pp. 728–54; N. E. Gallagher, 'Islamic and Indian Medicine', in K. F. Kiple (ed.), *The Cambridge World History of Human Disease* (Cambridge, 1993), pp. 27–34; D. Wujastyk, 'Indian Medicine', in Bynum and Porter (eds), *Companion Encyclopedia*, pp. 755–78.

Alongside these religious and magical meanings, there are some signs of speculation about disease. Egyptian medicine envisaged the body as a system irrigated by its fluids, on the analogy of the Nile and its canals serving the fields. Blockages would bring putrefaction. Such natural analogies spurred early pathological thinking as part of what may be called the transformation of animistic into rational thought.[10]

As in India and China, health became identified in Greece too as one of the supreme goods, being linked to cults of athleticism and beauty. By the fifth century BC, Greek physicians and philosophers were maintaining that disease was a natural occurrence, something stressed throughout the Hippocratic corpus, the name given to a collection of some forty medical treatises dating from as far back as 400 BC. These take a strongly personal approach to disease, in which the physician's art consists in organising symptoms into a prognosis in the case in question, according to the individual's constitution. Hippocratic medicine rarely ascribed diseases to particular organs, though with the development of dissection in Alexandria from the third century BC, anatomy was to assume greater consequence.[11]

The Hippocratic writings programmatically discounted divine or magical interference. All disease was seen to have its roots in the body and in human actions, being influenced also by such external factors as climate and environment. Epidemics were attributed to atmospheric pollutions (*miasmata*); individual maladies to errors in lifestyle, above all diet.

Health was viewed as balance and harmony, and disease as disturbance. Alcmaeon of Croton (fifth century BC) had taught that health was upheld by the balance of qualities (moist and dry, cold and hot, bitter and sweet). Such humours were the products of food and digestion, and bodily functions were governed by the anatomical centres of the liver, the heart and the brain — the seats of the natural soul, the vital soul and the rational soul respectively; from them originated the veins, arteries and nerves. Greek thinking about health and disease was teleological. All body parts were designed to interact to enable humans to lead a good life and to reproduce. Health was a state in harmony with Nature, disease was contrary to Nature.

The Greeks valued the cultivation of health, pursuing it through moderation (in eating, drinking, sex and other activities), and regarding it as a model for a healthy mind (*sōphrosynē*, wisdom). Antiquity likewise fostered the love of beauty. Christianity was, by contrast, indifferent to

[10] J. W. Estes, *The Medical Skills of Ancient Egypt* (Canton, MA, 1989).
[11] G. E. R. Lloyd (ed.), *Hippocratic Writings* (Harmondsworth, 1978); J. N. Longrigg, *Greek Rational Medicine* (London, 1993); V. Nutton, 'Humoralism', in Bynum and Porter (eds), *Companion Encyclopedia*, pp. 281–91; E. D. Phillips, *Greek Medicine* (London, 1973).

earthly well-being as an end in itself; rather spirituality was to be pursued, through the mortification of the flesh. In Christian theology, disease and suffering could be viewed as chastisements of the wicked or, as with Job, a trial of the chosen. Sickness might be a consequence of sin, and hence might require spiritual healing. The ascetic tradition regarded pain as salutary, and disease could be a purgation, a pilgrimage to holiness.[12]

Plague appeared under the Emperor Justinian (AD 527–65), then in the fourteenth-century Black Death, and later in torrents of subsequent outbreaks. Experience of epidemics encouraged the elucidation of hitherto fuzzy concepts of the contagiousness of disease. Infections were said to pollute the body or spread among a community like a poison (*virus*) or a dye, or rather as putrifying matter corrupted flesh. If spread by personal contact, a disease was contagious.[13]

From the 1490s, syphilis captured attention as a 'new disease', widely believed, then and by some nowadays, to have been imported into Europe by Columbus from the New World. This pox (that is, great pox, as distinct from smallpox) became widely known as the French disease, while the term syphilis appeared in a poem, 'Syphilis sive morbus gallicus' (1530), by Girolamo Fracastoro. In Fracastoro's theory, invisible particles (*seminaria*) spread contagion. This ontological model of diseases, which pictures them as real and distinct entities, gained support from the sixteenth century. The Swiss medical iconoclast Paracelsus and his Netherlandish follower van Helmont developed it by deeming disease an external invader. Opposing the old theory of diseases as humoral imbalances, the latter envisaged diseases as thorns in the flesh.[14]

In the Restoration era, Thomas Sydenham (1624–89) further developed the emergent ontological concept. Whilst in many ways a staunch Hippocratic, Sydenham also regarded diseases as distinct entities, and was one of the pioneers of nosology, the science of disease classification, which flourished in the eighteenth century amongst such systematists as Linnaeus, Bossier de Sauvages and William Cullen, all of whom created taxonomic

[12] P. Brown, *The Body and Society* (New York, 1988); K. Park, 'Medicine and Society in Medieval Europe, 500–1500', in A. Wear (ed.), *Medicine in Society: Historical Essays* (Cambridge, 1992), pp. 59–90; J. Preuss, *Biblical and Talmudic Medicine*, trans. F. Rosner (New York, 1978); O. Temkin, *Hippocrates in a World of Pagans and Christians* (Baltimore, MD, 1992).

[13] D. R. Brothwell and A. T. Sandison (eds), *Diseases in Antiquity: A Survey of the Diseases, Injuries and Surgery of Ancient Populations* (Springfield, IL, 1967); M. N. Cohen, *Health and the Rise of Civilization* (New Haven, CT, 1989); Kiple (ed.), *Cambridge World History of Human Disease*.

[14] C. Quétel, *History of Syphilis* (London, 1990); J. Arrizabalaga, J. Henderson and R. French, *The Great Pox: The French Disease in Renaissance Europe* (New Haven, CT, 1997); A. G. Debus, *The Chemical Philosophy: Paracelsian Science and Medicine in the Sixteenth and Seventeenth Centuries* (New York, 1977).

systems dividing diseases, like plants and animals, into orders, families, genera and species.[15]

The 'new philosophy' of the 'scientific revolution', which challenged Aristotelianism with a mechanical, mathematical view of nature, inevitably had an impact on disease theory. Iatrophysics (medical physics) and iatrochemistry (medical chemistry) dismissed the Galenic, humoral doctrine of health ('fluidism'), and stressed the primacy of the solid organs and fibres in the body machine.

Descartes viewed bodies as essentially mechanical, utterly unlike the mind. Cartesian philosophy promoted a mechanistic physiology and pathology, built upon a corpuscular theory of matter and chemical explanations. Envisaging disease as a breakdown, medical mechanists questioned the organism's capacity to mend or heal itself. No longer were diseases to be seen as purposive, functional healing processes.[16]

But though the mechanical philosophy carried the day in the physical sciences, it ultimately proved, if appealing, less persuasive in explaining the processes of life. Hence many eminent physicians, notably Georg Stahl, insisted that health and disease could be understood only by presuming the active participation of some sort of a soul (*anima*) or vital principle inherent in the body; while later thinkers like Albrecht von Haller endowed all fibres with irritability. No mere machine, the body was dynamically engaged in preserving life and restoring health. The eighteenth century witnessed impassioned controversies between mechanists, vitalists and animists.[17]

Concepts of disease were thus contested, and meanwhile they were being shaped by investigations in anatomy and physiology. In a tradition headed by Vesalius's *De humani corporis fabrica* (On the Structure of the Human Body, 1543), human dissection became touted as the key to understanding the body, and pathological anatomy, the study of morbid changes, developed in its wake. With Morgagni's *De sedibus et causis morborum* (On the Seats and Causes of Disease, 1761), pathology emerged as a discipline in its own right, correlating diseases and symptoms with changes noted upon autopsy, thereby linking particular diseases with specific bodily sites. Pathological

---

[15] L. S. King, *The Medical World of the Eighteenth Century* (Chicago, IL, 1958); idem, *The Road to Medical Enlightenment, 1650–1695* (London, 1970); idem, *The Philosophy of Medicine: The Early Eighteenth Century* (Cambridge, MA, 1978).

[16] R. B. Carter, *Descartes' Medical Philosphy: The Organic Solution to the Mind–Body Problem* (Baltimore, MD, 1983).

[17] L. S. King, 'Boissier de Sauvages and 18th Century Nosology', *Bulletin of the History of Medicine*, 46 (1966), 43–51; K. Faber, *Nosography: A History of Clinical Medicine* (New York, 1930); R. D. French, 'Sickness and Soul: Stahl, Hoffman and Sauvages on Pathology', in A. Cunningham and R. French (eds), *The Medical Enlightenment of the Eighteenth Century* (Cambridge, 1990), pp. 88–110.

anatomy was further assisted by new techniques and instruments for gauging the state of internal organs in living bodies, particularly the introduction of the stethoscope (1816) by René Laennec.[18]

This new approach to disease theory — stressing objective signs not subjective symptoms — flourished in hospitals, especially the huge Paris charity institutions, which housed legions of patients suffering from identical diseases, and in which dissection was encouraged. Large hospitals, notably the state-run institutions in Paris, encouraged statistical investigation too. In the 1820s Pierre Louis conducted trials to ascertain the influence of bleeding upon pneumonia. Some patients were bled early, others later. The findings showed that early bleeding did not improve recovery chances — indeed nothing did. Statistics were henceforth to play a growing role in disease thinking, while pointing towards the clinical trial as a means of evaluating therapies.[19]

The objective, quantitative view of illness gaining ground in hospitals matched a growing use of statistics to sound the health of populations at large. Clinical deployment of instruments like watches and thermometers also promoted objective approaches to disease. Forerunners of the diagnostic laboratory, such apparatus had been pioneered by Galileo's colleague Santorio, but their uptake was tardy. In the Galenic tradition, health had been viewed teleologically as an ideal natural state. But increasingly it was argued by Quetelet and other pioneers of statistics that medicine must be familiar with the numerical range of normal pulse rate or body temperature, obtained on the basis of measurements from large populations. Quantification lent health and disease a law-like aspect, and the profile of particular diseases might be expressed through charts and graphs.

Diagnostic use of tabular data seeded the idea that disease is a physiological process. Body activities could increase and diminish and still remain within the range of the 'normal', implying a continuum from positive health to full-blown disease. Such notions received early expression in the writings of the Scotsman John Brown (1735–88). In what became known as Brunonianism, he maintained that the interaction between the body's natural

[18] R. D. French, 'The Anatomical Tradition', in Bynum and Porter (eds), *Companion Encyclopedia*, pp. 81–101; S. Jarcho (trans. and ed.), *The Clinical Consultations of Giambattista Morgagni* (Boston, MA, 1984); R. C. Maulitz, *Morbid Appearances: The Anatomy of Pathology in the Early Nineteenth Century* (Cambridge, 1987); E. M. Tansey, 'The Physiological Tradition', in Bynum and Porter (eds), *Companion Encyclopedia*, pp. 120–52.

[19] E. H. Ackerknecht, *Medicine at the Paris Hospital, 1794–1848* (Baltimore, MD, 1967); W. F. Bynum, *Science and the Practice of Medicine in the Nineteenth Century* (New York, 1994); M. Foucault, *The Birth of the Clinic*, trans. A. M. S. Smith (orig. published 1973; London, 1994); J. R. Matthews, *Quantification and the Quest for Medical Certainty* (Princeton, NJ, 1995)

excitability and the external stimuli which it encountered determined health over a range between the extreme conditions of asthenia (dangerous under-stimulus) and sthenia (over-excitement). Disease was thus not an objective, external thing but represented life under changed circumstances — an idea later to assume great significance.[20]

Scepticism towards traditional therapies (whose inadequacies had been exposed by Pierre Louis's early clinical trials) led some physicians of the anatomico-clinical school to proclaim that the healing power of nature was superior to any medication. Against such 'therapeutic nihilists' with their ontological concept of disease, others argued that anatomy could not provide an understanding of true disease aetiology, which would be obtained only from physiology, or the experimental investigation of living beings. In Germany, Rudolf Virchow's epoch-making *Die Cellularpathologie* (1858) and, in France, Claude Bernard's *Introduction à l'étude de la médecine expérimentale* (1865) became classical expositions of this concept. Life involved a range of functions which could proceed normally or abnormally. Physiology's task was to find out how the body worked, and that, insisted Bernard, could only be done experimentally.[21]

Morgagni had looked to the organs as the seats of disease; Bichat had pointed to the tissues; Virchow, for his part, declared that it was cells which were responsible for health and disease. Drawing a liberal political comparison, he pictured the body as a social organism dependent on the functioning of its cells and sought to explain changes visible in the cells physiologically by referring to irritation and pathogenesis. The implied vitalism of Virchow's cellular pathology was inimical to a circle of physiologists led by Helmholtz, Du Bois-Reymond, Brücke and Carl Ludwig. They developed a radical programme of their own, reductionism: physiology would become truly scientific only once it were recast entirely in biophysicical and biochemical terms.[22]

All such physiological disease concepts challenged ontological thinking. Individuals differed, insisted the physiologists, and, since life could be subjected to an infinite variety of changed conditions, every sick person represented his or her own disease. Bernard laid renewed stress upon the

[20] W. F. Bynum and R. Porter (eds), *Brunonianism in Britain and Europe, Medical History*, suppl. 8 (London, 1989).

[21] E. H. Ackerknecht, *Rudolf Virchow: Doctor, Statesman, Anthropologist* (Madison, WI, 1953); C. Bernard, *Introduction to the Study of Experimental Medicine*, trans. H. Greene (New York, 1957); F. L. Holmes, *Claude Bernard and Animal Chemistry: The Emergence of a Scientist* (Cambridge, 1974).

[22] W. Coleman and F. L. Holmes (eds), *The Investigative Enterprise: Experimental Physiology in Nineteenth-century Medicine* (Berkeley, CA, 1988).

internal milieu — blood and electrolytes — which provided a stable environment for the cells composing the body, cushioning it against the external
environment. The constancy of the internal milieu was upheld by the
regulatory functions of the nervous system. Later, once the role played by
endocrine glands in the body's regulatory system had been elucidated,
Walter Cannon introduced the term 'homeostasis' for the actively sustained
equilibrium prevailing in the organism.[23]

Debates over the nature of disease were meanwhile given fresh impetus
by Robert Koch's discovery of the tubercle bacillus (1882), which, with
further micro-biological discoveries, lent immense authority to the germ
theory of disease promoted by Louis Pasteur. Pasteur, Koch and their
respective French and German followers demonstrated that specific micro-
organisms were responsible for specific diseases; diseases could now be
defined bacteriologically; tuberculosis was the disease caused by the tubercle
bacillus, and so forth. Koch's famous 'postulates' implied that the problem
of disease had finally been solved: it was all a matter of the identification of
specific micro-organisms.[24]

Bacteriology was to exercise an immense influence on disease theory,
with the study of microbes assuming priority over the idea of the
individual constitution or the role of socio-environmental factors. Bacteriology and immunology accorded huge prestige to the laboratory, seemingly
threatening the traditional clinical arts and the sanitarians' war on filth. The
germ theory of disease was further strengthened by the rapid development of
effective vaccines against anthrax, rabies, diphtheria and other conditions;
by Paul Ehrlich's 'magic bullet' (Salvarsan) against syphilis; and by the
discovery of antibiotics. All these, especially the 'miracle drugs', created the
image, widespread by the mid-twentieth century, that disease was an
'enemy' that modern scientific medicine was about to 'vanquish' — about
which more later.[25]

In truth, however, definitions and understandings of disease remain
highly contentious to this day: the rancorous row since the early 1980s as to
whether HIV is *the* cause — the *vera causa* — of AIDS is only the most

[23] W. B. Cannon, *The Wisdom of the Body* (New York, 1932); M. Neuberger, *The Doctrine of the Healing Power of Nature throughout the Course of Time*, trans. L. J. Boyd (New York, 1943); R. B. Welbourn, 'Endocrine Diseases', in Bynum and Porter (eds), *Companion Encyclopedia*, pp. 483–551.

[24] T. D. Brock, *Robert Koch: A Life in Medicine and Bacteriology* (Madison, WI, 1988); W. D. Foster, *A History of Medical Bacteriology and Immunology* (London, 1970); G. L. Geison, *The Private Science of Louis Pasteur* (Princeton, NJ, 1995).

[25] R. Hare, *The Birth of Penicillin* (London, 1970); G. Macfarlane, *Alexander Fleming: The Man and the Myth* (New York, 1985); B. Latour, *The Pasteurization of France*, trans. A. Sheridan and J. Law (Cambridge, MA, 1988).

spectacular instance nowadays of profound uncertainty.[26] More generally, debates as to whether it is possible to be sick without being diseased, or to have a disease without being sick, still carry crucial theoretical and practical implications. Doctrines of susceptibility and immunity are highly intricate and, some would say, inherently question-begging. And, in the end, who has the right to pronounce someone ill: the sufferer, the physician or society?

On top of this, the interplay between mind and body in sickness remains a minefield.[27] How far may disorders be deemed psychogenic or at least to have a psychosomatic component?[28] And larger questions loom about understanding the organism. What is to count as healthiness and what as sickness? What is 'normal', what 'pathological'?[29] In wider evolutionary terms, it is no easy matter to judge which biomedical events truly help or harm. Is fever a disease, a symptom, or the body's (and so Nature's) way of fighting sickness?[30] These questions have prompted disparate answers from sufferers and their physicians, as likewise from regulars or irregulars.[31] And such responses have hinged upon wider, extra-medical doctrines respecting order and harmony, good and evil; and upon deep-seated beliefs about the economy of Nature, the purposes of Providence and the meaning of life, ideas articulated in the West within the frameworks of Classical metaphysics, Christian eschatology, and evolutionary biology.

The problem of disease: the historical record

Thus it cannot be said, in any philosophical way, that we have arrived at the truth about the nature of health and disease. Almost the reverse: it is plausible to claim that the AIDS debate — with its triumphal cries of 'We've found the virus' — rather suggests just how crass medical thinking and public understanding can still be on this subject. Yet western medicine has undoubtedly, in world-historical terms, been uniquely successful.

To what is that success due? The ceaseless spread of western medicine throughout the world owes much, doubtless, to political and economic

[26] S. Epstein, *Impure Science: AIDS, Activism and the Politics of Knowledge* (Berkeley, CA, 1996).
[27] P. L. Entralgo, *Mind and Body, Psychosomatic Pathology: A Short History of the Evolution of Medical Thought* (London, 1995).
[28] E. Shorter, *From Paralysis to Fatigue: A History of Psychosomatic Illness in the Modern Era* (New York, 1992).
[29] G. Canguilhem, *On the Normal and the Pathological*, trans. Carolyn Fawcett (New York, 1991).
[30] R. M. Nesse and J. C. Williams, *Evolution and Healing: The New Science of Darwinian Medicine* (London, 1995).
[31] P. A. Nicholls, *Homeopathy and the Medical Profession* (London, 1988).

domination. But that dominance is also due to the fact that it is perceived to 'work' uniquely well. It is *conceivable* that in a hundred years time traditional Chinese medicine, shamanistic medicine or ayurvedic medicine will have swept the globe; in truth, however, there is every reason to expect that the medicine of the future will be an outgrowth of present western medicine. Why? What is so special about western medicine?[32]

Western medicine has developed a unique approach to, and radically distinctive techniques for exploring, the workings of the human body in sickness and in health; and these in turn have changed the ways our culture conceives of the body and of human life. To reduce the complex to the simple, most peoples and cultures the world over, throughout history, have sought to understand life — birth and death, sickness and health — primarily in context of a grasp of the relations of human beings to the cosmos: planets, stars, mountains, rivers, spirits and ancestors, gods and demons, the heavens and the underworld.

Modern western thinking, however, has become indifferent to all such elements. The West has evolved a culture preoccupied with the self, with the individual and his or her identity, and this quest has come to be equated with, or reduced to, the individual body and the embodied personality, expressed through body language.[33]

Explanations of how and why these modern, secular western attitudes have come about would need to take much into account. Their roots may be found in the philosophical and religious traditions they have grown out of, some of which have just been discussed. They have been enormously stimulated by the economic materialism of capitalism. But they are also intimately connected with the development of medicine — its promise, project and products.

Whereas most traditional healing systems the world over have sought to understand the relations of the sick person to the wider cosmos at large and on that basis to make the necessary readjustments between individual and world, or society and world, the West explains sickness principally in terms of the body itself — a cosmos of its own. Greek medicine, as we have seen, laid the foundations by dismissing supernatural powers — though not atmospheric and environmental influences; and the prestigious anatomical and physiological programmes of the Renaissance then created a new confidence amongst investigators that everything that needed to be known

---

[32] L. M. Magner, *A History of Medicine* (New York, 1992); L. Conrad, M. Neve, V. Nutton, R. Porter and W. Wear, *The Western Medical Tradition: 800 BC to AD 1800* (Cambridge, 1995); R. Porter, *'The Greatest Benefit to Mankind': A Medical History of Humanity* (London, 1997).

[33] R. Porter, 'History of the Body Reconsidered', in P. Burke (ed.), *New Perspectives on Historical Writing*, 2nd edn (Cambridge, 2001), pp. 233–60.

could essentially be discovered by delving ever more deeply, ever more minutely into the flesh, its organs, its tissues, its cells, its DNA.[34]

These have proved infinitely productive practices, generating first knowledge and then power, including on some occasions the power to conquer disease. The idea of probing into bodies, living and dead — and especially into *human* bodies — with a view to advancing medicine is quite distinctive to the European medical tradition. For reasons technical, cultural, religious and personal, it was not undertaken in ancient China or India, Mesopotamia or Pharaonic Egypt. Dissection and dissection-related experimentation were performed on animals alone in Classical Greece, and then rather rarely. A medicine that seriously and systematically investigated the materiality of bodies subsequently came into being — in Alexandria, then in the work of Galen, and subsequently in late medieval Italy. The key role of anatomising was then proclaimed in the Renaissance, and it became the foundation-stone for those later edifices of scientific medicine already mentioned: physiological experimentation, pathology, microscopy, biochemistry and all the other later specialisms, to say nothing of invasive surgery.

This was not the only course that medicine might have taken; it was not the course that the other great world medical systems took. Nor did it enjoy universal approval: protests in Britain around 1800 against the scandal of body-snatching, and the ongoing anti-vivisectionist protests, show how sceptical public opinion remained about the activities of anatomists and medical researchers. The fact, however, is that was the programme which western medicine pursued, and, bolstered by science at large, it generated a mode of medicine of unique power, substantially independent of its real efficacy as a rational social approach to good health.[35]

The triumph of this high-tech scientific medicine may be a prime example of what William Blake denounced as 'single vision', the kind of myopia which (literally and metaphorically) stems from looking doggedly down a microscope. Single vision has its limitations when it comes to explaining the human condition; this is why Samuel Coleridge described doctors as being '*shallow* animals', who 'having always employed their

---

[34] J. Sawday, *The Body Emblazoned: Dissection and the Human Body in Renaissance Culture* (London, 1995); W. R. Arney and B. J. Bergen, *Medicine and the Management of Living: Taming the Last Great Beast* (Chicago, IL, 1985).

[35] R. D. French, *Antivivisection and Medical Science in Victorian Society* (Princeton, NJ, 1975); R. Richardson, *Death, Dissection and the Destitute: A Political History of the Human Corpse* (London, 1987).

minds about Body and Gut, they imagine that in the whole system of things there is nothing but Gut and Body'.[36]

The success of modern western medicine has produced problems and paradoxes. It has peered more and ever more minutely into the body, and acquired greater powers. But all this has been at the risk of becoming blinkered about patients, about people, about society, and — so to speak — about the philosophy of medicine. Hence medicine today is arguably facing a fundamental crisis. It is losing its way, or having to redefine its goals.

Fifty years back things were simple. During the Second World War a publisher brought out 'The Conquest Series', with titles which included *The Conquest of Disease, The Conquest of Pain, The Conquest of Tuberculosis, The Conquest of Cancer, The Conquest of Brain Mysteries*. The publisher's blurb said they explained 'the many wonders of contemporary medical science today'. In a similar cast of mind, in the *British Medical Journal* in 1949, Lord Horder posed the question, 'Whither Medicine?', and returned the answer direct, 'Why, whither else but straight ahead'. Today, when many of the old diseases conspicuously have not been conquered, no thinking person any longer knows where 'straight ahead' is.

For centuries, the medical enterprise was too feeble to attract radical critiques of itself. From Cato to Chekhov, medicine was mocked;[37] yet most who could, called the doctor when sick. People did not have high expectations from medicine, and, when Doc typically achieved little, they did not blame him too much. Medicine was a profession, but it carried little prestige or power. Death humbled all.

In the twentieth century, by contrast, medicine grew conquering and commanding; it now costs a fortune; and, as its publicity has mushroomed, it has provoked a crescendo of criticism. Historians, social scientists, political analysts and the public pose searching questions. From the 1950s the new medical sociology put medicine under the microscope — and sometimes on the couch. One school of sociologists mounted assaults on professional dominance. Another contended that the categories of medicine — the very notions of health and sickness — were essentially social labels, often involving stigma, victim-blaming, and the designation of deviance with respect to class, race and gender. Sociologists have characterised medicine as

---

[36] E. L. Griggs (ed.), *Collected Letters of Samuel Taylor Coleridge* (Oxford, 1956), i, 256, Coleridge to Charles Lloyd Sr, 14 November 1796.

[37] J. Trautmann and C. Pollard, *Literature and Medicine: Topics, Titles and Notes* (Philadelphia, PA, 1975); H. Silvette, *The Doctor on Stage: Medicine and Medical Men in Seventeenth-century England* (Knoxville, TN, 1967).

a vehicle of social control, reproducing social norms, exercising social power.[38]

Medicine has also become the prisoner of its own success. Having conquered certain grave diseases and provided some relief from suffering, its mandate has become muddled. What are its aims? Where is it to stop? Is its prime duty to keep people alive as long as possible, willy-nilly, whatever the circumstances? Is its charge to *make* people lead healthy lives? Or is it but a service industry, on tap to fulfil whatever fantasies its clients may frame for their bodies, be this cosmetic surgery or the longing of post-menopausal women to have babies?[39]

Public alarm is bound to grow over the high-tech 'can do, will do' approach apparently embraced by cutting-edge scientific medicine — whose elite sometimes seems primarily interested in extending medicine's technical virtuosity. Where patients are seen as problems and reduced to biopsies and lab tests, 'tibs and fibs', no wonder many of the public vote with their feet, and opt for styles of holistic medicine which present themselves as more humane. And the irony is that, the healthier western society becomes, the more medicine it craves — indeed, it regards maximum access to medicine as a right and duty. Especially in free-market America, immense pressures are created — by the medical profession, by medi-business, the media, by the high-pressure advertising of pharmaceutical companies, and dutiful (or susceptible) individuals — to expand the diagnosis of treatable illnesses. Scares are created. People are bamboozled into lab tests, often of dubious reliability. Thanks to diagnostic creep or leap, ever more disorders are revealed.[40] Extensive and expensive treatments are then urged — the physician who chooses not to treat may be exposed to malpractice accusations. Anxieties and interventions spiral. Practitioners, lawyers and pharmaceutical companies do well, even if patients don't get well; and medicine spirals up in the atmosphere like a space-shot off-course.

The root of the trouble is structural. It is endemic to a medical system in which an expanding medical establishment, faced with a healthier population of its own creation, is driven to medicalising normal life events such as menopause, converting risks into diseases, and treating trivial complaints

[38] D. Armstrong, *Political Anatomy of the Body: Medical Knowledge in Britain in the Twentieth Century* (Cambridge, 1983); idem, 'Medical Sociology', in Bynum and Porter (eds), *Companion Encyclopedia*, pp. 1631–52.

[39] L. J. Schneiderman and N. S. Jecker, *Wrong Medicine: Doctors, Patients and Futile Treatment* (Baltimore, MD, 1995).

[40] L. Payer, *Disease-mongers: How Doctors, Drug Companies, and Insurers are Making You Feel Sick* (New York, 1992).

with fancy procedures.[41] Doctors and 'consumers' alike are becoming locked within the fantasy of technological perfectibilism: *everyone* has *something* wrong with them, everyone and everything can be cured.

It is at this point that medical empiricism fails us. Medicine must redefine its own philosophy; and, to do that, a critical account of the history and philosophy of medicines past would be of prime service.

---

[41] Illich, *Limits to Medicine*.

CHAPTER EIGHT

Class

DAVID FELDMAN

Introduction

British history and, in particular, British history between the late eighteenth and early twentieth centuries holds a place of special significance in the historiography of class. In part, this is because Friedrich Engels' account of social conditions in Manchester in 1844 helped to shape Karl Marx's thinking as he formulated both a theory of history and a programme of revolution driven by class struggles. But, more generally, Engels' book provides one example of the fascination with Britain as the first industrial nation, both among contemporaries and historians. Under this sign British history has exerted a recurrent attraction upon historians and theorists, Marxists and non-Marxists, eager to trace the impact of the industrial revolution on social relations and political movements. This history has not only had the force of a case-study but has also, at times, been endowed with emblematic significance. It has been the history of the English working class which, on occasion, has been raised as the yardstick of normal development against which the historical experience of other countries has been compared.[1]

But if the history of Britain has had a particular significance for historians of class, the concept of class has held a fluctuating and contested place within British historiography, particularly in recent decades. In the 1970s, with social history a self-confident presence, the concept of class stimulated both debate and research. It was characteristic of the moment that when, in 1976, the journal *Social History* announced its arrival, it proclaimed

---

[1] R. H. Tawney, 'The American Labour Movement', in J. Winter (ed.), *R. H. Tawney: The American Labour Movement and Other Essays* (Brighton, 1979), pp. 55–9. A more recent example of the influence of British history and historiography on the wider field of working-class history is I. Katznelson, 'Working-class Formation: Constructing Cases and Comparisons', in I. Katznelson and A. Zolberg (eds), *Working-class Formation: Nineteenth-century Patterns in Western Europe and the United States* (Princeton, NJ, 1986), pp. 3–41.

that 'social history' was not merely a new sub-discipline but, in the words of Lucien Febvre, 'a new land of history'. As it did so it pointed to two vital and inspirational currents: the *Annales* school in France and the Anglo-Marxist historians such as Eric Hobsbawm and Edward Thompson.[2] Indisputably, class mattered.

Two and a half decades later things look different. The view that 'class' is available to historians as a realist, albeit controversial, category of analysis has been brought radically into question. Rather than devote themselves to researching the processes of class formation, class conflict and accommodation, many historians now prefer to attend to how 'class' came into existence as a distinct category, how it developed and how it has structured our knowledge of the past.[3] Even historians who set out to defend or rehabilitate the significance of class in British history confess 'it has become increasingly unclear what the point of working-class history is'.[4] This essay examines the uses of class among British historians over the last century. In doing so it may help us to understand both the extent and the limits to the fall of class.

The industrial revolution

The terminology of class is embedded deeply within British historiography. It has been neither an invention of the post-1945 years, nor a monopoly of Marxists or historical sociologists. In the first four decades of the twentieth century class gave shape and direction to Whig accounts of political and social change during the industrial revolution. Even G. M. Young, who presented his elegiac and patrician portrait of Victorian England as 'the conversation of the people that counted', acknowledged that the 'ground-tone' of the decades was given by demographic, agrarian and industrial change which had created 'the visible splitting of society ... into possessors and a proletariat'.[5] G. M. Trevelyan similarly related the politics of the Reform Bill in class terms: 'the Whig followers of Grey and Althorp were

[2] 'Editorial', *Social History*, 1 (1976), 1.
[3] This shift can be followed in a useful reader: P. Joyce (ed.), *Class* (Oxford, 1995).
[4] M. Savage and A. Miles (eds), *The Remaking of the British Working Class 1840–1940* (London, 1994), p. ix. As this quotation hints, the diminishing presence and prestige of class-based history writing has been related to the intellectual and political failures of Marxism in the wider world. Accordingly, this decline is a widespread phenomenon and is by no means restricted to British history.
[5] G. M. Young, *Victorian England: Portrait of an Age* (London, 1936), pp. vi, 19, 22.

acting under the direct inspiration of middle-class opinion, and under the compelling fear of working-class revolt'.[6] According to the Oxford don and Conservative MP J. A. R. Marriott, whose *England since Waterloo* ran through eleven editions between 1913 and 1936, the Reform Act of 1832 'dethroned the landed aristocracy and committed supreme power to the commercial classes'. The remainder of the century too provided a political narrative that, at one level, Marriott related in class terms. By the accession of Edward VII, he explained, political supremacy had passed 'from the bourgeoisie to the manual workers'.[7]

These examples are taken from books aimed at students or general readers. Their scholarly source on the crisis of the early 1830s was J. R. Butler's *The Passing of the Great Reform Bill*, published in 1914. Butler possessed impeccable Whig credentials. He was born in the Master's lodge at Trinity College, Cambridge, went on to write Trevelyan's entry in the *Dictionary of National Biography* and, like Trevelyan, he eventually occupied the Regius Chair in History at the University of Cambridge. It is no great surprise, therefore, that he presented the Reform Bill as a necessary and wise adjustment to a changed world. The background to reform was 'a revolution in the social state of England' such that the system of parliamentary representation 'bore no longer any relation to the facts of national life'.[8]

In Butler's account the social and political drama was given a shape by class conflict. The dominant image he provides is one in which a class is ranged against the nation, the people against a ruling class.[9] This perspective drew on the categories and antinomies of Gladstonian Liberalism which sought to arouse popular sentiment against the selfish abuses of the 'upper 10,000'. But at times Butler also highlights both the middle and the working class separately as forces in conflict. Social change had intensified the division between capital and labour and the Bill itself introduced an 'era of middle-class domination of national life'. William Cobbett, we are told, appealed to the 'class consciousness' of 'the working classes', as did Robert Owen. The resolution of 1832, therefore, was inherently unstable.[10]

The industrial revolution and its social consequences provided the backcloth to these histories of political reform but elsewhere the economic and social changes received more sustained attention. The trilogy written by

[6] G. M. Trevelyan, *British History in the Nineteenth Century and After* (London, 1937), p. 225.
[7] J. A. R. Marriott, *England since Waterloo* (London, 1936), pp. 4–5.
[8] J. R. Butler, *The Passing of the Great Reform Bill* (London, 1914), p. 106.
[9] Ibid., pp. 425–6.
[10] Ibid., pp. 107, 122, 133, 138–9, 262.

Lawrence and Barbara Hammond was conceived as a whole but published
separately as *The Village Labourer, The Town Labourer* and *The Skilled
Labourer* in 1911, 1917 and 1919. Though little noticed initially by
academic reviewers, the three books shaped controversy in the inter-war
years and remained the starting-point for debate in the 1950s and 1960s on
the standard of life in industrialising England.[11]

Class and class domination provided a focus for the Hammonds' account
of social change in England between 1760 and 1830. Their histories were
predicated on (even if they did not examine) a pre-industrial society
dominated by communitarian values and practices. Enclosure in the
eighteenth century, engineered by an 'omnipotent' aristocracy, they argued,
destroyed the village community and 'alienated the soil from the whole
labouring class'.[12] In towns too the Industrial Revolution (always
capitalised) 'separated England from her past'.[13] The Hammonds acknowledged that large-scale industry, capitalist organisation and a proletariat were
not inventions of this period but, they claimed, in these years they became
'the most obvious and significant fact' about English society.[14]

For the Hammonds the political dimension of this process was of central
importance. The sub-title of *The Village Labourer* is *A Study of the
Government of England before the Reform Bill*. In the book they aimed to
show 'what was happening to the working classes under a government in
which they had no share'.[15] The rural revolt, the blazing ricks and machine-
wrecking of 1830 were the wages of sins committed by the ruling class. In
the case of the towns the social system produced by the industrial revolution
was deformed by a spirit which accepted the division of the country into
'two nations' as inevitable and which regarded men and women not as
citizens but as servants of economic power.[16] Class conflict for the
Hammonds, therefore, was not an inevitable feature of all societies but a
disfiguring fissure that could and should be repaired by a moralised and
reformed political community.[17]

[11] On the Hammonds see S. Weaver, *The Hammonds: A Marriage in History* (Stanford, CA, 1997);
P. Clarke, *Liberals and Social Democrats* (Cambridge, 1978). For an example of their influence see
G. M. Trevelyan, *English Social History* (London, 1946), pp. 463–85.
[12] J. L. Hammond and B. Hammond, *The Village Labourer* (London, 1911), p. 105.
[13] J. L. Hammond and B. Hammond, *The Town Labourer* (London, 1917), p. 3.
[14] Ibid., p. 4.
[15] Hammond and Hammond, *Village Labourer*, p. 7.
[16] Hammond and Hammond, *Town Labourer*, pp. vii–viii; J. L. Hammond and B. Hammond, *The
Skilled Labourer* (London, 1919), pp. 5–7.
[17] P. Clarke, 'The Social Democratic Theory of Class Struggle', in J. Winter (ed.), *The Working
Class in Modern British History* (Cambridge, 1983), pp. 3–18.

Unlike later Marxist historians, the Hammonds retained faith in the reforming capacities of the English governing classes. The separation of classes was an inevitable facet of modernity but it did not have to lead, as it had done, to a history which 'reads like a history of a civil war'.[18] This left a notable imprint on their history. *The Village Labourer* concludes with a striking assessment of the eighteenth-century ruling class and a recuperation of a Whig, national history. As a class of country gentlemen, accustomed to vigorous physical exercise, the English ruling class had not succumbed 'to the supreme vice of moral decadence' which had flourished in European court society; alone among the European aristocracies, the English ruling class did not crumble at once before Napoleon.[19]

This integration of class within a consensual national history — or at least a history which carried the hope that a consensual nation could be created — can be found more widely in early twentieth-century historio-graphy. It can be seen, for instance, in Mark Hovell's account, *The Chartist Movement*, published posthumously in 1918. Hovell drew a contrast between the emotional and violent character of Chartism and the early twentieth-century working-class movement, 'led by men of clear and shrewd, though perhaps limited outlook, of uncommon ability, backed by three generations of experience and a solid organisation'.[20] Like the Hammonds, he understood the 'divorce of classes' to have been an outcome of the industrial revolution. At the same time, he faced the apparent paradox that it was where production was still carried on under 'the domestic system' that doctrines promoting class conflict drew most support.[21] Chartism, he concluded, was not the product of 'the developed capitalistic system' but of a transitional phase. Its immaturity reflected both the incompleteness of economic change and the immaturity of the working-class movement which prevented its effective integration with the polity.[22]

Implicit here was a view of the factory as the location within which mature, stable relations between capital and labour could emerge. This idea was shared by Sidney and Beatrice Webb.[23] Indeed, the Webbs saw Chartism in terms almost identical to Hovell. In 1926 Beatrice Webb reflected as follows:

[18] Hammond and Hammond, *Skilled Labourer*, p. 1.
[19] Hammond and Hammond, *Village Labourer*, p. 328.
[20] M. Hovell, *The Chartist Movement* (Manchester, 1925), p. 27.
[21] Ibid., pp. 9, 17, 22.
[22] Ibid., p. 27.
[23] S. Webb and B. Webb, *Problems of Modern Industry* (London, 1898), pp. 143–9.

> The working-class revolt against the misery and humiliation brought about by the onset of the Industrial Revolution — a revolt, in spasmodic violence, apeing revolution — had its fling in the 'twenties and 'thirties and its apotheosis in the Chartist movement of the 'forties.[24]

However, by the 1850s 'the spread of education among the rank and file' and the steady expansion of industry led trade unionists to substitute 'Industrial Diplomacy for the ruder methods of the Class War'.[25]

The historical work of G. D. H. Cole offers a further instance of this narrative and analysis in which class was created by the industrial revolution. Cole was a socialist whereas the Hammonds remained tied to the liberal tradition. His preferences, which had drawn him to guild socialism, were voluntarist whereas the Webbs placed their faith in an elitist and instrumentalist pursuit of influence in government. Despite these political differences, like the other historians we have discussed thus far, Cole's histories presented the industrial revolution as an epochal caesura: it destroyed village life, created the problem of the factory town, compelled parliament to reform itself and raised the middle class to affluence and power. 'And, last but not least, it created the modern wage-earning class — the proletariat which nominally free, can live only by selling its labour for a wage'.[26]

These historians agreed that the industrial revolution created a new society divided by class but, with the partial exception of the Hammonds, they did not focus in detail on the economics of this transformation or its impact on social structure, social relations or a way of life. Instead, their central questions, though diverse, converged on the political meaning and consequences of the industrial revolution. We have already noted the way in which the Hammonds' first interest was the behaviour and morality of the nation's rulers. Cole's histories chronicled radical and working-class activism. The history of the labour movement, for Cole, was a record of the struggle to articulate and realise those ideals that might one day supersede the capitalist system. In this respect, the story itself was the message.[27] His interest in the history of working-class life was focused on the ways in which it fed into the labour movement in the most immediate ways. For him, as for Hovell, mass support for Chartism was seen as an instinctual response to hunger. In so far as either writer approached the

---

[24] B. Webb, *My Apprenticeship* (London, 1926), p. 179.

[25] Ibid., pp. 179–80.

[26] G. D. H. Cole, *A Short History of the British Working Class Movement 1789–1927, vol. 1* (London, 1932), p. 11.

[27] See A. Wright, *G. D. H. Cole and Socialist Democracy* (Oxford, 1979), pp. 144, 147.

history of working-class culture it was in the idealisation of rationalist figures such as William Lovett and Francis Place.[28] In the case of Sidney and Beatrice Webb, the way of life of the new proletariat — what a later generation would call their culture — was a distant concern. In the introduction to their *History of Trade Unionism* the Webbs defended their approach:

> In spite of all the pleas of modern historians for less history of the actions of government, and more descriptions of the manners and customs of the governed, it remains true that history, however it may relieve and enliven itself with descriptions of the manners and morals of the people, must, if it is to be history at all, follow the course of continuous organisations.[29]

Before the industrial revolution

The invocations of class we have discussed so far were united in their belief that it was a specifically modern phenomenon, a characteristic of industrial societies. It is symptomatic that the term had no place in accounts of the English Revolution written in the first four decades of the century. Although Trevelyan was content to use 'class' to describe and explain change in the late eighteenth and nineteenth centuries the absence of class conflict from the Civil War was, he argued, a key feature which distinguished it from the French Revolution. The English Revolution was characterised by a clash of ideas and principles; ultimately it was marked by the triumph of liberty.[30]

Nevertheless, the nature of the industrial revolution as well as its significance as the progenitor of class was brought into question by some historians in the inter-war period. The Hammonds' view of the industrial revolution was the object of direct criticism in *An Economic History of Modern Britain* published in 1926 by the Cambridge historian J. H. Clapham.[31] In contrast to the accounts we have discussed so far, Clapham emphasised 'the diversity of national economic life' and the unevenness of technological change. On the basis of statistical evidence Clapham argued that, except for those involved in dying trades such as handloom weaving,

---

[28] For both men this was also expressed in practical commitment to the Workers' Educational Association. On Cole and the WEA see L. Goldman, *Dons and Workers: Oxford and Adult Education since 1850* (Oxford, 1995). On Hovell see W. F. Tout, 'Preface', in Hovell, *The Chartist Movement*, p. xxi. See too G. Wallas, *The Life of Francis Place, 1771–1854* (London, 1898).

[29] S. Webb and B. Webb, *History of Trade Unionism* (London, 1894), p. viii.

[30] G. M. Trevelyan, *England under the Stuarts* (London, 1904), pp. 195–6.

[31] J. H. Clapham, *An Economic History of Modern Britain, vol. 1* (Oxford, 1926), pp. vii–viii.

living standards rose after the Napoleonic Wars. In this way he attacked two central tenets of the intepretation proposed by the Hammonds: that economic change in these years was dramatic and, for the mass of the people, calamitous.[32]

The work of some historians of sixteenth- and seventeeth-century England posed a different challenge to the idea that class was born with the industrial revolution. The writing of R. H. Tawney evolved in sympathy and in tension with the historical work of the Hammonds. Like them, he developed a moral critique of 'the acquisitive society' but in his case it was inspired by Anglican socialism. Tawney's chief interest was in the erosion of 'traditional standards of social behaviour'.[33] He was critical, therefore, of the Hammonds' 'disposition' to 'touch lightly, if at all, on those crucial antecedents [of late eighteenth- and early nineteenth-century enclosures], and to write at times as though the fall of man occurred in the reign of George III'.[34] Tawney traced back to the sixteenth and seventeenth centuries the attitudes and social divisions identified by the Hammonds. His first book, *The Agrarian Problem in the Sixteenth Century*, published in 1912, focused on the growth of rural capitalism in the sixteenth and early seventeenth centuries.[35] It also anticipated the triumph of capitalism in the Civil War and settlements of 1660 and 1689 which removed the last obstacles to the aggrandisement of the great landed proprietors. Tawney's second purely historical work, *Religion and the Rise of Capitalism*, traced the separation of economic and moral thinking in England to the rise of Puritanism, 'the schoolmaster of the English middle classes'.[36] The consequences of the rise of agricultural capitalism were analysed by Tawney in his 1941 essay, 'The Rise of the Gentry'. The relative decline of the aristocracy was part of a transition from feudal to bourgeois society which, he hinted loudly, had its political analogue in civil war and revolution.[37]

Tawney was not a lone scholar exploring the modernity of early modern society. This had been a major theme, before the First World War, for the leading historical economists William Cunningham, W. J. Ashley and George Unwin. Their theme was developed in the inter-war years by others

---

[32] Clapham, *Economic History*, pp. 447–507.

[33] J. Winter, 'Introduction', in idem, *History and Society: Essays by R. H. Tawney* (London, 1978), p. 24.

[34] R. H. Tawney, 'J. L. Hammond 1872–1949', in Winter (ed.), *History and Society: Essays by R. H. Tawney*, p. 237.

[35] R. H. Tawney, *The Agrarian Problem in the Sixteenth Century* (London, 1912).

[36] R. H. Tawney, *Religion and the Rise of Capitalism* (London, 1926).

[37] R. H. Tawney, 'The Rise of the Gentry', *Economic History Review*, 11 (1941), 1–38; see too idem, 'Harrington's Interpretation of his Age', *Proceedings of the British Academy*, 24 (1941), 199–223.

such as Ephraim Lipson. Lipson argued that, although the industrial revolution brought the application of motive power to industry and transport and led to the concentration of workers in factories, it did not 'give birth to a different kind of industrial society based on the division between employers and wage earners'.[38] His emphasis on the capitalist character of the early modern economy allowed him to suggest a society troubled by the intermittent eruption of 'class struggle'.[39] But this was a theme he mentioned rather than explored.

It was left for Marxist historians to insist on the importance of class for understanding pre-industrial England. In 1940, Christopher Hill, a young and recently appointed fellow at Balliol College, Oxford, and a member of the Communist Party, edited a thin volume titled *The English Revolution 1640* intended for a readership beyond the academy. The book contained three essays and Hill's own was by far the most substantial, taking up more than half of its 136 pages. Hill explicitly disparaged interpretations of the revolution repeated by 'Whig and Liberal historians': specifically, he dismissed as superficial the belief that 'the Parliamentary armies were fighting for the liberty of the individual and his rights against a tyrannical government'. Historians had paid too much attention to what people at the time had said and had penetrated too little below the surface.

> The English revolution of 1640–60 was a great social movement like the French Revolution of 1789. An old order that was essentially feudal was destroyed by violence, a new capitalist social order created in its place. The Civil War was a class war, in which the despotism of Charles I was defended by the reactionary forces of the established church and feudal landlords. Parliament beat the King because it could appeal to the enthusiastic support of the trading and industrial classes in town and countryside, to the yeoman and progressive gentry, and to wider masses of the population whenever they were able by free discussion to understand what the struggle was really about.[40]

Hill's book preceded Tawney's essay on the rise of the gentry by a year. Individually and together, the two interventions presented a serious challenge to the orthodox interpretation of the revolution and both, but particularly Hill, emphasised the role of class in history before the industrial revolution.

---

[38] E. Lipson, 'England in the Age of Mercantilism', *Journal of Economic and Business History*, 4 (1932), 692.

[39] On 'class struggle' see E. Lipson, *The Economic History of England: The Age of Mercantilism* (London, 1934), p. 409.

[40] C. Hill, 'The English Revolution', in idem (ed.), *The English Revolution 1640* (London, 1940), p. 9.

Hill's essay on 1640 prefigured one of the distinctive contributions of the Communist Party Historians Group in the post-war decade. The group, in which Hill was a leading figure, was officially constituted in 1946. It comprised a broad collection of activists but included a minority of established or aspiring academic historians. Among its members were Maurice Dobb, Victor Kiernan, Christopher Hill, Rodney Hilton, Eric Hobsbawm, John Saville and Edward Thompson. These figures, with the exception of Dobb who was older, were drawn from the student generations of the 1930s and 1940s. They formed the first cohort of Marxists within the British historical profession.[41]

Yet the concept of class did not provide the motor for the Communist historical project in the post-war decade. The primary term for these historians, disclosing the pattern of the past and present, was 'the mode of production'. This concept, which encompassed both the forces of production and the social relations of production, was what conferred on a society its particular shape.[42] This idea was elaborated most fully by Maurice Dobb in *Studies in the Development of Capitalism*, published in 1946. Dobb's work formulated the 'main and central problem' addressed by the Communist historians.[43]

Dobb defined class, conventionally enough, as the relationship to the process of production. He elaborated on the point decisively, however, by emphasising that this relationship amounted to a particular mode of extracting and distributing the fruits of surplus value. In this register, Marxist historians regarded the historical process as a succession of economic stages. Dobb argued that the form of extracting surplus labour had altered at different points of development 'and these varieties of form have been associated with the use of various methods and instruments of production and with different levels of productivity'.[44] The growth of industry thus engendered new classes because new instruments of production created novel problems, requiring new forms of appropriating surplus labour.

Dobb addressed class in the context of a history of economic transformation in the long term. In doing so he disconnected the history of class from a narrative set by political history. Accordingly it was capitalism, not the industrial revolution and its reflection in the political turbulence of the

---

[41] E. J. Hobsbawm, 'The Communist Party Historians Group', in M. Cornforth (ed.), *Rebels and their Causes: Essays in Honour of A. L. Morton* (London, 1978), pp. 22–6.

[42] M. Dobb, 'Historical Materialism and the Role of the Economic Factor in History', *History*, 36 (1951), 1.

[43] M. Dobb, *Studies in the Development of Capitalism* (London, 1946); Hobsbawm, 'The Historians Group', p. 38.

[44] Dobb, *Studies*, pp. 15–16.

early nineteenth century, which lay at the centre of Dobb's history. At the same time, however, Dobb adhered to a narrow treatment of class as an effect of the particular form of the exploitation of labour in the immediate process of production. In contrast to later formulations, class struggle was here conceived as a second-order phenomenon; a function of economic history.[45]

In general, it has not been this strand in the output of the Communist Party historians which a subsequent generation has emphasised. Recent assessments have highlighted a second aspect of their work: their role as pioneers researching the history of popular protest and popular politics.[46] Here their main focus of interest was on the forms of protest and revolt which preceded the struggles of the industrial working class. The Communist historians presented their party as the legatee of what they construed as a national radical tradition.[47] Rodney Hilton concluded his essay, 'Peasant Movements in England before 1381', with the following observation:

> When we read the statement of a Colonel Rainborough in 1647, 'The poorest he that is in England hath a life to live as the greatest he', we know that here is an expression of an English tradition as ancient as the more publicised traditions of reverence for old established institutions.[48]

The most celebrated contribution in this vein is Christopher Hill's essay, 'The Norman Yoke'. Hill traced the theory of Saxon rights — usurped by the Norman Conquest, but which the people continually strove to recover — as it was used to rally resistance to the Crown, aristocracy and privilege from the seventeenth to the late nineteenth centuries.[49]

At the same time as they identified their party as the inheritors of the national radical tradition, the Communist historians' relationship to that tradition remained critical and distanced. They retained a developmental perspective on the history of popular movements and sought to distinguish these earlier forms from mature class movements. Hill's conclusion to 'The Norman Yoke' was that 'Once the role of the working-class movement in modern industrial society has been grasped, nostalgic yearnings for an

---

[45] Dobb, *Studies*, p. 16; Simon Clarke, 'Socialist Historians and the Critique of Economism', *History Workshop Journal*, 10 (1978), 140, 149.

[46] B. Schwarz, ' "The People" in History: The Communist Party Historians Group, 1946–56', in R. Johnson, G. McLennan, B. Schwarz, D. Sutton (eds), *Making Histories: Studies in History-writing and Politics* (London, 1982), pp. 68–9; H. Kaye, *The British Marxist Historians: An Introductory Analysis* (Cambridge, 1984). D. Dworkin, *Cultural Marxism in Postwar Britain* (Durham, NC, 1997), pp. 15–26.

[47] Schwarz, ' "The People" in History', p. 56.

[48] R. Hilton, 'Peasant Movements in England before 1381', *Economic History Review*, 2, 11 (1949), 136.

[49] C. Hill, 'The Norman Yoke', in J. Saville (ed.), *Democracy and the Labour Movement* (London, 1954), pp. 11–66.

idealised past give place to a scientific programme of action for building the future out of the present.'[50]

This two-sided relationship to the history of popular protest is particularly clear in the work of the two Communist historians who researched and wrote most in this area: Eric Hobsbawm and George Rudé. Both Hobsbawm and Rudé rejected the idea that the history of pre-industrial popular protest consisted of irrational and futile gestures by ignorant and desperate men. Instead they emphasised the purposive character of popular protest and that ' "the mob" consisted of the ordinary urban poor'.[51] The Luddites, for example, were defended from the Webbs' dismissive verdict which saw machine-breaking as a 'blind' and 'groping' response to industrialism by the early labour movement. On the contrary, Luddism was seen as an appropriate and successful tactic in the boom conditions at the end of the Napoleonic Wars. Much of the machine-breaking did not betoken hostility to new technologies but was a tactic to secure higher wages: 'collective bargaining by riot'.[52]

At the same time as these historians were concerned to recover the rational and instrumental character of popular movements, however, they were also clear that the mob was both 'primitive' and 'pre-political'. The advent of modern industrial society had brought a new epoch in the history of protest. Industrialisation required workers to adapt themselves to a new pattern of life and struggle, and the modern labour movements 'are the most striking and universal result of their education'.[53] They were in no doubt as to the progressive character of this change. Hobsbawm observed wryly:

> The transformation of the *menu peuple* of large capital cities into a modern working class has meant a loss of colour, but whoever has seen the horrifying spectacle of the Neapolitan sub-proletariat will treat even Stoke-on-Trent with indulgence.[54]

Hobsbawm, Rudé and others thus developed an original and distinctive curiosity about the forms of protest which had preceded the modern movement. However, their understanding of pre-industrial forms of popular and 'primitive' protest was framed by a teleology whose endpoint was the emergence of the modern working class and labour movement.

---

[50] Hill, 'The Norman Yoke', p. 66.
[51] E. J. Hobsbawm, *Primitive Rebels* (Manchester, 1959), p. 114.
[52] E. J. Hobsbawm, 'The Machine Breakers' in idem (ed.), *Labouring Men* (London, 1964), pp. 6–8; G. Rudé, *The Crowd in History* (New York, NY, 1963), pp. 89–91.
[53] Hobsbawm, *Primitive Rebels*, p. 108; idem, 'Custom, Wages and Work Load', in *Labouring Men*, pp. 344–70.
[54] Hobsbawm, *Primitive Rebels*, p. 125.

This left them reluctant to describe these earlier phenomena as class movements.

The Communist historians approached class in two ways. First, class was meaningful within a history of economic development. Here it was conceived as a function of the relations of production: as a vital presence within human history but not as its motive force. Second, the Communist historians were interested in class as a political formation which characterised modern industrial society. The former of these two emphases was not developed by historians in subsequent decades. The historical sociology of transformation and change was little explored and the economic history of the industrial revolution was largely abandoned by historians for whom class was an important concept.[55] Instead, as we shall see, the history of class developed predominantly as a history of popular politics.

Making and breaking the English working class

Edward Thompson, along with many others in the Communist Party Historians Group, left the Communist Party in the crisis that followed the Soviet invasion of Hungary in 1956. Despite this political trajectory, Thompson's landmark volume, *The Making of the English Working Class*, published in 1963, has been praised as the finest single achievement of Anglo-Marxist historiography and identified as the belated offspring of the Historians Group.[56] In some respects there is good reason to emphasise this lineage. The history of English popular radicalism, central to the work of the Communist historians, is not only an integral part of Thompson's book but is pursued there with unprecedented attention to the content of those traditions as they were reshaped over time. Nevertheless, the argument here will be that, if we focus upon its treatment of class, *The Making of the English Working Class* is more notable for the way in which it departed from what had become the mainstream of Anglo-Marxist historiography.

In *The Making of the English Working Class*, Thompson presents the process of class formation in three phases. In the first section of the book he reconstructs the radical traditions among urban artisans and tradesmen — religious dissent, popular constitutionalism and riot. The second part of the

---

[55] There are, of course, important exceptions including E. J. Hobsbawm, *Industry and Empire* (London, 1968); R. Samuel, 'Workshop of the World: Steam Power and Hand Technology in Mid-Victorian Britain', *History Workshop Journal*, 3 (1997), 6–72.

[56] Schwarz, '"The People" in History', pp. 85–6; Dworkin, *Cultural Marxism*, pp. 108–9.

book deals with 'the truly catastrophic nature of the Industrial Revolution'.[57] It also traces the emergence of 'collective self-consciousness, with its corresponding theory, institutions, discipline and community values', as the emergent working class responded to both economic exploitation and political repression.[58] In the final section, Thompson charts the struggles of Luddites and the revolutionary underground, of trade unionists and political radicals, of Owenites and syndicalists, from the Napoleonic Wars to the Reform Act of 1832 and its immediate aftermath.

In general, Thompson reproduced a story familiar from Whig historiography and the catastrophist interpretation of the industrial revolution. Within this familiar framework he revisited episodes and consistently rewrote them in ways that recovered the creative activity of popular protest and also insisted on its importance upon the larger historical stage. Contrary to 'the classic Whig interpretation', for instance, Thompson argued that the physical force conspiracies of 1817 were not merely the invention of government spies and *provocateurs* but reflected the existence of a real revolutionary movement in Nottingham and Yorkshire.[59] Similarly, Butler's account of the crises of autumn 1831 and the 'days of May' the following year was criticised for its complacent failure to understand that the country was 'within an ace of revolution' and, more generally, to comprehend that it was the strength of the working-class radical movement that drove on the Reform crisis to its conclusion.[60]

This emphasis on the ways in which working people 'contributed by conscious efforts to the making of history' had still larger consequences for Thompson's analysis of class.[61] Thompson eschewed an understanding of class as a function of economic development. 'The working class', he wrote, 'did not rise like the sun at an appointed time. It was present at its own making.'[62] The idea of agency was at the heart of Thompson's reconfiguration of class and the mode of production was now displaced as the key and prior term for understanding class.

The stimulus for this creative process lay in men's experience and the conflicts which arose from them; these conflicts, in turn, generated an

---

[57] E. P. Thompson, *The Making of the English Working Class*, revised edn (Harmondsworth, 1968), pp. 217–18.
[58] Ibid., p. 463.
[59] Ibid., pp. 711–34.
[60] Ibid., pp. 888–90, 899.
[61] Ibid., p. 13.
[62] Ibid., p. 9.

awareness of class. Thompson did not depart from the view that class was a necessary consequence of a particular relationship to the means of production.[63] Rather, the concept of experience allowed him to move with illusive ease between class as a relationship to the means of production and class understood as class consciousness. The idea of 'experience' translated a structured economic relationship into a confrontation between a multitude of individuals and the world beyond them. Once the economy was approached at this level it was easily rendered as a cultural formation as individuals were seen to have made sense of their experience. In a famous passage Thompson wrote:

> Class happens when some men, as a result of common experiences (inherited or shared), feel and articulate the identity of their interests as between themselves, and as against other men whose interests are different from (and usually opposed to) theirs.[64]

It is this process of making sense which, for Thompson, rendered class a cultural as much as a social and economic phenomenon:

> Class consciousness is the way in which these experiences are handled in cultural terms: embodied in traditions, value-systems, ideas and institutional forms. If the experience appears as determined, class consciousness does not.[65]

There were limits to Thompson's turn to culture. Class could not be defined simply as a cultural formation, free from objective determinations.[66] At the same time, however, Thompson appeared to abandon any normative assessment of what a class movement was: 'Class is defined by men as they live their own history, and, in the end, this is its only definition.'[67] But when Thompson rejected the idea that there was any pre-given identity or consciousness that a class should have he also left open the question whether a class could have *any* consciousness or identity.

As he later acknowledged, in taking the case of the English working class in the late eighteenth and early nineteenth centuries this issue did not directly arise. This was because 'class in its modern usage ... became available to the cognitive system of people living at that time. Hence the concept not only enables us to organise and analyse the evidence; it is also, in a new sense, *present in the evidence itself.*'[68] However, when Thompson turned to work on

---

[63] He remained convinced that 'the class experience is largely determined by the productive relations into which men are born — or enter involuntarily', *The Making*, p. 10.
[64] Ibid., pp. 9–10.
[65] Ibid., p. 10.
[66] E. P. Thompson, 'Eighteenth-century English Society: Class Struggle Without Class', *Social History*, 3 (1978), 149.
[67] Thompson, *The Making*, p. 11.
[68] Thompson, 'Eighteenth-century English Society', 148.

the eighteenth century he no longer found documents containing class
terminology 'in its modern usage'. In this circumstance, while refusing a
structural definition of class as 'so many men who stand in a certain relation to
the means of production', Thompson was bound to face the question of whether
it was possible to apply the concept of class to such a society. His answer was to
label as 'class struggle' any conflict related to property relations and the
extraction of surplus value at any time.[69] In contrast to more orthodox Anglo-
Marxist historians, Thompson abandoned a prescriptive view of class and
found it possible to categorise pre-industrial movements of protest as class
struggles.[70]

This formulation offered historians both gains and losses. Thompson's
achievement was to release Marxist histories of pre-industrial protest from
the need to measure them against a political standard set by the modern
labour movement. At the same time, his formulation was both
reductive — capitalism produces class conflicts — and so capacious that it
provides no ground upon which to categorise cases, compare one with
another or to explain why one phase of class conflict faded and another
took hold.[71]

At this point we can summarise three of the distinctive features of
Thompson's approach to class. First, and most fundamentally, for
Thompson it was now class struggle and not the mode of production
that was the primary focus for analysis. Second, in contrast to a previous
generation of labour historians, Thompson's attention to experience led
him to attend not only to the history of formal politics and the institutions
of the labour movement but also to the ideas and signifying practices of
working-class culture more broadly.[72] Third, Thompson's focus on
experience and struggle as the foundations of class meant that the history
of class became identified with the history of protest and the history of
popular politics. It is characteristic that it was in the simultaneous struggle
for the Reform Bill, and the struggle with the middle class for control of
the radical movement, that the process of 'making' reached fruition and
the working class discovered itself.[73] Popular politics thus became an

---

[69] Thompson, 'Eighteenth-century English Society', 149

[70] We can contrast Thompson's position to the doubts expressed by Hobsbawm whether the term
working class could properly be applied to England in the 1820s and 1830s, while a working class
was still emerging from a 'mass of petty producers, small masters, countrymen etc'. 'The Labour
Aristocracy', in *Labouring Men*, p. 276.

[71] Katznelson, 'Working-class Formation', p. 11.

[72] R. Johnson, C. Critcher and J. Clarke (eds), *Working-class Culture: Studies in History and Theory*
(London, 1979).

[73] Thompson, *The Making*, pp. 887–8.

expression of the totality of experience. The place of class within a history of structural transformation and continuity over several centuries was lost from view.

The publication of *The Making of the English Working Class* did not eclipse other traditions of social history and working-class history in Britain in the 1960s and 1970s. Institutionally oriented labour history and the history of social policy, demography and family history all provided a significant impetus to a new social history; modernists borrowed from sociology, early-modernists from social anthropology. Moreover, a great deal of social history was written from an explicitly anti-Marxist position.[74] From another perspective, however, Thompson's influence was immense. To the extent that the social history of modern Britain, as it was written in the late 1960s and 1970s, possessed an integrating, synthesising theme then that theme was class: the emergence, development and containment of social and political conflicts between different classes. Class was employed by historians to organise research on topics from work to religion and from philanthropy to popular recreations, and to infuse particular and sometimes recondite topics with a larger significance. And, insofar as class was discussed, Thompson's formulations were central. There were, of course, other voices and other traditions: Harold Perkin's rendition, strongly influenced by Talcott Parsons, of class conflict and accommodation as an idealist struggle for hearts and minds between contending visions of the social order, the political sociology of class presented by Peter Clarke, and other Marxist versions such as the structural and quantitative analysis by John Foster of *Class Struggle and the Industrial Revolution*.[75] As with Thompson's work on the nineteenth century, each of these reflections on class located its ultimate significance in the dynamics of political conflict and stability. However, none of these alternative visions and formulations was as influential as *The Making of the English Working Class* or occupied a comparable point of reference.

One way of appraising that influence is to turn to two major essays on the working class at the end of the nineteenth century: Gareth Stedman Jones' 'Working-class Culture and Working-class Politics in London,

---

[74] M. Taylor, 'The Beginnings of Modern British Social History?', *History Workshop Journal*, 43 (1997), 155–76.
[75] H. Perkin, *The Origins of Modern English Society, 1780–1880* (London, 1969); P. Clarke, 'Electoral Sociology of Modern Britain', *History*, 57 (1972), 31–55; J. Foster, *Class Struggle and the Industrial Revolution* (London, 1974).

1870–1900: Notes on the Remaking of a Working Class' and Eric Hobsbawm's, 'The Making of the Working Class 1870–1914', the former first published in 1974, the latter in 1984.[76] Neither of these essays followed Thompson in any devotional sense and both adopted a more formal analytical structure than is present in *The Making of the English Working Class*. Nevertheless, the titles of both essays immediately declare their debt to Thompson. Both essays also emulated Thompson in their explicit attempts to combine an analysis of the history of the labour movement and the history of working-class culture: what Hobsbawm characterised as 'the working class of cup finals, fish-and-chip shops, palais-de-dance and Labour with a capital L'.[77] Like Thompson, these historians placed culture in the context of the material realities of working-class life. This context was approached in broad terms and encompassed changing living standards, patterns of residence and new habits of consumption but, as with Thompson, both historians gave causal precedence to changes in the structure of production. Both essays also understood the development of working-class consciousness and working-class politics as an expression of the totality — the economic, social and cultural history — of working-class life.

But, at the same time as Thompson's example was an inspiration to others, the pursuit of 'experience' produced results which proved hard to assimilate within a framework which privileged class as the shared experience of manual labourers and their families. Work on the 'labour aristocracy' was one focus for this research which explored the particular work experience, associational life and concern with respectability of a limited upper stratum of the working class.[78] Most damaging, however, was the work of historians on the supposedly 'mature' working class of the late nineteenth and early twentieth centuries. Historians now argued that there was no linear move towards deskilling and the simplification of work over the course of the nineteenth century: sectionalism was rife, subcontracting was widespread, penny capitalist activity commonplace and workers bound in a relationship with their employers characterised by

---

[76] G. Stedman Jones, 'Working-class Culture and Working-class Politics in London, 1870–1900: Notes on the Remaking of a Working Class', *Journal of Social History*, 7 (1974), 460–508; E. J. Hobsbawm, 'The Making of the Working Class 1870–1914', in idem, *Worlds of Labour* (London, 1984), pp. 194–213.

[77] Hobsbawm, 'Making of the Working Class', p. 194.

[78] See for instance R. Gray, *The Labour Aristocracy in Victorian Edinburgh* (Oxford, 1976); G. Crossick, *An Artisan Elite in Victorian Society* (London, 1978).

CLASS 199

cooperation as well as conflict. To some extent, attention also shifted from the minority of workers enrolled in trade unions to the large majority who were not.[79] Paul Johnson's research on patterns of saving and spending similarly emphasised internal divisions within the working class. In place of class and community, Johnson argued, consumption and display, competition and emulation underpinned collective institutions such as savings clubs and friendly societies.[80] This emphasis on diversity meant that the capacity of 'class' to account for political change in the late nineteenth and early twentieth centuries appeared decreasingly credible. By and large, the pursuit of 'experience' enriched social history empirically but undermined the coherence and explanatory power of the prevailing conception of class.

Thompson's call to rescue the poor and defeated from the 'enormous condescension of posterity' resonated powerfully with historians affiliated to new social movements: most significantly with feminist historians who were concerned to recover the history of their antecedents or to comprehend the ideological and material sources of female subordination.[81] Several historians explored the hostility of male workers to women in the workplace. Others emphasised conflicts or divisions between men and women in working-class homes and streets. Work by Barbara Taylor and Sally Alexander revealed the ways in which, among other things, the Chartist movement was an attempt to maintain masculine privilege.[82]

By the end of the 1970s work inspired by feminism was being supplemented by new research into the histories of immigrants in modern Britain. In general, these histories revealed the particularities of immigrant experiences and found that ethnicity was not reducible to class. Closely related to this, historians began to recover and analyse the hostile reception

[79] C. More, *Skill and the English Working Class* (London, 1980); J. Benson, *The Penny Capitalists* (London, 1983); R. Harrison and J. Zeitlin (eds), *Divisions of Labour* (Brighton, 1985); P. Joyce, *Work, Society and Politics: The Culture of the Factory in Later Victorian England* (Brighton, 1980); R. Mckibbin, 'Why was there no Marxism in Britain?', *English Historical Review*, 99 (1984); W. Lazonick, 'Industrial Relations and Technical Change: The Case of the Self-acting Mule', *Cambridge Journal of Economics*, 3 (1979).
[80] P. Johnson, *Saving and Spending: The Working-class Economy in England 1870–1939* (Oxford, 1985).
[81] S. Rowbotham, *Hidden from History* (London, 1973); A. Davin and S. Alexander, 'Feminist History', *History Workshop Journal*, 1 (1976), 4.
[82] B. Taylor, *Eve and the New Jerusalem: Socialism and Feminism in the Nineteenth Century* (London, 1983); S. Alexander, 'Women, Class and Sexual Difference in the 1830s and 1840s', *History Workshop Journal*, 17 (1984); Fine examples of the broader trends can be found in A. John (ed.), *Unequal Opportunities: Women's Employment in England, 1800–1914* (Oxford, 1986); J. Lewis (ed.), *Labour and Love: Women's Experience of Home and Family* (Oxford, 1986).

immigrants received, not only from politicians but also from, among others, trade unionists and working-class patriots.[83] For many historians, their search for experience and their recovery of agency had made it impossible to think of the working class as other than deeply divided by gender and ethnicity; at worst it became hard to conceive of a working class at all.

The difficulties surrounding the concept of the working class were, if anything, multiplied where historians turned to the history of the middle class. Here too historians discovered a diversity of economic interests, for instance, between professionals and entrepreneurs, retailers and merchants, and between the financial and industrial sectors. These fissures were supplemented by other divisions based on status and gender, religion and politics.[84] But unlike the working class, the middle class generated few leaders or intellectuals willing to announce the existence of the middle class and still fewer who were eager to promote an independent middle-class politics. In the face of this reticence historians have looked for new forms of collective action or ideology on which to locate middle-class identity. Morris, for instance, in his study of Leeds, has rested his claims for a class identity upon the practices of voluntary associations. Others have pointed to a characteristic middle-class economic ideology or religious outlook. But what emerges, from Morris's study is, at best, a highly attenuated assertion of class because his scrupulous research reveals the constant intrusion of divisions. Moreover, the timing of the growth of voluntary societies and a new public sphere which stretches into the eighteenth century fits poorly with the emergence of Morris's middle class in the second quarter of the nineteenth century.[85] Similarly, historians who emphasise evangelicalism or political economy find it hard to demonstrate that either was an invention or possession of the middle class.[86] An approach to class which sees politics and ideology as the touchstone of class identity has thus faced immense difficulties when it has confronted the history of the middle class in Britain.

[83] See for instance K. Lunn (ed.), *Hosts, Immigrants and Minorities: Historical Responses to Newcomers in British Society, 1870–1914* (Folkestone, 1980); S. Gilley and R. Swift, *The Irish in the Victorian City* (London, 1985).

[84] W. D. Rubinstein, *Men of Property* (London, 1981); V. A. C. Gatrell, 'Incorporation and the Pursuit of Liberal Hegemony in Manchester, 1790–1839', in D. Fraser (ed.), *Municipal Reform and the Industrial City* (Leicester, 1982); L. Davidoff and C. Hall, *Family Fortunes: Men and Women of the English Middle Class 1780–1850* (London, 1987); R. J. Morris, *Class, Sect and Party: The Making of the British Middle Class, Leeds 1820–50* (Manchester, 1990).

[85] R. J. Morris, *Class, Sect and Party*; J. Barry, 'The Making of the Middle Class', *Past and Present*, 145 (1994), 199–201.

[86] S. Gunn 'The "Failure" of the Victorian Middle Class', in J. Wolff and J. Seed, *The Culture of Capital: Art, Power and the Nineteenth-century Middle Class* (Manchester, 1984); Davidoff and Hall, *Family Fortunes*, part 1.

Language and class

The measure of class was politics. This left the exponents of class bound to demonstrate clear and direct connections between social groups and political ideologies, and between social and political change. Gareth Stedman Jones' *Languages of Class*, published in full in 1983, made clear in new ways how hard it is to make such connections. Stedman Jones identified Chartism as one version of a radical critique of society which can be traced back to the Wilkesite controversies of the 1770s. This tradition did not adhere exclusively to any one social group; it was not necessarily plebeian or artisanal, let alone proletarian. Stedman Jones thus presented Chartism as a working-class movement in the sense that following the Reform Act of 1832, those with little or no property, or those whose only property was their labour — the working classes — were the category of people whom the Whig government intended to exclude from the franchise. But, he insisted, it was not a working-class movement in the sense that this class identity was expressed in the politics of Chartism.[87] The mainspring of Chartist protest was not a distinction between capital and labour but between the victims and beneficiaries of a corrupt and monopolistic political power. 'The self-identity of radicalism was not that of any specific group but of the "people" or the "nation" against the monopolisers of political representation and power *and hence* financial and economic power.'[88]

The significance of *Languages of Class* arose not only from its particular interpretation of Chartism but also from its intervention at a theoretical level. Stedman Jones explicitly departed from Thompson's conception of class and its founding categories of 'experience' and 'agency'. His reassessment of Chartism was based on a close examination of the meanings of the terms and propositions within Chartist speeches and writings. This focus followed from his view that experience did not, *pace* Thompson, directly translate into consciousness. Influenced by structural linguistics, Stedman Jones argued: 'Consciousness cannot be related to experience except through the interposition of a particular language which organises the understanding of experience.'[89]

Stedman Jones was not the first historian of popular movements to attend to language. For instance, in 1960 Asa Briggs published a much cited essay, on 'The Language of Class in Early Nineteenth-century England'. Here he

---

[87] G. Stedman Jones, *Languages of Class* (Cambridge, 1983), pp. 90–178.
[88] Ibid., p. 104.
[89] Ibid., pp. 101–2.

traced the replacement of a lexicon of 'ranks', 'orders' and 'degrees' with the terminology of class. It was the industrial revolution and the rise of class consciousness, he argued, which required this new vocabulary.[90] Thompson too, as we have noted, in *The Making of the English Working Class* had found the concept of class in its modern usage 'present in the evidence itself'.[91] However, these and other attempts to analyse the emergence of class identities and interests saw language as the expression of a collective experience. They were united in their view that language reflected social changes taking place in a reality that stood apart from, and prior to, its expression in language. This model, Stedman Jones argued, failed to acknowledge that language itself was a part of social being. Identities and interests were themselves produced within language.[92] In the case of Chartism, it was not experience but its ordering within language that led people to believe that the disposition of wealth and poverty was the result of the concentration and abuse of political power.[93] This discussion of the rise and fall of Chartism also advanced a more general argument concerning the incapacity of social history in general, and in particular the social history of class, to offer an explanation of political change in nineteenth- and twentieth-century Britain.[94]

For Stedman Jones, as well as others who developed his lead, it was now difficult to conceive of politics as an expression of the social totality. In this spirit, historians began to focus on working-class attachment to the Liberal Party in the nineteenth century and the continuities between radicalism of this sort and the political programme of the Labour Party in the early twentieth century.[95] There was also a turn towards explanations of political change that were contingent and conjunctural rather than based on long-term trends and structural formations. Stedman Jones, for instance, argued that the decline of Chartist popularity was closely related to its failure to correspond to the changed character of state activity after the Peelite reforms of the 1840s.[96] The idea that the rise of the Labour Party between 1900 and 1929, or indeed the success of the Liberal Party before the First World War, was an expression of fundamental social change—

[90] A. Briggs, 'The Language of "Class" in Early Nineteenth-century England', in A. Briggs and J. Saville (eds), *Essays in Labour History* (London, 1960), pp. 43–73.
[91] Thompson, 'Eighteenth-century English Society', 248.
[92] Stedman Jones, *Languages of Class*, p. 22.
[93] Ibid., p. 101.
[94] Ibid., p. 8.
[95] E. Biagini and A. Reid, *Currents of Radicalism: Popular Radicalism, Organised Labour and Party Politics in Britain 1850–1914* (Cambridge, 1991). E. Biagini, *Liberty, Retrenchment and Reform: Popular Liberalism in the Age of Gladstone* (Cambridge, 1992).
[96] Stedman Jones, *Languages of Class*, pp. 168–78.

the remaking of the working class — was criticised by Alastair Reid and Duncan Tanner among others.[97] In place of social determinism, a growing number of historians have emphasised the formative role of the state, trade unions and the political parties themselves in constructing political allegiances and alliances across diverse social constituencies. Politics no longer appeared as the expression of the social totality. Increasingly, political change was explored in terms of shifts within the political realm itself.[98]

The 'linguistic turn' proved both controversial and influential: controversial because its derogation of the social history of popular politics was not universally accepted and influential because it reset the terms of debate on class in the first half of the nineteenth century. Indeed, over the next two decades approaches to class as discourse became ascendant.[99] David Cannadine's study, *Class in Britain* published in 1998, was symptomatic of this victory and contributed to it. It remains a singular attempt, following the turn to discourse, to provide a synoptic account of class in Britain over three centuries. It did not offer a social history of class. Instead, Cannadine chose to ask: 'How, across a long time span, and from a broad geographical perspective, can we recover the ways in which Britons saw and understood the manifestly unequal society in which they lived?'[100] He identified three persistent visions of the social order: a hierarchical ordering of social ranks, a three-fold division into upper, lower and middle tiers, and a dichotomous model of class which divides society between the exploiters and the exploited. One central problem for Cannadine, therefore, was why the appeal of these different models changed over time. Here too he aligned himself with others moving away from explanations rooted in changes in economic and social structures, emphasising instead the role of politics and politicians from John Wilkes to Margaret Thatcher in creating and articulating social identities.[101]

---

[97] A. Reid, 'The Division of Labour and Politics in Britain, 1880–1920', in H. J. Mommsen and H.-G. Husing (eds), *The Development of Trade Unionism in Britain and Germany* (London, 1985), pp. 150–65; D. Tanner, *Political Change and the Labour Party* (Cambridge, 1990).

[98] J. Gillespie, 'Poplarism and Proletarianism: Unemployment and Labour Politics in London, 1918–34', in D. Feldman and G. Stedman Jones (eds), *Metropolis London: Histories and Representations since 1800* (London, 1989); J. Lawrence and M. Taylor (eds), *Party, State and Society: Electoral Behaviour in Britain since 1820* (Aldershot, 1997); J. Lawrence, *Speaking for the People: Party, Language and Popular Politics in England, 1867–1914* (Cambridge, 1998).

[99] See for instance P. Corfield (ed.), *Language, History and Class* (Oxford, 1991); D. Wahrman, *Imagining the Middle Class: The Political Representation of Class in Britain, c. 1780–1840* (Cambridge, 1995).

[100] D. Cannadine, *Class in Britain* (London, 1998), p. 19.

[101] Ibid., pp. 21–2.

Both Stedman Jones and Cannadine promoted our understanding of class as a discursive phenomenon but neither of them questioned the centrality of class in this particular sense in modern Britain. However, once some historians excavated languages of social identity and visions of the social order others found that class was not the only seam to mine. In *Visions of the People*, published in 1991, Patrick Joyce's stated aim was to displace class from its central place in the historiography of nineteenth-century England and to restore other identities and discourses which, he argued, were generally 'stronger and more fully part of their time'.[102] In place of class, Joyce emphasised 'populism': an anti-aristocratic and anti-statist discourse which construed a virtuous people struggling against corruption and privilege. Class had not merely been derogated from a way of grasping the totality of social experience to a linguistic construct, it was now revealed to be just one construct — one identity — among many.

The fall of class among historians has been hailed and mourned as marking a crisis for social history.[103] Historians influenced by postmodernism have extended the linguistic turn to question the possibility of conventional historical knowledge. According to Patrick Joyce, 'the salutary effect of postmodernist thought might be said to lie in its invitation to question the idea of a clear distinction between representation and the "real"'.[104] This critique of historical practice claims that our perception of the reality of the past is so completely permeated by our cultural or discursive categories that it can never be apprehended apart from them.[105] Alongside other categories such as 'the individual' and 'society', 'class' is now placed as a product of the history it claims to explain. The role of the historian is now to 'trace the discursivities of the social'; in this way, it is suggested, histories of 'society' and even of 'class' may survive.[106]

If this were the case then the future for history, let alone class, would be constrained indeed. But the argument fails to convince. First, a number of its proponents have found that although the 'status or meaning of the social

---

[102] P. Joyce, *Visions of the People* (Cambridge, 1991), pp. 1, 29.

[103] S. Thorne and D. Mayfield, 'Social History and its Discontents: Gareth Stedman Jones and the Politics of Language', *Social History*, 17 (1992), 165–88; J. Vernon, 'Who's Afraid of the Linguistic Turn?', *Social History*, 19 (1994), 81–97; P. Joyce, 'The End of Social History?', *Social History*, 20 (1995).

[104] P. Joyce, 'The Imaginary Discontents of Social History: A Note of Response to Mayfield and Thorne, and Lawrence and Taylor', *Social History*, 18 (1993), 83.

[105] Joyce, 'The End of Social History?', 78; Vernon, 'Who's Afraid', 89.

[106] Joyce, 'The End of Social History?', 83–4.

may be in question ... life without it has proved impossible'.[107] Second, although these postmodern scholars sometimes set about their less adventurous colleagues with intolerant scorn this belligerence is supplemented by professions of intellectual pluralism. Such pluralism rightly privileges historians' curiosity about the past and the legitimacy of numerous questions, some of which the linguistic turn and postmodern thought cannot address. Rather than announcing the impossibility of writing a history of society, therefore, the fall of class challenges a *certain sort* of social history: the social history of industrial society which sees politics as emblematic of the totality of economic, social and cultural forces.[108]

In particular, the challenge of understanding the emergence and development of modern society remains for anyone prepared to address it. Rather than capitulate to the claims of postmodernity, historians might better address the challenge and opportunity offered by a new chronology of 'the great transformation'. The idea that the late eighteenth and early nineteenth centuries witnessed a dramatic discontinuity in demographic, agrarian, urban and industrial structures has been questioned and reformulated in new ways as historians now see the process of modernisation over a period of centuries not decades.[109] What is required, therefore, is a renewed analysis of the 'great transformation' which spans the early-modern and modern periods and which reexamines the interactions between agrarian capitalism, urbanisation and industrialism. This would encompass not only the commodification of land, labour and money but would also extend to the familial, demographic and cultural framework of the transformation. It would encompass the ways in which modernity not only changed structures but also the ways in which it shaped lives at a micro-level. This analysis would not ignore politics, geopolitics and the state. On the contrary, historians now have a renewed awareness of the formative role both can play in social and economic change. It could even suggest how structures of

---

[107] V. S. Bonnell and L. Hunt, 'Introduction', in idem, *Beyond the Cultural Turn: New Directions in the Study of Society and Culture* (Berkeley, CA, 1999), p. 11. On Joyce's own failure to live without social history, despite his best intentions, see D. Wahrman, 'The New Political History', *Social History*, 21 (1996), 344–5.

[108] Even here, though, the capacity of historians to produce grand and creative narratives which stress class relations and which conceive of them as the foundations of politics has not yet been blunted. The end of the 1990s saw the publication of two such major studies: R. Price, *British Society 1680–1880* (Cambridge, 1999); R. Mckibbin, *Classes and Cultures: England 1918–1951* (Oxford, 1998).

[109] E. A. Wrigley, *The Population History of England, 1541–1870* (Cambridge, 1981); idem, *People, Cities and Wealth: The Transformation of Traditional Society* (Oxford, 1986); R. C. Allen, *Enclosure and the Yeoman* (Oxford, 1992); P. Clark (ed.), *The Cambridge Urban History of Britain, vol. 2* (Cambridge, 2000).

governance and politics were reshaped as people moved from a predominantly rural and religious society to one that was neither. At the same time, the history of politics and the state would not now be presented as the crystallisation of the whole.

In recent years, it has been Malthus not Marx who has inspired the most substantial achievements in historical sociology and who has done most to promote our understanding of some of these changes.[110] Predictably, however, the major achievements in this tradition have been for the period before 1800. It is also the case that the Malthusian approach has not been able to illumine the sources and articulation of social power. It is this, of course, which Marxists have claimed to do and which the concept of class has been intended to express. It remains to be seen how or even whether a new history of modernity will be able to manage without it.

Note.   I am grateful to Gareth Stedman Jones, Miles Taylor and Frank Trentmann who read and commented on earlier versions of this essay and to Ira Katznelson for helpfully discussing some of the issues with me.

---

[110] For instance Wrigley, *People, Cities and Wealth.*

CHAPTER NINE

The History of Art History in Britain: A Critical Context for Recent Developments and Debates

STEPHEN BANN

It is by no means an easy task to assess the development of art history in Britain in the twentieth century. This is for reasons that govern the history of the discipline as a whole, but are applicable in a specially acute form—so it may seem—within the British context. At the beginning of the century, art history as a form of academic inquiry had virtually no institutionalised existence in Britain although (as will be argued here) the tradition of aesthetic criticism provided an alternative base for understanding and evaluating the arts. By the end of the century, this dearth had been succeeded by a flood. Art history had followed English literature (and preceded film studies) as a new, popular and highly visible addition to the panorama of disciplines in the humanities.

Yet, by this recent stage, it is open to question whether the concept of a 'national' art history makes much sense at all. All areas of academic inquiry have been internationalised, to a greater or less extent, in the half-century following the Second World War. But, for the fledgling discipline of art history, the process has been particularly dramatic. This is because, on the one hand, the English-speaking world has been so extensively pollinated by German art history, and thus brought into contact with the first and most substantial tradition of scholarly writing in the domain.[1] On the other hand, it is the result of an extensive cross-fertilisation between Britain and the United

---

[1] It has been calculated by Heinrich Dilly that 252 art historians emigrated from the German-speaking countries in the period preceding the war, the number being roughly one-quarter of the total profession. The majority settled in Britain and the United States.

States in the subsequent decades. Of the living scholars to be mentioned here, a high proportion have held posts on both sides of the Atlantic.[2] This makes it difficult to isolate a specifically British strain, though the differences *vis-à-vis* the continental nations are still discernible. In this brief essay, I shall not attempt to review in depth the existence of a sophisticated native tradition of writing on the visual arts which, in the first years of the century, diverged markedly from the historicism of the German tradition. Nor will I look in detail at the fascinating story of the reception and domestication in Britain of German art history. These aspects will only be lightly touched on. My main focus will be on the recent debates within a broadly 'Anglo-Saxon' community of scholars. These, however, clearly have their roots in the specific conditions of art history's development over the entire century.

British art writing and German art history

Art history happens to have one of the longest established disciplinary associations in the world. Founded in 1873, the Comité international d'histoire de l'art (CIHA) partly belies its name in that its main base was originally central Europe. Its fourth international congress, taking place at Budapest in 1896, was the first to receive French participants. When the fifteenth congress took place at University College, London, in 1939, British art history had, to all intents and purposes, come of age. The Courtauld Institute, founded in London in 1931, was on the way to establishing itself as Britain's premier establishment for teaching and research in the subject. In the issue of *The Times* which covered the CIHA congress, a parallel column announced that the Barber Institute had been founded at Birmingham University.[3] Also by this stage, a nucleus of émigré German art historians including Edgar Wind and Fritz Saxl had already formed around the library of the independent scholar Aby Warburg, transported to London from his native Hamburg. Shortly after the end of the war, this would result in the establishment of the Warburg Institute as a research centre within the University of London.

---

[2] These include, among the art historians most discussed here, Michael Baxandall, Richard Wollheim, T. J. Clark, Thomas Crow and Norman Bryson.

[3] See *The Times*, 25 July 1939. The Barber Institute was, however, not advertised as a place for teaching and research in art history, but as 'a cultural centre for Birmingham'. Only in the comparatively recent past has it begun to nurture a full programme of art historical study within the university.

Having noted these promising beginnings, it is however right to sound a note of caution. By the early 1930s, Britain's leading art journal, originally called *The Burlington Magazine for Connoisseurs*, had lasted three decades since its foundation in 1903. Under the editorship of Herbert Read, and subsequently Benedict Nicolson, it would add scholars like Kenneth Clark and Ellis Waterhouse to its earlier contributors, among whom Roger Fry had been prominent. These names, however, only emphasise the fact that, throughout the inter-war period, art history in Britain was still predominantly the preserve of the major museums and their staff. Their directors and aristocratic trustees were as well represented on the editorial board of the *Burlington* as they were on the honorary committee of the 1939 CIHA conference. Of Britain's outstanding university collections, both the Ashmolean at Oxford and the Fitzwilliam at Cambridge had continued to consolidate their collections throughout the early twentieth century, but there was no corresponding local development of art history as an independent academic discipline. Cambridge was to initiate art history in the 1960s, as a partner with architecture in a new faculty. Oxford, whose Slade professorship offered Wind a post when he decided not to rejoin his Warburg colleagues after the war, would keep art history firmly under the tutelage of the Faculty of History.

Noting this disparity between art history in continental Europe and Britain would serve no useful purpose if it were not to be accompanied by a more positive gloss on the situation. In nineteenth-century Britain, artistic culture had thrived precisely through the example of figures who bridged the gap between practice and scholarship, the museum and the academy: one obvious case would be the redoutable Sir Charles Eastlake, president of the Royal Academy and first director of the National Gallery, to whose discerning eye the exceptional quality of the national collection can be in large part credited.[4] At the same time, the particular conditions of British culture gave rise, over the century, to a unique tradition of writing about the visual arts, which accurately proclaims its literary character by being called 'aesthetic criticism', but deserves recognition if only for the prestige and influence that it rapidly acquired throughout Europe and North America. Ruskin is the most salient representative of this tradition of writing, which in his hands developed a moral intensity and a contemporary urgency inevitably at odds with its value as history. Pater, on the other hand, reflects most clearly the extent to which

---

[4] For Eastlake's career, see David Robertson, *Sir Charles Eastlake and the Victorian Art World* (Princeton, NJ, 1978). He writes: 'No Englishman of his time was better informed in art' (p. 244). He extends the comparison to include museum directors in Paris and Berlin, and notes Bernard Berenson's acknowledged indebtedness to Eastlake's *Materials for a History of Oil Painting* (1847).

aesthetic criticism could act as a critique of positivist art history. His polite but firm dismissal of the 'new Vasari' — Crowe's and Cavalcaselle's work of connoisseurship on the history of Italian painting — is, however, not so much a licence for ahistorical attitudes, as a plea for the consideration of broader cultural issues in the assessment of stylistic influence. In this sense, Pater can genuinely be seen as anticipating the concept of a 'visual culture' as an alternative to the narrow object-based connoisseurship.[5]

Of course, aesthetic criticism did not (and does not) exist wholly in contradistinction to art history. In the last years of the nineteenth century, John Addington Symonds was one of the leading writers who chose a historical and narrative, rather than essayistic, mode for his brilliant and influential writings on Italian Renaissance art, culminating in his last major work, *The Life of Michelangelo Buonarotti*, in three volumes (1893).[6] Yet it would be fair to say that many of the major contributions to art history by British authors continued to reflect, well into the twentieth century, the ambivalence inherent in the choice of an essayistic mode — implying a connection with art criticism — rather than a historicist mode, let alone a study based on philosophy and theory. This is certainly true of Roger Fry, whose pre-eminence as a critic of contemporary art frames his approach, whether he writes of Giotto or of Cézanne. It also applies to the writer who, more than any other, took on the mantle of the nineteenth-century aesthetic critics, Adrian Stokes. Indeed the varied fortune of Stokes' writings since his death in 1972 reflects precisely the difficulty of accommodating so substantial and complex a figure within a paradigm of art historical writing increasingly dominated by the precedent of the German theorists.

In the long run, it seems likely that many of the abiding values in the tradition of British writing about art will be rediscovered in the work of some of its most distinguished present-day practitioners. One of the most original

[5] See in particular the famous essay on 'The School of Giorgione', where Pater queries 'all that negative criticism of the "new Vasari"' which has had the effect of reducing the corpus of authentic paintings by the artist. Pater values instead 'an influence, a spirit or type in art, active in men so different as those to whom many of his supposed works are really assignable': at a later stage in the essay, he identifies this spirit with 'such as in England we call "park scenery"'; in Walter Pater, *The Renaissance* (London, 1925), pp. 154, 159. The first version of this essay was published in 1877. Sir Joseph Archer Crowe and Giovanni Battista Cavalcaselle had published their *New History of Painting in Italy* (London) in 1864.

[6] Alex Potts comments on the difference between Pater and Symonds in this respect: 'For Symonds the Renaissance was identifiable as a concrete historical moment when political changes ... enabled humanity to discover a new freedom to act and to think ... With Pater, what was at issue was the formation of a new way of existing in and relating to the world'. See Alex Potts, 'Pungent Prophecies of Art: Symonds, Pater and Michelangelo', in John Pemble (ed.), *John Addington Symonds: Culture and the Demon Desire* (London, 2000), p. 106.

and admired studies of the past two decades, Richard Wollheim's *Painting as an Art* (1987), is the work of a friend and follower of Adrian Stokes, who has applied similar intuitions to a range of important paintings, while respecting their historical context. Even where there exist the clearest connections between the methods of German art history and those of their British followers, these need not exclude attention to their other distinctive qualities. The patent influence of Frederick Antal's Marxist approach on Anthony Blunt need not obscure the very different world-view which is distilled in Blunt's writing on Poussin. Nor should the recognition of Michael Baxandall's debt to E. H. Gombrich divert attention from the entirely new direction in which he has taken his subtle materialist analyses.[7]

To take a further telling example, the recent death of Francis Haskell provides a sad but illuminating occasion to look back on a career which adopted a very different pattern to that of the German mentors of the earlier generation. In Haskell's work, there are many resonances which evoke the British tradition of the nineteenth century: not indeed the musical cadences of the aesthetic critics but the robust and strongly argued essays of their predecessor, William Hazlitt, who was one of the first writers of any nation to convey the fascination of art as displayed in the specific context of the gallery and the collection.[8] Where his predecessor as Professor of the History of Art at Oxford, Edgar Wind, sought to unravel the complex iconography of Renaissance masterpieces, Haskell paid close attention to the intricacies of patronage and the continual vagaries of taste to which even such masterpieces had been subject over the years. In his last, magisterial work on *History and its Images* (1993), the elusiveness and unreliability of the image as a vehicle for historical truth itself became the chief subject of debate. Haskell opened up the issue of whether the image had ever been, or could ever become, a reliable source for the general historian. But, in so doing, he made his colleagues all the more keenly aware of the problematic status of historical representation. In terms of the argument of this study, Haskell's legacy has a double importance: it is both an indication of the historiographical turn which art history has adopted in the last quarter-century, and a guide to some of the wider possibilities of engagement with the history of visual culture.

---

[7] See the useful collection of essays on Baxandall's work in *Art History*, 21, 4 (1998), where Allan Langdale discusses Baxandall's difference of opinion with Gombrich over the concept of the 'period eye' (p. 483). Baxandall's contribution to establishing the 'cognitive style' of an epoch, which will be noted later in this study, clearly differs from Gombrich's resolutely anti-Hegelian stance.

[8] By an inspired choice, the readings in Francis Haskell's memorial service in King's College Chapel, Cambridge on 10 June 2000 included the passage in which Hazlitt recounts his first visit to the Louvre, in the essay *On the Pleasure of Painting*.

The historiographical turn

These are but a few examples of the ways in which the British tradition of writing on art can be detected, sometimes as an underground stream, in the work of contemporary practitioners. It remains true, nevertheless, that the most momentous factor in the half-century following the Second World War was the opportunity, and need, to catch up with the intellectually demanding approach developed in the German-speaking countries. The intersection between émigré German art historians and those individual scholars who learned from them, in Britain as well as the United States, is indeed a complex subject which cannot be covered in detail here. What sets the scene, however, for my end-of-century perspective is the further stage in the process of reception, when English speakers have been offered the opportunity to catch up with the full range of sources which the German mentors had taken for granted. This is what I am calling the historiographical turn. The works published in English in the previous quarter-century by prominent figures like Panofsky, Gombrich and Wind implicitly referred back to earlier debates that they, and their own predecessors, had taken for granted. Consequently a great deal of new exegesis had to be undertaken to bring essential studies by the German pioneers back into circulation.

Leading this development at its outset, Michael Podro's influential study, *The Critical Historians of Art* (1982), acknowledged in its preface that the great Germanic tradition of thinking and writing about images 'continued to exert an influence largely through shadowy reminiscence, the texts themselves having slipped from view'.[9] Similarly, Michael Ann Holly's *Panofsky and the Foundations of Art History*, published two years later, aspired to recover the full intellectual profile of the figure universally regarded as central to the development of the discipline, and to assess his contribution against the contemporary context.[10]

Proceeding through the 1990s, introductory works like these, which provide the groundwork for an understanding of the art historian's method, have been complemented by a new selection of important texts republished in translation. Any brief list would include Alois Riegl's *Problems of Style* which appeared in English in 1992, with the comment in Henri Zerner's

---

[9] Michael Podro, *The Critical Historians of Art* (Oxford, 1982), p. v.

[10] Michael Ann Holly, *Panofsky and the Foundations of Art History* (Ithaca, NY, 1984). Holly sets the style of her inquiry by putting the question: 'How, then, can we confidently speak of the history of art as a "science" — and for that matter, how can we even call it a "history" if we refuse to acknowledge the historical character of its own principles and techniques?' (quoted in my review of the study in *History and Theory*, 25, 2 (1986), 200).

preface that it had 'not been replaced or superseded as an exposition of the history of ornamental art in antiquity and the medieval period';[11] Panofsky's *Perspective as Symbolic Form*, which had indeed triumphed over its inaccessibility in English to achieve 'a reputation well outside the professional territory of art history', as Christopher S. Wood remarked in the introduction to his timely translation;[12] and, in the more recent past, such a study as *The Practice of Art History* by the little-known Otto Pächt, once again introduced by Wood, who comments on 'the ingenuity and creativity of his eye', and the relative strength of his distinctive methods of analysis, judged against the approaches of more accessible contemporaries such as Panofsky and Gombrich.[13]

From the point of view of the English-speaking world, at any rate, this progressive accumulation of earlier, essential texts might seem to constitute the belated formation of a canon. To the observer from outside the discipline, it might appear as if the necessary critical and historical instruments were deemed to be already in existence (despite being temporarily inaccessible). Hence a judicious overview of the whole field would succeed in balancing the record, correcting any random inequalities and distortions that might have crept in. Consistent with this historiographical reprise, and logically developing from it, has been the publication of a sequence of helpful synthetic works, usually in the form of collections of essays, which seek to apply the methodological dividends of this expanded view to the concrete tasks of art historical scholarship. I cite three of these in particular, noting that their titles point to this ambition for synthesis: *Essential Art History* (1992), *Critical Terms for Art History* (1996) and *The Subjects of Art History* (1998).[14]

It is too early to estimate the long-term utility of such collections. Clearly they are the outcome of what academic publishers believe to be the appropriate provision for larger and more diverse groups of university students. What should also be stressed, however, is the inevitable degree of self-consciousness about method which such composite collections take for granted. From this evidence alone, one might venture to think that art history

---

[11] Alois Riegl, *Problems of Style: Foundations for a History of Ornament*, trans. Evelyn Kain (Princeton, NJ, 1992), p. xxiii.

[12] Erwin Panofsky, *Perspective as Symbolic Form*, trans. Christopher S. Wood (New York, 1991), p. 7.

[13] Otto Pächt, *The Practice of Art History: Reflections on Method*, trans. David Britt (London, 1999), p. 13.

[14] See Paul Duro and Michael Greenhalgh (eds), *Essential Art History* (London, 1992); Robert S. Nelson and Richard Shiff (eds), *Critical Terms for Art History* (Chicago, IL, 1996); Mark A. Cheetham, Michael Ann Holly and Keith Moxey (eds), *The Subjects of Art History: Historical Objects in Contemporary Perspective* (Cambridge, 1998). I should note in passing the helpful bibliography of suggested readings in the 'Historiography and Methodology of Art History (1972–1994)' included in Nelson and Shiff, pp. xv–xvi.

has been going through a rite of passage over the last two decades of the twentieth century. This has involved, in turn, the fuller acknowledgement of the 'foundations' laid by successive generations of scholars in the German tradition, and the attempt to apply their insights systematically across a broad spectrum of different types of material.

Although I offer this phenomenon as one immediate way of reading the balance sheet at the end of the millennium, I should add that this is far from being the whole story. Such indications of the recent focusing of the discipline in intrinsic terms, as it were, must not leave out of account its situation relative to other disciplines and other adjacent fields of study. It may appear that art history has earned the right to consider itself as an autonomous discipline. As far as the institutional and pedagogic basis of the discipline is concerned, this is a justifiable claim, even though there remain great national disparities in the teaching and placement of art historical studies, which come into view when we direct our attention to just a few of the leading countries involved.[15] But academic disciplines cannot just will themselves into intellectual autonomy. It is perhaps the predicament — as it is also the great opportunity — of art history that it is intimately involved in a cultural transformation too vast for it, in any real sense, to control. This transformation remains, however, too integrally rooted in the conflictual identity of the discipline to be merely dismissed or disregarded.

The pictorial turn in the human sciences

My last point referred to the recent 'historiographical turn' of art history. The American scholar W. J. T. Mitchell has written, by contrast, of the 'pictorial turn' which is taking place throughout the human sciences. Himself a notable example of a specialist from the adjacent field of English studies who has contributed significantly to enriching the techniques of art history, Mitchell expresses the predicament (and opportunity) of the art historian in a particularly incisive way:

[15] As might be expected, Germany has been foremost in studying the development of its own art historical tradition. See Willibald Sauerländer, 'L'Allemagne et la "Kunstgeschichte"', *Revue de l'Art*, 45 (1979), 4–8: this largely summarises the material of Heinrich Dilly, *Kunstgeschichte als Institution* (Frankfurt, 1979). See also Thomas Gaehtgens, 'Etudier l'histoire de l'art en Allemagne', *Revue de l'Art*, 126 (1999), 4–8, for a buoyant statement of the present situation in Germany. France has been slow to follow, but the remarkable and distinctive development of art history in France has recently been revealed for the first time in Lyne Therrien, *L'histoire de l'art en France* (Paris, 1998).

If a pictorial turn is indeed occurring in the human sciences, art history could very well find its theoretical marginality transformed into a position of intellectual centrality, in the form of a challenge to offer an account of its principal theoretical object — visual representation — that will be usable by other disciplines in the human sciences. Tending to the masterpieces of Western painting will clearly not be enough. A broad, interdisciplinary critique will be required, one that takes into account parallel efforts such as the long struggle of film studies to come up with an adequate mediation of linguistic and imagistic models for cinema and to situate the film medium in the larger context of visual culture.[16]

One could easily quibble with some of the points taken for granted in this statement. Mitchell first published his essay on the 'pictorial turn' in 1992, and his comment about the 'theoretical marginality' of history of art takes up the dyspeptic view of the state of the discipline in the English-speaking world advanced four years earlier by Norman Bryson, at the launch of his *Calligram: Essays in New Art History from France*.[17] It is doubtful if any impartial observer would today repeat so confidently the claim that film studies has set its house in order, and formed an agreed disciplinary paradigm to which art history should aspire. Nevertheless, the critical force of what Mitchell is asserting remains undiminished. In blunt terms, the overwhelming attraction of the 'image' both within and beyond the established fields of the humanities puts the art historian on the spot. Art history cannot expect to insulate itself from the demands directed to visual data by historians and literary scholars, let alone students of film, photography and the other visual media. On the other hand, if art history shifts its parameters to take a more catholic view of its disciplinary field, this will arguably be at the expense of the more tried and tested conceptions of its role.

I intend to look at some of the recent debates in art history in the light of this dilemma. This may well be a sort of concern not so strongly affecting the other historical topics studied in this volume. For instance, the contribution of British historians over the last century to our knowledge of class, or city life, or the Middle Ages, can still be seen quite legitimately as a subsection within the general development of historical scholarship, however specific or

---

[16] W. J. T. Mitchell, *Picture Theory* (Chicago, IL, 1994), p. 15. Mitchell's contribution to art history has been specially notable in fields like *ekphrasis* and art criticism, and the social history of landscape. Under his editorship, the Chicago-based journal *Critical Inquiry*, predominantly devoted to the critical study of literature, has also become a place for the publication for major art historical essays, such as those of Michael Fried.

[17] See Norman Bryson (ed.), *Calligram: Essays in New Art History from France* (Cambridge, 1988). He is, however, very conscious of describing a quickly evolving situation: 'There can be little doubt: the discipline of art history, having for so long lagged behind, having been among the humanities perhaps the slowest to develop and the last to hear of changes as these took place among even its closest neighbours, is now unmistakably beginning to alter' (p. xiii).

novel the methodology may be. It is not so obvious that art history could, or should, be regarded in this way. Indeed one might say that this necessary connection of art history with issues of representation and imaging may ensure that it is, and will remain, a highly polarised field of study, perpetually traversed by new debates about the nature of its objects and the uncertain limits of its competence.

This is not exclusively, or even primarily, a matter of the conflict between 'conservative' and 'avant-garde' tendencies, as the earlier quotation from Bryson's anthology of 1988 might lead one to suppose. It is endemic in the different degrees to which art historians are prepared to allow for the image's resistance to language. The recently published translation of Pächt, to which reference has already been made, takes as the by-line for its back cover the quotation: 'My credo for Art History is: In the beginning was the eye, not the word.' This implies, of course, that Pächt is questioning the mismatch between linguistically based interpretations and the supposedly more primary demands of visual experience that he detects in the work of some of the German pioneers.[18] I cannot deal here with the substantive issues that lie at the root of such arguments about representation and the image. These have been debated many times, and in considerably greater depth than is possible in this study. What I propose to do is to observe how some of the arguments referring to these issues were employed contextually in the staging of a number of polemical confrontations over the last quarter of the past century. The lines of debate have been drawn up very differently on each occasion. But the arguments have tended to fall into similar patterns, not least in their explicit or implicit reference to the heritage of German historical scholarship, but also in their invocation of more venerable approaches to the problem of writing about images.

A simple way of introducing these debates would be to state from the outset the consequences that flow from the Janus-like status of the discipline. In so far as history of art is history, it must inevitably be seen as a specialised branch of an all-encompassing scholarly pursuit that has successively split off into specific areas of expertise, but still retains its identity *vis-à-vis* the philosophical and language-based disciplines of the humanities. We would expect history of art, in other words, to reflect some of the disciplinary developments of historical science, and particularly those at the 'cultural' and 'intellectual' end of the spectrum. At the same time, history of art, being concerned with specific art objects, cannot be

---

[18] See Wood's introduction to Pächt, *Practice of Art History*, pp. 9–18, and also his introduction to Panofsky, *Perspective*, where the relation between Panofsky's iconology and philological method is investigated (pp. 7–24).

completely divorced from the evolution, over the last three centuries in particular, of specialised languages for describing and evaluating the effects of art works, which may be classed under the general heading of 'art criticism'.[19] Nor can it be entirely detached from the historical view which present-day artists, and art critics, hold as being relevant to the judgement of the art of their times. As we shall see, the way in which the debates traced here have proceeded implies the inclusion of questions such as the following in the art historical agenda. What is to determine the criteria for the kinds of objects that the art historian chooses to write about? Is the category of the 'visual' sufficient on its own to determine where the line is drawn? How far can perceptions of the current state of art be related to the historical view of the art historian? Such questions, and particularly the latter, might in the end prove to be unanswerable. But that does not mean that they have to be abandoned at the outset.

Social History of Art and New Art History

A generally agreed starting-point for the debates which have opened up the discipline in the past quarter-century might be the clarion call of the young British art historian T. J. Clark, published in the *Times Literary Supplement* on 24 May 1974. Clark declared there that art history was not perhaps in crisis but '[o]ut of breath, in a state of genteel dissolution'; it had forfeited the right it once held (in Germany at any rate) to rank among the most advanced of scholarly disciplines, and it had successively narrowed its field of intellectual inquiry.[20] The fact that Clark draws a stark contrast between the pioneering work of the German art historians in the first half of the century and the decadence of his own period is of course worth noting. But the new orientation that he himself succeeded in giving to art history cannot be seen, in any sense, merely as a revival of the discourses of Riegl, Wölfflin, Warburg and their fellow theorists. What he proposed was a new

[19] The work of Winckelmann is generally acknowledged to be of crucial importance for both areas. See Alex Potts, *Flesh and the Ideal: Winckelmann and the Origins of Art History* (Yale, CT, 1994), and idem, ' "Sans tête, ni bras, ni jambes", La description du Torse du Belvédère de Winckelmann', in Larys Frogier and Jean-Marc Poinsot, *La description* (Châteaugiron, 1997), pp. 19–33.

[20] Quoted in Nelson and Shiff, *Critical Terms*, p. xii. Robert Nelson also notes the parallel observation of Hubert Damisch, in 1975, that art history had declined from its 'great period' and was '"totally incapable of renovating its method" by reference to theoretical developments in other fields'. Clark's article is reprinted in full in Eric Fernie (ed.), *Art History and its Methods* (London, 1995), pp. 248–53.

critique based on sophisticated recent notions of ideology. As he put it, 'Ideology is what the picture is, and what the picture is not.' To gloss this elegant formula, he chose a terminology taken directly from Freud's *Interpretation of Dreams*: 'ideology is the dream-content, without the dream work'.[21] The model that he advocated for a reinvigorated concept of artistic creation was not the well-worn concept of the 'representative' artist, dear to old-fashioned Marxists, but the more elusive and self-contradictory model of subjectivity explored by writings such as Walter Benjamin's on Baudelaire, and Sartre's on Flaubert.

Clark's call to action did not occur in a vacuum. The two books that he himself had published in the year preceding this article, *The Absolute Bourgeois* and *The Image of the People*, bore as their respective subtitles: 'Artists and Politics in France 1848–51' and 'Gustave Courbet and the 1848 Revolution'. No less than his striking article, these set the agenda for an intensive scrutiny of the political and social investment of the artist which would also involve a thorough investigation of the primary sources. Without any doubt, Clark's advocacy proved an inspiring precedent for young English and American art historians in the period that followed. It may now be difficult not to see his attention to the involvement of artists in failed revolutions in the light of the political history of Europe, and France in particular, in the late 1960s. Revisionist readings, based on archival sources, have disclosed a rather different picture of art and patronage in mid-nineteenth-century France.[22] But the very production of such new versions is, in a real sense, a tribute to the fertility of his position. Certainly Clark has continued to engage our attention in works which refine and revise his concept of the social engagement of the modern artist.[23]

---

[21] Quoted Fernie (ed.), *Art History and its Methods*, p. 251.

[22] I refer specifically to a recent study by a French art historian: Chantal Georget, *1848 — La République et l'art vivant* (Paris, 1998). Georget claims to be pursuing the 'inverse' strategy to Clark: 'starting from the hypothesis that there had to be an art specific to the Republic, after studying the objectives of the Administration of the Fine Arts, he lengthily examines the works of artists susceptible to have been influenced by the new ideas or by the events — Delacroix, Daumier ... — in order to discern the existence of a "republican art" of which he finally discovers little trace. So he takes it as a failure ... We on the other hand look at the full breadth of the archives, in order to see if the State itself, by means of its artistic administration, can be held or not held responsible for the new artistic orientations. In other words, we do not take as our point of departure the artists or their work contemporary with the Republic; we do not look to analyse how the events or the "spirit of the times" might or might not have influenced their work, but on the contrary how the Republic itself believed it had an influence on the course of artistic life'(p. 9). [My translation]

[23] For a good account of his notion of social mediation, in the light of his most recent study, *Farewell to an Idea: Episodes from a History of Modernism* (Yale, CT, 1999), see Gail Day, 'Persisting and Mediating: T. J. Clark and the Pain of "the Unattainable Beyond"', *Art History*, 23, 1 (2000), 1–18.

There remains, however, some confusion about the significance of the new orientation which Clark, and a number of like-minded scholars, managed to achieve. This is perhaps due to the fact that Clark's work became specifically identified, in the English-speaking world, with the term 'Social History of Art'. At a recent symposium entitled 'Whatever Happened to the Social Art History?', it soon became plain that the positions of these scholars as historians were not always fully appreciated, and that this confusion related in part to their affiliations with what might be called 'mainstream' history.[24] An intellectual historian from outside the province of art history viewed the aspirations of the 'social art historians' as if their work drew its impetus essentially from the mid-century social history with a Marxist orientation associated with such British scholars as E. P. Thompson and Eric Hobsbawm. Yet the American art historian, Thomas Crow (a respondent chosen for his own personal links with the 'Social History of Art') protested that this was a complete misconception: the historians with whom he had felt an affiliation, and from whom he had learned, were the American scholars with a broadly cultural, rather than a specifically political and economic brief, such as Natalie Zemon Davis and Carl Schorske.[25]

This difference of interpretation seems to me symptomatic of the complex mapping that is necessary to track the development of art history over the recent period. It has already been made clear that the 'social history of art' in its 1970s version differed fundamentally from the Marxist tradition epitomised by scholars in the German tradition like Arnold Hauser, whose view of the correspondence of the artist to society presupposed a much more direct 'reflection'.[26] It also has to be said that the dominant English-speaking Marxist historians mentioned above were not specially noteworthy for their informed interest in art. Their work — if it addressed artistic achievement at

[24] The symposium took place at the meeting in New York of the College Art Association, 24–26 February 2000, and was chaired by Marc Gotlieb.

[25] For Schorske's pervasive effect on cultural history, see Michael Roth (ed.), *Rediscovering History: Culture, Politics and the Psyche* (Stanford, CA, 1994), a volume of essays published in his honour, to which both Clark and Crow contributed. Natalie Zemon Davis's interest in the image was well attested by 1982, when she published her thoughts on the French historical film, *Le Retour de Martin Guerre*, on which she had collaborated. See Daniel Vigne, Natalie Zemon Davis and Jean-Claude Carrière, *Le retour de Martin Guerre* (Paris, 1982).

[26] Hauser's own ideas, of course, were themselves developed in relation to the perception of a lack of social engagement by the pioneers of the discipline. For pertinent comments on Hauser's critique of Wölfflin in his *Philosophy of Art* (1963), see Paul Mattick Jr, in Nelson and Shiff, *Critical Terms*, pp. 73–4.

all — tended to view it essentially as a superstructural phenomenon.[27] Crow was thus right to insist that the type of historical inquiry which appealed to him was the more adventurous new social history, with a pronounced cultural slant, which was itself responsive to recent developments in European historiography, such as the French *nouvelle histoire*. The names of Davis and Schorske, both extremely attentive to visual representation, could not be bettered as an index for this type of inquiry.

What has to be acknowledged, however, is the fact that, by the early 1970s, the promise of a social history of art was being subsumed within a more widespread and diffuse phenomenon, which would become widely known as the 'New Art History'. Within this broad collocation, there was ample room for a variety of very different orientations to find expression. These were, in fact, characterised more by the fact that they all shared negative attitudes to much that had been written recently in the name of art history, than by their unanimity in seeking to plot the new way forward. 'New Art History' proved a highly useful slogan for rallying conference delegates, packaging new books, and attracting contributors to write for essay collections. This is however not to disparage it. The fact that such conferences were held, and numerous books and essays published under this aegis, makes it possible to gauge in retrospect some of the changes that were under way.

It is accepted that the first public use of the term (with a question mark appended) was at a conference organised in 1982 by the editors of *Block*, an art journal published at Middlesex Polytechnic and described a few years later as '[packing] a political punch more often found in Nanterre than in the National Gallery'.[28] By 1986, the term was sufficiently well grounded for seventeen contributors to respond to a call for essays on the topic, by this time divested of its question mark. And by 1994 it had already acquired a certain mythology of its own on both sides of the Atlantic, as attested by the exceptionally well attended conference held in

---

[27] This does not of course mean that their historical work is irrelevant as a framework for interpreting works of art in their social and economic context. The curators of the recent major exhibition, *Global Conceptualism: Points of Origin, 1950s–1980s*, clearly expressed their debt to Hobsbawm's *Age of Extremes* (1994) in enabling them to periodise and contextualise the wide range of works on exhibition. Yet, as I pointed out in my catalogue introduction to this show, it has to be admitted that Hobsbawm's specific comments on the type of work exhibited are invariably negative and uninteresting. See *Global Conceptualism: Points of Origin, 1950s–1980s* (New York, 1999), p. 4.

[28] A. L. Rees and Frances Borzello (eds), *The New Art History* (London, 1986), p. 3. The introduction to this collection of essays also makes clear the indebtedness of the *Block* group to the teaching developed at Leeds University by T. J. Clark in the previous decade, in particular his MA course on the social history of art.

that year by the Musée d'Art contemporain de Montréal under the title 'The New Art History — Revisited'. However selectively pitched and unrepresentative these events and publications may seem in retrospect, they make it possible for a number of parallel currents of development to be singled out for attention.

One of these is the issue, touched on before in this essay, of the relationship of art history to history. By this may be understood not simply the relationship of the discipline to its own past, but also its connection to simultaneous developments in the field of the historical sciences. It might appear obvious, but it bears restating, that the perception of the need for a 'New Art History' was intimately associated with the conviction that the discipline had suffered a disastrous lapse from its earlier high standards in the early years of the post-war period. Few obvious successors had appeared to take on the mantle of the German scholars. In 1994, Thomas Crow narrowed down this general complaint to the specific failure of senior American scholars to measure up to the challenge set by their teachers: 'The greatest damage was done by the poor performance of a whole generation of American scholars, many of them trained after World War II by the émigré Europeans. Finding students who were unprepared to work at the highest level, these teachers consciously or unconsciously lowered their demands.'[29] For Crow, it was not simply a matter of the post-war generation throwing overboard the high seriousness and philosophical concern of the émigré art historians, but of 'actual skills in historical research' being abandoned in the course of a wholesale retreat from hard intellectual effort.

However justified it may have been to represent art history in America as having lost its intellectual nerve in the third quarter of the century, the same could not be applied to history as a whole, particularly in its European manifestations. To me, it seemed clear, when I responded to the questions of the editors of The New Art History in 1986, that 'the destiny of the "new art history" [was] integrally bound up with what has come to be called the New History ... There can be no "new art history" except to the extent that it participates in a "new history".'[30] Under the rubric of 'new history', I placed, not surprisingly, members of the French Annales school like Braudel, Duby and Le Roy Ladurie, as well as Natalie Zemon Davis and Keith Thomas. I was less concerned than Crow turned out to be about the loss of basic techniques of archival research, preferring to draw attention to the

---

[29] Revoir la New Art History (Montreal, 1995), p. 30.
[30] Rees and Borzello, New Art History, p. 28.

need for art historians to 'have a self-critical estimate of the rhetorical underpinning of the historical craft, such as might be obtained from reading Foucault, or Barthes, or Hayden White'.[31]

Yet the cluster of concerns that animated the contributors to *The New Art History* in 1986 went far beyond this issue of the relation of art history to history, in its 'new' and in its traditional forms. By carefully keeping individual contributors in ignorance of the issues tackled by the others, the editors succeeded in getting an eclectic spread of approaches which seems all the more indicative in retrospect. Topics ranged from the advocacy of 'little magazines' for the study of the history of avant-garde movements (Dawn Ades), and reflections on the 'mutual implications of art history and curatorship' (Charles Harrison), to the consequences for art history of semiotics (Margaret Iversen), feminism (Lynda Nead), aesthetic criticism (Michael O'Pray) and the state of the undergraduate syllabus (Marcia Pointon). Especially significant, since they recurred in several contributions, were the mentions of a select group of interdisciplinary fields that were then in the process of being opened up, and would rapidly acquire their own momentum: among them, landscape (in the sense of both landscape painting and garden history), museum studies and the history and theory of photography.[32]

In this respect, *The New Art History* certainly reflected the wealth of new concerns which were developing at that stage both inside and on the fringes of the discipline. These were finding expression through strategically planned new journals, as well as through individually authored studies. *Critical Inquiry* has already been mentioned as a major journal which would open its pages to art historical material. *Representations*, which began publication from the University of California Press in 1983 under the co-

[31] It is interesting to note that in 1983 Peter Burke concluded his brief essay on 'Rethinking Cultural History' with a plea for the renewed study of rhetoric in its historical context, summoning cultural historians to an involvement with 'the rhetoric of everyday life'. This was offered as an antidote to the 'literal-minded' attitude to historical information sometimes exemplified by classic cultural historians like Burckhardt and Huizinga. See *The Cambridge Review*, 104, 2277 (18 November 1983), 208.

[32] Landscape studies had been reinvigorated, at the start of the decade, by John Barrell's *The Dark Side of the Landscape* (Cambridge, 1980), and the influence of this powerful analysis by a scholar in English studies had been reflected in the public debate over David Solkin's recent Richard Wilson exhibition at the Tate Gallery (discussed by Alex Potts and Neil McWilliam). Museum studies were not explicitly the subject of an individual contribution, but relevant to several; by the end of the 1980s, they had generated their own interdisciplinary impetus, as evidenced by Peter Vergo's anthology, *The New Museology* (London, 1989). Photography was the primary subject of the essays by Victor Burgin and Ian Jeffrey, and also mentioned, together with feminism, by Adrian Rifkin.

chairmanship of the 'New Historicist' Stephen Greenblatt and the art historian Svetlana Alpers, was to offer a valuable bridge between scholars in literary studies, 'new historicism' and the 'cultural poetics' associated with the anthropologist Clifford Geertz. In addition to drawing attention to its recent emergence in my article of 1986, I also singled out the recent publication of two other new journals, both based in Britain and edited by the British scholar John Dixon Hunt: *Journal of Garden History* and *Word & Image*.[33] The former has proved exemplary in focusing a previously diffuse debate, and immeasurably raising the critical standards of work on the history of gardens and designed landscapes. The latter has also been remarkable, not only in attracting a continuing flow of excellent individual articles, but also in attracting special issues on a wide range of topics. These range from medieval illuminated manuscripts to emblem studies, from semiotics and cartography to advertising and the history of book illustration. It is clear that the success of these new journals has not affected the fortunes of existing publications. In fact, they have helped to reinvigorate the 'house journals' of the discipline, in particular *Art History*, the organ of the British Art Historians' Association since the 1970s, and *The Art Bulletin*, published by the College Art Association of America.

One way in which many of those associated with the 'New Art History' marked their divergence from the disciplinary concerns of the post-war period was in proclaiming their openness to 'theory'. This, however, was not only a matter of catching up with the classic German texts already mentioned here, but of assimilating the new material on the visual arts — both historical and critical — which had been published in France from the 1960s onwards. In 1988 Norman Bryson launched his series with Cambridge University Press, entitled 'New Art History and Criticism', with a collection of translations from the French featuring authors such as Julia Kristeva, Louis Marin, Roland Barthes and Michel Foucault. Not one of these authors would have been regarded in the strict sense as an art historian by the French profession. Bryson was, however, making the point (as firmly emphasised in his editorial introduction) that the brilliant and resourceful analysis of works of visual art carried out by a poet like Yves Bonnefoy, a historian and

---

[33] Rees and Borzello, *New Art History*, pp. 28–9. *Journal of Garden History* is now known under the new title of *Studies in the History of Gardens and Designed Landscapes*. I should add that the previous decade was notable particularly for the foundation of two journals which combined the historical treatment of modern and contemporary art with an exceptionally high level of committed criticism: *October*, originally edited in New York by Jeremy Gilbert-Rolfe, Rosalind Krauss and Annette Michaelson and first appearing in Spring 1976; and *Macula*, originally edited in Paris by Yve-Alain Bois, Guy Brett, Jean Clay and Raymonde Hébraud-Carasco and first appearing in Summer 1976.

philosopher of science like Michel Serres, or an art critic like Jean-Claude Lebensztejn, not to mention the internationally celebrated figures already listed, could be a source of inspiration for new art historians practising in the English-speaking world.[34]

Bryson's strategy implied a new and productive focus on French theory, which complemented but also, to some extent, challenged the hegemony of German art historical scholarship.[35] His own work in the l980s had laid some of the groundwork for this new orientation, with *Word & Image: French Painting of the Ancien Régime* (1981) placing a special focus on the art criticism of Diderot, and *Vision and Painting: The Logic of the Gaze* (1983) seeking to supplant the psychological focus of Gombrich's *Art and Illusion* with a semiotic and psychoanalytic analysis of representation based on the theories of Jacques Lacan. In 'The Pictorial Turn', Mitchell credits him with having managed to 'bring the latest news from France and shake art history out of its dogmatic slumber'.[36] However, he acknowledges that 'a more broadly conceived account' of the development of Anglo-American art history would have to trace the 'path-breaking work' of a number of other important figures who were publishing from the 1960s onwards: Svetlana Alpers, Michael Baxandall, Rosalind Krauss, Ronald Paulson, Leo Steinberg, T. J. Clark and Michael Fried. It is difficult to quarrel with this list, all of whose members can be credited with playing a central role in the construction of the new art history in its broader sense. It is also impossible to do justice here, even in a summary way, to the range of contributions to art history which each has made. Nevertheless, a few of those mentioned above will take centre stage in the final debate that I shall be summarising. This debate can be seen as subsuming many of the issues that have already been raised here.

---

[34] See Bryson (ed.), *Calligram: Essays in New Art History*. The only essay not drawn from recent French writing on the arts was the Czech semiotician Jan Mukarovsky's 'Art as Semiological Fact' (1934), which was, however, a text originally written in French for presentation at an international congress. The commitment of the Cambridge series to new French writing was particularly exemplified by the publication of such works as the selected texts of Jean-Louis Schefer, ed. and trans. Paul Smith, *The Enigmatic Body* (Cambridge, 1995).

[35] It is worth emphasising that the fragmented state of French art history, and its conspicuous lack of cross-fertilisation of the kind proposed in *Calligram*, derives in part from an institutional development involving essentially independent bodies as diverse as the Ecole des Beaux-Arts, the Ecole du Louvre, the Collège de France and the Sorbonne over a long period. The different strands are carefully unpicked in Therrien, *L'histoire de l'art en France*, chs 2, 3, 4, 6.

[36] Mitchell, 'The Pictorial Turn', p. 14. He draws an interesting comparison with Jonathan Culler, who in the previous decade provided a similar 'service' for 'Anglo-American literary criticism'. It is worth pointing out that both Culler, whose *Structuralist Poetics* was published in 1975, and Bryson himself, moved from a British to an American university in the period when their work was performing this role.

Visual culture versus the autonomy of art

In the untidy sequence of stages which I have tried to map up to this point, the terms 'Social History of Art' and 'New Art History' have served as symptoms of a changing climate of opinion, the first relating to the mid-1970s and the second to the mid-1980s. The former concept was not supplanted by the latter; rather, a mass of new ingredients entered the mix.[37] Differences of generation undoubtedly played their part in overemphasising the dialectical movement between these, and subsequent, shifts of art historical focus. Indeed at the symposium on 'Whatever Happened to the Social Art History?', already mentioned above, it was noticeable that art historians of the present middle generation took there to be much more clear-cut issues at stake in this development over two decades than Thomas Crow was willing to admit as respondent. James Elkins suggested that new visual and media studies had simply taken over from the earlier emphasis on social history, and that a plurality of new authorities had supplanted the monolithic tyranny exercised by Marx. Anne Higonnet accused the Social Art History of making objects a function of issues, rather than issues a function of objects, and attacked a reading of the nineteenth century which seemed to turn a select number of major artists into heroes.[38] Thomas Crow resisted the attempt to impugn these choices of subject matter as essentially subjective ones, and considered that the only sufficient justification for the art history practised in the 1970s (as at the present day) was its intellectual depth and its genuine quality as scholarship.

These brief comments from a recent panel discussion are quoted to demonstrate a simple point: that the issues that have dominated debates in art history over the past quarter-century inevitably change in their substance and relative importance, in accord with the generation of the person who considers them. I began by signalling a 'historiographical turn' in art history as evidence for the increased self-confidence of the discipline in institutional

---

[37] It is interesting to note that, among the contributors to the 1986 anthology, only John Tagg saw his task as querying the mission of the Social History of Art. Quoting Clark's statement in 1974 that this was 'the place where the questions have to be asked', he lists various criticisms of 'the once confident expectations of the Social History of Art' (*New Art History*, pp. 165–6).

[38] It is certainly the case that Clark and Crow have not seen it as their task to challenge the canon of accepted masters, at least for the nineteenth century. This means that, however high the quality of the analysis of major painters like David, Courbet and Manet, there turn out to be large gaps when an attempt is made to extend the 'social history' beyond the privileged epochs. Stephen Eisenman's confidently titled *Nineteenth-century Art: A Critical History* (London, 1994) includes excellent sections written by Crow, but wears threadbare in the editor's dismissive chapter on 'The July Monarchy and the Art of *Juste Milieu*'.

terms. But, of course, the accessibility of German sources and the provision of student guides to methodology have given no guarantee that a more brilliant and intellectually distinguished art history would be written. I spent some time looking at the successive debates around 'Social History of Art' and 'New Art History'. These certainly provide firm evidence of a broadly based movement of renewal, which has fixed on new areas and new interdisciplinary methods, as well as restoring some of its lost prestige to traditional archival research. But a problem still lurks within the expanded field of history of art, which Mitchell diagnosed when he alluded to the 'visual turn' of the human sciences. This is already implicit in many of the contributions to the debate on 'New Art History' which I have summarised. It can be expressed quite simply. Is art history destined to lose its own identity, and be subsumed within the study of 'visual culture'?

This has been a central issue of the 1990s, and has to some extent taken the place of the two debates already summarised. It can be viewed as an irreversible outcome of disciplinary developments adjacent to the field of art history, as well as being a feature of the broad context evoked by Mitchell. To take one instance, the current position of film studies, which Bryson rightly regarded in 1988 as having stolen a march on art history in its recently acquired theoretical sophistication, now seems to be in much closer proximity to the art historian's field. Film historians have developed a considerable interest in nineteenth-century spectacle, and in the technical and institutional aspects of such manifestations as the panorama and the diorama, which presaged the invention of cinematography. This confluence is also clearly to be observed in the recent rapid development of the history and theory of photography, however halting its earlier progress may have been on the European side of the Atlantic. It is now much more difficult than it was in the 1970s to draw a line around 'art', and not least in the social context of the nineteenth century. There is a steady accumulation of studies which treat not only photography, but also the neglected field of printmaking, as powerful engines for the circulation of communicative images rather than pale reflections of the 'high' arts.[39]

Yet the arguments for a focus on 'visual culture' have been challenged in the 1990s, and not only so by the traditional art historians whose mission is

---

[39] See for example the remarkable study by Anthony Hamber, *'A Higher Branch of the Art': Photographing the Fine Arts in England 1839–1880* (Amsterdam, 1996). The recent exhibition of the work of Paul Delaroche at the Musée des Beaux-Arts, Nantes, and the Musée Fabre, Montpellier, is probably the first in which a nineteenth-century painter is presented together with the full range of printed and photographic material associated with his work. See *Paul Delaroche: Un peintre dans l'histoire* (Paris, 1999).

to tend the 'masterpieces' of western painting. In a special issue of *October*, published in Summer 1996, Rosalind Krauss and Hal Foster brought together a number of important contributions to this debate, in the form of answers to a questionnaire on visual culture by American academics, as well as a group of strategically argued articles.[40] Opening the issue is a contribution by Kurt W. Forster on the historical figure most generally credited with anticipating the study of visual culture, Aby Warburg. Forster analyses Warburg's interest in ethnography, and looks at his comparisons between features of the culture of the American Indians in Arizona and the prevalence of wax votive images in Renaissance Florence, previously neglected by art historians with their 'sanitised image of the Renaissance as an age of refinement'.[41] This gives a significant depth of perspective to the present-day argument, which W. J. T. Mitchell also considerably broadens in his own article for the collection. Mitchell is ready to acknowledge that 'visual culture' as it has been advocated over the previous decade has 'produced a remarkable transformation in the sleepy confines of academic art history'. But he also questions the need for art history to insist upon 'a rhetoric of innovation and modernisation': to play at catching up with 'the text-based disciplines and the study of film and mass culture'. In his view, 'Pictures want equal rights with language, not to be turned into language. They want neither to be levelled into a "history of images" nor elevated into a "history of art" but to be seen as complex individuals occupying multiple subject positions and identities.'[42]

Mitchell's comments should not be taken as repudiating his earlier remarks on the 'pictorial turn'. But they do invite art historians to make a careful self-scrutiny before they venture to lay claim to the expanded field of visual culture. Those who have offered answers to the *October* questionnaire, several of them from adjacent fields like film and cultural studies, rise very well to the opportunity. What is worth noting — since *October* has been from its inception a journal committed to contemporary art practice as well as to the historical analysis of modernism — is the importance that they attach to the rise of a parallel phenomenon in the visual arts. In their

---

[40] See *October*, 77 (Summer 1996). Among those who responded to the questionnaire are several art historians mentioned in this essay: Svetlana Alpers, Thomas Crow, Michael Ann Holly, Keith Moxey and Christopher Wood.

[41] Ibid., 17.

[42] Ibid., 82. Mitchell acknowledges that he is arguing against the claims made editorially by Norman Bryson, Michael Ann Holly and Keith Moxey in the collection of essays, *Visual Culture: Images and Interpretations* (Hanover, NH, 1994).

statement on behalf of the editors, Rosalind Krauss and Hal Foster note the existence of a 'mutation in the avant-garde: a strange cross-over between the worlds of artistic production and exhibition and of academic teaching and publishing'.[43] Hal Foster develops this perception in an eloquent essay which pleads, in the end, for a new concept of art's 'strategic autonomy': this will not simply repeat Kant's gesture of '[wresting] institutions away from the *ancien régime*', or the modernist attack on 'the priority of iconographic texts', but recognises the special challenge posed to the arts by information technology as it builds up 'an archive without museums'.[44]

This being said, it is important to recognise at the same time the very considerable degree to which 'visual culture' has become embedded in the study of art history, over the course of the recent period under discussion here. Svetlana Alpers affirms in her answer to the *October* questionnaire that her use of the term in *The Art of Describing* (1983) was derived from the historical work of Michael Baxandall. She also correctly remarks that her use of the concept was different in its specific reference to the art of the Dutch seventeenth century, where (according to her argument) notions of vision connected with optics, devices like microscopes and cameras, and skills like map-making, were closely related to the practice of painting. To repeat her formulation: 'I was not only attending to those visual skills particular to a culture, but claiming that in that place and time these skills were definitive.'[45] In spite of these legitimate reservations, it would be hard to deny the strategic importance of Alpers' decision to focus, at the time, on this exemplary period and practice. Nor would be possible to exclude from any general account of the construction of visual culture as an area of study over the last three decades the vital contribution of Michael Baxandall. Whether he discusses the visual effect of volume in Piero's *Madonna del Parto* with reference to the Renaissance skill of gauging the content of a barrel, or tests the limits of iconographic interpretation with reference to the same artist's *Baptism of Christ*, Baxandall is constantly reaffirming the intellectual dignity, as well as the historical specificity, of the act of vision.[46]

It may indeed be somewhat of a distortion to single out the element of 'visual culture' as a destabilising tension within the field of art history, when the roots of the difference of approach extend so deep, indeed as far as the

[43] *October*, 77 (Summer 1996), 4.
[44] Ibid., 97, 118–19.
[45] Ibid., 26.
[46] The first reference is to Baxandall's *Painting and Experience in Fifteenth-century Italy* (Oxford, 1972), and the second to *Patterns of Intention: On the Historical Explanation of Pictures* (Yale, CT, 1985).

founding fathers. It has been said more than once in the recent past that the
art historian of the present day can choose to follow either Panofsky or
Warburg, and some of the most innovative scholars of the middle generation
show that important new findings can be derived from either line of descent.
This study has sought to emphasise, on a number of levels, that art history in
Britain lies at the intersection of competing and converging traditions, none
of which can legitimately be taken as canonical. The option of 'visual
culture' characterises the discipline as a fox, making forays into the territory
of the social sciences, and indeed of mainstream history. But hedgehog art
history will not disappear, any more than the fundamental (and still hotly
debated) issue of art's 'autonomy'.

CHAPTER TEN

Historiography and Philosophy of History

PETER BURKE

Just as Britain was once regarded — at least by Germans — as a *Land ohne Musik*, so it is still sometimes viewed by foreigners as a land without historiography, in the sense of a place in which historians show unusually little concern for the past of their own discipline. A similar point might be made about the relative lack of interest of British historians (and, to a lesser extent, of British philosophers as well) in the philosophy of history.

There is indeed something to be said in favour of these views. Until quite recently, for example, there was, as far as I know, no journal published in Britain devoted either to the history of historical writing or historical thought (*Rethinking History* began to appear as recently as 1996), so that scholars with articles to publish in these areas had to send them to *History and Theory* in the USA or *Storia della Storiografia* in Italy. Unlike Germany, the USA and other countries, posts in British universities are rarely if ever allocated to historiography or the philosophy of history.

Courses in the philosophy of history are also rare, and the formal study of historical method has not been encouraged in history departments, at any rate until recently. In the early 1960s, some Oxford students (myself included) complained about the lack of attention given to historiography in the Faculty. Oxford now offers first-year undergraduates a choice between 'Approaches to History', 'Quantification' or 'Historiography from Tacitus to Weber'. The University of Sussex has a first-year course, 'Historical Controversy', and the University of Warwick a third-year 'core course' on historiography. The University of Newcastle used to have a first-year class on 'The Study of History' which inspired one of its professors to edit a collection of essays on famous historians.[1] On the other hand, some British universities still give little or no time

---

[1] John Cannon (ed.), *The Historian at Work* (London, 1980).

to these topics. The lack of courses may be read as an expression of cultural resistance to historiography and philosophy of history, but it also functions as a constraint, discouraging the next generation from entering this field. A similar point may be made about the lack of journals and university posts.

Again, there is no real British rival to Bernheim or Langlois and Seignebos, for example, introductions to method which were for a long time historians' bibles in Germany and France, respectively. The German medievalist Ernst Bernheim's *Lehrbuch der historische Methode* (1889) had reached its sixth edition by 1908 as well as being translated into Spanish and (more freely) into Italian, but not into English. The more pragmatic treatise by the French historians Charles Langlois and Charles Seignobos, *Introduction aux études historiques* (1879), was also regularly reprinted.

Langlois and Seignobos appeared in English in 1898 with a laudatory preface by the Regius Professor of Modern History at Oxford, F. York Powell. Among the successors of this virtually canonical text available to British readers was *History, its Purpose and Method*, by the Dutchman Gustaaf Renier, and *The Historian's Craft* by the Frenchman Marc Bloch.[2] Even G. R. Elton, whose *Practice of History* (1967) articulates a common-sense, no-nonsense view of method, was German by origin. The major exception to the rule that the British leave this topic to foreigners is E. H. Carr. Although he was best known for his history of the Soviet Union, Carr's Trevelyan lectures, *What is History?* (delivered in Cambridge in 1961 and published in book form soon afterwards), have been widely read.

That the lack of journals and chairs in the subject is no accident is suggested by the fact that a substantial proportion of the books and articles published on British historiography in the course of the twentieth century were written by foreign scholars, especially Americans (among them Joseph Levine, Fritz Levy, Frank Fussner, David Lowenthal, and the Canadians Mark Phillips and Daniel Woolf). The book-length monographs on the leading British philosopher of history, R. G. Collingwood, have not been written by British scholars but by Americans (Louis Mink and William Dray), a Dutchman (W. J. van der Dussen), a Finn (Heikki Saari), a Frenchman (A. Shalom), a Norwegian (Peter Skagestad) and an Indian (C. Kanichai).[3] The most famous

---

[2] G. Renier, *History, its Purpose and Method* (London, 1950); Marc Bloch, *The Historian's Craft* (1949, English trans. Manchester, 1954).

[3] Louis Mink, *Mind, History and Dialectic: The Philosophy of R. G. Collingwood* (Bloomington, IN, 1969); W. H. Dray, *History as Re-enactment* (Oxford, 1995); W. J. van der Dussen, *History as a Science: The Philosophy of R. G. Collingwood* (The Hague, 1981); Heikki Saari, *Re-enactment: A Study in R. G. Collingwood's Philosophy of History* (Åbo, 1984); A. Shalom, *R. G. Collingwood: Philosophe et Historien* (Paris, 1967); Peter Skagestad, *Making Sense of History* (Oslo, 1975); C. Kanichai, *Collingwood's Philosophy of History* (Alwaye, 1981).

scholar in the field of historiography working in twentieth-century Britain was an Italian, Arnaldo Momigliano, and the most famous philosopher of history after Collingwood was a Russian, Isaiah Berlin.

It is tempting, and indeed not unreasonable, to seek an explanation for what Gareth Stedman Jones once called 'the peculiar myopia of English historians' (their relative lack of interest in general interpretations of the past, in historical method and in the past of the discipline) in the 'peculiarities of the English' in general, notably empiricism and the cult of common sense and the amateur.[4] Hence, perhaps, the notorious 'absence of an English Durkheim, Pareto or Weber' noted by Perry Anderson, and the apparent insulation of Britain from the crisis of European positivism.[5]

As for the cult of the amateur, it should be noted that Oxford and Cambridge long resisted the apparatus of German historical scholarship. In Oxford, for instance, the D. Phil. was introduced as late as 1917, 'partly in the hope of attracting to Britain ... Americans in search of the higher degrees', and in the 1940s and 1950s it was, we are told, 'still viewed by many arts dons as a distasteful medium of dry Teutonic pedantry'. In Cambridge, shortly before the First World War, G. M. Trevelyan described the methods of 'German learning' as 'a strait waistcoat to English limbs and faculties', and denounced attempts 'to drill us into so many Potsdam Guards of Learning'.[6]

Even today, studies of historiography still appear to many British historians to be unnecessarily inward-looking and navel-contemplating. Publishing studies of historical method, or even lecturing on the topic, smacks of telling one's colleagues how to do their job. Even in the age of so-called 'postmodernism', references to 'the facts', to 'brass tacks' and so on still flow easily from the mouths, the pens and the PCs of British historians. The existence of national styles in science has been a matter of academic debate, but the phenomenon would appear to be obvious enough in historiography, whether it should be explained by the lack of courses in philosophy in British schools (in contrast to at least some schools in

---

[4] Gareth Stedman Jones, 'The Pathology of English History', *New Left Review*, 46 (1967), 29–43, at 30; E. P. Thompson, 'The Peculiarities of the English', *Socialist Register* (1965), 311–62, a critique of the emphasis placed on these peculiarities by Perry Anderson and Tom Nairn.

[5] P. Anderson, 'Components of the National Culture' (1968), rpr. with revisions in his *English Questions* (London, 1992), pp. 48–104, the quotation at p. 56; Jones, 'Pathology', 33.

[6] Brian Harrison (ed.), *History of the University of Oxford: The Twentieth Century* (Oxford, 1994), pp. 6, 218; G. M. Trevelyan, *Clio: A Muse* (London, 1913). See Dorothy S. Goldstein, 'History at Oxford and Cambridge: Professionalisation and the Influence of Ranke', in George Iggers and James Powell (eds), *Leopold von Ranke and the Shaping of the Historical Discipline* (Syracuse, NY, 1990), pp. 141–53, concluding that, although there was a tendency to professionalisation in the period 1870–1900, 'the compelling image remained that of the brilliant amateur'.

France, Germany and Italy), or more generally by the local culture of empiricism.

This essay has two themes: the history of historiography and the philosophy of history, linked interests in practice and also in principle, since one is concerned with what historians have done and the other with what historians should do. It is divided into four sections, dealing in turn with the history of historical writing, with discussions of method, and with debates and assumptions about the pattern of the past. The changes which took place in the course of the twentieth century will be discussed in each section and in more general fashion in the conclusion.

The history of historical writing

Before 1950, relatively few studies on historiography were published in Britain, although this handful included some works of distinction, three in particular. F. M. Cornford, a classicist in the circle of Gilbert Murray, Jane Harrison and the young Arnold Toynbee, discussed what would later be known as 'mythistory' in his *Thucydides Mythistoricus* (1907); G. P. Gooch produced a survey of *History and Historians in the Nineteenth Century* (1913); and the young medievalist David Douglas wrote about seventeenth-century studies of the Middle Ages in his *English Scholars* (1939).

The 1950s was a turning-point in this respect, a decade in which a remarkable amount of work on the history of history was published, remarkable considering the remoteness of the topic from the university teaching of the authors. *The Hedgehog and the Fox*, an essay (originally a lecture) by Isaiah Berlin, concerned with Tolstoy's attitude to history in *War and Peace*, was probably the study which attracted attention most widely. This was also the age of the polymath Arnaldo Momigliano, whose many essays on the history of historical writing began to appear in English at this time.[7] Momigliano was also important as an inspiration and as a model for younger scholars, whose interest in historiography he did much to encourage, whether they focused on classical antiquity, the Renaissance or later periods.[8]

In Cambridge, Herbert Butterfield was the centre of a similar network of scholars, including Brian Wormald, author of *Clarendon* (1951), and Duncan

---

[7] Arnaldo Momigliano, 'Ancient History and the Antiquarian' (1950), 'George Grote and the Study of Greek History' (1952) and other essays of the 1950s repr. in A. D. Momigliano, *Studies in Historiography* (London, 1966).

[8] Among them Fergus Millar, Michael Crawford and myself.

Forbes, who acknowledged the encouragement of Butterfield in his *Liberal Anglican Idea of History* (1952). In Oxford, Hugh Trevor-Roper wrote essays on historians from Camden to Carlyle, and also encouraged graduate students to enter the field.[9] In Edinburgh, Denys Hay's life-long interest in historiography may be illustrated by his *Polydore Vergil* (1952) and *Annalists and Historians* (1977).

From the 1980s onwards, a rapidly increasing number of studies have been published in this area. The only general survey — limited to England — John Kenyon's *The History Men* (1983), exemplified a sturdy empiricist approach to the subject from the point of view of an historian of seventeenth-century English politics. However, John Burrow's study of nineteenth-century historians, *A Liberal Descent* (1981), offered a more intellectual history of 'the Whig tradition', 'the ancient constitution' and other topics. Stephen Bann's *The Clothing of Clio* (1984) was essentially concerned, as the title-page made clear, with 'the representation of history' in the nineteenth century. In the 1980s and 1990s a series of short studies of Maitland, Gibbon, Hume and Namier, together with books on G. M. Trevelyan, Eileen Power and others, introduced the history of historical thought and writing to a wider public.[10]

The recent rise of interest in historiography is associated with an increasing openness to different approaches to the past in a profession in which there is considerably less consensus than there was fifty years ago. There have been lively exchanges on topics such as history from below, women's history and post-colonial history, and the disagreements show no signs of abating.

As it has become less marginal, historiography itself has developed. Contributions to the subject have been made by scholars in a broad range of disciplines, including archaeology (Stuart Piggott, for instance), geography (David Lowenthal), anthropology (Elizabeth Tonkin) and literature (David Womersley).[11] The object of historiographical studies has been reconstructed. It is less and less confined to the study of major texts by major

[9] Trevor-Roper was the supervisor of my never-completed doctoral thesis on 'New Trends in European Historical Writing, 1500–1700'.
[10] G. R. Elton, *F. W. Maitland* (London, 1985); Roy Porter, *Gibbon* (London, 1988); Nicholas Phillipson, *Hume* (London, 1989); Linda Colley, *Namier* (London, 1989); David Cannadine, *G. M. Trevelyan: A Life in History* (London, 1993); Maxine Berg, *A Woman in History: Eileen Power 1889–1940* (Cambridge, 1996). Historians are also represented in the 'Past Masters' series, including John Burrow, *Gibbon* (Oxford, 1985), and Peter Burke, *Vico* (Oxford, 1985).
[11] Stuart Piggott, *Ancient Britons and the Antiquarian Imagination* (London, 1989); David Lowenthal, *The Past is a Foreign Country* (Cambridge, 1985); Elizabeth Tonkin, *Narrating Our Pasts* (Cambridge, 1992); David J. Womersley, *The Transformation of the Decline and Fall* (Cambridge, 1988).

historians but now includes what might be called the 'historical culture' of the past, including the views of ordinary people as well as academics, readers as well as writers, and paintings, museums, monuments and memories as well as texts.[12] Although space does not permit a serious discussion of popularisations, of historical publishing, of the teaching of history in schools and other relevant topics, the essay which you are now reading is itself conceived as a study of British historical culture, defined by contrast to that of other countries such as France, Germany and the United States.

Historical methods

If there is now more interest in Britain than ever before in the history of historiography, the reason may well be that historians are becoming more self-conscious about their methods. It used to be the case, as was remarked earlier, that British historians did not publish books on this topic, although the role of inaugural lectures of professors of history is worth noting as a licensed occasion for general reflections on both method and historiography. The opportunity provided by such occasions was not always taken, but R. H. Tawney's inaugural lecture at the London School of Economics in 1932, to quote one famous example, was one of the rare British contributions of the time to the discussion of the relative importance of events and structures which exercised so many historians in France.

A few methodological topics have long been open to debate in college essay societies and elsewhere, including 'bias' in history and the question whether history should be regarded as an art or a science. Beyond this, historical method has usually been discussed either by philosophers or by the practitioners of new sub-disciplines, notably intellectual history and economic history. Let us take these groups in order.

The first and still the most important figure in this field is of course R. G. Collingwood.[13] Collingwood, who was most active in the 1920s and 1930s, was a unique combination of a practising historian (and archae-ologist), specialising in Roman Britain, and a philosopher, an idealist particularly interested in Croce and in Vico. A special post of 'Lecturer in Philosophy and Roman History' was created for him at Oxford.

---

[12] Lowenthal, *The Past*; Raphael Samuel, *Theatres of Memory* (London, 1994).

[13] Michael Oakeshott, *Experience and its Modes* (1933) and *On History* (1983); W. H. Walsh, *An Introduction to the Philosophy of History* (London, 1951); Patrick Gardiner, *The Nature of Historical Explanation* (Oxford, 1952); W. B. Gallie, *Philosophy and the Historical Understanding* (1964).

Collingwood's most famous study, *The Idea of History*, developed out of his lectures and was published posthumously in a fragmentary form. It is perhaps most famous for its claim that 'all history is the history of thought' (in other words, 'the re-enactment of past experience'); for its stress on what the author called 'the questioning activity'; and for its contrast, in the tradition of German neo-Kantian philosophy, between historical and scientific method. As Collingwood put it, in one of the most famous passages of *The Idea of History*, 'When a scientist asks "Why did that piece of litmus paper turn pink?", he means "On what kinds of occasions do pieces of litmus paper turn pink?" When an historian asks "Why did Brutus stab Caesar?", he means "What did Brutus think, which made him decide to stab Caesar?"' It should be emphasised that Collingwood viewed thought not *in vacuo* but as a response to a situation. To understand an edict of the emperor Theodosius, for example, the historian 'must envisage the situation with which the emperor was trying to deal, and he must envisage it as that emperor envisaged it'.[14]

Another influential section of the *Idea of History*, entitled 'Who killed John Doe?', comes in the chapter on historical evidence. Today, the comparison between historians and detectives almost immediately conjures up the name of Carlo Ginzburg and his celebrated parallel between the methods of Sherlock Holmes, Sigmund Freud and Giovanni Morelli. In the 1930s, however, in the heyday of the detective novel, Collingwood — inspired by Agatha Christie rather than by Sir Arthur Conan Doyle — was already drawing analogies between legal methods and historical methods.[15]

It is surely revealing of the lacunae in British historical culture that, when the *English Historical Review* received *The Idea of History*, the editor sent it for review to a philosopher, Michael Oakeshott. Oakeshott's verdict was that, had he lived, the author might have become the Kant of historical knowledge, and that the last hundred pages of the book were 'enough to put him ahead of every other writer on the subject'.[16] Isaiah Berlin's position was also close to that of Collingwood (who had once urged him to read Croce's book on Vico). One of the few criticisms came from Arnold Toynbee, who considered that the claim that all history is the history of thought neglected the importance of impulse and emotion in the past.[17]

---

[14] R. G. Collingwood, *The Idea of History* (1946, revised edn, ed. J. van der Dussen, Oxford, 1993), pp. 214, 283.
[15] Ibid., pp. 266–8; see Joseph M. Levine, 'The Autonomy of History: R. G. Collingwood and Agatha Christie', *Clio*, 7 (1978), 253–64.
[16] Michael Oakeshott, *English Historical Review*, 62 (1947), 84–6.
[17] Toynbee, *A Study of History, vol. 9* (London, 1954), pp. 718–37, at p. 721.

Since Collingwood's day, despite contributions from Oakeshott, Berlin, W. H. Walsh, Patrick Gardiner and W. B. Gallie, analytical philosophy of history has largely been left to philosophers on the other side of the Atlantic such as William Dray and Arthur Danto, who have made the subject their main academic concern.[18] Although some historians have been sympathetic, and Collingwood's lectures were attended by future historians such as C. V. Wedgwood and Max Beloff, admiration did not lead to emulation.[19]

The major exception to this rule is that of the practitioners of a new discipline or sub-discipline which emerged in Britain in the 1950s and 1960s, the history of ideas or intellectual history, developing out of the courses on the history of political thought taught at Oxford, Cambridge and elsewhere. An MA in the History of Ideas was established at the new University of Sussex, in 1963. Collingwood was and is a hero to the dominant figures in the field, John Pocock (a New Zealander who practised history in Britain before moving to the United States) and Quentin Skinner. In their histories of political thought, Pocock and Skinner often treat texts (by Edmund Burke, for example, or by Thomas Hobbes) in Collingwoodian style as responses to situations. They are also concerned with what they variously call the 'languages' or 'conventions' of political thought. Thanks to Skinner, the problems of method raised by attempts to write the history of political thought in particular have become the object of an extended debate, in Britain as well as the United States, and it is no longer unusual to find historians referring to the work of philosophers such as John Austin, John Searle and Richard Rorty.[20]

Another kind of intellectual history which has been the site of some fruitful recent debates over method, in Britain as well as in the USA and elsewhere, is the history of science, provoked by the cultural relativism of Thomas Kuhn's *Structure of Scientific Revolutions* (1962) and, more recently, by the 'sociology of scientific knowledge' (known as SSK), with its emphasis on scientific knowledge as local knowledge produced in environments such as laboratories. The debate over the relative importance of microsocial or microhistorical approaches to the history of science versus the more traditional macrohistorical ones is still in progress.[21]

The closest parallel to the methodologically self-conscious approach of the intellectual historians is to be found in economic history. At much the

---

[18] William H. Dray, *Laws and Explanation in History* (Oxford, 1957); Arthur C. Danto, *Analytical Philosophy of History* (Cambridge, 1965).

[19] Dussen, *Collingwood*, p. 2.

[20] James Tully (ed.), *Meaning and Context: Quentin Skinner and his Critics* (Cambridge, 1988).

[21] Jan Golinsky, *Making Natural Knowledge* (Cambridge, 1988).

same time as their colleagues in intellectual history, the 1950s and 1960s, British economic historians began to reassess their methods, stimulated by a debate on the other side of the Atlantic associated with the so-called 'New Economic History', as well as by changes in economics, notably the rise of econometrics. Quantitative methods, which were becoming increasingly sophisticated at this time, were the major focus of this debate. However, the new economic historians also questioned traditional types of historical explanation by introducing the idea of the 'counter-factual', in other words taking might-have-beens in history more seriously than before and attempting to calculate the economic consequences of different courses of action (building or not building railways, abolishing slavery or retaining it, and so on).

Other kinds of historian have followed in the wake of these developments. Social historians, another group in search of autonomy, were interested — for a while, at least — in quantitative methods for the study of social change. A recent collection of essays on 'virtual history' shows even the traditionally more conservative military and political historians arguing in explicitly counter-factual terms.[22]

Most recently of all, British professional historians have begun to confront the problems of epistemology raised by the postmodernist denial of the 'facts' which generations of scholars believed to be the building-blocks of their interpretations of the past, emphasising instead how historians like other scholars 'construct' the objects they study. It was, characteristically, Lawrence Stone who provoked a discussion of postmodernism in the pages of *Past and Present* by writing to the journal denouncing it.[23] Introductions to historical method are, finally, springing up like mushrooms and some of them are very different from the pragmatic empiricist approach exemplified by G. R. Elton's *The Practice of History*.[24]

Scepticism concerning the possibility of knowing the past is of course nothing new. The movement of 'historical pyrrhonism', as it was described at the time, was an influential one in the seventeenth century. Even what is now known as 'constructivism', the idea that historians and other scholars construct or invent rather than find or observe the objects of their study, has its own history, going back well before the late twentieth century (see the Introduction to this volume).

This sense of construction, obviously part of the 'postmodern condition', may also have been been encouraged by a rise of interest in comparative

---

[22] Nial Ferguson (ed.), *Virtual History* (London, 1997).

[23] Lawrence Stone, 'History and Post-Modernism', *Past and Present*, 131 (1991), 217–18

[24] Keith Jenkins, *Rethinking History* (London, 1991); Ludmilla Jordanova, *History in Practice* (London, 2000).

history. In Britain, this approach has generally been practised by anthropologists and sociologists such as Jack Goody, for example, and by the triple alliance of Ernest Gellner, John Hall and Michael Mann, rather than by working historians.[25] However, some historians have been sympathetic to this approach. A series of studies in comparative history was launched in the 1970s.[26] More recently, thematic courses on comparative history have multiplied in British universities. The comparative approach was recommended by one of the leaders of the profession, John Elliott, in his inaugural lecture as Regius Professor of Modern History at Oxford, *National and Comparative History* (1991). It had already been practised by the same author in his *Richelieu and Olivares* (1984).

General interpretations of the past

The main point to make about general interpretations of the past by British historians is reminiscent of the remark about snakes in Iceland. Interpretations on this scale are rarely made and often rejected. A famous statement of agnosticism in this respect is H. A. L. Fisher's preface to his *History of Europe* (1935), confessing his inability to find in history 'a plot, a rhythm, a pre-determined pattern', and emphasising 'the play of the contingent and the unforeseen'. It might be compared with G. N. Clark's inaugural lecture of 1944, claiming to articulate a 'consensus' of 'working historians' with his statement 'we work with limited aims', or with Alan Bullock's critique of what he called 'metahistory' (a term he had borrowed from Isaiah Berlin), in 1951 in the recently founded journal *History Today*.[27] Bullock's article provoked a debate in the pages of the journal in which Christopher Dawson and Max Beloff defended metahistory and Gustaaf Renier pleaded for a compromise. (After this, even the word disappeared from use until it was revived by Hayden White in 1973.)[28] However, in the twentieth century the

[25] Jack Goody, *Technology, Tradition and the State in Africa* (London, 1971), and many other studies; Ernest Gellner, *Nations and Nationalism* (Oxford, 1983); John A. Hall, *Powers and Liberties: The Causes and Consequences of the Rise of the West* (Oxford, 1985); Michael Mann, *The Sources of Social Power, vol. 1* (Cambridge, 1986).

[26] The British contributors to the series were Peter Burke, *Venice and Amsterdam* (London, 1974); Robert Browning, *Byzantium and Bulgaria* (London, 1975); and Daniel Snowman, *Kissing Cousins: An Interpretation of British and American Culture, 1945–75* (London, 1975).

[27] G. N. Clark, *Historical Scholarship and Historical Thought* (Cambridge, 1944), p. 11; Alan Bullock, 'The Historian's Purpose: History and Meta-history', *History Today* (February 1951), 5–11.

[28] C. Dawson, 'The Problem of Meta-history', *History Today* (June 1951), 9–12; G. J. Reiner, 'Plain History and Meta-history', *History Today* (July, 1951), 69–70; M. Beloff, 'Plain History and Meta-history II', *History Today* (September, 1951), 57.

main British contributions to grand interpretations of the past came from
the margin of the profession, from H. G. Wells and from Arnold Toynbee.
Wells, turning from novels to an *Outline of History* (1919–20), distinguished
in the manner of Ibn Khaldun (though without reference to him) between two
conflicting traditions, that of the agricultural 'communities of obedience' and
that of the pastoral 'communities of will', and discussed the attempts to
combine them, aided by Christianity and the state.[29] Wells' book aroused
considerable interest and controversy for the next decade or so. It was attacked
by Catholics, notably Hilaire Belloc, had its errors concerning the ancient
world pointed out by a classicist (Arnold Gomme), and passed through seven
editions by 1930.

The most memorable twentieth-century British attempt to describe the
patterns of the past on a grand scale is of course Arnold Toynbee's *Study of
History* (1934–61), a monumental work in twelve volumes. Trained as a
classicist and pursuing a career in an institute of contemporary international
affairs, Toynbee was better qualified for the task than most of his colleagues.
Compared to Hegel (say) or to his recent predecessor Oswald Spengler,
Toynbee was relatively empiricist. He had read Spengler in 1920 (borrowing
the book from Lewis Namier), but criticised the author as 'dogmatic and
determinist'. Toynbee's volumes are packed with detailed information as
well as with reflections on themes such as 'law and freedom in history', or
the idea that material and spiritual achievement are antithetical and so occur
at different times. The phrases he coined to describe recurrent historical
patterns ('challenge and response', 'withdrawal and return', 'external
proletariat' and so on) gave his version of the cyclical interpretation of
history an air of novelty.

When the early volumes appeared in the 1930s, the general reaction was at
first respectful or even enthusiastic, but it turned increasingly critical. The
philosopher R. G. Collingwood, for instance, who had already dismissed the
work of Spengler as anti-historical, described Toynbee as a 'positivist' who
tried to apply the method of natural science to history. Although he admitted
that 'in the detail of his work, Toynbee shows a very fine historical sense',
Collingwood castigated him for following the wrong principles.[30] Isaiah
Berlin agreed with Collingwood, claiming that, although Toynbee's work
might be magnificent, it was not history but 'historiosophy' or even 'theodicy'.

---

[29] H. G. Wells, *Outline of History* (1920, revised edn London, 1932), especially pp. 728–32. These
general themes are emphasised in C. Dawson, 'H. G. Wells and the *Outline of History*', *History
Today* (October 1951), 29–32.

[30] R. G. Collingwood, 'Oswald Spengler and the Theory of Historical Cycles', *Antiquity* (1927),
311–25; idem, *The Idea of History*, revised edn (Oxford, 1993), 159–65.

William Dray entitled the chapter on Toynbee in his *Philosophy of History* (1964), 'An Empirical Approach'. British historians, on the other hand, found Toynbee far from empirical enough. He had submitted his work in advance to some specialists (Geoffrey Hudson on China, Norman Baynes on Byzantium and Hamilton Gibb on Islam), but his knowledge was obviously patchy. Strong on classical antiquity, the history of religions and empires, the Balkans and what used to be called the 'Near East', he was weak on Africa, on South America and, above all, on science and technology.

Richard Pares, who reviewed the book at length in the *English Historical Review*, did focus on the central ideas of *A Study of History*, noting for example the problem of defining civilisations and the danger of hypostatising them. The verdict of Pares was characteristically balanced and cautious: 'Like other grandiose failures, Dr Toynbee's work contains many excellent ideas which other historians can use as clues in the construction of that intermediate kind of sense which is the most that they can safely try to make of history.'[31] All the same, it tells one something about British historical culture in the mid-twentieth century that it should have been left to a Dutch historian, Pieter Geyl, to debate with Toynbee on the radio (a discussion organised by the BBC in 1949) as well as to write the most influential refutation of *A Study of History*.[32] The British reaction to the book was very different from the serious discussion which its general ideas provoked on the continent, from Raymond Aron in France and José Ortega y Gasset in Spain to Eugene Kosminsky in Russia.

There was something heroic about Toynbee's enterprise, however flawed. It was as eclectic or syncretist as late Roman religion, taking its conceptual apparatus from thinkers as diverse as Spengler, Bergson, Frazer, Teggart, Berdyaev and Jung. Criticising his predecessors for describing society as an organism, the author spoke of cultural 'growth' all the same. He virtually refused to engage with the ideas of Marx, and made no reference to those of Max Weber, who had once debated with Spengler.

Some of Toynbee's cultural comparisons and contrasts retain their value. The points he made about 'the relativity of historical thought', the need to escape from the framework of the nation-state and to realise that western civilisation is only one among many, command more assent today than when he originally made them. Indeed, it is hard to dissent from Momigliano's

---

[31] A. J. Toynbee, *A Study of History*, 10 vols (Oxford, 1934–54); Richard Pares, *English Historical Review*, 71 (1956), 256–72, the quotation at 272. Another sympathetic review, despite criticisms, came from Albert Hourani, 'A Vision of History' (1955, repr. idem, *A Vision of History*, Beirut, 1961), pp. 1–34. Hugh Trevor-Roper, 'Arnold Toynbee's Millennium', *Encounter*, 45 (1957), 14–28, claimed that Toynbee saw himself as a Messiah.

[32] P. Geyl, *Debates with Historians* (The Hague, 1955), chs 5–8.

positive verdict on Toynbee's 'single-handed achievement in deprovincialis-
ing history'.[33] Toynbee's own analogy between himself and Sir James Frazer is
not an inappropriate one. They were both classicists who turned to comparison
on a broad scale, and were both denounced and pillaged by their successors.

A distrust of generalisations also underlay the suspicion of sociology to
be found in the British historical profession before 1950 and in some places
long after, despite the fact that most British sociologists were as empiricist as
their colleagues in history departments and disinclined to produce grand
interpretations of the past in the manner of Hegel, Marx or Comte. Namier's
interest in the ideas of Vilfredo Pareto was exceptional for its time. Tawney
was one of the few English historians to take the ideas of Max Weber
seriously as early as 1922, when he gave the lectures which turned into his
best-selling *Religion and the Rise of Capitalism* (a Pelican book as early as
1938).[34] In the 1960s, Weber's *Protestant Ethic* was regularly discussed and
refuted, but his more ambitious studies of bureaucracy and charisma were
still virtually ignored.

The reception — or more exactly the 'non-reception' — of the ideas of
the sociologist Norbert Elias is another litmus paper revealing the attitudes
and interests of British historians in his day. Although Elias came to live in
England in the 1930s and taught at the University of Leicester after the war,
his major study in historical sociology, *The Civilising Process* (1939), was
virtually ignored for forty years. Only following its translation in 1981–2
was the book discussed or mentioned by a substantial number of British
historians. The exceptions to this case of non-reception may also be
revealing. *The Civilising Process* was praised in an article published in 1945
by Patrick Gordon Walker, who was a Marxist history don at Oxford before
he gave up his academic career for a political one, becoming home secretary
in a Labour government. Elias was mentioned by Ernst Gombrich in 1952
and quoted several times with approval by Toynbee in 1954. Then silence
seems to have descended until his ideas were discussed in an inaugural
lecture by Hellmut Koenigsberger in 1975, rapidly followed by Keith
Thomas in his Neale Lecture of 1977.[35]

---

[33] A. Momigliano, review of Toynbee, *English Historical Review*, 78 (1963), 725.

[34] See R. H. Tawney, 'The Study of Economic History', *Economica*, 13 (1933), 1–21, rpr. *History and Society* (London, 1978), pp. 47–65.

[35] Patrick Gordon Walker, 'History and Psychology', *Sociological Review*, 37 (1945), 37–49; Ernst Gombrich, 'Visual Metaphors of Value in Art', rpr. in his *Meditations on a Hobby-horse* (London, 1963), pp. 12–29; Toynbee, *Study of History, vol. 9*, pp. 249, 329, 335–6, 361; Hellmut G. Koenigsberger, *Dominium regale or dominium politicum et regale* (London, 1975); Keith Thomas, 'The Place of Laughter in Tudor and Stuart England', *Times Literary Supplement*, 21 January 1977, 77–81.

Anthropology has of course come to have a warmer reception from British historians than sociology ever did, ever since Thomas argued in its favour in the early 1960s.[36] The reason for this difference in reception is probably that, despite the example of Frazer, anthropology was more readily associated than sociology with fieldwork in particular societies, while the emphasis on what used to be called 'the native's point of view' and is now known as 'local knowledge' fitted in well with Ranke's injunction to study the past on its own terms. The right anthropologists were discovered at the right time — not Radcliffe-Brown or even Lévi-Strauss, but Evans-Pritchard and, by the 1970s, Clifford Geertz, whose stress on interpretation did not so much challenge the assumptions of historians as encourage them to be more self-conscious about what they were already doing.

The Toynbee debate was the one occasion in twentieth-century Britain when substantive philosophy of history was discussed seriously within the historical profession. Even the philosophers generally preferred to concentrate on historical method. Among the apparent exceptions, Isaiah Berlin's *The Hedgehog and the Fox* (1953), a dazzling essay on Tolstoy's view of history, was more of a contribution to the history of nineteenth-century ideas, while his *Historical Inevitability* (1954) was essentially the work of a moralist concerned to defend the notion of human responsibility against its critics.

Toynbee apart, for explicit interpretations of the past on the part of British historians in the twentieth century it is necessary to turn to the Marxists and their sympathisers. Historians showed little interest in Marx before the 1930s, although the English socialist E. Belfort Bax had already published a trilogy of books on 'The Social Side of the German Reformation' in which he quoted Kautsky, if not Marx or Engels. After the Second World War, however, the situation changed. It was the period 1945–56 which was the high point of the Communist Party Historians Group, including Christopher Hill, Eric Hobsbawm, Edward Thompson and Rodney Hilton. It was out of the discussions of this group that the journal *Past and Present* (founded in 1952 and subtitled 'a journal of scientific history') developed. When *Past and Present* became established and respectable, it was a former member of the Communist Party Historians Group, Raphael Samuel, who founded *History Workshop Journal* (1976), which formerly described itself as a journal of 'socialist' (and later of 'socialist and feminist') history.

Within the culture of British Marxism, there were lively debates, at their height in the 1960s and 1970s, about the place of agency and structure in

---

[36] Keith Thomas, 'History and Anthropology', *Past and Present*, 24 (1963), 3–18.

history, with Edward Thompson at the centre and rival accusations of 'economism' and 'culturalism' flying about. More recently, Perry Anderson has been virtually alone among British intellectuals in taking the substantive philosophy of history seriously enough to write about it, notably in his essay on the idea of the 'ends of history'.[37]

A few debates also took place between Marxist and non-Marxist historians, notably the one between T. S. Ashton and Eric Hobsbawm known as the 'standard of living controversy'. For the most part, however, the two groups avoided each other or, if they did discuss their ideas, failed to communicate, as in the case of a conference of urban historians in the mid-1960s in which the protagonists of one debate were described in the proceedings as 'boxing vigorously but hardly touching each other'.[38] A sympathetic assessment of Marxist history from outside, like Herbert Butterfield's in the 1930s, was rare, and it may well be significant that this assessment was not published in a historical journal but in the pages of a literary periodical, Scrutiny, which also carried a long and essentially favourable review of Christopher Hill's early essay on the English Revolution.[39]

From a continental point of view, the empiricist heritage of the English Marxists is extremely striking, the local equivalent of the Marxist idealism of Gramsci and his followers in Italy. Edward Thompson, for instance, used to describe himself as a 'Marxist empiricist' and in 1978 published a characteristically vehement denunciation of what he called 'the Poverty of Theory' (especially French theory, from Althusser to Foucault).[40] Even the most theoretical of English historians accommodated themselves to the dominant culture of empiricism.

Implicit interpretations

In a sense it is impossible not to have a philosophy of history, just as it is impossible not to have a philosophy of life, since actions reveal assumptions

---

[37] Perry Anderson, 'The Ends of History', in A Zone of Engagement (London, 1992), pp. 279–375.

[38] Report by W. G. Hoskins on an exchange between John Foster and W. H. Chaloner in H. J. Dyos (ed.), The Study of Urban History (London, 1968), p. 342.

[39] Herbert Butterfield, 'History and the Marxian Method', Scrutiny, 1 (1932–3), 339–55; Hill was reviewed by L. C. Knights in Scrutiny, 9 (1940–1), 166–9.

[40] Edward P. Thompson, The Poverty of Theory (London, 1978); see Perry Anderson, Arguments within English Marxism (London, 1980), pp. 5–58. At a conference in Cambridge I once heard Thompson describe himself as a Marxist empiricist, provoking an immediate reaction from his neighbour, Ernest Gellner, 'You can't be!'

about progress and decline, the role of individuals and other major themes of debate. If there is, or at any rate was, something of a taboo in Britain against self-conscious discussions of the pattern of the past, implicit interpretations can of course be found everywhere.

In the first half of the twentieth century, ideas of progress and evolution were virtually taken for granted. The leading Tudor historian A. F. Pollard, for example, called one of his books *The Evolution of Parliament* (1920). If it was less than a theory, the term was more than a metaphor, since Pollard was arguing that changes in the parliamentary system had taken place in a gradual and impersonal way rather than as a result of specific acts of creation. As for progress, it was discussed in a relatively explicit manner in a chapter in E. H. Carr's *What is History?* and also in J. H. Plumb's *The Death of the Past* (1969). Plumb's book, stimulated by an invitation to give a series of lectures at City College New York, claimed that advances were visible both in history and historiography.[41]

For other more or less implicit interpretations of the past we may turn to the fortunes of Whig and Tory history after 1900. Herbert Butterfield's *Whig Interpretation of History* (1931) drew attention to some traditional assumptions in British history: 'the tendency in many historians', as the preface put it, 'to write on the side of Protestants and Whigs, to praise revolutions provided they have been successful, to emphasise certain principles of progress in the past and to produce a story which is the ratification if not the glorification of the present'. Butterfield launched a phrase which resonated for decades. It may sometimes have given the false impression that the controversy is uniquely English rather than a local version of a broader debate on teleology or what the French call 'finalisme', but it has made generations of students more conscious of rival interpretations of history than they might otherwise have been.[42]

There has been no dissection of Tory or conservative history along the lines of Butterfield's book on the Whig interpretation. The varieties of conservative history make the task a difficult one. Several of these varieties have been particularly associated with Peterhouse, in three different phases in the life of the college. The first, in the 1930s, was the age of Butterfield himself, whose *Whig Interpretation* may be viewed as a guided missile launched from Peterhouse in the direction of Trinity College, where G. M. Trevelyan, a historian in the tradition of his ancestor Macaulay, was a fellow. The second, in the 1960s, was the age of Maurice Cowling, whose

---

[41] On Plumb, Maurice Cowling, *Religion and Public Doctrine in Modern England* (Cambridge, 1980), pp. 396–9.
[42] On Butterfield, ibid., pp. 220–50.

view of history as the realm of chaos and contingency might be described as an anti-theoretical theory. The third, in the 1980s, was the age of J. C. D. Clark, whose interpretation of eighteenth-century England, defined against the rival views of J. H. Plumb and E. P. Thompson, presents it as an *ancien régime*, thus illustrating the link between interpretation and periodisation.

Periodisation, especially the definition of the modern period, is a major domain of more or less implicit interpretations of the past. The concept of 'modern' history has long been enshrined in many university courses as well as in the titles of some well-known historical studies, among them Lord Acton's *Lectures on Modern History* (1906), Sir John Clapham's *Economic History of Modern Britain* (1926), Dennis Brogan's *The Development of Modern France* (1940) and Quentin Skinner's *Foundations of Modern Political Thought* (1978). The problem is of course what these authors and other British historians meant by the term 'modern'. To answer this question it may be useful to compare and contrast attitudes around the years 1900, when the *Cambridge Modern History* began to be published, and 1961, when it began to be replaced by the *New Cambridge Modern History*.

Mandell Creighton's introductory note to the first volume of the *Cambridge Modern History* explained why the year 1500 had been taken as a starting-point, arguing that 'Anyone who works through the records of the fifteenth and sixteenth centuries becomes conscious of an extraordinary change in mental attitude' at that time, notably 'the growth of national feeling' and 'the growth of individual freedom'. His conclusion was that 'Modern history professes to deal with mankind in a period when they had reached the stage of civilisation which is in its broad outlines familiar to us, during the period in which the problems that still occupy us came into conscious recognition, and were dealt with in ways intelligible to us as resembling our own. It is this sense of familiarity which leads us to draw a line and mark out the beginnings of modern history.'

Volume 1 of the *New Cambridge Modern History*, edited by G. R. Potter, bore the same title as the first volume of its predecessor, 'The Renaissance'. However, Denys Hay's introductory reflections reveal the rise of a certain detachment from the idea of modernity. 'By 1900', he claimed, 'the current view of the break between modern and medieval had hardened into a pedagogical dogma.' Hay went on to point out the many 'flaws' in the scheme. Compared to the force of this critique, the displacement of the beginning of modernity (or at any rate the beginning of the volume) from 1500 to 1450 comes as something of an anticlimax.

Other proposed redatings of the onset of the modern world have been more radical. The proposals have come in the main from two groups of historians who gradually acquired disciplinary autonomy in the twentieth century: economic historians, who viewed the 'industrial revolution' as the great breakthrough, and historians of science, who preferred the 'scientific revolution' of the seventeenth century.

'Industrial revolution', a term used in France in the 1820s and by Marx in the 1860s, was taken up by Arnold Toynbee senior (uncle of the world historian) in the 1880s and used without much heart-searching until the middle of the twentieth century. (More recently, it has been argued more and more frequently that there was no revolution but a gradual transition to industrial society.) Originally a way of describing certain economic and social changes in Britain, the term broadened its meaning with the rise of the concept of 'pre-industrial society' (a phrase used by Aldous Huxley in 1934 to describe the interests of William Morris). The implication of the concept is that 'modern' history began not in 1500 but at the end of the eighteenth century or even later.

The idea of the 'scientific revolution' goes back to the 1940s, and is linked with discussions of the shift from 'magic' to 'science', or 'alchemy' to 'chemistry'. As in the case of the industrial revolution, historians have become more and more doubtful about the 'revolutionary' character of changes in what was known at the time as 'natural philosophy'. What deserves emphasis here is the effect of studies of the history of science on the periodisation of history in general. In this context, two key witnesses are G. N. Clark and Herbert Butterfield, precisely because they were not historians of science but general historians who took the history of science seriously.

In his book *The Seventeenth Century* (1929), G. N. Clark, already interested in what he called the 'scientific revival' of the period, argued the case for the years around 1650 as 'one of the great watersheds in modern history'. In similar fashion, Butterfield's *Origins of Modern Science* (1949) claimed in its preface that the scientific 'revolution' (a long revolution which he associated with the period 1300–1800) 'outshines everything since the rise of Christianity and reduces the Renaissance and the Reformation to mere episodes'.

The debates about the timing of industrialisation and the rise of science were important ones. Linked to these debates, but still more fundamental, was a decline in what Creighton, quoted above, called the 'sense of familiarity' of the fifteenth and sixteenth centuries. In the second half of the twentieth century it was becoming increasingly difficult for historians to see the years around 1500 as the beginning of their world. 1500 was still treated as a watershed but the late eighteenth century seemed to mark a still more important rupture with the past. Hence the concept of 'early modern' gradually came into use among British historians after the Second World War (although it has not been recognised in the second edition of the *Oxford English Dictionary*). An early example of the new usage is G. N. Clark's chapter on 'the early modern period' in *The European Inheritance* (1954), published in book form as *Early Modern Europe* (1957). Clark chose the dates *c.* 1450–*c.* 1720, but since his time it has become more common to end the period in the middle of the eighteenth century or even later. Introducing Keith Thomas's lecture on 'Age and Authority in Early Modern England', at the British Academy in 1976, the president, Sir Isaiah Berlin, joked about what obviously appeared to him as a very strange idea.[43] If it was not an indirect way of noting the self-contradiction of the concept, Berlin's surprise suggests that the term had not yet spread beyond teachers and students of the period.

The relative lack of a British historical contribution to the debate over 'postmodernity' (the period, not the movement of self-conscious 'post-modernism') deserves to be noted here. After all, periods are what historians are supposed to know about. One of the first references to the 'post-modern Age of Western History' came from a British historian as early as 1954, Arnold Toynbee, but it elicited few echoes.[44] Perry Anderson, who has recently published what he calls a 'historical account' of the origins of postmodernity, emphasising 'temporal sequence' as well as social settings, stands virtually alone. In this context it may be significant that Anderson has always been on the margin of the British historical profession, whether as an independent man of letters, as a publisher or as a professor of history in California.[45]

Conclusions

It has been argued that the assertion that British historians lack a serious interest in historiography and philosophy of history needs to be qualified in a number of ways, for example by paying attention to sub-disciplines and also to chronology. Was there a turning-point in the studies described here, and, if so, when? Some interests and ideas have a longer history than is usually

---

[43] Personal memories of this incident.
[44] A. J. Toynbee (1954) cited in the *OED Supplement*, s.v. 'Post-Modern'. The term was used in D. C. Somervell's abridgement of Toynbee as early as 1947. See Perry Anderson, *The Origins of Postmodernity* (London, 1998), pp. 5–6.
[45] Anderson, *Postmodernity*.

thought. Maitland's concern with what he called 'German Theory', notably Otto Gierke, goes back before 1900 and might usefully be compared and contrasted with recent interest in (say) the ideas of Jürgen Habermas. An interest in Marxism on the part of a few scholars goes back to the beginning of the twentieth century. The English historian Cornford's book on the place of myth in historical writing (in his case that of Thucydides) came sixty years before the studies by Hayden White.

Suppose that we try to think in decades. Between 1900 and 1930, there is relatively little to report, but the most important British contributions to both analytical and substantive philosophy of history were made by Collingwood and Toynbee, who were working out their ideas in the 1930s. Namier turned to Freud and Pareto at much the same time, when other historians were turning to Marx. In the 1950s, more serious studies of historiography were produced than in the previous half-century. In the 1960s came the 'invasion' of social and cultural theory from the continent (often via the USA), and books by Gramsci, Lukács, Lévi-Strauss and Foucault began to be translated into English. These books were read by some historians as well as sociologists and literary critics, just as works by Gadamer, Habermas, Elias and Ricoeur would all be translated and read in the 1970s and 1980s. In the 1990s, postmodernity and postmodernism were finally discussed by some British historians, especially outside the older universities, making students of history familiar, perhaps for the first time, with the fictional elements in historical writing and the ideological cargo of all 'Grand Narratives', Whig or Tory, radical or conservative, feminist or 'male chauvinist'.

The 1950s or 1960s looks like the best candidate for a general turning-point. (I must confess to having believed in the 1960s that the change was beginning at that time, but retrospectively the case for the 1950s seems stronger.) Even today, though, I have the impression that there is less interest in the topics discussed in this essay in Britain than in most European countries. Most British historians would probably raise an eyebrow if they were asked to describe their epistemology, while many continental historians would not. Like many stereotypes, the one of Britain as a culture of empiricism or even a land without historiography or philosophy of history contains a kernel of truth. Although globalisation has been undermining insularity, British historians remain distinctive — if not peculiar — in their approaches to their subject.

Note. My thanks to Mark Phillips for his perceptive comments on a draft version of this essay.

Index